Lecture Notes in Computer Science 2708
Edited by G. Goos, J. Hartmanis, and J. van Leeuwen

Springer
Berlin
Heidelberg
New York
Hong Kong
London
Milan
Paris
Tokyo

Rick Reed   Jeanne Reed (Eds.)

SDL 2003: System Design

11th International SDL Forum
Stuttgart, Germany, July 1-4, 2003
Proceedings

 Springer

Series Editors

Gerhard Goos, Karlsruhe University, Germany
Juris Hartmanis, Cornell University, NY, USA
Jan van Leeuwen, Utrecht University, The Netherlands

Volume Editors

Rick Reed
Jeanne Reed
Telecommunications Software Engineering Limited
The Laurels, Victoria Road
Windermere, Cumbria, LA23 2DL, UK
E-mail: {rickreed/jeanne}@tseng.co.uk

Cataloging-in-Publication Data applied for

A catalog record for this book is available from the Library of Congress

Bibliographic information published by Die Deutsche Bibliothek
Die Deutsche Bibliothek lists this publication in the Deutsche Nationalbibliografie;
detailed bibliographic data is available in the Internet at <http://dnb.ddb.de>.

CR Subject Classification (1998): C.2, D.2, D.3, F.3, C.3, H.4

ISSN 0302-9743
ISBN 3-540-40539-9 Springer-Verlag Berlin Heidelberg New York

Springer-Verlag Berlin Heidelberg New York
a member of BertelsmannSpringer Science+Business Media GmbH

http://www.springer.de

© Springer-Verlag Berlin Heidelberg 2003
Printed in Germany

Typesetting: Camera-ready by author, data conversion by DA-TeX Gerd Blumenstein
Printed on acid-free paper   SPIN 10928738   06/3142   5 4 3 2 1 0

Preface

This volume contains the papers presented at the 11th SDL Forum, Stuttgart.

As well as the papers, the 11th SDL Forum also hosted a system design competition sponsored by Solinet with a cash prize for the "best" design. This follows a similar competition at the SAM 2002 workshop (papers published in LNCS 2599). The winning entry from SAM 2002 is described in the last paper in this volume.

The SDL Forum was first held in 1982, and then every two years from 1985. Initially the Forum was concerned only with the Specification and Description Language first standardized in the 1976 Orange Book of the International Telecommunication Union (ITU).

From the start this graphical CEFSM (communicating extended finite state machines) notation was used both to describe the implementation of systems and to specify systems (especially protocol systems in standards). In the early days both types of description were quite informal, though specifications were certainly more formal than the main alternative: natural language with some ad hoc figures. Implementations were usually written in assembly language, which is at too low a level to reason well about the interaction between communicating agents within a system. In this case the notation provided an intermediate description that gave an overview of how the implementation worked, and often the actual logical development was done at the graphical level with hand coding of that description.

In the 20 years since the first SDL Forum there have been many advances in technology, but the CEFSM paradigm has stood the test of time. Moreover, whereas in 1982 only a few systems actually needed to be described in this way, nearly all systems are now considered to consist of communicating objects that can benefit from being defined in the CEFSM way. The approach is used to develop complete end-to-end systems in telecommunications, and is also used for other component systems such as vehicle engine management.

Fortunately one of the advances has been software development systems that allow engineers to use graphical notations directly for definition, with the implementation being derived directly from the graphical description. One might imagine that such developments have made the engineers' work easier, but what has happened is that it has enabled engineers to develop more complex systems, so the work has remained just as challenging. An engineer or engineering team is likely to be concerned with much more than just the logic of the state machines. They will be expected to describe various scenarios and sequences of operation, the formal testing of the system, dimensioning and deployment, encoding on interfaces, fault tolerance and possibly the ergonomics of the user interface. While the logical operation of components is still vital, it is only part of the overall system design.

For system design the ITU recommends a set of notations (ASN.1, URN, MSC, eODL and TTCN) to be used with the CEFSM notation. As the set of languages used by engineers has increased, so has the scope of the SDL Forum. The ITU SDL+ methodology published of 1996 included most of the previously mentioned notations, plus the object model notation familiar from UML: indeed many seem to think that UML is just the object model notation. UML (in the guise of OMT) was included to some extent in the 1997 SDL Forum, and four years later the 2001 SDL Forum was entitled "Meeting UML" (LNCS 2078). The trend is expected to continue beyond 2003, because there are plans to provide UML profiles for ITU languages. As a side effect UML will then be a framework that provides "glue" between the ITU languages. This is quite natural, because much of UML2.0 is based on the Message Sequence Chart and Specification and Description Language standards of ITU, and the UML Testing Profile is related to TTCN-3.

The 11th SDL Forum was therefore about System Design Languages, as reflected in the title of this volume and suggested as a new meaning for the acronym SDL. In some cases SDL is already used in this sense as engineers rarely use just one notation. For example, the third paper in this volume has SDL in the title but also includes collaboration diagrams, and message sequence charts. You can read the papers in this volume and come to your own conclusion, but do not be surprised to find others using SDL to mean System Design Languages rather than the CEFSM notation defined by the ITU-T Recommendations in the Z.100 to Z.109 series for the Specification and Description Language.

April 2003

Rick Reed
Chairman
SDL Forum Society
www.sdl-forum.org

SDL Forum Society

The SDL Forum Society is a not-for-profit organization that, in addition to running the SDL Forum:

- runs the SAM (SDL and MSC) workshop every 2 years between SDL Forum years;
- is a body recognized by ITU-T as co-developing the Z.100 to Z.109 and Z.120 to Z.129 standards; and
- promotes the ITU-T system design languages.

For more information on the SDL Forum Society, see http://www.sdl-forum.org.

Organization

Each SDL Forum is organized by the SDL Forum Society with the help of local organizers. The Organizing Committee consists of the Board of the SDL Forum Society plus the local organizers, and others as needed depending on the actual event. For SDL 2003 the local organizers from Solinet need to be thanked for their effort to ensure that everything was in place for the papers in this book.

Organizing Committee

Chairman, SDL Forum Society: Rick Reed (TSE Ltd.)
Treasurer, SDL Forum Society: Uwe Glässer (Paderborn University)
Secretary, SDL Forum Society: Andreas Prinz (DResearch)
Local Organizers, Solinet: Lisa Ritchie and William Skelton

Programme Committee

Daniel Amyot, University of Ottawa, Canada
Gyula Csopaki, Budapest University, Hungary
Sarolta Dibuz, Ericsson, Hungary
Fabrice Dubois, France Telecom, France
Anders Ek, Telelogic Technologies, Sweden
Joachim Fischer, Humboldt University, Berlin, Germany
Uwe Glässer, Visiting Fellow, Microsoft Research, Redmond, USA
Reinhard Gotzhein, University of Kaiserslautern, Germany
Jens Grabowski, Institute for Telematics, Lübeck, Germany
Peter Graubmann, Siemens, Germany
Øysten Haugen, Ericsson, Norway
Dieter Hogrefe, Georg-August University, Göttingen, Germany
Eckhardt Holz, Humboldt University, Berlin, Germany
Olle Hydbom, Telelogic Technologies, Sweden
Clive Jervis, Motorola, UK
Ferhat Khendek, Concordia University, Canada
Yair Lahav, Textology, Israel
Nikolai Mansurov, KLOCwork, Canada
Sjouke Mauw, University of Eindhoven, The Netherlands
Birger Møller-Pederson, Ericsson, Norway
Ostap Monkewich, Nortel Networks, Canada
Anders Olsen, Cinderella, Denmark
Andreas Prinz, DResearch, Germany
Bob Probert, University of Ottawa, Canada
Steve Randall, PQM Consultants, UK

Rick Reed, TSE Ltd., UK
Lisa Ritchie, Solinet, Germany
Amardeo Sarma, NEC, Germany
Richard Sanders, SINTEF, Norway
Ina Schieferdecker, GMD Fokus, Germany
Edel Sherratt, University of Wales, Aberystwyth, UK
William Skelton, Solinet, Germany
Daniel Vincent, France Telecom, France
Thomas Weigert, Motorola, USA
Milan Zoric, ETSI, France

Reviewers

The Programme Committee arranged for most of the reviews of papers within
their own organizations. However, a few reviews were undertaken by additional
reviewers at short notice. These reviewers were:

Gregor v. Bochmann, University of Ottawa, Canada
Ahmed Bouabdallah, ENST-Bretagne, France
Rolv Bræk, NTNU, Norway
Ken Chan, University of Ottawa, Canada
Laurent Doldi, Transmeth, France
Jaqueline Floch, SINTEF, Norway
Birgit Geppert, Avaya Labs, USA
Pedro Merino Gómez, UMA, Spain
Javier Poncela Gonzalez, UMA, Spain
Paul Herber, Paul Herber Systems Ltd., UK
Jozef Hooman, University of Nijmegen, The Netherlands
Nisse Husberg, Technical University, Helsinki, Finland
Finn Kristoffersen, Cinderella, Denmark
Shashi Kumar, Jönköping University, Sweden
Bruno Müller-Clostermann, University of Essen, Germany
Dagbjorn Nogva, Braodpark, Norway
Ken Turner, Stirling University, UK
John Sarallo, Appairent, USA
Rui Miguel Soares Silva, ESTG, Portugal
Hasan Ural, University of Ottawa, Canada
Gerardo Padilla Zárate, CIMAT, Mexico

Thanks

A volume such as this could not, of course, exist without the contributions of
the authors who are thanked for their work.

Table of Contents

Timing

Validation

Design

Applications

SAM 2002 Design Winner

Looking for Better Integration of Design and Performance Engineering

Wei Monin, Fabrice Dubois, Daniel Vincent, and Pierre Combes

France Telecom R&D/DTL
Laboratory of Advanced Techniques for Software Systems
Technopole Anticipa, avenue Pierre-Marzin, 22301 Lannion, France
{wei.monin,fabrice.dubois,daniel.vincent,
pierre.combes}@rd.francetelecom.com

Abstract. In various domains, performance evaluation has proved very valuable, especially when done at early stages of the development process; the simulation technique, in particular, combines good properties (flexibility, low-cost, relevance of results) for the prediction of software systems performance. However, too often performance engineering is kept separate from the design process of software systems. We try to analyze reasons for that, and discuss ways to better motivate designers to tackle performance evaluation. We then present an approach that aims at producing performance models from design-oriented specifications (based on scenario and/or automata formalisms, such as MSC/SDL). The approach is well adapted to the study of service platforms, and targets basic queuing networks that offer a flexible and powerful framework for modeling performance, as well as mature simulators on the market.

1 Introduction

The purpose of performance evaluation for software systems is twofold:

1. it is an efficient way to identify satisfactory configurations of the system, with respect to some well-defined Quality of Service (QoS in the following) requirements;
2. it allows for detection of faulty behavior due to congestion, or more generally to inadequate resources management.

More precisely, performance evaluation helps to make good decisions regarding buffering capacities, tasks distribution onto processing resources, number and respective power of processors, etc. The goal is often to find the cheapest solution that fulfills the given requirements. When associated with relevant methodology and tools, performance evaluation should definitely be seen as a fundamental software engineering technique.

Designers have often neglected performance engineering for software systems because learning these techniques is judged to represent a significant effort ("we will fix it later"). [1] states that 80% of client/server applications have to be redesigned, because performance requirements are not fulfilled. With appropriate

R. Reed (Ed.): SDL 2003, LNCS 2708, pp. 1–17, 2003.

techniques, the cost of a performance evaluation is generally less than 5% of the overall project budget. Thus, there is a need to better integrate performance engineering, associated tools and methodology, into the overall design process. In particular, functional specifications that are elaborated during the design phase should be considered valuable work towards performance analysis, because performance modeling conceptually relies (but not exclusively) on behavioral description.

Our goal in this paper is to discuss some possibilities to perform both design and performance evaluation more consistently, by deriving performance models from design (functional) oriented models. We do not intend to provide direct solutions here, but rather to present our feeling of what should be investigated in future research.

The performance technique that we target is the simulation of queuing systems, for which we first present benefits compared to other approaches. Then we try to understand why performance engineering is usually not well harmonized with the design phase, and finally we present our assessment of MSC and SDL as the possible basis for an appropriate bridge formalism to capture both functional and performance aspects. We have experimented with our approach on two (real) case studies. Although much simplified here for clarity, these examples are typical telecom service-oriented platforms with respect to the complexity of the application, and the type of requirements expressed in the model.

2   Approaches for Performance Evaluation

2.1   Overview

We identified three basic types of techniques for performance evaluation: the **analytic approach**, the **real testing approach**, and the **simulation approach**.

The choice of an approach depends on criteria such as: the application characteristics, the level of complexity, the availability of experts in the technique, and the general quality of results the technique can offer (in terms of reliability, precision, etc.).

Analytic Approach: The idea behind analytic techniques is to define the system's evolution in terms of pure mathematics. Very briefly, performance results are obtained by solving sets of equations, according to certain parameters. This is convenient in early phases of the design, when working with a simplified model is still possible. Indeed, the analytic approach needs to make assumptions about aspects such as independence of requests arrivals (Markovian assumptions). However, as the complexity grows – which happens quickly when describing software systems – such assumptions no longer hold.

Real Testing: The opposite solution strategy is the "heavy testing" approach. Testing requires the real system to be running (or at least a version very similar to the final one) and providing it with a realistic environment. This is of course necessary, because it is the only way to reveal implementation-dependent faults. But in practice, it is very difficult to generate a realistic environment artificially: for some applications designed to face very high load rates, for instance, it is just technically impossible. In any case, studying the system under various configurations (to find the best one) implies an obvious cost, in time as well as in money, because it is the real system that has to be reconfigured or dimensioned.

Simulation: As the precision of the design and the complexity of functional behavior grow, the simulation approach proves to be more realistic and more reliable. Of course, real tests are still useful during and after the implementation phase. Simulation is the most used technique for performance evaluation and this seems to be true for every kind of software system [2, 3, 4, 5, 6, 7]. In order to allow for simulation, system modeling is usually based on appropriate formalisms, such as queuing systems or Petri nets. Once the model is elaborated, it can be intensively simulated, under different configurations. For software systems, configuration parameters are processor speed, transmission throughput, task scheduling policy, processing resources topology, distribution of requests arrivals, etc. Reconfiguration is cheap, because it is virtual.

Simulation appears to be both easier to understand, and more efficient than analytic techniques [6]. The model is not described by a set of equations, but with programming constructs. These allow elaboration of a model as close as possible to the real system, while not requiring the complete software and hardware implementation, as is the case for the real testing approach. Moreover, simulation can be used in all steps of the design process. General-purpose simulators appeared in early 80's, such as QNAP [8], SIMSCRIPT [9], OPNET [10], and SES/Workbench [11]. Some of them mix analytic modules and simulation modules.

An obvious advantage of simulation, compared with real tests, is that simulation time is not related to real execution time. Simulation can perform a huge number of scenarios just by making some model parameters vary, and without installing new equipment. It is even possible to validate the model in extreme configurations, or under some lossy channels conditions, that could be impossible to realize in the real world at a given time (such as a storm effect). In most of the cases, simulation is a good compromise between use costs and results value. Moreover, the quality of results is fairly constant whatever the level of complexity of the system. This technique is especially efficient when one wants to compare different products or technologies that have to appear at a given place in a system, or when dimensioning a system. In the following we focus on the simulation approach.

2.2   Obstacles

Performance engineering still has some obstacles, that are not specific to the simulation approach.

The first obstacle concerns the capture of the internal behavior of the system. As explained below, although performance modeling is not really focused on functional aspects, there is still a minimal level of logic to be expressed in a performance model. Some parts of the system to be evaluated may be "black boxes" and it is sometimes not possible to obtain the information needed for these items.

The second obstacle relates to the acquisition of unit measurements (task execution times, channel delays, etc.). Here again, the "black box" effect is a problem, because measuring often requires the introduction of probes in the source code. In some applications, the performance engineer can overcome these drawbacks by increasing the abstraction level of the model.

Finally, obtaining a good knowledge of the behavior of end users is not easy either. User behavior is important too with request arrival repartition and scenarios distribution. This kind of information can only be gained by observations on a real system. For innovative applications, it is sometimes necessary to give and to quantify usage models.

3   Design vs. Performance: Different Concepts

Our experience is that design experts and performance experts, quite often, do not communicate so easily. One reason is the difference in concepts they manipulate: these two groups of people do not look at the system from the same viewpoint. This partly explains why the activities are usually kept separate from each other. Typically, performance evaluation is done (when it is done!) *after* functional design, when most of the architectural decisions have already been taken, and after the system implementation has already been committed in that direction. Ideally, the results of a performance analysis should influence such decisions, rather than just coming afterwards.

A lot of valuable work has already been done about transformation of a functional model into a performance-oriented model. However, in some cases (Timed SDL [12], SDL-net [13]), some important assumptions are made, dealing for instance with independence between arrival of requests. Such assumptions may hold for simplified examples, but usually they no longer hold when the complexity grows, so that the models appear to over-approximate of the real system. In other cases, such as SPECS [14], SPEET [15], HIT [16, 17], QUEST [18], DO-IT [19], Easy-Sim [20], Configuration Planner [21], SPEED [22], TLC [23], temporal annotations are introduced inside the reference functional specification. The resulting performance model is generally too detailed with respect to functional aspects, which generally prevents simulators from performing a deep analysis. In addition, these approaches often use ad-hoc analysis tools, whereas powerful analyzers on the market have proved very mature and well maintained. We share many points of view with [24] in particular, although we do not target exactly the same kind of performance models.

3.1   What is in a Performance Model?

Functional and performance models have basically different goals. For performance, we assume that the system works correctly and has previously been validated from a functional point of view; therefore many functional details are not relevant. What really matters is how the system uses resources – quantitatively, and under what basic logic – and not precisely what it does or how.

Actually, the only functional parts that must be captured are the ones that obviously influence performance. Though it may seem quite intuitive for humans, that filtering process is not easy to formalize, but still directly influences the quality of performance models, in terms of conciseness. As for other kinds of analysis techniques (for example model checking) the more compact the model is, the more efficient simulation is.

In order to enable computation of performance results (servers load, response times, rates of loss, etc.) performance modeling also contains environment modeling and resource modeling. Briefly, these respectively express what the clients traffic looks like (in terms of statistical laws, rate, etc.) and processing and communication capabilities (tasks scheduling policies, unitary execution times, etc.). These aspects are less crucial, because they do not deal with dynamics directly, therefore we do not subsequently address them.

In contrast to other approaches (such as [24] where Layer Queuing Networks are targeted) we are particularly interested in basic queuing networks: they use elementary and generic constructs, which open doors to the best level of expressiveness and flexibility. In particular, information on SES/Workbench queuing models is given in Sect. 4.5.

3.2   Key Issues to Make Performance Evaluation More Accessible

Elaborating an efficient performance model is not straightforward, at least from a designer perspective. Thus, it seems that there is room for improving the way such models can be obtained. In the following, we define requirements on a "performance-oriented" design formalism that could play such a role.

- The first key issue is to identify a language that would propose a reasonable set of constructs to model execution flows: that is, flows of more or less abstract tasks that have an impact in terms of resource consumption.
- Second, the language should be intuitive enough so that it is accepted by designers who are not familiar with concepts from the performance engineering area (the ultimate goal really is to popularize performance evaluation).
- Then, the language would preferably be based on existing, well-established design languages, with obvious benefits.
- Last, but not least, the mapping from that language to performance models should be defined formally to enable a rigorous extraction process, and as independent as possible from concrete performance formalisms and tools. We believe that the *basic queuing theory* is an appropriate concept space to target, as a powerful and very generic base that mature simulators on the market share (even though they don't concretize it in the same way). In particular, SES/Workbench, SIMSCRIPT, QNAP and OPNET have been used for years at France Telecom.

In the following, we present our experiment with MSC and SDL, as a possible basis for such a language.

4   Modeling Execution Flows with MSC and SDL

The approach we present here is particularly adapted to service-oriented platforms. This is of obvious interest from a network operator or service provider viewpoint.

4.1   Application Field: Service Platforms

Because they provide high-level and well defined services to end users, usually such systems can be reasonably characterized by a finite number of scenarios, corresponding to nominal use cases. The fact that the application can be summarized that way is a good starting point for mapping to the performance model. The execution flow triggered by a client request (that is, what concretely happens in the system when the scenario is running) is heavily determined by the nature of the request, while the influence of other factors is very weak. Another frequent property of service platforms is the weak inter-dependence, in the sense that the execution flow implied by a request does not depend on the way the other kinds of requests are treated. Even though, for some particular applications, such dependencies exist, they are usually easy to identify. The audio-conference example presented below contains such dependencies. These characteristics tend to facilitate the extraction of an efficient queuing model efficiently approximated, because the system's behavior is light.

4.2   Identification and Organization of Execution Flows

The first step is to identify a reasonable usage model for the system: a limited set of scenarios (use cases), that we call execution flows when looked at from the system tasks viewpoint. As explained above, that process seems to be quite natural for service platforms. Every scenario – or flow – is determined by the nature of the initial client request, and may generate at some points parallel branches, which in turn may synchronize at other points. In addition, scenarios often have fragments (phases) in common, thus it makes sense to compose scenarios in a global usage model, on the base of their shared phases[1]. HMSC, for instance, can help to produce such a structure. Once execution flows are well identified, we have to formalize them in order to enable their translation into queuing systems. In the following we discuss to what extent MSC and SDL are good candidates for that purpose.

Our ambition here is just to give a feeling of the concepts that are missing in the assessed languages, and we are aware that some significant work still has to be done regarding the rigorous definition of semantics.

---

[1] For clarity, however, the examples in that paper are presented flattened.

4.3   Formalization of Execution Flows: Scenario-Oriented (MSC)

Scenario languages such as MSC look appropriate for our needs: their purpose is to describe possible system executions, which somehow is closely related to our notion of execution flow. To better capture the information needed for performance-oriented modeling, we specialize MSC by introducing the following abstract constructs, to be used on MSC instances.

- **exec(t)** represents a task executed on the processor assigned to the instance, and that lasts t time units when the processor is 100% available to that task.
- **delay(t)** represents a simple delay, where time passes without implying business of the associated processor. This is used to model the fact that the system can slow down because of actions performed on external entities (database access, for example).
- **expect(c)** represents a sequencing condition for the instance. It means that the instance is blocked at that point until condition c – basically a predicate on global variables – evaluates to true. The condition can be seen as a door that has to be passed before the instance execution can continue, and the variables involved in the condition expression as the keys needed to open the door. Those variables, to be defined as global indicators by the designer, serve to indicate that some facts have been realized within the system (see **publish**).
- **publish(f)** represents an announcement to the whole system that some particular event happened. That announcement contributes to unblock instances that are waiting for that fact (f) to be realized. Announcing a fact is concretely achieved by giving new values to some shared variables that are used to represent the fact (through a predicate).
- **end** indicates the end of the current flow branch.

To concretely represent those events on MSCs, actions can be used for **exec** and **publish**, conditions for **delay** and **expect** (actually, both correspond to sequencing conditions), and a predefined message output for **end**.

Let us illustrate these concepts with the audio-conference example. This platform allows users to join an audio-conference bridge at a given date. The conference can only begin when a particular user, the *Organizer*, is connected (but the other participants can call before, in which case their call is hanging). In addition to a classical service controller, there is an entity that manages data about conference reservations (*DataFunction*). When a participant calls while the *Organizer* is absent, a message is played to the user, asking him/her to wait. In any case, if the number of participants (*nbp*) has already reached *max*, the call is rejected. When the *Organizer* joins, all pending participants are advised (welcome) and the conference is open. The diagram in Fig. 1 shows the execution flow implied by a simple participant's call. On reception of a call, the *Controller* processes it and asks the *DataFunction* to identify the caller. Both processing and identification are resource-consuming tasks, as specified with the **exec** clauses. The caller is recognized as a participant, then if no more participants can be accepted, the caller is rejected; otherwise, the number of connected

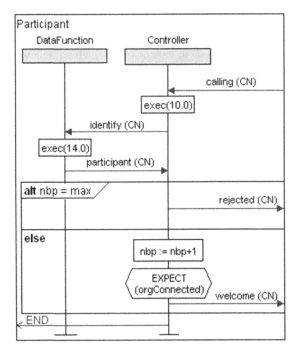

Fig. 1. Execution Flow Triggered by Participant

is incremented, and the controller is blocked until the *Organizer* is connected (**expect**(*orgConnected*)). When this fact happens (when it is **publish**ed), a welcome message is sent to the participant, indicating the conference is starting. The **end** message indicates the end of the flow branch (unique here).

When executing the flow resulting from the connection of the *Organizer* (Fig. 2), the system behaves almost the same, until the caller is identified as the *Organizer*. In that case, the fact that the *Organizer* is now in has to be announced, which is the purpose of the **publish** action.

The major difficulty with MSC is the notion of causality, which is particularly strict in an MSC diagram. An execution flow is a sequence of events triggered by the arrival of a client request, and performance evaluation consists in simulating such flows. That sequence is fully determined by causal links between events of the flow, or with events of other flows. These causal links are essential to enable a realistic performance analysis; therefore it must be possible to derive them from the design-level model (the MSC). The problem is that on an MSC, it is very difficult to distinguish the different branches of the flow from each other.

Let us consider the flow represented by the MSC on Fig. 3. That flow is split in two branches after event *e1*: the first one is materialized by the sequence of events *e2*, *e4*, *e10*, *e11*, *e12*, and *e13*; the second one by the sequence *e3*, *e5*, *e6*, *e7*, *e8*, and *e9*. In addition, imagine the system is known to behave

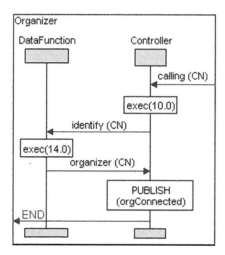

Fig. 2. Execution Flow Triggered by Organizer

in such a way that these branches are actually independent, which means that there is no synchronization between them.[2] In that case, the MSC proposed here only depicts one possible interleaving of events, but interpreting it in a strict manner would lead to the following conclusion: event $e11$, for that flow, always occur after $e7$. That is right for that MSC, but not for *that flow* in the real system. Other orderings may happen on the middle instance: $e11$ can occur before $e7$, for example, because those events belong to causally independent branches of the flow. The problem is that we would like simulation of the resulting queuing network to consider that possibility too! The strict interpretation of this MSC would lead to a constrained performance model, in the sense that some interleavings, although possible in the real system, are forbidden by construction.

Besides, we also know from the real system that $e7$ always occurs after e1. More precisely: for all executions of that flow, $e7$ comes after $e1$, because that is how the system is specified (input $e7$ can only occur if output $e3$ has been done before, which in turn is a reaction to input $e1$). We say we have a constant causal relation.

What we try to point out is the difficulty to produce a single representation of a flow that actually covers multiple possibilities of execution. When interpreting the MSC in order to produce the associated queuing model, the key issue is to manage to filter out apparent causal links (that indeed may happen as specified in the MSC, but might as well happen differently), and to keep only constant ones (that are inherent to the system's behavior).

In a general manner, what we need is a way to express exact triggering conditions of events, and that is the purpose of constructs presented above (**publish**,

---

[2] This can also be expressed in MSC (for example with a **par** expression), but this particular chart does not have that meaning.

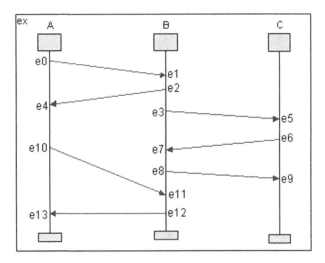

Fig. 3. A Flow Evolving in two Independent Branches

expect, delay). In fact, other notions such as co-region in MSC could be used to some extent to identify flexible orderings, but that would lead to complex diagrams. Moreover, because our objective is to identify constant triggering conditions, it is more natural and easier to specify their presence than their absence by means such as co-regions. In other terms, we specify significant - constant - causality rather than non-significant causality. In addition, by making constant conditions explicit, we express not only their existence, but also their exact nature: MSCs usually show that events occur, but not why. What we need in the performance model is to capture the basic logic that makes the underlying automata behave that way.

Another issue: even if we could express all possibilities for flexible orderings, we would still know nothing about their probability of occurrence and distribution, and that is why it is essential to let simulation naturally generate those possible interleavings.

MSC also has limitations in terms of algorithmic constructs. Behaviors like the one presented in the next section can hardly be captured with a scenario approach.

HMSC could help to face those problems: parallel branches of flows can be separated at that level, which makes each basic MSC easier to interpret. HMSC also may facilitate the expression of complex algorithmic constructs, but that needs further experiments, and anyway would often lead to unreadable diagrams. One risk, for specific applications, is to have to split flows in too many pieces, leading to some excessively complex HMSCs.

4.4 Formalization of Execution Flows: State-Machine Oriented (SDL)

As stated above, the MSC approach is limited in terms of algorithmic constructs, therefore we explored a more control-flow oriented formalism, like SDL.

Let's introduce the CoWS (Cooperating Web Services) platform, as a case study for the SDL approach. This platform dynamically builds web services by assembling basic bricks that are searched locally and on distant servers via Internet. The required functionalities (agenda, storage, mail, etc.) are specified in client requests (see Fig. 4).

The *XSL transformer* server processes requests by executing various tasks: URL decoding, identification, session update, external references composition, etc. As a result, two search campaigns are prepared and launched in parallel: one for local search, and the other for distant search. Both local and Internet search campaigns are driven by a dedicated handler. A handler sequentially submits all requests of its campaign, setting a timer each time to bound response time. On time-out, the handler aborts all remaining requests, builds a partial response aggregating all responses obtained so far, then asks the other handler to do the same thing. Specifying such a behavior with MSC is difficult, because control aspects play a significant role (counting, looping, etc.).

In the SDL approach, designers still have to identify a set of significant use cases. SDL is used to describe the associated execution flows. Extracting flows from a unique global SDL model of the system is an open issue, because it might be very difficult to decide which flows correspond what parts of behavior (at least statically).

Therefore we suggest, for each flow, to produce one specific view of the system that only describes handling of that flow. One drawback of that method might be that it leads designers to produce quite "unusual" functional views, because SDL is here used to produce a layered model rather than a global model, but

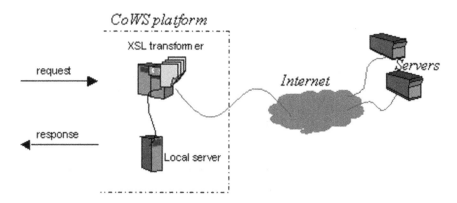

Fig. 4. Architecture of the CoWS Platform

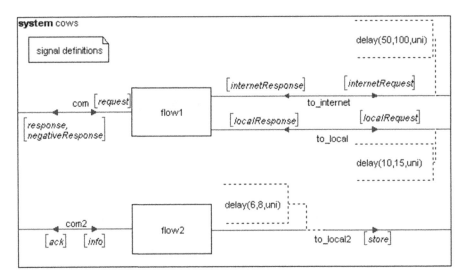

Fig. 5. Outside SDL View of Flows

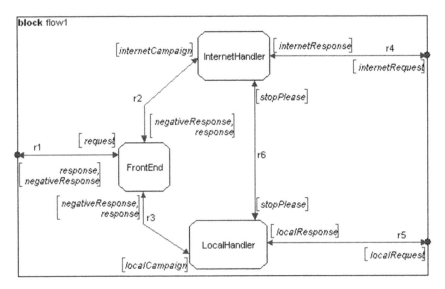

Fig. 6. Software Architecture for *flow1*

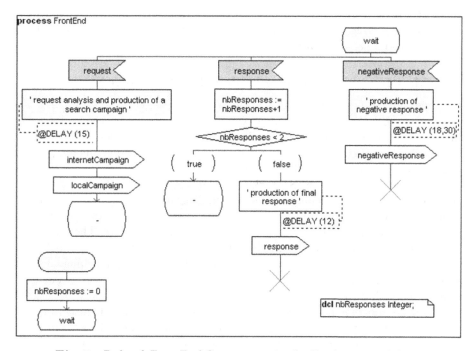

Fig. 7. Role of *FrontEnd* Component in the Realization of *flow1*

it is pragmatic and useful while the problem of inferring flows from a global model is under study. This method is depicted on Fig. 5, where one block is still used to describe one flow; note that each block accepts a unique signal from the environment: the flow's triggering request.

Each flow is then refined by describing what components of the system are involved in its realization (Fig. 6), and finally by giving the behavior of each component (Fig. 7). Again, our goal is not to specify the complete behavior, but just the essential logic that orients the flow in one direction or another. Therefore, the use of informal constructs is encouraged as far as possible, so that an appropriate level of abstraction (from the performance modeling point of view) can be reached. Typically, resource-consuming tasks are abstracted by informal tasks, to which we attach quantified delay annotations.

The advantage with the SDL approach is that arbitrary complex behavior can be specified, thus it is very natural to express precise triggering conditions of tasks. On the other hand, we lose the data-flow dimension and this has to be inferred by tracking outputs/inputs of signals from one instance to another. To facilitate this operation, the model should be statically unambiguous regarding routing. We also note some difficulties with this approach: expressing dependencies between flows might imply an important overhead of communication, because shared variables are not handled in a straightforward way by SDL, but as an explicit message exchange (from the execution point of view). We conclude, there is a need to define a rigorous framework (an "SDL profile") that would naturally lead designers to produce well-formed flow models, as expected by a performance model generator.

4.5   Mapping to Performance Models (SES/Workbench)

Here we roughly describe how execution flows represented in MSC or SDL are mapped to SES/Workbench queuing systems. The mapping procedure has been implemented in prototypes. The results obtained on the presented case studies are much promising. The mapping should also work for other queuing based tools, where the basic concepts are identical.

The formalism used in SES/Workbench contains both graphical and textual constructs, like SDL. Queuing models are built graphically, by interconnecting elementary nodes such as the service node with queue, user node, delay node, traffic generator node, blocking node, source and sink nodes, etc. Then behavior is specified inside nodes, using a C-based textual language. Typically, behavior defines actions to be carried out by a user node (such as publishing of facts through shared variables), unblocking conditions for blocking nodes, traffic generation algorithms, etc. Queuing models can also be hierarchically structured thanks to submodel nodes, that encapsulate lower-level models. Transactions are named stimuli that materialize client requests follow-ups into the system; they move from node to node, where they trigger the execution of tasks according to their nature (often determined by the data they carry). Nodes can communicate with each other thanks to a shared variable mechanism. SES/Workbench is presented in more detail in [11].

Mapping from MSC. To each execution flow (represented by a single MSC diagram) is associated one SES submodel, that we develop by mapping MSC clauses to SES primitives:

- the arrival of the client request is represented by a source node;
- **exec** actions are mapped to service nodes, preceded by a user node where time consumption is specified; service nodes also refer to their allocated processing node in the underlying resource model (not presented here);
- **publish** actions are mapped to user nodes that assign the concerned shared variables;
- **end** messages are mapped to sink nodes, denoting the end of a flow branch;
- **delay** conditions are mapped to delay nodes;
- **expect** conditions are mapped to blocking nodes parameterized with the corresponding predicate on shared variables; such nodes retain transactions until their predicate evaluates to true;
- outputs are mapped to edges from the sender node to the receiving one;
- output sequences (when an output is immediately followed by other outputs, from the same instance) are mapped to split nodes, which create multiple parallel branches in the flow;
- an alternative is mapped to a fork of conditional edges, where conditions are used to orient transactions in one direction or another.

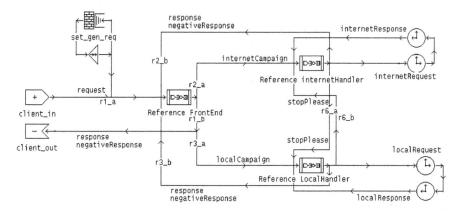

Fig. 8. Queuing System Derived for *flow1* of the CoWS Platform

Mapping from SDL As for MSC, we associate one SES submodel to each SDL execution flow. Mapping the architecture of flows is quite straightforward. The flow architecture is mapped to a similar hierarchy of submodels that are interconnected/encapsulated in the same way including routing indications.

As an example, Fig. 8 shows the submodel architecture reflecting *flow1* of the CoWS platform.

Describing the whole mapping procedure in detail would be too long here. However, the treatment of behavioral parts deserves some comments. SDL state machines are "state-driven", which means that given a state, the machine defines how to react to some expected signals. On the contrary, SES/Workbench models are event-driven, in the sense that nodes first consider the nature of the transaction that is submitted, then they select the appropriate reaction according to their own state. Therefore, the first step is to interpret SDL state machines in that way, so that for each possible input, the possible reactions are specified. Then, the state-machine is mapped to a queuing structure, that reflects the sequence of tasks (user and service nodes) to execute for each event.

5   Conclusion

The main purpose of this article was to raise and discuss an issue: how to facilitate the access to powerful performance evaluation techniques, in particular for engineers who are used to manipulating functional representations of systems.

A major obstacle lies in the fact that expected performance models - as far as the queuing systems simulation technique is concerned - represent the system from a viewpoint that is very different from the traditional functional viewpoint. The notion of execution flow, however, appears to be key concept; execution flows define chain reactions that are implied when a system is stimulated by a typical event. It appears that such flows, fortunately enough, are usually easy to identify in the case of service platforms.

Therefore, we try to adapt well-accepted design languages to the purpose of capturing execution flows, in order to ease a smooth derivation of queuing models. MSC, as a scenario language, appears very natural to capture the "event" flow side of execution flows, whereas SDL is more suited to the expression of non-trivial control aspects. In both cases, beyond validation of the ideas, a rigorous framework has to be defined, specially regarding the soundness of semantics and of the mapping to the queuing systems model.

The goal of this paper was to suggest orientations for deeper research rather than solutions, and we are now preparing a collaborative project that will precisely address theoretical issues, and keep user-friendliness as a strong requirement, as well as applicability of the approach to commercial simulators.

References

[1] C. U. Smith and L. G. Williams. Software performance engineering: A case study including performance comparison with design alternatives. IEEE Transactions on Software Engineering, 19(7):720-741, July 1993. 1

[2] S. Fdida and G. Pujolle. Modèles de Systèmes et de Réseaux - Tome 1: Performance, Eyrolles, 1986. 3

[3] A. M. Law and W. D. Kelton. Simulation modeling and analysis, McGraw-Hill, 2nd ed., 1991. 3

[4] P. Fishwick. Simulation model design and execution. Prentice Hall, 1995. 3

[5] M. Polo and B. Rumpler. Méthode et outil d'aide au dimensionnement d'un serveur de base de données, Ingénierie des Systèmes d'Information, Vol.5, No.4, October 1997. 3

[6] D. M. Neuse. Why simulate?, Capacity Management Review, Vol.36, No.2, Feb. 1998. 3

[7] O. Catrina and S. Budkowski. Simulation guiding and validation based on dependence relations between events. Proceedings of the 13th European Simulation Multiconference (ESM'99), Warsaw, June 1999. 3

[8] QNAP tool (http://www.simulog.fr). 3

[9] Simscript tool (http://www.caci.com). 3

[10] OPNET tool (http://www.opnet.com). 3

[11] SES/Workbench tool, Hyperformix (http://www.hyperformix.com). 3, 14

[12] F. Bause and P. Buchholz. Qualitative and Quantitative Analysis of Timed SDL Specifications. In Proc. KiVS'93, Springer Informatik aktuell (1993) 486-500. 4

[13] H. M. Kabutz, Analytical performance evaluation of concurrent communicating systems using SDL and stochastic Petri nets. Doctoral thesis, department of Computer science, University of Cape Town, Republic of south Africa, 1997. 4

[14] M. Butow, M. Mestern, C. Schapiro, and P. S. Kritzinger. Performance modelling with the formal specification language SDL. Proceedings of the FORTE/PSTV'96 Conference on Formal Description Techniques, Kaiserslautern, Germany, 1996. 4

[15] M. Steppler and M. Lott, SPEET - SDL Performance Evaluation Tool. SDL'97 - Time for Testing, Proceedings of the 8th SDL Forum, Elsevier, 1997. 4

[16] E. Heck. Performance Evaluation of Formally Specified Systems - the integration of SDL with HIT. Doctoral thesis, University of Dortmund, Krehl Verlag, 1996. 4

[17] J. Martins. A system Engineering Methodology Integrating performance evaluation and Formal Specification. PhD Thesis, Ecole Polytechnique Fédérale de Lausanne, April 1996. 4

[18] M. Diefenbruch. Functional and Quantitative Verification of Time-and resource Extended SDL Systems with Model-checking. Proceeding of Messung, Modellierung und Bewertung von Rechen- und Kommunikationssystemen, Freiberg, Germany, VDE-Verlag, 1997. 4

[19] A. Mitschele-Thiel and B. Müller-Clostermann. Performance Engineering of SDL/MSC systems, Journal on Computer Networks and ISDN Systems, Elsevier, Vol. 31 No. 17, June 1999. pp 1801-1816. 4

[20] C. Schaffer, R. Raschhofer and A. Simma. EaSy-Sim: A Tool Environment for the design of Complex, Real-Time systems. Proceedings International Conference on Computer Aided Systems Technologies. Innsbruck, Springer-Verlag, 1995. 4

[21] H. M. EI-Sayed, D. Cameron and C. M. Woodside, Automated performance modeling from scenarios and SDL design of distributed systems. Proceedings of International Symposium on Software Engineering for Parallel and Distributed Systems (PDSE'98), Kyoto, April 1998. 4

[22] C. U. Smith and L. G. Williams. Performance Engineering Evaluation of Object-Oriented Systems with SPEED, Computer Performance Evaluation: Modeling Techniques and Tools, No. 1245, Springer-Verlag, Berlin, 1997. 4

[23] C. E. Hrischuk, C. M. Woodside, J. A. Rolia and R. Iversen, Trace-based load characterization for generating performance software models. IEEE Transactions on Software Engineering, Feb 1999, Vol 25 No.1. 4

[24] D. Petriu and M. Woodside, Software Performance Models from Systems Scenarios in Use Case Maps, Performance TOOLS 2002, Springer Verlag. 4, 5

Scenario-Based Performance Engineering with UCMNav

Dorin Petriu[1], Daniel Amyot[2], and Murray Woodside[1]

[1] Department of Systems and Computer Engineering
Carleton University
Ottawa, ON K1S 5B6, Canada
{dorin,cmw}@sce.carleton.ca
[2] School of Information Technology and Engineering
University of Ottawa
Ottawa, ON K1N 6N5, Canada
damyot@site.uottawa.ca

Abstract. The analysis of a scenario specification for a new system can address some questions of system performance, in the sense of delay and capacity estimation. To assist the analyst, a performance model can be generated automatically from a Use Case Map specification in the UCM Navigator (UCMNav). This paper describes the process, and the information that must be supplied in the way of scenario annotations. It illustrates the tool-supported process with a substantial example related to electronic commerce, which demonstrates the impact of provisioning the software architecture for concurrency.

1 Introduction

Software performance engineering (SPE) is concerned with performance characteristics (metrics) such as response times, delays and throughput, and it aims to insure that software products under development will meet their performance requirements. SPE uses predictive performance models to analyze the effect of software features on performance metrics for systems with timing and capacity requirements. SPE should begin early in the software life cycle, before serious barriers to performance are frozen into the design and implementation. Although existing methods for early analysis are successful, the transfer of designer knowledge into the performance model is slow and expensive [1].

Scenario specifications provide a powerful starting point for system design and for analysis of various kinds of requirements. *Use Case Maps* (UCMs) are a graphical language specifically used for expressing scenarios, and for experimenting with scenario interactions and architecture [2, 3]. The UCM notation is part of the User Requirements Notation, currently standardized by ITU-T [4]. Among the numerous scenario notations surveyed in [5], UCMs are notably fit for many requirements engineering activities and for transformations to other modeling languages. A UCM tool, the *UCM Navigator* (UCMNav [6]) has been

R. Reed (Ed.): SDL 2003, LNCS 2708, pp. 18–35, 2003.

augmented to assist with the early analysis of performance questions, from scenario specifications. This tool has already been used in various SPE case studies [7, 8, 9] and in SPE graduate courses. This paper addresses the details of how to begin such an analysis, by considering the performance attributes of scenarios and how they are represented in tools.

The analysis of performance from scenario specifications is an active area of investigation [1]. Many other approaches are based on adding performance attributes to behavior models, with scenario-based and state-based languages. For instance, Message Sequence Charts (MSCs) [10] can be supplemented with performance information to generate SDL [11] specifications, as suggested by Dulz et al. [12] and by Kerber [13]. UML behavior models [14] can also have such annotations. Kähkipuro uses performance-oriented UML models (in addition to the design model) to generate performance models [15], whereas Woodside et al. extract performance models from UML designs in a CASE tool [16]. A survey of methods for building performance models from UML specifications is given in [17]. The advantages of UCMs for SPE are the capture of scenario interactions and of architecture issues, the ability to describe scenarios without specifying explicit inter-component collaborations, and the flexibility to rapidly modify the architecture and to re-analyze, as studied by Scratchley in [9].

There exist many families of performance modeling languages. A very recent study showed that queueing networks (QN) provide higher scalability and adequacy for performance analysis than process algebras and generalized stochastic Petri Nets [18]. *Layered Queueing Networks* (LQNs) are supersets of QNs [20]. They capture the workload within activities (operations connected in sequence or in parallel) which belong to an entry of a task (method of an operating system process) running on a host device (usually a processor). The host device is usually a processor, a task is often an operating system process, but may also be an object, and an entry is like a method.

The following sections describe the steps needed to do a performance analysis of scenarios specified with the UCMNAV editor. A tutorial example of an electronic commerce system (e-bookstore) is presented in order to illustrate these steps, which are:

- start with a UCM model that is "sufficiently complete" for performance analysis;
- augment the UCM with performance-related data;
- generate a Layered Queueing Network performance model and solve the model (this step is automated);
- analyze the LQN results with reference to performance requirements and goals, and revise the UCM if needed.

The reader unfamiliar with UCMs or LQNs can find additional tutorial material in [2, 3, 19, 20, 21].

2   UCM Model

A UCM describes a system as a set of *paths* that traverse a set of *components*. The operations of the system are captured as *responsibilities* along a path, allocated to particular components. The sequence in the path represents causality and control, including forking into parallel subpaths. The movement of the path from one component to another represents transfer of control, without showing details of how this is accomplished. Path detail can be hidden in sub-diagrams called *plug-ins*, contained in *stubs* (diamonds) on a path. More details on the UCM semantics can be found in [3].

The steps required for performance analysis will be presented using an example of a Web-based bookstore called the RADSbookstore (for selling books on Real-time And Distributed Systems), also described in [8]. The RADSbookstore provides the following facilities:

- an interface for customers - to browse the catalogue and to buy books;
- an interface for bookstore administrators - to examine the inventory and the sales data;
- separate databases for the inventory and the customer accounts;
- applications to manage customer accounts, shopping cart objects, and the inventory;
- a subsystem to track and fill back-orders (orders to be filled for books that are not in stock).

Figure 1 shows the RADSbookstore root (top-level) map. The parallelogram shaped components represent concurrent processes, while the rectangle shapes are uncommitted architectural elements. The details of service operations are entirely hidden in the stubs; indeed there are seven different client operations and two different administrator operations. These are *dynamic stubs* with selection of the appropriate plug-in UCM according to a request type. In this style, the

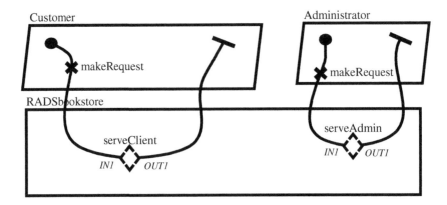

Fig. 1. UCM Root Map for the RADSbookstore

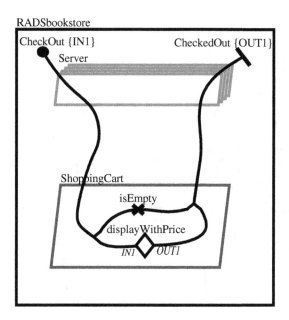

Fig. 2. First Level Plug-in for the checkout Scenario, in Stub serveClient

root UCM represents a large number of scenarios. Because of space limitations here, we will illustrate only the checkout scenario for customers, which has two levels of plug-ins as shown in Fig. 2 and Fig. 3, and the fill backorders scenario for administrators, shown in Fig. 4.

2.1   UCM Style Constraints for Generating Performance Models

The UCMNav tool has a performance model generation capability, but it can only be used on a UCM which satisfies certain constraints on completeness and style. (To encourage the capture of incomplete scenarios, the default style of a legal UCM is relatively unconstrained.) In particular, a UCM **must** be *properly formed*, meaning:

– it must have at least one point, empty or otherwise, inside each component that is crossed by a path;
– it must have all loops expressed by the explicit loop construct
  • this means avoiding "informal" looping structures formed by using an OR-fork followed by a path looping back to an OR-join at an earlier point on the path (see Fig. 5);
– it should not have paths branching from a loop that join with paths that did not branch off the same loop;
– plug-ins must be properly bound to their stubs;
  • that is, each input to a stub must be bound to a start point in the plug-in map, and each output to an end point in the plug-in.

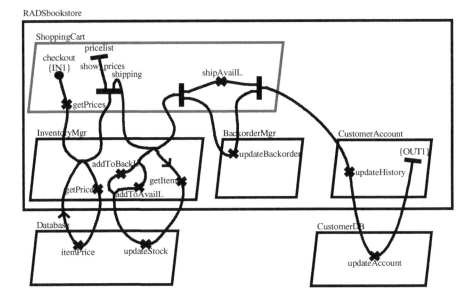

Fig. 3. Second Level Plug-in for the checkout Scenario, in Stub displayWithPrice

– plug-in maps must not also be identified as root maps.

In addition, UCMs for performance **should** also:

– have paths that fully cover the scenario interactions of the system that are to be modeled;
– be augmented with the necessary performance-related data, as listed below. Some of the parameters have default values.

UCMNAV has the capability of automatically generating LQN models for any well-formed UCM, triggered by selecting the menu Performance → Generate LQN. The *scenario to performance transformation algorithm* (SPT, [7]) used to generate LQNs uses a point to point traversal of the UCM paths and infers a calling structure between the components based on the order in which they are traversed by the path. If a path crosses a component but does not have a point inside that component, then the path traversal will not detect the component, and the entire set of calling relationships between components may be misinterpreted. Thus, if the designer does not intend a path to touch a component, it is recommended not to draw the path over the component at all.

The requirement to use the loop construct relieves the SPT algorithm of the need to interpret some very complex constructs which can be created by allowing paths to branch and rejoin in any way at all. In effect it is a "good structure" constraint similar to the use of a *while..do*. Figure 5 shows some valid loop constructs and indicates whether they are interpreted as being properly formed for the performance model transformation.

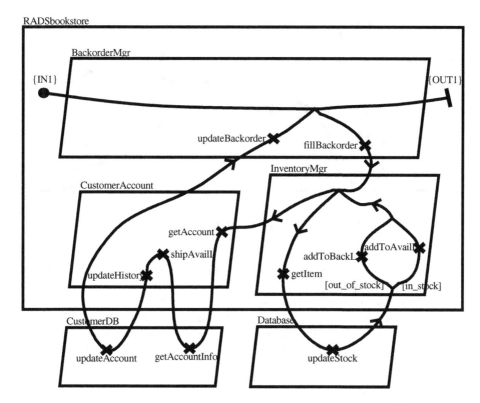

Fig. 4. Plug-in for the fill backorders Scenario, in Stub serveAdmin

When used informally, plug-in maps can be associated with a stub without explicitly binding the input and output path segments. However, the SPT algorithm relies on the bindings to traverse the path into the stub, and out again. For a set of plug-ins in a dynamic stub, it treats the input segment as an OR-fork to choose between possible plug-ins. The binding dialog window for a stub is shown in Fig. 6 and is accessed by opening the Applicable Transformations pop-up menu for the stub and selecting the Bind Plugin to Stub entry. Existing bindings are shown in the Stub Bindings text box. To create an entry binding, one needs to select a stub entry and a plug-in map start point before clicking on the Bind Entries button. Similarly, to create an exit binding one needs to select a stub exit and a plug-in map stop point before clicking on the Bind Exits button. Binding a plug-in map into a stub also requires that the plug-in start and end points have unique names in order to distinguish which point to use in a binding.

A given UCM model can include multiple maps of both *Root* and *Plug-in* type, and a root map can even be used as a plug-in map in any stub. However this will confuse the interpretation by the current SPT algorithm. If the same map is to be used both as a root map and a plug-in map, then it is best to avoid confusion by exporting the map and then importing back as a plug-in for

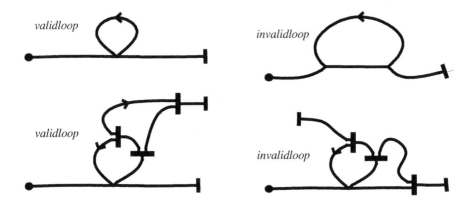

Fig. 5. Valid and Invalid Loop Structures

the desired stub. There will be two copies of the map, but each copy will have a clearly defined type.

There is also a more subtle issue regarding the interactions between components when generating an LQN model from a UCM. Calling relationships between components are determined by the order in which they are traversed by a path. As a path crosses new components, it is assumed that calls are being made from component to component. Whenever a path returns to a component it has previously crossed, it is assumed that a reply to a call is being received. The SPT algorithm attempts to maximize the synchronous interpretation of interactions between components, but this interpretation requires that the path return to components that are supposed to make synchronous calls. Thus, the performance model is based on the more restricted interpretation that inter-component communication is determined solely by the order in which components are crossed along a path. This is not necessarily an interpretation that is assumed in other types of UCM usage.

2.2 UCM Performance-Related Parameters

The generation of performance models requires that the UCM be augmented with adequate performance-related data to enable meaningful analysis. The following steps must be performed in order:

- create processors and disks or other devices;
- assign UCM components to processors;
- assign service demands to UCM responsibilities.

The following steps should also be done but their order does not matter:

- define arrival characteristics for start points;
- assign probabilities/weights to branches on OR-forks;
- assign probabilities/weights to plug-ins for dynamic stubs;

– assign loop repetition counts to loops.

Time values used for parameters do not show units and can be interpreted to be of whatever time unit the designer chooses (typically milliseconds or seconds). However, it is important that the time unit used be consistent throughout the entire UCM.

Processors and devices need to be created in UCMNAV prior to LQN generation. To create a device, one should open the Device Characteristics dialog box (Performance menu) as shown in Fig. 7 (left).

The type of device to be edited can be selected from the Device Type drop-down menu. Devices can be:

– **Processor**: processing device that acts as a host to components;
– **Disk**: disk device;
– **DSP**: digital signal processor;
– **Service**: any external service.

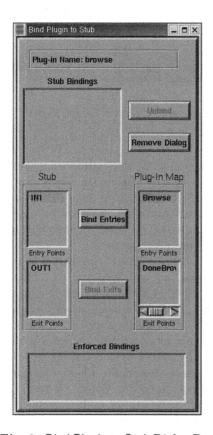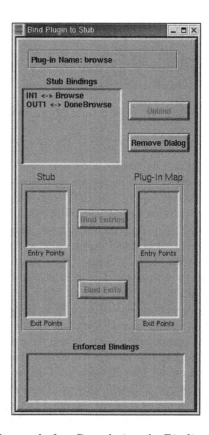

Fig. 6. Bind Plugin to Stub Dialog Box before and after Completing the Bindings

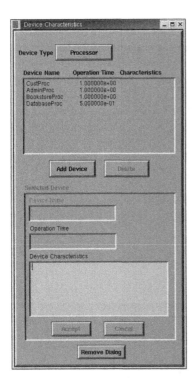 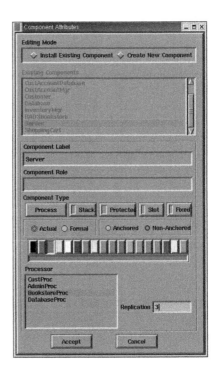

Fig. 7. Device Characteristics and Component Attributes Dialog Boxes

Each device must be specified to have an associated operation time that is a relative scale factor for its processing speed. A larger operation time indicates a slower device. The SPT algorithm also creates a default infinite processor (a multiprocessor with an unlimited number of replicas) with an operation time of 1. All the components that do not have a processor assigned in the UCM are generated as LQN tasks assigned to this infinite processor.

Components in the UCM should have a host processor specified. Figure 7 (right) shows the Component Attributes dialog box which is used to configure components. The *Editing Mode* determines whether the component is a stand-alone component (Create New Component) or a reference to an already existing component (*Install Existing Component*). The Component Label is the name of the component - if the component is a reference of an existing component then changing the label will change that name of the component and all its other references. The Component Type drop-down menu determines whether the component is a Team, Object, Process, ISR, Pool, Agent, or Other. However, all component types are mapped to LQN tasks. In the case of multiple references to the same component, only one LQN task is generated for the component and visits to any of the references are assumed to generate messages to that one task. The Stack checkbox indicates whether or not the component is replicated, and

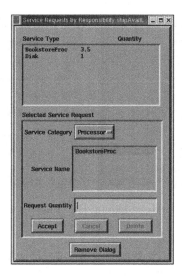

Fig. 8. Service Requests by Responsibility Dialog Box

it activates the Replication field which specifies the number of copies. Multiple components are generated as multi-threaded tasks in the LQN. If the Replication field is set to * then the corresponding LQN task is infinitely-threaded. The Processor text field shows all the processors defined in the UCM, with the highlighted processor being the host for the component. If no processor is selected for the component then the LQN generated will make the corresponding task run on the infinite processor.

Responsibilities can make specific demands on the various services defined. Figure 8 shows the Service Requests by Responsibility dialog box (invoked from the Edit Responsibility dialog box by pressing the Service Requests button). The Service Type column in the top text field shows the services that are called and the Quantity column indicates the number of requests made. To add a new service request, one selects the Service Category to be used from the drop-down box and then selects the actual device in the Service Name field. If the service type is processor, then only the name of the host processor for the component that contains the responsibility will be shown, but it must still be explicitly selected by highlighting it in the Service Name field. The request quantity must also be entered in the Request Quantity field.

Deciding upon the right values for service demands can be a delicate undertaking, and there are different strategies used to find them. A value can come from a known value or benchmark, a performance budget for the maximum/average time that may be taken by the responsibility [22], or maybe just an estimate by the designer that can be fine-tuned later [23]. Any responsibility that does not have service demands specified is generated as an LQN activity with a default demand of 1. This default means that even an incompletely spec-

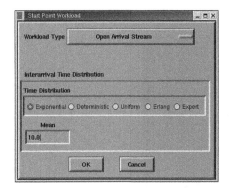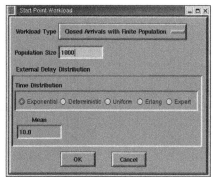

Fig. 9. Start Point Workload Dialog Boxes for Open and Closed Arrivals

ified UCM generates an LQN that can be solved, although the solution is only a very rough approximation.

The arrival process for each start point needs to be specified using the Start Point Workload dialog box, shown in Fig. 9, which is accessed from each start point's transformation menu. The arrivals can be specified as either open streams with no limit on the job population or as closed streams with a finite job population. In order to be picked up by the SPT algorithm, the distribution of the interarrival time for open arrival streams and the think time for closed streams should be specified as either exponential with a mean, deterministic with a mean, or uniform with a value. Erlang distributions with a high and low value or expert distribution with a string descriptor are not currently handled. Start points with closed arrivals imply a return path for each job and as such should be connected to an end point along the same path or be contained in the same component as an end point. In the absence of such an end point, the SPT algorithm will generate the required return path from the first end point encountered as the path is traversed. By default, start points with no specified arrival process are generated as having open arrivals with an exponential distribution with a mean of 1.

Probabilities for OR-fork branches should be specified using the Specification of OR-Fork dialog box accessed from each OR-fork's transformation menu. The branches are labelled as BR1, BR2, and so on, and those labels are shown on the UCM whenever the window is open. Branch probabilities can be specified as decimal fractions or as relative weights for each branch, and they are normalized during the LQN generation process. Similarly, plug-ins for dynamic stubs are also traversed like branches between a virtual OR-fork at each stub entry point and a virtual OR-join at each stub exit point. Each plug-in should also have a specified selection probability, which are specified in the Choose Plugin dialog box of each dynamic stub. Any missing branch or plug-in selection probabilities are given a relative weight of 1. If all the branch or plug-in selection probabilities for an OR-fork or dynamic stub are missing, then each branch or plug-in will be generated with an equal probability in the LQN.

The number of loop repetitions for each loop construct needs to be specified as a loop count in the Edit Loop Characteristics dialog box. Loops with missing loop counts are generated with a default value of 1.

2.3 Verification of Parameter Completion

UCMNAV provides the capability of verifying whether all the performance-related parameters have been entered for all relevant elements in a UCM. Selecting the Performance menu → Verify Annotation Completeness entry highlights in red all the UCM elements that have missing parameters. Selecting the Performance menu → Remove Annotation Highlighting entry removes the highlighting.

3 LQN Performance Model

Figure 10 shows the LQN model generated from the annotated RADSbookstore UCMs. The details of entries and activities, and the workload parameters are suppressed for presentation purposes. The multiple interaction arrows show the numbers of different kinds of access made from one task to another. For example, tracing the paths in Figs. 1, 2 and 3 leads us from the set of Customer tasks, to the RADSbookstore task representing the system as a whole (a task without functions) to the Server. The Checkout scenario then calls the ShoppingCart, which manages the checkout. The ShoppingCart calls the InventoryMgr (twice), the BackorderMgr, and the CustomerAccount. The InventoryMgr in turn calls the Database, and the CustomerAccount calls the CustomerDB.

The forwarding path, shown by the dashed arrow from the InventoryMgr to the CustomerAccount, is part of the Administrator's backorder scenario, as shown by the Administrator path in Fig. 1 and the fill backorders plug-in in Fig. 4. The forwarding occurs when the InventoryMgr is updated, initiates the shipping, and then passes on the information to the CustomerAccount for the accounting and billing. The CustomerAccount then forwards the reply back to the RADSbookstore.

3.1 Solving LQNs

LQN models can be solved using tools such as the *LQNS analytic solver* and the *LQSim* simulator [20]. Both solvers accept the same input LQN file format, which is automatically generated from UCMNAV, and generate similar output files with the following sections:

- **General Solver Statistics**: elapsed time, system time, blocks, simulation length for LQSim, etc.
- **Echo of the Specified Service Demands**: specified service demands for every entry and activity.

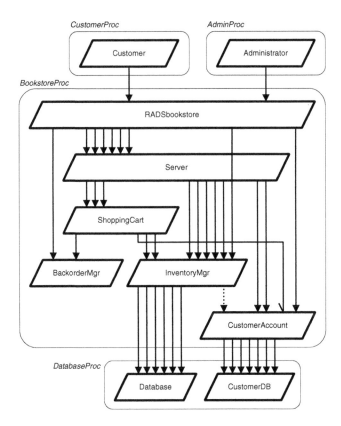

Fig. 10. LQN Model of the RADSbookstore

- **Measured Quantities**: measured service demands, number of blocking and non-blocking calls, call delays, synchronization delays.
- **Service Times**: solved service times for every entry and activity, includes confidence intervals when simulated with multiple blocks.
- **Service Time Variances**: variances and squared coefficients of variance for the service times calculated in the section above.
- **Throughput and Utilizations**: solved throughput and utilizations for every entry and activity, includes confidence intervals when simulated with multiple blocks.
- **Utilizations and Waiting Times for Devices**: solved hardware utilizations and waiting times by every entry.

LQNS is faster but more limited than LQSim in the models it can handle. Some LQN models do not have a stable analytical solution and therefore they need to be solved using simulations with LQSim.

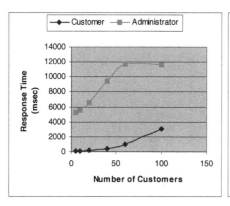 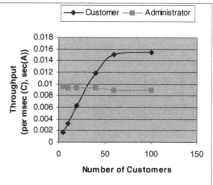

Fig. 11. Response time and throughput simulation results for the RADSbook-store

The layered nature of LQNs and the fact that the solvers provide results for both software and hardware resources means this approach is suitable for detecting both software and hardware performance bottlenecks.

Figure 11 shows the response time and throughput results for the RADS-Bookstore. The bookstore was solved as a closed system with a variable client population and a single administrator. The results show that this system becomes saturated with about 50 clients.

4   Performance Analysis

The LQN performance model can be used as a basis for exploring the performance solution space of the system. The kinds of analysis that can be performed include, but are not limited to, the following:

- **Sensitivity Analysis**: how important are different values for certain parameters to the solution. This is useful to estimate the performance impact of the uncertainty in estimated values.
- **Scalability Analysis**: how well does the system cope with more users, how does the system throughput, response times and utilization behave as the workload is increased.
- **Concurrency Analysis**: how does the system respond to changes in the number of threads or replicas for certain tasks.
- **Deployment/Configuration Analysis**: how does the system respond to different deployment configurations, what are the effects of bandwidth limitations, network delays, or reallocating the system hardware.

4.1   Example of Concurrency Analysis for the RADSbookstore

The results for the base case of the RADSbookstore indicate that Customers are queueing up at the Server task, which has 5 threads. This suggests that increasing

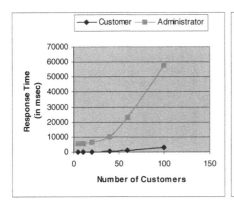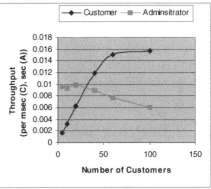

Fig. 12. Response Time and Throughput Simulation Results for the RADS-bookstore with 50 Server Threads

the number of Server threads would remove a software bottleneck. Figure 12 shows the results of increasing the number of Server threads to 50. Instead of improving the overall performance of the system, increasing the number of Server threads actually degrades it. The response time and throughput for Customers remains essentially unchanged, but the response time for the Administrator rises from 12 seconds with 100 Customers to 60 seconds with 100 Customers. Thus the increase in threads consumes resources and makes the Administrator response much worse, giving absolutely no benefits.

A deeper analysis of the performance results for the base case of the RADS-bookstore shows that within the system the Inventory Manager task is 100i% saturated, mostly due to waiting for the Database which is 80% busy. Thus the Customers queueing at the Server are actually held up by the InventoryMgr and the Database. Therefore the limited number of Server threads provides a kind of admission control, keeping congestion out of the system without actually slowing it down. This indicates that a better way of improving the performance of the system is to improve the InventoryMgr and the Database.

An examination of the way in which Customers interact with the RADS-bookstore shows that they mostly browse the catalogue of books, and do not really need full database capability and concurrency control. The catalogue is rarely updated, and could be separated out as a read-only database without complex concurrency control. Indeed, creating a separate Catalogue server inside the RADSbookstore to replace the catalogue accesses to the InventoryMgr and the Database significantly improves the system performance, as shown in Fig. 13.

5   Conclusions

Software Performance Engineering from requirements descriptions is very challenging and demanding. However, several developments such as those presented

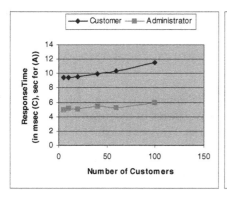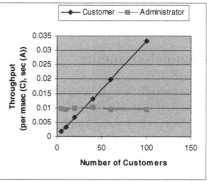

Fig. 13. Response Time and Throughput Simulation Results for the RADS-bookstore with a Catalogue Server

in this paper indicate that automated generation of performance models early in the development process is not only possible but also useful.

This paper presented systematically the steps involved in the construction of UCM models annotated with performance information, as supported in UCM-Nav. Once all the required information is provided, a situation that can be verified by the tool, UCMNav can automatically generate a performance model suitable for various kinds of performance analysis. Traceability between the two models is preserved through the use of common names. Default values are provided by the SPT algorithm for several categories of parameters if they are not specified by the designer. Analysis reports for the resulting LQN model are produced automatically with tools such as the LQNS analytic solver and the LQSim simulator. The e-commerce example illustrated typical situations of parameter provision and analysis results. Many variants of an UCM model (such as a different underlying architecture, or different values for the performance parameters) can quickly be generated, evaluated, and compared.

The two languages selected here (UCM and LQN) proved to be a good match for performance engineering based on requirement scenarios. Queueing networks are known to be abstract, like UCMs, but they are usually difficult to obtain from behavioral descriptions [18]. With UCMNav, they are generated automatically from the requirements specification, at the cost of some stylistic constraints. The addition of performance annotations is not really costly because such information is typically needed by any performance model.

Many of the parameter annotations for UML models have been inspired from existing work on UCMs and are now part of the performance profile for UML [24]. Recent work also suggests that the SPT algorithm used in UCMNav can likely be applied to scenario specifications in other languages, including MSC and UML sequence, collaboration, and activity diagrams [8]. This will be investigated, together with transformations to variants of queueing networks other than LQNs. We also plan to study how best to use UCM scenario definitions in a performance engineering context, as well as the verification of soft real-time requirements (captured with pairs of *timestamps* on UCM paths [9]) through LQN analysis.

Acknowledgments

This research was funded by the Natural Sciences and Engineering Research Council of Canada (NSERC), through its programs of Strategic and Collaborative Research Grants, and by Nortel Networks. We are thankful to Don Cameron and Os Monkewich for their collaboration.

References

[1] R. Pooley. Software Engineering and Performance: a Roadmap. The Future of Software Engineering, ICSE'2000, Limerick, Ireland, pp. 189-200, 2000   18, 19

[2] R. J. A. Buhr. Use Case Maps as Architectural Entities for Complex Systems. IEEE Transactions on Software Engineering. Vol. 24, No. 12, December 1998, 1131-1155, 1998   18, 19

[3] ITU-T, URN Focus Group. Draft Rec. Z.152 - UCM: Use Case Map Notation (UCM). Geneva, 2002   18, 19, 20

[4] ITU-T. Recommendation Z.150 (02/03), User Requirements Notation (URN) - Language Requirements and Framework. International Telecommunication Union, Geneva. (see also http://www.UseCaseMaps.org/urn/)   18

[5] D. Amyot and E. Eberlein. An Evaluation of Scenario Notations and Construction Approaches for Telecommunication Systems Development. To appear in Telecommunication Systems Journal, 2003   18

[6] A. Miga. Application of Use Case Maps to System Design with Tool Support. M.Eng. thesis, Dept. of Systems and Computer Engineering, Carleton University, Ottawa, Canada, 1998   18

[7] D. Petriu and C. M. Woodside. Software Performance Models from System Scenarios in Use Case Maps. 12th Int. Conf. on Modelling Tools and Techniques for Computer and Communication System Performance Evaluation, London, U. K., April, 2002. (http://www.UseCaseMaps.org/pub/tools02.pdf)   19, 22

[8] D. Petriu and C. M. Woodside. Analysing Software Requirements Specifications for Performance. Third International Workshop on Software and Performance (WOSP), Rome, Italy, 2002   19, 20, 33

[9] W. C. Scratchley. Evaluation and Diagnosis of Concurrency Architectures. Ph.D. thesis, Department of Systems and Computer Engineering, Carleton University, Ottawa, Canada, 2000   19, 34

[10] ITU-T. Recommendation Z.120 (11/99), Message Sequence Chart (MSC). International Telecommunication Union, Geneva   19

[11] ITU-T. Recommendation Z.100 (08/02), Specification and Description Language (SDL). International Telecommunication Union, Geneva   19

[12] W. Dulz, S. Gruhl, L. Lambert, and M. Sollner. Early performance prediction of SDL/MSC specified systems by automated synthetic code generation. SDL'99: Meeting UML, Proc. of the Ninth SDL Forum, Montréal, Canada, Elsevier, 1999   19

[13] L. Kerber. Scenario-based Performance Evaluation of SDL/MSC-Specified Systems. Performance Engineering, LNCS 2047, Springer, pp. 185-201, 2001   19

[14] Object Management Group. Unified Modeling Language Specification, Version 1.5. March 2003. (http://www.omg.org) 19

[15] P. Kähkipuro. UML-Based Performance Modeling Framework for Component-Based Distributed Systems. Performance Engineering, LNCS 2047, Springer, pp. 167-184, 2001 19

[16] C. M. Woodside, C. Hrischuk, B. Selic, and S. Bayarov. Automated Performance Modeling of Software Generated by a Design Environment. Performance Evaluation, vol. 45, pp 107-124, July 2001 19

[17] S. Balsamo and M. Simeoni. On transforming UML models into performance models. Workshop on Transformations in the Unified Modeling Language, Genova, Italy, April 2001 19

[18] V. Cortellessa, A. Di Marco, and P. Inverardi. Comparing Performance Models from a Software Designer Perspective. TR SAH/042, Universita di L'Aquila, Italy, 2003. (http://sahara.di.univaq.it/tech.php?id_tech=42) 19, 33

[19] D. Amyot. Introduction to the User Requirements Notation: Learning by Example. Computer Networks, Vol.24/2, Elsevier, June 2003 19

[20] Layered Queues for Software and Hardware Performance Modeling: Resource Page (http://www.layeredqueues.org/) 19, 29

[21] C. M. Woodside. Tutorial Introduction to Layered Performance Modeling of Software Performance. On-line, May 2002.
(http://www.sce.carleton.ca/rads/lqn/lqn-documentation/tutorialf.pdf)
19

[22] K. Siddiqui and C. M. Woodside. Performance-Aware Software Development (PASD) Using Resource Demand Budgets. Third International Workshop on Software and Performance (WOSP), Rome, Italy, 2002 27

[23] C. U. Smith and L. G. Williams. Performance Solutions. Addison-Wesley, 2001 27

[24] Object Management Group. UML Profile for Scheduling, Performance and Time. Document ad/2001-06-14, http://www.omg.org/cgi-bin/doc?ad/2001-06-14, June 2001 33

Using SDL for Modeling Behavior Composition

Jacqueline Floch[1,2] and Rolv Bræk[2]

[1] SINTEF Telecom and Informatics
N-7465 Trondheim, Norway
jacqueline.floch@sintef.no
[2] Department of Telematics
Norwegian University of Science and Technology (NTNU)
N-7491 Trondheim, Norway
{jacqueline.floch,rolv.braek}@item.ntnu.no

Abstract. Behavior composition is a means to achieve modularity and adaptability. Unlike process algebra, SDL does not explicitly define composition operators. In this paper, we propose design patterns and rules for expressing elementary behaviors called roles and their composition in SDL. The composite state concept newly introduced in SDL-2000 is used in an original and innovative way to model roles and their composition. Simple SDL extensions are also discussed that facilitate composition. These extensions do not require changes to be made to the SDL semantics.

1 Introduction

Because a short time-to-market is increasingly important for new services, telecommunications operators and manufacturers are in constant search for better frameworks and methods for the rapid construction and deployment of services. Reuse, adaptation, dynamic composition and configuration are some techniques that can contribute to rapid service construction and deployment. At NTNU, the PaP project has explored these techniques in order to define a framework for service development and execution that enables services to be designed separately, and then composed dynamically using Plug-and-Play techniques [1]. In that project, our work has addressed the following question:

> How can we model services so that they can be easily composed and adapted – possibly at run-time?

Composition and adaptation is simplified when services are designed in a modular way, and functionality can be reused. Services usually involve the interaction of several components, allowing adaptation to be performed at different levels. In a coarse-grained approach to adaptation, service components are replaced, or new components added. In a fine-grained approach, existing service components are partially modified. We have chosen to address a fine-grained approach, and seek to produce services by composing small behavioral elements in various ways. Our choice is inspired from existing service architectures such

R. Reed (Ed.): SDL 2003, LNCS 2708, pp. 36–54, 2003.

as IN (Intelligent Network), where a fine-grained approach has been successfully adopted [2], and TINA (Telecommunications Information Networking Architecture), that defines a set of service scenarios and interfaces as basic elements of a service [3]. Another reason for adopting a fine-grained approach is that small adaptations are typically required in the provision of customizable services to the mobile users.

We adopt a role based design approach [4]. Roles and role collaborations focus on behaviors across a system boundary. Experience suggests that role modeling provides better support for system adaptation and reuse than class modeling. The unit of reuse is seldom a class, but rather a slice of behavior [5]. In our approach, services are modeled as collaborations between functional roles. Complex roles may be decomposed into small elementary roles in order to break down behavior complexity. Conversely, more complex roles, and thus behaviors, can be produced by composition.

This paper presents our approach to service role modeling and composition using SDL [6]. Describing system behaviors in terms of state machines has proved to be of great value, and is widely adopted in most teleservice engineering approaches. We favor the use of the modeling language SDL because of its formal semantics that enables an unambiguous interpretation of the service specification. Using SDL, we are able to reason completely about service role behaviors and interactions between roles at the design level. There exist various types of dependencies between roles that constrain how they may be composed. Although SDL does not define explicitly any composition operators, we here use SDL to describe different composition classes. A set of SDL concepts is selected for the realization of role composition, and general guidelines are drawn out for the specification of the roles to be composed.

In this paper, we first introduce to the modeling concepts of actor and service role. The assignment of roles to actors is presented in Sect. 3. Sections 4, 5 and 6 present the composition approach. Design rules and patterns are proposed, and some extensions to SDL are introduced. The advantages of the composition approach are discussed in Sect. 7.

2   Actors, Roles and Collaborations

Service design is complex. Communication services normally require the coordinated effort of several distributed components that execute concurrently, and some components may be involved in several services. In a PaP context, this complexity even increases as services should be designed such that they can be dynamically adapted.

Our approach to service design makes use of roles [7, 8]. A service is seen as a collaboration between service roles where a role is the part a computational object plays in a service. A computational object that is involved in several services plays several roles that are composed to form the object behavior. By using roles, we are able to better comprehend the collaborations between the computational objects involved in a service, and to break down the complexity

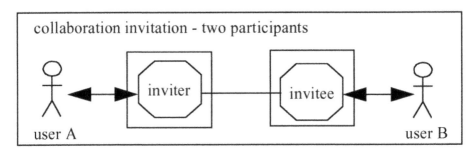

Fig. 1. Collaboration Structure Diagram for the Service invitation

of service specification. We are also able to compose roles to provide new services in a flexible way.

In a PaP context, roles are allocated dynamically to computational objects. We call these computational objects actors. Service execution requires the assignment of roles to actors.

2.1   Modeling Collaborations

Collaborations describe the interactions between actors; they focus on behaviors across a system rather than the behaviors of individual objects. As services are described in terms of roles, collaborations are primarily used to describe interactions between roles rather than interactions between objects. We describe collaborations using two diagram types:

- *Collaboration structure diagrams* describe structures in terms of roles involved in a collaboration and interaction associations between these roles. Actors playing the roles may also be represented. We propose a new graphical notation for collaboration structures (Fig. 1). The invitation collaboration shown in this figure enables a user to invite another user to participate in some service activity.
- *Collaboration sequence diagrams* describe the interactions between roles. We use the MSC language to describe collaborations sequences [9]. We do not detail this kind of diagram here as the focus is set on SDL. An example is however shown in Fig. 13.

2.2   Modeling Service Roles

The behavior of roles is described using state machines. Because SDL does not define the concept of role, an SDL feature that fits the concept of role has to be selected. SDL systems consist of a structure of communicating agents; SDL agents are meant to represent computational objects. SDL composite states allow the structuring of state machines. As they represent parts of behavior, we find them well suited to represent elementary roles. We use state types so that roles

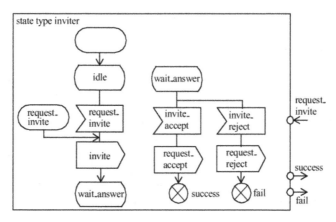

Fig. 2. Service Role inviter Modeled as an SDL Composite State

can be instantiated in multiple combinations with other roles to form a complete behavior.

In Fig. 2, the role inviter is specified using a composite state. The definition of labeled entry and exit points will be justified later. Signal parameters and variables are not represented in this state machine diagram. Variables may be declared as part of the role definition or as part of the actor playing the role. When elementary roles are composed within an actor, shared variables should be declared at the actor level.

2.3   Modeling Actors

Service roles are played by actors. We represent actors using SDL process agents (see Fig. 3). The assignment of roles to agents is specified by instantiating composite states within these agents, and, in the case of parallel composition (see Sect. 6), using inner process agents.

3   Service Role Assignment

Actors may play several roles. Role management is the behavior that describes the assignment of roles to actors, and the selection of a specific role among several alternative roles. Role management may require coordination between interacting actors, and can be described using roles.

Fig. 3. Actor inviter Playing the Role inviter

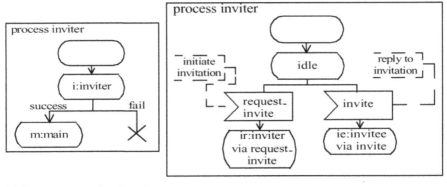

(a) Spontaneous role triggering   **(b) Implicit role triggering**

Fig. 4. Spontaneous and Implicit Role Triggering

The separation between role management and the behavior of the role(s) being managed is beneficial. It augments the understanding of the system behavior, and contributes to reducing the complexity of extending the system. Alternative behaviors may be introduced by extending the role management without making changes to the existing roles. Conversely, the roles being assigned may be modified without changing role management. Role management consists of two main elements: role triggering and role assignment indication, introduced below.

3.1   Service Role Triggering

The assignment of a role to be played may be decided internally in an actor, or triggered by a request from another actor. In the latter case, a request may either be expressed explicitly or implicitly. We propose three main role triggering patterns:

1. *Spontaneous Role Triggering.* We say that a role is triggered spontaneously when it is instantiated as part of the logical action sequence of an actor, i.e. when the actor reaches a specific state. In Fig. 4(a), the role inviter and main are triggered spontaneously.
2. *Implicit Role Triggering.* A role is triggered implicitly when its invocation is requested by another actor, and expressed by a stimulus defined as part of the collaboration to be started and of the role to be assigned. In Fig. 4(b), the message requestinvite triggers the actor to play the role inviter.
3. *Explicit Role Triggering.* A role is explicitly triggered when its triggering is requested by another actor, and expressed by a stimulus defined explicitly for triggering purposes. This stimulus specifies the role to be played. In Fig. 5, the message "play" represents the explicit request.

Explicit role triggering introduces supplementary signalling leading to increased traffic and processing loads. However, the explicit approach is attractive when there is a need for negotiating and learning the role to be played.

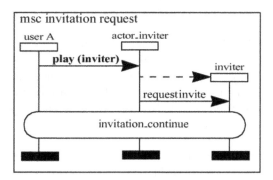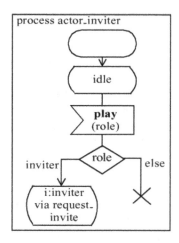

Fig. 5. Explicit Role Triggering

3.2   Service Role Assignment Indication

The assignment of roles needs to be coordinated between actors. Role assignment indication is used to report the assignment of a role. Similarly to triggering, several behavior patterns for assignment indication may be defined:

- *Implicit Role Assignment Indication.* Indication about the role assignment is implicitly expressed by a stimulus defined as part of the collaboration being started and of the role being assigned.
- *Explicit Role Assignment Indication.* The role management played by the actor, indicates, by a stimulus defined explicitly for indication purposes, whether or not the requested role has been instantiated.

3.3   Extension to the MSC Language

Explicit triggering and assignment indication require the actors to be represented in the collaboration sequences. The MSC language does not provide any notation for expressing structural relations between instances in a chart. We have introduced an extension to MSC allowing us to group instances, more specifically actors and roles in our work. We omit to detail this extension here as the focus is set on SDL. An example is however shown in Fig. 13.

4   Role Composition

There exist various types of dependencies between roles that constrain the form of composition that can be applied on roles. While sequential composition enforces behavior ordering, concurrent composition supports simultaneous behaviors. Sequential composition encompasses true sequential composition, guarded sequential composition, choice and disabling. Roles that are composed concurrently may execute more or less independently. We show that one can use SDL to model all these different composition classes.

Ideally roles should be specified without making assumptions about how they are going to be composed with other roles. We define simple general design rules that enable roles to be easily composed. Using these rules, no supplementary behavior needs to be specified within the roles being composed sequentially. On the other hand, roles that are composed concurrently may require explicit coordination behavior. We propose design patterns for the coordination of concurrent roles.

The introduction of new services can be achieved by defining new elementary roles, and by composing new and existing roles in different ways. Composition may be applied incrementally. Service features usually result from the collaboration between elementary roles. Roles obtained from the composition of elementary roles may themselves be composed with other roles either sequentially or concurrently. In multiphase services, roles are usually composed sequentially.

Sequential and concurrent composition can both be applied statically at role design time. Dynamic concurrent composition (see Sect. 6), on the other hand, is applied at run-time. This form of composition suits a plug-and-play approach where roles are designed off-line, and deployed dynamically. Sequential composition with choice (see Sect. 5.2) can also be applied at run-time when the execution platform provides support for behavior selection and adaptation.

5   Sequential Composition

Two roles are sequentially composed if the execution of one of them precedes the execution of the other. The role executing first must be completed before the other can start its execution. The sequential composition of roles leads to a new role, a composite role that may itself be composed with other roles. We represent true sequential composition in SDL by linking the elementary role states in a composite state. The ordering of execution of the composed roles is enforced by the definition of the composite state. No adaptation needs to be done in the roles to be composed in order to deal with the composition.

Guarded sequential composition, choice and disabling are all extended forms of sequential composition. They all ensure mutual exclusion between the roles being composed and impose an order of execution. They are also described in SDL by linking the elementary role states in a composite state. Guards and disabling triggers are added that control the execution of roles. These composition classes are described below.

5.1   Guarded Sequential Composition

Guards describe preconditions that prefix the execution of roles. Guards may either be expressed as predicates over local conditions (conditions set within the actor executing the role), or external conditions (conditions set by other actors).

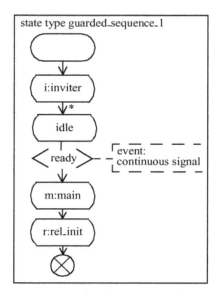

(a) guarded spontaneous triggering

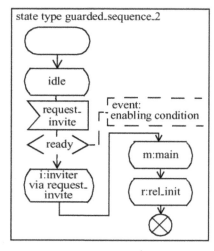

(b) guarded implicit triggering

Fig. 6. Guarded Sequential Composition

Guards based on internal conditions are typically used when the composite role executes concurrently with other roles within the same actor. External conditions may be used to facilitate the coordination of composition across actors.

In SDL, we describe guards as continuous signals or enabling conditions. Fig. 6 shows an example of both, where the condition ready may represent an internal condition such as the state of a stream channel, or an external condition such as the state of another actor. In sequence (a), the basic state idle is introduced so that the continuous signal does not force the exit of the role inviter. In the case where roles are triggered spontaneously, only continuous signals are used. Note the use of the "*" symbol in that sequence meaning that the state "idle" is entered after inviter for any exit point of inviter that is not otherwise mentioned (all exits in this case – assuming (a) represents the whole of guarded_sequence_1).

5.2   Choice among Alternative Behaviors

Using choice, alternative roles can be specified in a sequential composite role. The selection of a behavior among the alternative behaviors in a choice may be controlled by guards or external triggers. An external trigger either belongs to the interaction with other roles (implicit triggering) or actors (explicit triggering).

Choice Based on a Condition. In SDL, guards are either specified using a named return (from a state), a set of continuous signals, or a combination

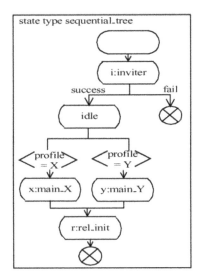

Fig. 7. Choice among Alternative Behaviors using Conditions

of these mechanisms. While a named return reflects a condition set by the role immediately preceding the occurrence of a choice, continuous signals may be related to actions that have taken place at any time before the occurrence of a choice, or that are taking place within another role executing concurrently. The resolution of a condition specified using a continuous signal may require an interaction with other actors. This increases the complexity of the validation analysis and should be restricted to the synchronization of role composition across actors.

In Fig. 7 the exit conditions from the service role inviter control the selection of the further behavior. On success, the selection of a main activity is based on a set of continuous signals representing the content of the user profile.

Modeling a choice based on a condition is straightforward. No supplementary signalling is needed to control the choice. The roles specified as alternative behaviors do not need any adaptation. Labeled exit points facilitate the specification of choices. Labeled exit points may be defined that are not used in the composite state. Therefore we recommend defining them in any case. We state this recommendation in our first design rule.

> **Design Rule: Exit Conditions**. Labels that express exit conditions should be attached to the exit points of the state's modeling roles.

Choice Based on an External Trigger. In SDL external triggers are specified using signals. The consumption of these signals is specified as part of the composite state where the choice is made. In the case of implicit triggering, triggering signals belong to the role to be selected. The triggered role is then entered through a state entry point allowing one to enter the triggered state

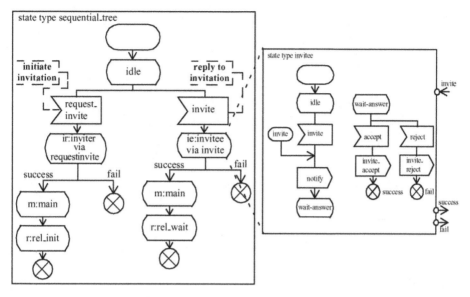

Fig. 8. Choice among Alternative Behaviors using External Triggers

after the consumption of the signal. No major specification change of the role is required in order to deal with the composition. Labeled entry points facilitate the specification of choices, and should be defined in any role.

Design Rule: Entry Conditions. Entry points that represent entry through external triggering should be defined with names in the states representing roles.

Any initialization to be performed when entering the triggered roles through the default start node should also be performed when entering through entry conditions. A procedure named entry in a state is an *Entry procedure* and is interpreted on entering the state. Such entry procedures can be defined to describe initialization tasks.

Design Rule: Entry Procedure. An entry procedure should be defined that describes the tasks to be performed when entering a role.

Figure 8 illustrates a choice based on external triggers. Here a service user may either initiate an invitation or reply to an invitation. The user is represented by a single actor in the service framework, that either plays the service role inviter or invitee. The selection of a service role is triggered by the external signals requestinvite or invite.

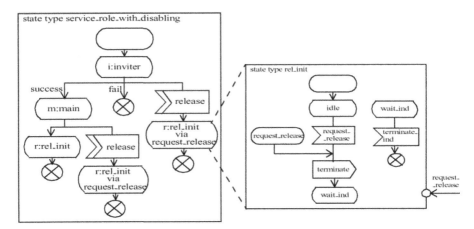

Fig. 9. Disabling

5.3   Disabling

A role disables another role if its execution inhibits the execution of this other role. Unlike suspension (see Sect. 6.4), disabling has a permanent interruption effect. The disabled role is forced to complete execution.

We represent disabling in SDL by linking the elementary role states in a composite state, where the disabling role state is triggered by the reception of a signal. The reception of the disabling signal should take priority over the reception of other signals. This is expressed by means of a priority signal. No major specification change of the disabling role is required. The same design rules as for choice based on an external trigger apply.

Figure 9 illustrates disabling of the service role inviter. In this example, release may be forced when the invitation or the main service activity have not yet completed, or it may take place as a normal case after the completion of the main activity.

In the case where an exit procedure is defined in the disabled role, the exit procedure is executed upon disabling. This enables the designer to describe termination operations of the disabled state. However, SDL exit procedures can only contain a single transition, and therefore do not allow one to describe two-way interactions with other actors.

> **Design Rule: Exit Procedure.** When designing an exit procedure, take into account that the state may be exited through an exit node, or when a transition attached to the composite state is interpreted.

6   Concurrent Composition

With concurrency, we do not mean true concurrency, but rather interleaving. Two or more roles are composed concurrently if their execution interleaves. As

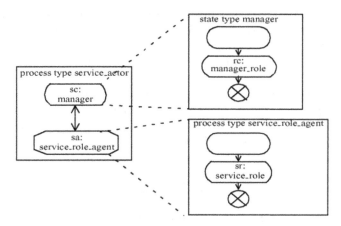

Fig. 10. Concurrent Composition using Process Agents

roles are composed within a computational object and share processing resources, simultaneity is neither necessary nor desirable. Roles composed concurrently have overlapping lifetimes. They may execute in an independent manner, or their execution may require explicit coordination. We distinguish between *static* concurrent composition, where the roles and the number of roles that are being composed are set at design time, and *dynamic* concurrent composition, where roles are created dynamically upon decisions made at run-time.

We propose to represent concurrent composition using process agents in SDL. A process agent representing an actor may contain other process agents representing roles. Inner process agents execute in alternating manner. It is possible to specify several levels of concurrency, as inner process agents may themselves contain process agents. In the case of dynamic concurrent composition, the role process agents are created dynamically at run-time.

An alternative to process agents is provided by state aggregation. State aggregation has many limitations, and can only be used to model some cases of static independent concurrent composition of instances of distinct roles. We propose simple extensions to SDL that make state aggregation easier to apply.

6.1   Using Process Agents

The concurrent execution of multiple role instances increases the complexity of a specification. We propose structural design rules that contribute to an orderly design and ease the readability of the descriptions. A new role responsible for managing the set of concurrent roles is introduced. This manager role and the concurrent roles are specified within the same process agent as shown in the generic model in Fig. 10:

- The managing role, manager, can be composed with other service roles.
- The roles to be composed, service_role, are defined using composite states that are instantiated within the role process agents service_role_agent.

Different manager roles may be introduced. We define the allocation manager as a role that assigns a role to a request. A mediation manager is another kind of manager that in addition to role assignment, also mediates messages to and from that role. It may also support other functions such as the grouping of multiple requests.

The introduction of an allocator role may influence the initial addressing scheme. Using SDL gates, channels and connections, it is also possible to specify a system structure that enforces the correct addressing of the signals. However, such an approach provides a limited addressing support. It cannot be applied when the requesting instance is a member of an instance set, and is not appropriate for dynamic system structures. Using the following design rule, no supplementary behavior needs to be specified in the roles being composed.

> **Design Rule: Addressing Information.** Request messages should contain the addresses of the roles waiting for a reply.

6.2 Using State Aggregation

State aggregation provides a simple approach to the modeling of the static concurrent composition of instances of distinct roles. It defines a partitioning of a state into multiple states that execute in an interleaving manner. Using state aggregation, sequential and concurrent composition can easily be combined in a state graph. However, state aggregation is difficult to apply. The SDL definition of state aggregation introduces several restrictions:

- The input signal sets of the state partitions must be disjoint. Thus state aggregation is not the appropriate technique to model static independent concurrent composition of instances of the same role.
- The composite state terminates when all state partitions have terminated, or when a transition is triggered at the composite state level. SDL does not provide any support for specifying that a state partition (or a group of state partitions) forces the exit of the composite state. [1]
- Although the exit points from the state partitions may be connected to the exit points of the state aggregation, SDL restricts the appearance of each exit point in exactly one connection. Thus it is not possible to define exit conditions of the state aggregation from the exit conditions of the state partitions in a flexible way.

Extensions to the SDL Language. We suggest introducing simple extensions to SDL to facilitate using state aggregation for modeling the static concurrent composition of instances of distinct roles. We propose two sets of extensions:

---

[1] Editorial note: This can probably be achieved by a Boolean variable in the composite state that is used for continuous signals to exit any of the internal states.

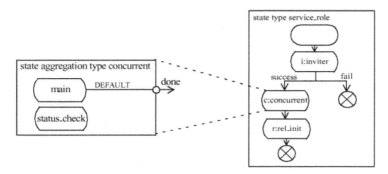

Fig. 11. Extension to State Aggregation: Termination

- The termination of a state partition (or a group of state partitions) may force the termination of the state aggregation. This can be modeled as shown in Fig. 11. The exit point done of the state aggregation is connected to an exit point of the state partition main (here DEFAULT), but not to any exit point of status_check. The connection of an exit point to a single state partition indicates that the termination of the partition forces the termination of the state aggregation.
- Exit points may appear in multiple connections, and exit conditions of the state aggregation can be expressed as logical expressions of the exit conditions of the state partitions. Connection lines need not be represented graphically here. We prefer a textual representation. Qualifiers are used that refer to the state partitions.

We have also considered a set of extensions for supporting non-disjoint input signal sets of the state partitions. Such an extension requires support for the identification and addressing of sub-states. Furthermore, the creation of states would enable dynamic concurrent composition to be described using state aggregation. In that way, it would be possible to use a single SDL concept, the composite state, to model sequential and concurrent compositions. However, with these extensions, the state concept becomes identical to the process agent concept, the main difference being that states can be linked sequentially. As this set of extensions is complex, we suggest representing concurrent composition using process agents when state aggregation cannot be used.

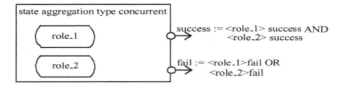

Fig. 12. Extension to State Aggregation: Exit Conditions

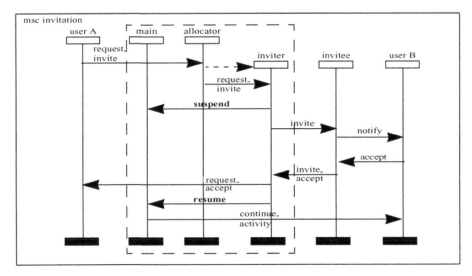

Fig. 13. Extension to State Aggregation: Exit Conditions

6.3   Coordination Behavior Patterns

Roles that are composed concurrently may execute more or less independently. Their composition may require explicit coordination behavior. Coordination often requires behavior to be added to the roles that are composed. Coordination is often application dependent. We have proposed a set of coordination patterns for the coordination of roles.

As an example, alternating execution is shown in Fig. 13. Here, for logical reasons, the main activity in the service has to be suspended while a new invitation takes place. The roles main and inviter have overlapping lifetimes, but the role main is suspended during invitation request.

Coordination Events. Coordination events trigger the coordination of concurrent roles. They may be related to the state of a shared resource or the stage of a service phase. Coordination events are often service dependent. Generic events may however be defined for a set of services. Generic user states such as *busy*, *not responding* are defined in Parlay [10]. In SDL, coordination events may be modeled by input signals, enabling conditions, or continuous signals.

Coordination Modes. The composed roles may execute concurrently between two coordination events, or alternating: In the first case, the roles evolve independently until they reach coordination points, where they wait for some coordination event to occur. In the second case, only one of the roles can execute at a time; the other roles are suspended until a coordination event is reached where, possibly, one of the suspended role resumes while the activated role is suspended.

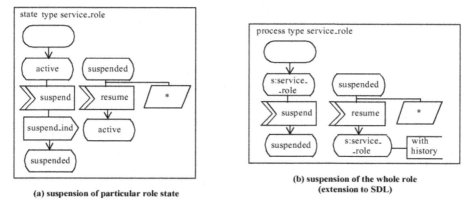

(a) suspension of particular role state

(b) suspension of the whole role
(extension to SDL)

Fig. 14. Suspension and Resumption at Different Levels

Coordination Interaction. Coordination between concurrent roles may be communicated directly between the concurrent roles or through a coordinator.

6.4   Role Suspension and Resumption

The alternating execution of concurrent roles requires mechanisms for the suspension and resumption of roles. Suspension and resumption are triggered by the notification of coordination events. A suspended role enters a suspended state where all signals expected by the role (except the resumption trigger) should be saved. Particular signals, such as exceptions, may also be enabled in a suspended state. Suspension can only take place in a stable role state: suspension may be enabled in a subset of the role states or any role state. In the first case, suspension has to be modeled as part of the role definition; suspension is application-dependent. In the second case, suspension may be modeled as part of the role definition or at the role level. In the latter approach, no supplementary behavior needs to be specified within the role being composed.

In Fig. 14 case (a), suspension applies to one state. As it is not possible in SDL to test the value of a state, the value of the suspended state should either be stored in a variable, or distinct suspended states should be defined for the distinct active states that can be suspended. In case (b), the definition of SDL composite states makes the specification of a simple design pattern for role suspension intricate. On resumption, the role should be re-entered in the state it was left. The SDL history concept supports the re-entering of a composite state. However, the state specified in the nextstate node with history must be the state in which the transition was activated. Thus, using history is normally not allowed in case (b). The intermediate state suspended introduced between leaving and re-entering active prevents us from using history.[2]

---

[2] Editorial note: It is possible to hide intermediate states in a procedure.

Another difficulty is introduced by the SDL definition of entry procedure. When re-entering a composite state with history, the entry procedure of the composite state is invoked. No mechanism in SDL is provided to distinguish between entering or re-entering a state (apart from different entry points). Some intricate work-arounds using flags may be introduced. However such work-arounds introduce dependencies between composite roles and sub-roles. This is not desirable.

While suspension is defined as a temporary interruption, disabling is permanent. Suspension may be modeled in the same manner as disabling using triggering at the composite level. In that way, we try to model suspension and disabling without introducing changes to the role behaviors. A new difficulty is introduced by the SDL definition of exit procedure. When exiting a composite state, the exit procedure is invoked. No mechanism in SDL is provided to catch the cause of exit. It is not possible to test whether a return node has been reached, or a signal at the composite level has triggered the exit. In the latter case, it is not possible to test the type of the signal. These limitations of SDL also makes the definition of generic composition behaviors intricate.

Extensions to the SDL Language. We propose the following extensions to SDL that facilitate the specification of suspension at the role level:

- Several transitions may be executed between leaving a composite state and re-entering this state with history.
- The boolean variable re_enter is defined for all composite states; this variable is set to true when re-entering a state. Testing this variable, it is easy to determine which tasks should be performed.
- The variable exit_cause is defined for all composite states, that distinguishes between exits through a return node and exits triggered at the composite level. It should also be possible to test exit conditions attached to return nodes, and the trigger types and values.

In general, we lack simple mechanisms in SDL for testing state and signal names, for testing entry and exit conditions, etc. This lacking support makes the specification of general patterns cumbersome. Such mechanisms do not require changes to be made to the SDL semantics.

7   Conclusion

This paper has described a role modeling and composition approach that uses SDL. Two main composition schemes are defined: sequential and concurrent composition.

Sequential composition ensures mutual exclusion between the service roles (roles) being composed and imposes an order of execution. The modeling of sequential composition is straightforward in SDL. Simple design rules have been introduced. When these rules are followed, no supplementary behavior needs to be specified within the roles being composed in order to deal with the composition.

Concurrent composition is used to compose roles that have overlapping life-times. Static concurrent composition applies at design time. It requires the roles and the number of instances to be set at design time. Dynamic concurrent composition is applied at run-time. Roles are created dynamically upon decisions made at run-time. Concurrent composition is modeled using process agents or state aggregation. State aggregation however involves many limitations that restrict its application to the composition of static composition of instances of distinct roles. Simple extensions to SDL are suggested that would facilitate using state aggregation.

Roles composed concurrently may execute more or less independently. When roles are dependent, composition requires explicit coordination behavior. We propose design patterns for the coordination of concurrent roles. SDL provides rather poor support to the definition of generic coordination behaviors. This lacking support makes the specification of general patterns cumbersome. We have proposed simple extensions that do not require changes to the SDL semantics.

The composition approach is attractive for several reasons:

- It encourages the designer to produce modular service descriptions. The elementary roles and collaborations are simple and can be easily understood.
- By nature, it provides a method for adding or replacing elementary behaviors. New functionality can also be added at run-time. In that way, the composition approach supports incremental service development and deployment.
- Dependencies between roles are highlighted during composition. Thus, the composition approach contributes to the understanding of dependencies between roles and services.
- When components are involved in several services, the contribution to different services can be modeled by different roles that are composed in order to obtain the whole component behavior. In that way, role composition enables one to concentrate on individual services, and break down complex component behaviors.
- Composition can be exploited during validation. This helps to reduce the complexity of the analysis. As validation takes into account the compositional properties of a system, it is also suited for the validation of components bound at run-time.

The power of expression of SDL is not restricted by the design patterns and rules that have been proposed. In that way, the composition approach does not introduce any restriction to the functionality that can be defined.

Acknowledgments

We would especially like to thank Richard Sanders for inspiring discussions and thorough comments. The work presented here has been supported by the Norwegian Foundation for Research (project grant 119395/431).

References

[1] F. A. Aagesen et al. Towards a Plug and Play Architecture for Telecommunications. Fifth International Conference on Intelligence in Networks (1999). 36

[2] ITU-T. Recommendation I.329/Q.1203 Intelligent Network – Global Functional Plane Architecture. International Telecommunication Union, Geneva, October 1992. 37

[3] TINA-C. Service Component Specification, version 1.0b. January 1998. 37

[4] T. Reenskaug. Perspectives on the Unified Modeling Language semantics. Presented at the 10th SDL Forum (2001). 37

[5] M. Mezini and K. Lieberherr Adaptative Plug-and-Play Components for Evolutionary Software Development. Proceedings of OOPSLA'98. 37

[6] Recommendation Z.100 (11/99), Specification and Description Language (SDL). International Telecommunication Union, Geneva. 37

[7] T. Reenskaug et al. OORASS: Seamless support for the creation and maintenance of object oriented systems. Journal of O-O programming (1992). 37

[8] B. B. Kristensen and K. Østerbye. Roles: Conceptual Abstraction Theory and Practical Language Issues. Theory and Practice of Object Systems, Vol. 2. 1996. 37

[9] ITU-T. Recommendation Z.120 (11/99), Message Sequence Chart (MSC). International Telecommunication Union, Geneva. 38

[10] The Parlay Group. Parlay APIs 2.1. Generic Call Control Service Data Definitions 2000. 50

A Real-Time Profile for UML
and How to Adapt It to SDL*

Susanne Graf and Ileana Ober

VERIMAG**, Centre Equation
2 avenue de Vignate, 38610 Gières, France
{Susanne.Graf,Ileana.Ober}@imag.fr

Abstract. This paper presents work of the IST project OMEGA, where
we have defined a UML profile for real-time that is compatible with the
Profile for Performance, Scheduling and Real-time recently accepted at
OMG. In contrast to this OMG profile, we put emphasis on semantics
and on its use in the context of timed analysis of real-time embedded
systems. The defined profile is compatible with the time concepts existing
in SDL, and we show how we can also adapt these notations to SDL and
MSC, which do not yet have a notation for this purpose.

1 Introduction

Today's embedded applications have often strong constraints with respect to
deadlines, response time and other non-functional aspects[1]. They may be distributed and run on different execution platforms and this influences strongly
the non-functional characteristics. To allow early analysis of timing properties,
we propose to lift the choices and constraints coming from a given run-time system, as well as assumptions on the environment, to the abstract model level in
terms of a set of annotations which can be interpreted by timed validation tools.
To make this approach feasible, the annotation language must be flexible and
orthogonal to the functional description. It must allow the expression of global
constraints and their refinement into a set of local constraints.

The Aim: Our aim is to provide means not only for describing systems with
time dependent choices, but also for defining timed models of systems. We include time related assumptions on the environment, for example the arrival time
of inputs of the environment and (platform dependent) durations of tasks. Thus,
the idea is to perform validation (simulation, symbolic test or verification) on
a timed *model*, built from knowledge of or assumptions on the environment and
the platform. Aspects include resource sharing and scheduling (which have to

---

* This work has been partially supported by the IST-2002-33522 OMEGA project.
** A research laboratory of CNRS, Université Joseph Fourier and Institut National
Polytechnique de Grenoble.
[1] We restrict ourselves here exclusively to timing aspects.

R. Reed (Ed.): SDL 2003, LNCS 2708, pp. 55–76, 2003.

be confirmed later by testing, run-time monitoring or code analysis). At requirement level, this approach can be used to validate the consistency of a set of requirements and to build the loosest timed model satisfying all requirements. This model can then be further refined compositionally[2].

Overview of Existing Approaches: Modeling languages and tools that are used in the domain of embedded and real-time software, usually do have time related concepts. However, these concepts are generally not sufficient for timed analysis at model level. The existence of analysis tools is crucial in this context, but presently only partially covered.

Languages using an *asynchronous event driven approach* (such as SDL [1], ROOM [2], State charts [3]) use a notion of global and external time. In SDL and ROOM, global time is available within the system through a special expression, and can be stored in variables or sent as parameters of messages. In Unified Modeling Language UML [4] the semantics of time progress is not stated definitively, with the aim of being flexible enough to accommodate all possible approaches.

The development tools existing for SDL, such as [5, 6], allow code generation and some restricted form of analysis. Properties are expressed in terms of MSC [7] or by means of a tool internal observer language. These tools define a particular time model and special profiles for limited performance and timing analysis based on simulation of scenarios. Most approaches for enriching SDL with time constraints and providing tools for performance or timing analysis are scenario based [8, 9]. For SDL there have been studies of a methodology for the development of real-time systems [10] and extension of SDL with time constraints for timing and performance analysis [11, 12].

Although standard UML does not include any particular time framework, a number of tool supported frameworks have been proposed. For example, Rose RT (a variant of the ROOM framework), the Real-Time Studio of Artisan [13], Rhapsody [14] and, more recently, the tool TAU Generation 2 [15] propose UML frameworks including real time aspects. These tools allow automatic or semi-automatic code generation and have facilities for simulation and restricted functional analysis, but almost no support for timing analysis. For instance, Rhapsody validation tools [16] exist only for a rather deterministic, external time semantics and not for time dependent properties.

Recently, a UML Profile for Schedulability, Performance and Time Specifications [17] has been defined. It integrates the ideas and concepts from most of the previously named approaches. It is very general, in order to be able to adapt to any possible real-time framework and for all kinds of diagrams. It essentially defines a vocabulary, is very much tailored towards timed scenarios, and for the moment, it exists only on paper.

Timed automata [18, 19] have been used for modeling real-time aspects of systems, for defining semantics of modeling languages and for studying controller synthesis [20, 21] and scheduling frameworks [22, 23]. A number of validation and

---

[2] The traffic light example in Sect. 4 is an instance of this type of use.

analysis tools – such as Hytech [24], Kronos/IF [25, 26, 27] or Uppaal/Time [28, 29] – exist for the framework of timed automata (extended with data), but they are in general not closely coupled with development environments.

In the OMEGA IST project (http://www-omega.imag.fr), which is creating *the definition of a development methodology for embedded and real-time systems in UML based on formal techniques*, we have started to refine the UML Profile for Schedulability, Performance and Time in order to make it usable for efficient analysis. In this article, we report on this work and show how it can be adapted for the definition of a real-time profile for SDL which is compatible with the already existing time related features of SDL and MSC.

We start, in Sect. 2, with an overview of the concepts necessary in a real-time framework. In Sect. 3.1, we define the *basic time concepts* of the UML real-time profile of the Omega project and their semantics. They are expressive enough to express all time related elements of a model. An increase in expressiveness can be obtained by an extension with probabilistic features, as used in the context of performance analysis. In Sect. 3.2, we define the semantics of the basic time concepts as an extension of any untimed formalism which can be interpreted as an event labeled transition system. In particular, we distinguish two different interpretations of Boolean expressions, either as predicates or as constraints. In Sect. 3.3, we define a set of derived notations, intended to give the user a convenient means for the expression of common constraint patterns. They can be expressed in terms of basic concepts, at least in the context of the expression language OCL [30], allowing powerful quantifications. Finally, in Sect. 5, we propose a way to adapt this UML profile to SDL.

2   Needs for Timed Specifications

A minimal set of real-time related concepts necessary for a modeling language with the aim of supporting all the stages of the development of a real-time system, contains just the following concepts:

A global notion of time. If necessary, local time can be defined by means of local clocks which have a well-defined relationship to global time (which might be defined in terms of drift (maximal deviation of speed), offset (max. deviation of value), ...).

Explicit *functional use of time* by means of access to time through *timers*, *clocks* and a construct like *now* (allowing access to global time), allowing control- or data- flow to be explicitly made time dependent. It is desirable that the necessary discretization can be decided as late as possible in order to avoid unnecessary complexity.

Means for the specification of time constraints. To represent requirements or assumptions on the environment. For the underlying execution platform assumptions (or knowledge) on the execution time of activities must be expressible and taken into account at model level. We propose constraints on durations between *events* as the basic means for expressing time constraints, as is the case in Sequence Charts and in Timed Automata. This is also in line with the UML RT profile.

Timing issues are strongly influenced by the *execution mode* and *the type of concurrency* between different parts of the system. Concerning parallelism one can distinguish *simulated parallelism* (concurrent entities sharing computing resources) and *distributed parallelism*. This distinction is generally not made in modeling languages focusing on functional aspects, but it is important when assumptions on execution times and effects of resource sharing should be taken into account.

For entities composed by *simulated parallelism*, one may define restrictions on the level of granularity at which computations of concurrent objects are interleaved: in the case of *functionally independent behaviors*, the choice of this granularity has no influence on the functional properties; at the level of the implementation, this granularity is defined by the *preemptibility* or non-preemptibility of steps of computations. When interleaving a set of *functionally dependent parallel behaviors*, the choice of the granularity influences not only the timed but also the functional behavior. It defines when stimuli from outside can be taken into account. Extreme choices consist of:

- making no hypothesis on the granularity (as in Java): any parallel behavior of the set can accept stimuli at any time, independently of all others. This obliges the designer to handle mutual exclusion and access of shared variables explicitly;
- run-to-completion semantics: stimuli from the outside of each entity are only accepted when all the parallel behaviors of the set are stable (waiting for a stimulus) and no stimulus from within the entity is present.

In the context of the second solution, activities are insensitive to their environment before they are terminated, that is *atomic* as seen from outside. In this context, it is important to have an *interrupt* concept, allowing for example to terminate useless activities without cutting all the atomic steps into smaller pieces (and adding corresponding locks, etc.). In this article, we focus only on purely time related aspects, and we consider the execution model to be part of the functional model. In the subset of UML we consider in Omega, a notion of *activity group* (basically an active object and several passive objects, executing like an SDL process in a run-to-completion fashion) defines how activities within a group can interleave.

Scheduling. For schedulability analysis, one needs to distinguish between simulated and distributed parallelism between *activity groups*, as this determines which execution times add up and which ones do not. We introduce the following notations[3]:

- a notion of *resource* and a *deployment mapping* from activity groups to resources

---

[3] Partly described in Sect. 3.3, but still to be worked out in detail.

- the distinction between *preemptible* and *non preemptible* resources, actions and objects for the definition of a notion of atomicity.
- the distinction between *execution delay* and *execution time* of actions or transitions, where the first refers to the time elapsing between the start time and the end time of an action, and the second refers to pure execution time[4] which is necessary for an analysis taking into account scheduling issues.
- *priorities* within or between concurrent behaviors, defined in a hierarchical fashion, are a powerful means to eliminate non determinism and can be used at model level to define any scheduling policy. At implementation level, priorities might either be reflected by a run-time scheduler (possibly a hierarchy of explicit event handlers) or by sequential code generated according to the defined priority rules.

3   Ingredients for a UML Profile for Timed Verification

We start by defining a set of basic time related concepts that give expressiveness to the framework. In Sect. 3.2 we define their semantics. Finally in Sect. 3.3, derived concepts are introduced to make use of the framework easier.

3.1   Basic Time Related Concepts

The only time related concept existing in standard UML is the *Time* data type. UML defines no mechanisms for representing time progress nor operations on *Time*. The *Profile for Schedulability, Performance and Time* [17] defines a large vocabulary of time related concepts, which is not completely worked out and which is more or less syntax so far. We consider here only the subset concerned with real-time, add some missing concepts, and propose a semantic framework.

Primitives for modeling time. As in SDL, the time model is based on two data types: *Time*, relating to time *instances*, and *Duration*, relating to the time elapsing between two instances of time. These data types can be used, like any UML data type, in attributes, parameters, etc.

A particular instance of time is *now*. It always holds the *current time* and is visible in all parts of the model. Using the vocabulary of ASM [32], *now* is a *monitored* variable: some external mechanism changes its value. A general constraint imposes its values to monotonically grow, and model dependent *time constraints* can introduce additional restrictions on time progress as compared with system progress.

Timing mechanisms. In the UML RT Profile, two related timing mechanisms are introduced, informing the system on time progress: *timer* and *clock*. A *timer* is an extension of its homonym in SDL (as it can be *set*, *reset* and sends *timeout* signals). Additionally, timers can be periodic, can be paused or restarted. *Clocks* are similar to periodic timers and emit *Ticks*.

---

[4] Obtained by measurements on the target platform or by static timing analysis as done, for example, in [31].

Events play an important role in the UML RT profile. They are defined in UML as a "specification of a type of observable occurrence": that is, as an (observable) state change. There exists no explicit notion of event in SDL, but MSC defines behaviors in terms of events. We use *TimedEvents* with a *time stamp* holding their occurrence time. We define a rich set of events allowing reference to all relevant time points of a behavior. For instance, three events are associated with any transmission of a signal *sig*:

> *send(sig)* the instant at which the signal is sent by the sender;
> *receive(sig)* the point of time at which the signal is received by the receiver (in its input queue);
> *consume(sig)* the instant at which the signal is consumed and a transition is triggered (or the signal is discarded).

Not all three events associated with a signal must necessarily be distinct. For example, if *receive(sig)* and the corresponding *consume(sig)* occur at the same time, they represent a single event, and this corresponds to non buffered communication. Every *action* has the associated events *start(action)* and *end(action)*. In the case of an *instantaneous* action, the *start* and *end* event are always simultaneous and denoted by the event *start-end(action)*. The complete list of predefined events (associated with operation calls, signal exchange, actions, transitions, timers, etc.) is given in the Appendix.

As an event is an instance of state change, it is defined by a triple of the form *(occurrence time, current state, next state)* where the *next state* is defined by the *current state*, or equivalently by a triple of the form *(occurrence time, current state, action)* where the *action* defines the rules that determine the state after the event. We chose the second type of representation, by encoding the relevant part of the current state and the action in an *event name*, thus allowing constraints on an event to depend only on its *occurrence time*, *current state* and the parameters of its *action*.

For instance, a *send event* associated with a call is identified by: the relevant part of the state in which the call is issued (that is, the object initiating the call); the target object; the operation that is called and its parameters; and possibly the place in the control flow of the state machine in which the call takes place, as well as some condition on the local or global state.

Example: The expression *cond:send(o#tr@lab:target!sig)* identifies all the events, where provided the condition *cond* holds on the global state when the event occurs, the event is a *send* event in the object identified by *o* and the transition named *tr* (of the state machine associated with *o*), and the execution of an action labeled *lab* sends *target* the signal *sig*. Events can be specified partially, so that *send(o:sig)* represents any event in which the signal *sig* is sent by an object *o*, regardless of target, action that generated it, parameters or the global state.

Note that, even if all the parameters are identified, the event may have multiple *occurrences* in a given execution. Thus, for any given execution, an *event specification* defines a *sequence* of *event occurrences*. In order to be able to distinguish different occurrences of an event and to to talk about the history of a given event, previous occurrences of an event can be referred to by means of expressions of the form *pre(event)*, *pre(pre(ev))*,. . . .

Time Expressions evaluate to *Time* instances. A particular time expression, evaluated only in events, is *now*. In any state, the expression *time(ev)* evaluates to the time point of the last occurrence of an event matching *ev*, whereas *time(pre(ev))* evaluates to the point of time of the occurrence before the last one. Simple arithmetic expressions, as in SDL, are other examples of time expressions. *Example:* t : *Time* $\pm$ d : *Duration*, t : *Time* $\pm$ *real* $\times$ d : *Duration* .

Duration Expressions evaluate to *Duration* instances. All evaluations of features of type *Duration* are duration expressions. Other duration expressions are, as in SDL, simple arithmetic expressions, such as time instance subtraction. *Examples*:

t_1: *Time* - t_2: *Time*   (under the condition that $t_1 \geq t_2$)
pos_real $\times$ *d:Duration* (a scalar product)
now - time(ev) (time elapsed since the last occurrence of event *ev*)
time(ev) - time(pre(ev)) (time elapsed between the very last and the
     previous occurrence of event *ev*)

Predicates on Time and Duration: Any Boolean expression containing duration or time instances is a time dependent predicate. It can be used (just as any Boolean expression) as guard or test within an action, or as a predicate in a property to be checked. Although in principle arbitrary time dependent Boolean expressions can be used, in practice only simple forms of predicates are really useful. Indeed, the type of predicates used in properties or guards determine the possibility of analysis (see Sect. 5). *Examples:*

t_1 : *Time* - t_2 : *Time* $\leq$ *d:Duration* (simple duration constraint)
time(ev_1) - time(ev_2) $\leq$ *d* (simple duration constraint)
now - time(event) $\leq$ *time(pre(event)) - time(pre(pre(event)))* (constraint on
     difference of durations, as used in auto adaptive algorithms).

Time Dependent Predicates are evaluated in events, and the fact that an event satisfies some predicate amounts to the evaluation of an assertion of the form $(s, t, a) \models p$[5] which is equivalent to the assertion $(s, a) \models p[t/now]$ or $s \models p[t/now]$ if p is independent of the parameters of the action. The interpretation of time dependent predicates can be extended to states:

$s \models p$ iff $\forall t \in [time(enter(s)), time(exit(s))]$. $(s, t) \models p$

that is if p holds in all time points in which the system stays in state s.

We distinguish between *predicates*, which are evaluated to *true* or *false* in individual events (or states), and *invariants* - of the form *invariant(p)* (where p is a predicate) - which hold if p has been *true* ever since the initial state. Interesting

---

[5] Where s is a *state*, t a *time* value, and a represents the parameters of the *action* represented by the event.

invariants are often of the form $invariant(in(s) \Rightarrow p)$ or $invariant(at(e) \Rightarrow p)$, requiring p to hold at each occurrence of event e, respectively in all time points in which the system is in state s. In order to ease the expression of such invariants, we allow to "attach" $invariant(p)$ with states s or events e as a short hand.

3.2   Semantics

The semantics of time related concepts is defined independently of the semantics of the formalism used for expressing functional behavior. We only suppose that the semantics of the functional behavior of systems can be viewed as a labeled transition system, where transitions represent *events*. An additional requirement is that all referenced events are identifiable in the transition system defining the functional semantics.

We define the semantics of the time related concepts by a set of timed automata with urgency [19][6] constraining the *occurrence time* (and only on the occurrence time) of all the events whose possible occurrence ordering are given by the untimed semantics.

Thus, the *timed behavior* of a system can be represented by the synchronized product of the possibly infinite event labeled transition system defining its behaviors in terms of state changes and (partial) order of events, and a set of time automata defining allowed occurrence times of events.

How time related concepts can be represented as timed automata is relatively straightforward for most constructs. We present here the timed automaton associated with a timer to demonstrate that this way of defining time extension has the expected effect, and we discuss the interpretation of time dependent Boolean expressions, because for them several interpretations coexist.

The time automaton associated with any timer instance is given in Fig. 1a. It does not express any constraint on the occurrence times of the actions *set* and *reset*, but we suppose that they occur immediately after the preceding action (in the same sequential behavior), which in the timed automaton is expressed by an *eager* transition. Also, given an occurrence of *set*, this automaton constrains the occurrence time of the *timeout* (that is, the *occur* event) to exactly the defined timeout time *time(set(timer,delay)) + delay* which is also expressed by an *eager* transition.

The point of time of the consumption of the timeout, however, is not restricted by the timer itself, but possibly by some additional constraint, for example "*always the time between the timeout and the corresponding consumption is smaller than d*" [7], which can be expressed by an invariant of the form

$invariant(\ at(consume(t)) \Rightarrow now - time(occur(t)) \leq consume\text{-}delay\ )$

---

[6] Alternatively, we could have used another formalism, such as ASM, but the advantage of timed automata is that they have as predefined concepts, all the primitives making the expression of the semantics easy.

[7] Under the condition on the functional model that the timer is only set again after the timeout has been consumed.

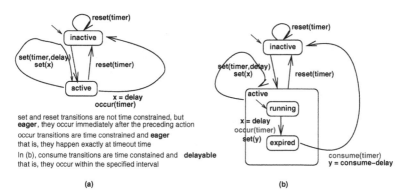

Fig. 1. Timed Automaton: (a) For a Timer (b) With Constraint Consumption Delay

or, as we will see in the next section, by the shorthand

$$invariant(\ duration(occur(t),\ consume(t)) \leq consume\text{-}delay\ )\ )$$

Figure 1b shows the timed automaton corresponding to the composition of the timer timed automaton and the timed automata associated with this constraint, where the transition associated with the consume event is *delayable*, meaning that it will occur somewhere within the specified delay.

Interpretations of Time Dependent Boolean Expressions
Boolean expressions can be interpreted in different ways, depending on their use:

Predicates: Time dependent Boolean expressions used as guards of transition triggers or in decisions are predicates, which take at each occurrence of the transition either a value *true* or *false* depending on the value of time at the instance the *trigger event* occurs. The value of complex predicates can be combined from basic ones and can be used in other event based property formalisms: for example in sequence charts, predicates are used as *conditions*. A timed automaton representing a time dependent predicate, is an observer which, depending on the point of time at which the concerned events are observed, provides a Boolean value. In such a timed automata all transitions are *lazy*, meaning that no constraint on possible time progress is expressed, but the Boolean value (the value of the predicate) depends on time progress. As an example, see the timed automaton representing the predicate *duration(start, end)* in Figure 2.

Invariants: The value of a (time dependent) invariant of the form *invariant(p)* is *true* only if *p* holds on the entire execution leading to the current state or event. Invariants can be used as *properties*, meaning that they should be derivable from a given system description. Live Sequence Charts [33, 34], as they are used in Omega, provide an intuitive means to express complex invariants as well as liveness properties. The timed automaton associated

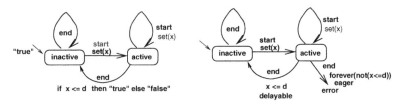

a) Automaton representing a predicate on duration(start,end)   b) Automaton representing a constraint on duration(start,end)

Fig. 2. Timed Automata Representing (a) a Predicate (b) an Invariance Constraint

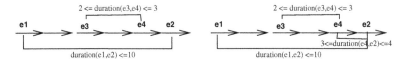

Fig. 3. Incomplete Time Constraints

with *invariant*(*p*) is that of *p*, except that, once it takes the value *false*, its value remains *false* forever.

Constraints: invariants can also be used as *constraints* or *(assumed) facts* on the system under consideration, its environment or the underlying execution platform. An assignment $x := 0$ represents the invariant *whenever this step is executed, in the state just after the execution the variable x has the value* 0 without necessarily saying how this is achieved exactly. Analogously, an invariant of the form $duration(action) \leq 5^8$ can be used to restrict the model to the set of executions satisfying the functional constraints in which not more than 5 time units pass between the event *start*(*action*) and the corresponding event *end*(*action*).

Such a constraint on the time elapsing between two events, *forces* time progress or waiting in accordance with the constraint. In timed automata, this is obtained by means of *eager* or *delayable* transitions. Whenever it is impossible to force time progress in such a way as to satisfy some constraint, this means that the set of time constraints is either inconsistent or incomplete and can be represented in the timed automaton implicitly by a timelock or explicitly by an error condition (see Fig. 2b for an example).

Constraints restrict the model on which *properties* are verified. Constraints are consistent if they are *non overlapping*: that is, in every possible execution, any event is under the scope of at most one time constraint.In this case, the set of associated timed automata define an executable model, in the sense that any computation satisfying the constraints up to some point of time, can be continued by satisfying all constraints. When constraints are overlapping, they might be inconsistent or incomplete. Inconsistency must lead to some redesign. Figure 3

---

[8] See next section for the definition.

shows two incomplete sets of (overlapping) constraints. Both sets of constraints are satisfiable, but must be completed by a constraint on the occurrence time of the event e_3 (relative to the occurrence time of e_1) in order to guarantee that all other constraints remain satisfiable. Most existing tools, such as the simulation tools for SDL or the tool for executing timed live sequence charts of [34], avoid this problem by a priori choosing the earliest point of time at which an event is possible. This corresponds often to a possible execution (at least when the set of constraints is consistent), but not always, as the second example of Fig. 3 shows. Moreover, our aim is to keep constraints as loose as possible, and thus to characterize the largest set of timed behaviors of (sequential) subsystems and to enable compositional analysis.

In [35] a framework is described for more flexible composition of duration constraints than conjunction which could be used to further extend the real-time profile presented here.

3.3 Derived Duration Expressions

Our approach is based on duration constraints between the occurrences of an event *ev1* and a subsequent event *ev2*. In a sequence of occurrences of *ev1* and *ev2*, several options exist to identify the "matching" pairs between which to impose the constraint. We propose expressions for three different ways of identifying such matching pairs.

1. *duration(ev1, ev2)* represents the duration between an occurrence of *ev1* and the next occurrence of *ev2* such that there is no other occurrence of *ev1* in between. Only at the occurrence of the first *ev2* after a (series of) *ev1*, is the value of *duration(ev1, ev2)* that of *now - time(ev1)*: that is, the time passed since the **last** event *ev1*. At other points of time, its value is difficult to express only in terms of occurrence times of events: $time(pre^n(ev2))$ - *time(ev1)* where n is chosen such that $time(pre^{n-1}(ev2)) \leq time(ev1) \leq time(pre^n(ev2))$. Using additional time stamp variables or a timed automaton makes the expression of this constraint easy (see Fig. 2 for the expression of *duration(start,end)* $\leq d$).
   A particular instance is *duration(ev1,now)* which represents at any point of time the duration since the last occurrence of *ev1*: that is, *now - time(ev1)*. This expression corresponds to an implicit duration counter associated with event *ev1*, and it can alternatively be expressed by means of a time stamp at each occurrence of *ev1*.
2. When several request events (each corresponding to *ev1*), may all be answered by a single *effect* event (corresponding to *ev2*), and this should happen within a limited time starting from the first request, the time elapsed between the **first** event of a series of occurrences of *ev1* and the first consecutive *ev2* is relevant. The expression *duration-first(ev1, ev2)* can be used in this case (the timed automaton associated with *duration-first(start,end)* $\leq d$ is obtained by eliminating in the timed automaton of Fig. 2 the *set(x)* action in case of repeated *start* events).

3. Finally, the case where several observations on pairs *(ev1,ev2)* are "active" simultaneously, must be considered. In most cases, one can find a parameter x (or combination of parameters) identifying the matching pairs, and express the required constraint by a constraint of the form

    for any x: duration(ev1(*,x,*),ev2(*,x,*)) ≤ d.

    Nevertheless, due to the implicit use of FIFO buffers for storing signals in objects, it might be impossible to always find the matching parameters, and for this purpose *pipelineDuration(ev1, ev2)* is introduced, where the matching pairs may be overlapping, observed in a pipelined fashion. In any case, such a set of constraints cannot be expressed by a single timed automaton, but by multiple instances of a parameterized timed automaton, such that at every occurrence of *ev1*, a new instance (with appropriate values of parameters) is instantiated, constraining only its corresponding *ev2* event; each instance is killed when the constrained event *ev2* occurs.

Moreover, we propose some convenient shorthands

1. Instead of *duration(enter(state),exit(state))* shorthand *duration(in(state))* can be used. For *duration(trued(cond),falsed(cond))* the *duration(in(cond))* shorthand can be used. Analogues exist for any type of "duration".
2. We allow also expressions of the form *duration(SE1,SE2)*, where *SE1, SE2* are lists of events, representing the distance between any occurrence of an event in *SE* and the next instance of any event in *SE2*.

Additionally, duration expressions are defined that correspond to frequently used duration patterns with semantics defined in terms of basic duration expressions:

Client response time attached to operation calls and signals with some specified response, is defined as *duration(invoke(op),consume-return(op))*, that is, the time elapsed between the moment at which the operation call (respectively the initiating signal) is emitted and the moment at which the response (return or defined response signal) is consumed by the client.

    Example: ClientresponseTime(sourceObj:sig1, sig2)≤ 7, means that each time the object *o* sends *sig1*, then, **if** it receives a response *sig2* some time later, this will happen within less than 7 time units.

Server response time attached to operation calls or signals with specified response, is defined by *duration(receive(op),invoke-return(op))*, that is, the time between the reception of a request (in the input queue) and the moment at which the response (or return) is sent back (from the server point of view).

Duration can be associated with some behavior (action, transition, operation, or signal with specified response), as a shorthand for the duration between the start and the termination time of the behavior. That is, one can simply write *duration(act)* for *duration(start(act),end(act))*. It does not include waiting time in the event queue when the execution refers to the treatment of a signal, but it does include potential preemption time during the execution of the behavior.

Execution time associated with a behavior, is similar to its *duration*, except that it also takes deployment issues into account and accounts only for the time during which the object is executing and neither preempted nor waiting for some response from external objects.

Period attached to an event, is defined as the duration between successive occurrences of the event, that is *duration(pre(event),event)*.

Reactivity is attached to objects or groups of objects and is defined as the maximum delay between any event of the form *Receive(req)* and the corresponding event *Consume(Req)*, that is the maximal delay which may elapse between the moment at which a request reaches the object and the moment at which it starts to treat it. This feature is useful, when the size of input queue can be statically bounded.

Transmission delay attached to associations stereotyped as communication paths (similar to SDL channels), defines a communication delay.

The list of derived duration expressions has the status of an initial proposal. It contains a number of concepts likely to be interesting and serves to illustrate the general idea. Nevertheless, a larger discussion and more feedback from users is necessary. Some of the concepts may need adaptation. For instance, the more restricted notion of *Worst case execution time* might be more useful than *Execution time*. It might be interesting to distinguish different kinds of transmission delays. Also predefined notions of *jitter* might be introduced explicitly, instead of asking the user to write down his preferred formula relating the occurrence times of n consecutive events ev, $pre(ev)$, ..., $pre^n(ev)$.

4   Example

We illustrate a possible use of time annotations by modeling a part of the traffic light system of the SDL design contest. Given the level of description of this example, execution times, response times, etc. play no role. At control level, only expressions of type *duration()* and the distinction of different types of invariants are relevant. The main idea is to illustrate the possibility of complete separation of functional and time dependent specifications and of the expression of time constraints by means of a set of relative simple constraints, each one depending on not more than a few events.

A traffic light controller consists of a set of traffic light controller proxies (TLCP). Each TLCP controls the light switches of all its associated traffic lights and gets information about the presence or absence of traffic on its controlled lanes from a number of sensors (at different distances from the lights on all the lanes) by means of signals *traffic* and *notraffic* from a *traffic sensor handler* associated with each TLCP, not described here. The information about the status is stored in a Boolean variable *traffic*. The state machine of TLCP described using SDL (see Fig. 4) has only two states, *red* and *green*, and it can pass from *green* to *red* on other lanes without any condition, and from *red* to *green* when traffic has been detected and all other traffic lights are *red* (this requires a global variable *AllRed* updated by all the TCLPs at every transition). Each traffic light

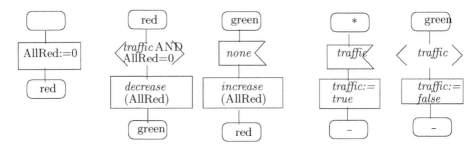

Fig. 4. TLCP Functional Behavior

has an additional *orange* phase of some fixed length, but this is handled in the traffic lights themselves (not described here).

The state machine of Fig. 4 describing the functional behavior is totally time independent. In addition, a number of time constraints need to be satisfied. We show that also for this type of "functional" time constraints, it can be advantageous to use a constraint based approach, instead of starting immediately with an *implementation* in terms of timers or some cyclic environment observation.

The first constraint prevents livelocks: whenever there is traffic, the light will be turned *green* within some delay max_r. This is expressed by an invariant of the following form, where we omit the context $TLCP(i)$ to simplify the expressions:

$$duration(\{enter(red), trued(traffic)\},\ enter(red)) \leq max_r \qquad (1)$$

Due to the existence of an *orange* phase, and in order to avoid unstable behavior, a minimal duration of both the *green* and the *red* phase must be fixed:

$$duration(in(green)) \geq min_g \qquad (2)$$
$$duration(in(red)) \geq min_r \qquad (3)$$

Constraint (1) implies a constraint on the "nominal" length of the *green* phase, depending on the number N of "directions". Once the minimal delay has passed, as soon as there is no traffic anymore on the lanes of $TLCP(i)$, the *green* phase should be terminated within a delay ϵ (except if within ϵ new traffic arrives). When there is traffic all the time (with the exception of some durations not longer than ϵ), the *green* phase takes its nominal length $max_g \leq max_r/(N-1)$. We express this as an invariant[9] attached with the *green-to-red* transition:

$$
\begin{aligned}
&(duration(in(green)) = min_g &\Rightarrow\quad& duration(trued(notraffic), now) \geq \epsilon)\\
\wedge\ &(min_g \leq duration(in(green)) \leq max_g &\Rightarrow\quad& duration(trued(notraffic), now) = \epsilon)\\
\wedge\ &(duration(in(green)) \geq max_g &\Rightarrow\quad& duration(trued(notraffic), now) \leq \epsilon\ )\\
\wedge\ &(duration(in(green)) \leq max_g) &&\qquad\qquad\qquad\qquad\qquad (4)
\end{aligned}
$$

---

[9] Using the "min-synchronization" of the framework of [35] instead of conjunction with constraint (2), would allow simplification of the expression of constraint (4).

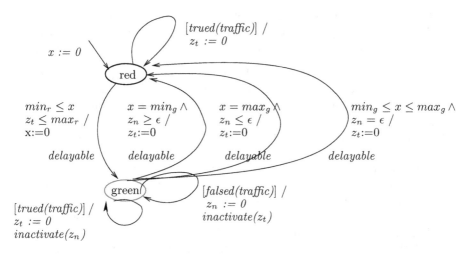

Fig. 5. TLCP Behavior: Time Constraints

The composition of the timed automata associated with all constraints[10] is given in Fig. 5. The traffic light never turns *green* without traffic and stays *green* a limited amount of time. In order to make sure that even with permanent traffic on all directions each light turns *green* after at most max_g time, the order in which the lights turn *green* cannot be chosen non deterministically[11]. Instead of choosing some fixed order, we propose a more flexible solution based on a dynamic *priority*, initialized arbitrarily to

$$init(priority) = forall\ j\ (priority(j):=j) \tag{5}$$

and updated each time $TLCP(i)$ changes to *green* by

$$update(i,priority) = forall\ j\ (priority(j):= (if\ j=i\ then\ 0\ else\ priority(j)+1)) \tag{6}$$

that is, the longer a light remains *red*, even in the absence of traffic on its lanes, the higher its priority gets, allowing occasional traffic to pass quickly without disturbing lanes with heavy traffic.

Figure 6 shows a possible run for 3 directions, depending on traffic. If permanent traffic is present on all directions, each traffic light spends the maximum time in *red* and in *green* (the first period in Fig. 6). If there is no traffic on direction 2 before the end of the nominal green phase, its light turns *red* earlier. If no traffic is present on some direction (here 2), even if it has the highest priority, it passes its turn keeping its priority.

The timed traffic light behavior is defined by the conjunction of the behaviors defined by Fig. 4 and Fig. 5. It cannot be directly translated into SDL by replacing *clocks* by time stamps, for two reasons:

---

[10] The *red* and *green* phases alternate, and traffic cannot go away in the *red* phase.

[11] To allow a non deterministic choice, the condition for *turn green* must also depend on the waiting time of all the TLCP(i).

- the use of *urgency* is essential to obtain the expected behavior
- SDL transitions represent actions or activities that might take time, whereas timed automata transitions represent *events*: instantaneous state changes.

An actual traffic light satisfying all the constraints can finally be implemented in different ways. One consists in introducing signals *trued/falsed(traffic)* and timers for the ϵ waiting period. A second solution consists in a process scanning every ϵ for changes of the *traffic* variable, where the length ϵ of the cycle is induced by the required minimal reaction time. Notice that the cycle length is not necessarily constant: during the *red phase*, it depends on the precision with which one wants to determine the time of traffic occurrence, and, as long as the minimal waiting time (min_g, min_r) has not been reached, there is no need to scrutinize for changes of *traffic* at all.

Choosing $max_g = max_r/(N-1)$ allows constraint (1) to be respected. Nevertheless, in the case of high traffic on all lanes, no flexibility is possible: the only solution satisfying all the constraints consists in turning the lights *green* in a round robin fashion. A smaller value of max_g, would allow modification of the priority rules and to provide additional green phases to those lanes with the highest traffic.

Another flexibility could be obtained by not a priori fixing the maximal length of the *green* phase: there is no need to quit the *green* phase if there is no traffic on any other line. This can be done by relaxing constraint (4) when there is no traffic on any other line.

Notice also that the proposed solution using a global variable *priority* would be made easy by the introduction of a flexible notion of global priority in SDL.

5   Discussion: Adapt this Profile to SDL

SDL already contains most primitives for dealing with time. Nevertheless, SDL suffers from some deficiencies which are discussed in this section.

SDL does not offer the possibility to define local time. Timers are less powerful as they cannot be periodic and they cannot express clocks which "tick" periodically, where ticks are consumed instantaneously or lost. The extension of SDL with more powerful timers and UML clocks has already been proposed previously [12, 36]. Also the introduction of local time is straightforward by having a different *now* attached with each "locality". The values of different local

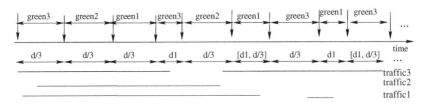

Fig. 6. A Possible Evolution of Traffic Lights over Time

times need not evolve strictly synchronously, but by respecting some specified drift, offset,.... Nevertheless, explicit modeling of local clocks should be avoided whenever possible, and the uncertainty on the relative speed or values of local clocks expressed in terms of uncertainties on the occurrence times or durations.

In SDL, it is left open how concurrent activities are sequentialized (when they do not run in a distributed fashion). It is however specified that activities within a process agent are executed in a run-to-completion fashion. This makes the definition of "interrupts" in principle impossible. It has been proposed (see [12]) to use the exception mechanism of SDL, which can be considered as a kind of exception to the run-to-completion principle, for the definition of interrupts.

Our main concern is the expression of time constraints on execution times and durations between events. The SDL semantics says that time passes in actions and not in states[12], but no means is provided to specify constraints on the time passed in actions. Waiting can be forced by means of timers and time guards. Existing tools implement a different interpretation: As in MSC or timed automata, "atomic" parts of transitions are viewed as *instantaneous events*. Moreover, time passes only where explicitly required by waiting conditions. This view allows the expression of time *constraints* by means of time guards, decisions and explicit *error states*. Nevertheless, such error states do not exist in SDL, and they make the models cumbersome. Moreover, some of the identified events, such as "reception of a signal in the input queue" has no syntactic representation and can therefore not be constrained.

Alternatives for the expression of time constraints exist, which can be extended in such a way as to serve our purpose.

MSC: is an event based formalism allowing the expressing of constraints on time elapsing between events. By introducing instances of agents which are implicit in SDL, such as the input queue of a process or the agent associated with a process set, all introduced events can be represented. MSC is already used in practice to express time constraints on SDL specifications. But MSC is not expressive enough for this purpose. For example, MSC does not allow the expression of constraints of the form "**if** the entire scenario in between two constraint events occurs, **then** the time constraint *must* hold, otherwise no constraint is imposed". Live Sequence Charts (LSC) [33] are more powerful as they allow expression of such implications by means of *cold* event occurrences and *hot* time constraints.

An extension of MSC, with the concepts of LSC would be very useful and allow the expression of timed scenarios in practice. Notice however, that scenario based formalisms can be very cumbersome when the number of possible alternative scenarios is high or when only events at the interface of a single agent are constrained, and they should not be the only means for expressing time constraints.

Annotations: Some tools allow the expression of duration constraints on actions in the form of special comments. The inconvenience is that each tool defines its own notation and semantics.

---

[12] Editorial note: This is obviously *not* the case. While waiting in a state time passes.

Annotations (using the event names and duration expressions defined in Sect. 3.3) are convenient for simple constraints associated with processes tasks, signals,... specifying execution times of tasks or durations such as response times, process execution periods ..., because they occur (for example) in contracts specifying interfaces. These annotations can take the form of special comments, but their syntax and semantics should not be left open as a tool issue.

Observers: Some SDL tools provide the facility to define *observers* as a means for defining constraints and properties. Observers allow constraints to be imposed on occurrences of events as in MSC. They can also observe and constrain the global state of the observed system, and then look almost like SDL processes. Observers are a very powerful means for expressing properties and constraints, but exist only in particular tools. SDL does not provide any standard notation for them.

Triggers for observers are any of the defined events, and they define constraints on their occurrence time using time stamps (such as $now - t \leq 3$) or the duration expressions defined in Sect. 3.3 (such as *duration(ev,now)* ≤ 3). To define properties and constraints, they may use the error states mentioned above or an explicit urgency as in timed automata.

So that modeling languages can be used in practice, it is very important that the user has the freedom to express time constraints in the most convenient manner, depending on each situation. For this reason, all three above mentioned approaches are useful. Separation of functional specification and timing information is motivated by the fact that timing information is mostly platform or implementation dependent, and makes it easier to adapt the time related specifications to a different platform. In all three types of formalism, we distinguish between *constraints* which are part of the definition of the system, and *properties* which must be derivable from the system definition and constraints.

To take into account scheduling and deployment related information, new notations have to be introduced in SDL. The simplest way is almost the one proposed in QSDL [11]. At the architecture level, a list of *resources* with an attribute defining their preemptibility is defined. For block and process agents as well as tasks, it is specified on which resource they are executed. Inner agents and tasks run on the same resource, if not otherwise stated. Scheduling policies are defined by keywords, such as RMA or EDF, or by priority rules. They are attached to resources or agents in a hierarchical fashion. Within a process, priorities are defined between transitions or their triggers, and within a block, they are defined between sub-agents. Priorities may be dynamic, where dynamic priorities can be specified in a declarative way (that is, depending on some precondition) or by means of an *observer* (attached to the concerned agent) that explicitly updates priorities depending on the observed states and events.

Perspectives of Simulation and Validation

In Sect. 3.2 we have already discussed the simulation issue: any SDL model with time constraints can be simulated. This is an important property, because this means that such a model can be used for model based testing.

Obviously, any interesting property is in general undecidable on an SDL specification due to infiniteness of data domains, and unbounded message buffers and agent creation. Nevertheless, the verification of time related properties can often been done on a finite control abstraction: that is, a system with finite data domains, bounded message buffers and bounded agent creation. A number of interesting verification problems are decidable on such a finite control abstraction under the conditions that in the timed automata obtained by translation: clocks can only be reset to zero, stopped and restarted; and the only allowed tests are comparisons of clock values or differences of clock values with **constants**. This means that the only allowed constraints imposed on events are Boolean combinations of comparisons of the type "duration since the occurrence of some event lays within an interval" or "the difference of occurrence times between two passed events lays within an interval".

MSC constraints are in this restricted set: they constrain only intervals on occurrence times of events or durations between pairs of events and timers.

Observers satisfy the restrictions if they use only constraints that are Boolean combinations of interval constraints on expressions of the form $duration(e_1,e_2)$[13]. An alternative, is using time stamps of the form "$t := now$" and comparisons of the form "$now - t \in [2,3]$" or "$t_2 - t_1 \in [2,3]$". The general time stamping mechanism – which allows the *comparison* of time distances with different end points as in "$(now - t_2) \leq (t_2 - t_1)$" used in auto-adaptive algorithms – is more expressive but outside the decidable set.

Schedulers make use of *integrators*: they imply clocks used for counting execution time which are stopped when the process is suspended and restarted when it becomes executing again. Decidability is preserved if only interval constraints on such integrators are tested, which is typically the case when worst-case execution times and deadlines are specified.

There exist several tools based on timed automata allowing some verification under the above mentioned restrictions, such as Hytech [24], the Kronos/IF tool [25, 26] and Uppaal [28].

Let us consider a number of relevant time related verification problems:

- Consistency checking of a time constraint system and verification of properties expressing requirements of the same kind, that is interval constraints on distances between events are very similar in nature, and can be done with the same tools.

  Notice that, when execution time constraints and deadlines are specified, and several concurrent behaviors are executed on the same resource, consistency checking and verification includes schedulability checking.

---

[13] Or *first-duration*(e_1,e_2) or any of the predefined duration expression. Notice that *pipeline-duration* poses a problem when no bound on the maximal number of concurrently active constraints can be given a-priori.

- Incomplete specifications, as in Figure 3, are problematic, as they may require backtracking during simulation. Under the before mentioned restrictions, the verification algorithm does synthesize for any transition the weakest constraint guaranteeing the satisfaction of all future constraints. When constraints are not "cyclically overlapping", completing an incomplete sequential specification can be done in linear time, even when interval bounds have parameters. This is useful for simplifying simulation, even in the case where the overall system is infinite.

  Nevertheless, constraint propagation can be done automatically with a reasonable effort only within a sequential behavior defined by an agent or a small set of agents. In general, budgeting over concurrent agents, must be provided by the user.

Notice that in the case where the intervals defining constraints are closed, there always exists an exact discretization. Thus which time model is used is not important. In practise, dense time leads often to more tractable models.

What to do when the system does not satisfy the requirements making the verification problem decidable? As long as all constraints are expressible by linear inequalities on time points or durations, the above mentioned verification problems are "semi-decidable". That is, successor sets can still be computed and termination detected, but there is no guarantee that the underlying model is finite and the verification procedure terminates. For these systems, one can still hope that the actually generated model is finite and small enough to be verified. Other remedies consist in using approximations of fixpoints or approximations based on reformulation of the constraints so that they can be analyzed by the above mentioned tools which use a more restricted internal representation than general linear inequalities.

References

[1] ITU-T. Recommendation Z.100 (08/02), Specification and Description Language (SDL). International Telecommunication Union, Geneva. 56
[2] B. Selic, G. Gullekson, P. T. Ward. Real-Time Object-Oriented Modeling. John Wiley & Sons, 1994. 56
[3] D. Harel. Statecharts : A visual approach to complex systems. Science of Computer Programming, 8:231–275, 1987. 56
[4] OMG Unified Modeling Language Specification, Version 1.3, June 1999. 56
[5] Telelogic. Objectgeode 4-1 reference manual, 1999. 56
[6] Telelogic. TAU Reference Manual, 1999. 56
[7] ITU-T. Recommendation Z.120 (11/99), Message Sequence Chart (MSC). International Telecommunication Union, Geneva. 56
[8] S. Leue. Specifying real-time requirements for SDL. PSTV, 1995. 56
[9] H. Ben-Abdalla, S. Leue. Expressing and analysing timing constraints in message sequence chart specifications. Tech. report, U. Waterloo, 1997. 56
[10] J. M. Alvarez, M. Diaz, L. M. Llopis, E. Pimentel, J. M. Troya. Deriving hard-real time embedded systems implementations directly from SDL specifications. Int. Symposium on Hardware/Software Codesign CODES, 2001. 56

[11] A. Mitschele-Thiel, B. Müller-Clostermann. Performance engineering of SDL/MSC systems. Computer Networks 31(17), 1999. 56, 72

[12] M. Bozga, S. Graf, L. Mounier, Iulian Ober, D. Vincent. Timed extensions for SDL. SDL Forum 2001, LNCS 2078, 2001. 56, 70, 71

[13] ARTiSAN, 2001. 56

[14] Ilogix. Rhapsody development environment. 56

[15] Telelogic. TAU Generation 2 Reference Manual, 2002. 56

[16] T. Bienmüller, W. Damm, H. Wittke. The Statemate Verification Environment – Making it real. Conf. Computer Aided Verification, CAV, LNCS 1855, 2000. 56

[17] OMG. Response to the OMG RFP for Schedulability, Performance and Time, v. 2.0. OMG document ad/2002-03-04, March 2002. 56, 59

[18] T. Henzinger, X. Nicollin, J. Sifakis, S. Yovine. Symbolic model checking for real-time systems. Symp. on Logic in Computer Science, 1992. 56

[19] S. Bornot, J. Sifakis, S. Tripakis. Modeling urgency in timed systems. Int. Symp. Compositionality - The Significant Difference, LNCS 1536, 1998. 56, 62

[20] O. Maler, A. Pnueli, J. Sifakis. On the synthesis of discrete controllers for timed systems. STACS'95, LNCS 900, 1995. 56

[21] E. Asarin, O. Maler, A. Pnueli. Symbolic controller synthesis for discrete and timed systems. Proc. Hybrid Systems II, LNCS 999, 1995. 56

[22] S. Bornot, G. Gössler, J. Sifakis. On the construction of live timed systems. Proc. TACAS 2000, LNCS 1785, 2000. 56

[23] T. Henzinger, B. Horowitz, Ch. Kirsch. Giotto: A time-triggered language for embedded programming. Embedded Software, LNCS 2211, 2001. 56

[24] T. Henzinger, Pei-Hsin Ho, H. Wong-Toi. HYTECH: A model checker for hybrid systems. J. on Software Tools for Techn. Transfer, 1(1-2), 1997. 57, 73

[25] S. Yovine. KRONOS: A verification tool for real-time systems. Springer Int. Journal of Software Tools for Technology Transfer, 1(1-2), 1997. 57, 73

[26] M. Bozga, L. Ghirvu, S. Graf, L. Mounier. IF: A validation environment for timed asynchronous systems. Comp. Aided Verification, CAV, LNCS 1855, 2000. 57, 73

[27] M. Bozga, S. Graf, L. Mounier. IF-2.0: A validation environment for component-based real-time systems. CAV, LNCS, 2002. 57

[28] K. Larsen, P. Petterson, W. Yi. Uppaal: Status & Developments. CAV'97, LNCS 1254, 1997. 57, 73

[29] E. Fersman, P. Pettersson, W. Yi. Timed automata with asynchronous processes: schedulability and decidability. TACAS, LNCS 2280, 2002. 57

[30] J. Warmer, A. Kleppe. The Object Constraint Language: Precise Modeling with UML. Addison-Wesley, 1998. 57

[31] Mooly Sagiv, Thomas W. Reps, Reinhard Wilhelm. Parametric shape analysis via 3-valued logic. TOPLAS 24(3): 217-298, 2002. 59

[32] Y. Gurevich. Evolving Algebras 1993: Lipari Guide. E. Börger, editor, Specification and Validation Methods. Oxford Univ. Press, 1995. 59

[33] W. Damm, D. Harel. LSCs: Breathing life into Message Sequence Charts. FMOODS'99 IFIP TC6/WG6.1 Conference on Formal Methods for Open Object-Based Distributed Systems. 1999. 63, 71

[34] D. Harel, R. Marelly. Playing with time: on the specification and execution of time-enriched LSC. Proc. Symp. on Modeling, Analysis and Simulation of Computer and Telecommunication Systems (MASCOTS 2002), 2002. 63, 65

[35] S. Bornot, J. Sifakis. An algebraic framework for urgency. Information and Computation, 163, 2000. 65, 68

[36] R. Münzenberger, F. Slomka, M. Dörfel, R. Hofmann. General approach for the specification of real-time systems with SDL. SDL forum, LNCS 2078, 2001. 70

Appendix: Predefined Events

The set of predefined events which can be used in time-constraints are the following ones. Moreover, the user can define additional events by means of "named" instantaneous skip actions (corresponding to SDL informal tasks) The events associated with an *operation call* are:

1. *Invoke*: emission of the call request;
2. *Receive*: reception of the call by the provider
3. *Accept*: start of the actual processing of the call by the provider;
4. *Invokereturn*: emission of the return reply;
5. *Receivereturn*: reception of the return by the caller;
6. *Acceptreturn*: consumption of the return[14].

Events associated with a *signal exchange* are:

1. *Send*: sending a signal;
2. *Receive*: reception of the signal by the target (i.e. when the signal is added in the queue);
3. *Consume*: start of treatment of the signal (triggering of transition or the moment the signal isdiscarded).

The events associated with an *action* are:

1. *Start*: starting time of the action;
2. *End*; termination time of the action;
3. *Startend*: simultaneous start and an termination of an *instantaneous* action.

The events associated with a *transition* of a state machine are:

1. *Start*: starting time of a transition;
2. *End*: termination of a transition (and entering the next state);

The events associated with a *state* of a state machine are:

1. *Entry*: time at which a state is entered;
2. *Exit*: time at which a state is exited;

The *change events* associated with *Boolean conditions* are:

1. *Trued* time at which the condition becomes true;
2. *Falsed* time at which the condition becomes false.

The events associated with *timers and clocks* are (some of can be seen as synonyms for some other kinds of events described above):

1. *set/reset/start/stop* (a timer or clock): events corresponding to the instantaneous actions defined for timers and clocks;
2. *Occur* : reaching of timeout time and notification of timeout;
3. *Tick*: equivalent to occur, but related to clocks;
4. *Consume*: timeout or tick consumption.

---

[14] In blocking call semantics *Acceptreturn* it is the same as *Receivereturn* or *Invokereturn*.

MSC Connectors – The Chamber of Secrets

Peter Graubmann

Siemens AG, Corporate Technology, Software and Engineering
Otto-Hahn-Ring 6, D-81739 München, Germany
peter.graubmann@siemens.com

Abstract. MSC Connectors as abstractions of the flow of messages between MSC constructs have two fields of application. They show their usefulness in the area of the component-oriented system development where the communication between MSC components, mostly given as MSC references in High Level MSCs or as decomposed instances, is designed as interface protocol of the involved components. But they also provide a means to describe the interaction between MSC constructs such as inline operator expressions or plain instances. This paper elaborates on the semantics definition of the MSC connectors and the specific rules for their application to individual MSC constructs.

Keywords: Component, Interface, Interface Protocol, Compositionality, Message Sequence Chart (MSC), MSC Connector, Component Oriented Software Development, System Family Engineering

Abbreviations: BMSC: Basic Message Sequence Chart; MSC: Message Se-quence Chart; LPO: Labeled Partial Ordering; TTCN-3: Test and Test Control Notation Version-3

1 Introduction

From a system engineering point of view, MSC connectors have been introduced as a means for describing interfaces and the interactions between components [1, 2, 3, 4]. System development today is more and more based on the composition, configuration, and re-use of components. Thus, interfaces or, more precisely, the interactions between the components, are a focal point in each development. In particular for system families, where a group of related products (products with the same main characteristics but differentiating features) are derived from a set of common assets, a description technique is needed which is capable to clearly specify the interactions between components, because they are (1) the basis of component selection, (2) prerequisite for an efficient component adaptation, and (3) the starting point for any system family evolution when new components have to be constructed in a way that ensures their compatibility with the components already existing in the asset space. Within such a system engineering context, MSC connectors are mainly viewed as a means to describe the interactions occurring between MSC components which usually are represented by MSC references or decomposed instances [5, 6, 7].

R. Reed (Ed.): SDL 2003, LNCS 2708, pp. 77–101, 2003.
© Springer-Verlag Berlin Heidelberg 2003

However, MSC connectors can be exploited not only for the description of and the reasoning about component interactions, but also as a well-suited means for determining the message flow between arbitrary constructs in any MSC. Like MSC references, which are used to structure MSCs by combining instances and describing related sequences of events on the appropriate abstraction level, MSC connectors may be used to abstract interaction sequences and to structure the message flow. Considerations with respect to this level have originally been stimulated by the development of a graphical format for TTCN-3 [8, 9] and the attempt to replace the complex and not much used MSC gate concept by a more intuitive mechanism [1, 3].

This paper focuses on the second kind of connector usage, where MSC constructs rather than MSC components are considered. Nevertheless, the component oriented view of MSC connectors and their usage for "interface engineering" should be kept in mind. Connectors are based upon *one* concept and both ways of connector usage rely on the same principles. The actual connector definitions however may very well look rather different. For the connection of components, various component interfaces are combined to form an interaction protocol between several components. The association of the connector with the available component interfaces thus becomes an important issue. For the connection of MSC constructs, simple interaction abstractions are needed which can be easily adapted to a concrete message exchange. The development of appropriate connector patterns will be crucial in this case.

In this paper, the basic connector concept (as presented in [2, 3]) is enhanced and further elaborated. The connector semantics is presented in a less formalistic but rather more graphical manner which facilitates the perception of the essential features. The semantics is extended to multiple connector applications with additional rules. The failure of connector applications is discussed. The necessary specialization of the connector application for the various "connectable" MSC constructs is presented. Section 2 describes briefly the building blocks of the MSC connector concept: environmental instances, MSC connector definition with external instances, MSC connector application and connector semantics. Section 3 discusses in more detail the application of connectors to the individual MSC constructs with the respective additional rules. Section 4 provides a conclusion and an outlook together with a list of issues still open.

2   The MSC Connector Concept

In this paper, we focus on MSC connectors as a concise and easy means to describe message flow abstraction between arbitrary (structural) MSC constructs. As interaction abstractions, connectors are obviously intended to be applicable more than once. To enable this multi-usability, they have to have features that allow their adaptation to slightly changed application contexts. These features are the *external instance mapping* and the *message mapping* (see Sect 2.3). Message mapping allows abstraction from concrete message names in the connector definition. The external instance mapping identifies for each connector endpoint which messages of the connected MSC construct go through the connector.

Connected MSC constructs have to be comprehensible even if not viewed together with the connector. So it seems natural that messages originally intended to be exchanged via a connector with another MSC construct are considered to be sent to or received from the environment as long as the MSC construct itself is not viewed in its full (connection) context. To achieve a flexible association of connectors with MSC constructs, we need a structured environment. This concept – another slight extension to MSC-2000 [6, 7] – is provided by the *environmental instances*.

2.1 Environmental Instances

The MSC environment as currently defined in the standard is a monolithic construct. We propose to structure it into several, logically distinct environments, each with its own name, the *environment identifier*, and described by its own *environmental instance axis*. The concept behind the standard MSC environment still remains valid. It is now referred to as *general environment*, does not have a particular name, and is, as it was, represented by the MSC diagram frame. Due to the environment semantics, there is no message exchange between environmental instances or between environmental instances and the general environment.

The environmental instances are discriminated from the normal, so-called *internal instances* by the keyword **env** in the instance header (see Fig. 1a). There is no event ordering on environmental instance axes. To visualize this also in the graphical form, we draw the environmental instance axis as dashed line.[1] The environmental instances of an MSC together with its general environment form a partitioning of the total environment. Thus, each message event in the (total) environment belongs to exactly one environmental instance or to the general environment.

In some cases, particularly within nested operator expressions, the introduction of additional environmental instances may rather blur the clarity of the MSC diagrams. So, two alternative representations are proposed: the so-called *arrow mechanism* and the so-called *attached environment identifier*. In both alternatives, the message arrow is drawn between (internal) instance and environment frame (as done in the standard MSC). For the arrow mechanism, a small arrow and the environment identifier is attached to the message name and the optional parameter list (see Fig. 1b). For the other variant, the environment identifier is attached to the arrow endpoint at the diagram frame (see Fig. 1c). These variants may help to produce intuitive and clear MSC diagrams, however, their use is not acceptable if the environment is already at the same time represented as instance axis.

---

[1] In [2, 3] it is proposed as solid line; the change was suggested by several reviewers.

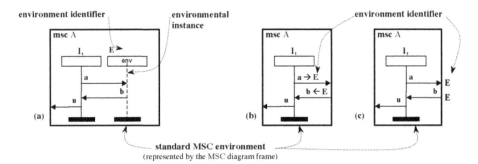

Fig. 1. The Structured Environment and Presentation Variants: (a) Environmental Instance E; (b) "Arrow mechanism"; (c) "Attached environment identifier"

2.2   Connector Definition

MSC Connector definitions present a potential interaction behavior. The "actual" behavior only comes into existence through the connector application (see Sect. 2.3). To point to the slight differences, MSC connectors are distinguished from MSCs by their own keyword **con**. Syntactically, MSC connectors can nevertheless be seen as a variant of the MSC reference definition [4]. The same constructs that constitute the MSC references are also available for the definition of MSC connectors.

There is, however, an additional construct: to comprehend the interaction described by a connector, the connected entities need to be represented. This is done by the so-called *external* instances.[2] They are distinguished by the keyword **ext** in their instance header (see Fig. 2).

It should be emphasized that, albeit external instances will be related to environmental instances during the connector application (see Sect. 2.3), they are quite different: external instances resemble the standard instances in all respect (save the **ext** keyword). In particular, they show the usual event ordering which is needed to reflect the behavior of the connected MSC constructs.

Figure 2 also shows an internal instance. Internal instances are used to incorporate interaction services into connector definitions for components. In the case of connecting arbitrary MSC constructs, internal instances may be rarely relevant.

---

[2] In the component-oriented view, external instances represent connected component roles or interfaces. For connecting MSC constructs, external instances can be understood as proxies for the behavior of the constructs that is visible to the connector.

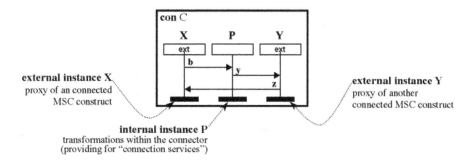

Fig. 2. Definition of the MSC Connector C

2.3   Connector Application

MSC connectors can be applied to MSC references, MSC reference expressions and decomposed instances, but also to plain instances with their co-regions, inline operator expressions and the environment.

The MSC connector application is syntactically expressed by a special graphical symbol: a double lined arrow (see Fig. 3a). This seems to adequately express that a connector can be viewed as a kind of high-level message. The obligatory connector name is attached to the arrow symbol. The *external instance mapping* associates the environmental instances in an connected MSC construct with the respective external instances in the connector. In Fig. 3a, the external instance mapping is expressed by $E \leftarrow X$ and Y beneath the arrowheads at each connector endpoint. The *message mapping* identifies message names in the connector with the messages in the connected constructs. An example is given also in Fig. 3a by the expression "$[c \leftarrow z;\ d \leftarrow y]$" which identifies the messages z and y in the connector definition with the respective messages c and d in the definition of the decomposed instances A and B in Fig. 3b.

The MSC connector application eventually describes the exchange of messages between the so-called *connected instances* in the connected MSC constructs. Connected instances are the instances, which exchange messages with environmental instances, that are associated with external instances in the connector by the external instance mapping. The respective messages are called *connected messages*. They are supposed to go through the connector.

MSC connectors are capable of connecting more then two MSC constructs. Branching points in the connector arrow allow the drawing of appropriate connector applications; for more details see [2].

External Instance Mapping The external instance mapping identifies for each endpoint of the connector symbol how the environmental instances of the connected MSC construct are to be associated with the external instances of the MSC connector. A specified message exchange with an environmental instance thus becomes a message exchange through the connector via the associated external instance.

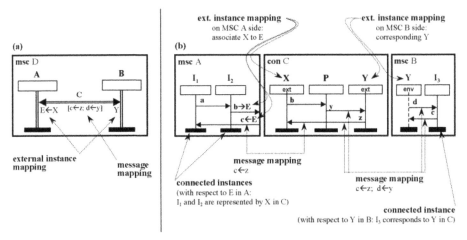

(a) the Connector Application; (b) the Respective Definitions of A, B and C.
In analogy to the graphical presentation of the connector, we propose to denote a decomposed instance with a double lined instance axis.

Fig. 3. MSC Connector C Connecting the Decomposed Instances A and B

In the simplest case, the external instance mapping associates two instances that bear the same name. This can be seen in Fig. 3, where the external instance Y in C is associated with the environmental instance Y in the decomposed instance B.

Equally simple is the case, where external and environmental instances are considered corresponding albeit they are differently named. An example can also be found in Fig. 3, where the association between the environmental instance E of the decomposed instance A with the external instance X of connector C is expressed by the simple mapping $E \leftarrow X$.

Identifying *one* external instance in the connector with *one* environmental instance in the MSC construct, is very likely to be sufficient to describe the external instance mapping in most cases. If there are two or more pairs of external and environmental instances to be associated, this is written as "$E_1 \leftarrow X_1$; $E_2 \leftarrow X_2$" with E_i environmental and X_i external instances.

Sometimes the situation may be slightly more complicated. Admittedly, this is more likely the case when several component variants of a product family are combined by an MSC connector. Yet, if a connector defining a certain interaction abstraction is intended to be applicable to a large number of MSC constructs without restrictions, some more flexibility is necessary. Therefore several external instances in the connector may be mapped onto one environmental instance (the connector provides the possibility to distinguish between several interacting MSC constructs which, in the current application, are all subsumed by the unstructured one that is actually connected). Alternatively, one external connector instance is mapped onto several or even all environmental instances of a connected MSC construct. This means, the more fine grained and better structured

MSC construct can nevertheless communicate by the given connector (being used in a different context, the refined structure of the MSC construct however is probably necessary).

The general definition of the external instance mapping takes into account the need for this flexibility, but ensures the correctness of the association:

> For each connector endpoint and the respective MSC construct, a non-empty subset of a partition of the external connector instances has to be mapped injectively into a partition of the environmental instances of the MSC construct. There is no message exchange among instances of the same partition element.

In Sect. 2.4, where the connector semantics will be discussed, we will see that each defined association between a set of external connector instances and a set of environmental instances in the MSC construct actually identifies the respective partial behavior of the MSC construct and the connector that has to be merged in order to determine the behavior of the entire connector application.

More details about the external instance mapping can be found in [2, 3] where also several shorthand notations are defined.

Message Mapping The message mapping adapts the message names of an MSC connector to its application context and thus allows definition of interaction abstractions without referring to concrete message names. It provides a rather sophisticated procedure to rename so-called *external connector messages*: that is, those messages in an MSC connector which come from or go to an external instance. The message mapping is enclosed in square brackets and attached to the connector symbol (see Fig. 3). The mechanism allows specification of several substitution alternatives, one of which has to be applied. Due to a lack of space we do not elaborate on the message mapping here. More details about it can be found in [2, 3] where also shorthand notations are discussed.

2.4   Connector Semantics

The behavior defined by a connector application is the result of a merging of the behaviors specified by the MSC connector and the MSC constructs. The *basic* merging procedure can be defined in the following manner:

> Each connector in/out message event on an external connector instance has to be identified with a corresponding equally named in/out message event that is received from, respectively sent to one of the environmental instances in the connected MSC that are associated to the external connector instance through the external instance mapping.
> The message mapping has to be performed prior to the merging.

For this merging procedure, it is assumed that messages with identical names also have to correspond with respect to their parameters. The explicit definition of this correspondence will be detailed in a later paper.

The Merging Procedure MSC connectors as well as connected MSC constructs may contain inline operator expressions, co-regions, or other structural concepts. Each of them represents a complex behavior usually including several alternatives. Merging the behavior of connector and MSC constructs will thus result in merging behavior alternatives. Obviously, only a few "corresponding" branches of the respective connector and MSC construct behavior can fit together. To determine the behavior of the connector application requires identification of the behavior alternatives that can be merged.

According to the MSC-2000 standard Z.120 [6, 7], a basic MSC describes the causal ordering of the contained communication events which can be provided suitably by a partial order semantics. This semantics can be extended in a straightforward manner to MSCs containing structural constructs by using sets of partial orders which are interpreted as alternatives using the delayed choice operator [10].

For the definition of the merging procedure, the notion of events and actions play a crucial role. Actions (which are identified as message types[3]) and their possibly recurring occurrences, the message events, have to be strictly distinguished. Several message events identified by the same message name (that is, related to the same action) may occur within one MSC. Therefore, labeled partial orderings are chosen as the underlying structure for the formal MSC connector semantics [10]: A labeled partial ordering (LPO) is a structure, consisting of a set of events, a reflexive, anti-symmetric and transitive order relation on this set of events, and a labeling function that provides the mapping of the event set onto the corresponding set of actions, which are essentially the message types, as already stated above.

According to this approach, it is assumed that the MSC connector and each of the connected MSC constructs are represented by a set of LPOs. These LPO sets have to be mutually merged whereby in general only a few combinations fit together, in which case they are called consistent. There is no merging result for non-consistent combinations (the merging procedure is considered to have failed in this case). The set of consistent LPOs represents the resulting behavior of the connector application.

The main step for the definition of the connector semantics is thus, to characterize the appropriate merge functions which map the events in the LPOs of the connector and the connected MSC constructs onto the events of the merged behavior. Obviously, a merge function has to preserve the message events of the connected MSC constructs with their labeling and their ordering; it also has to preserve the internal message events of the connector and the thereby defined labels and orderings; and eventually, it has to identify the corresponding message events on the external instances of the connector with connected message events on the corresponding connected instances. Thus, merge functions turn out to be partially identity mappings, but at their heart they are based upon bijective

---

[3] Message types are declared by a name, the direction indication ("sending" or "consumption"), and possibly further information (as, for instance, timing constraints).

mappings between external and corresponding connected message events which are called *external event mappings*.

External event mappings carry the external instance mapping over to LPOs. For each basic statement of the external instance mapping in a connector application, which is given as "$E_1, \ldots, E_n \leftarrow X_1, \ldots, X_m$" we identify a set of external message events M_X in the given connector LPO and a set of connected message events M_E in the given LPO of the connected MSC construct. M_X collects the message events occurring along the connector instances $X_1, \ldots, X_m$. M_E consists of message events corresponding to messages from and to the $E_1, \ldots, E_n$. Each mapping from M_X to M_E is called external event mapping. Obviously, only bijective external event mappings can contribute to the merging of the behavior of a connector and a connected MSC.

However, to simply use arbitrary bijective external event mappings would (in general) not yield a correct merging (labeling and ordering preservation requirements might be violated). Further constraints have to ensure that the result of the merging is again an LPO. Thus, we require that a merge function has to be consistent. This means, it has to show the following three properties:

(a) Compliance with the external instance mapping;
(b) Message type consistency;
(c) Ordering consistency.

Using the MSC connector application given in Fig. 3, we now will show (a) how the merge functions can be constructed out of the external instance mapping (thus, they are naturally compliant with it), (b) that message type consistency requires the correspondence of the labeling of the identified message events, and (c) that ordering consistency ensures that the merge procedure has not produced a violation of the event ordering.

The first step for determining the behavior of a connector application is to apply the message mapping to all LPOs of the connector. Since the message mapping allows for alternative substitutions, the number of resulting LPOs may increase.

In the next step, one LPO of each of the connected MSC constructs and one of the connector LPOs (after message substitution) have to be merged. This step eventually has to be repeated until all possible combinations are exhausted. In addition, there may exist several consistent merge functions for one combination. All of them have to be determined. The collected results of the merging procedure then define the behavior of the connector application.

In the example connector application of Fig. 3, MSC A, MSC B and connector C are each described by one LPO only (see Fig. 4). The external instance mapping for the application of C at the side of the MSC construct A determines which external messages in the connector can possibly be merged with which connected messages in A. The external instance mapping is defined by "$E \leftarrow X$". Thus, the connector message events $M_X = \{$C-X: *send b*, C-X: *receive c*$\}$ on the instance X are associated with the connected message events $M_E = \{$A-I_2: *send b*, A-I_1: *receive c*$\}$ on instances I_1 and I_2 which are exchanged with the

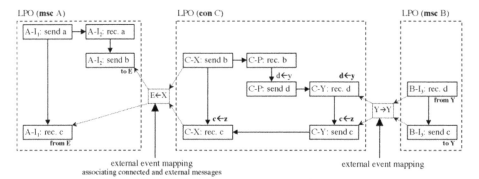

external event mapping
associating connected and external messages

external event mapping

LPO representation of the connector application of Fig. 3. Message events are represented by rectangles inscribed with the labeling and an additional indication of instance axis and MSC construct, to which the event belongs. The partial order relation is denoted by solid arrows. Message mapping or interaction with an environmental instance is indicated above/below the respective message events.

Fig. 4.   Labeled Partial Order (LPO) Representation: Connector Application

environmental instance E. This provides for two bijective external event mappings between these sets of message events: $\boldsymbol{f}_{A1}$ and $\boldsymbol{f}_{A2}$ (they are depicted in Fig. 5 and Fig. 6, respectively). For the connector application to MSC B, we have $M_X = \{ C\text{-}Y\text{: } receive\ d,\ C\text{-}Y\text{: } send\ c \}$ associated with $M_E = \{ B\text{-}I_3\text{: } receive\ d,\ B\text{-}I_3\text{: } send\ c \}$ with again two external event mappings $\boldsymbol{f}_{B1}$ and $\boldsymbol{f}_{B2}$ (to be also found in the same figures).

The merge functions are constructed out of the partially defined identity functions on the LPOs of the connected MSC constructs and a partially defined function on the connector message events which itself is a composition of the partially defined bijective external event mappings and the identity on the inter-

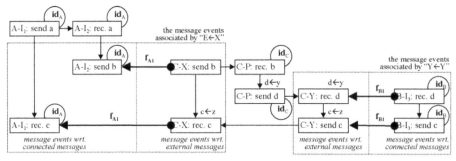

Consistent merge function defined by $\boldsymbol{f}_{A1}$, $\boldsymbol{f}_{B1}$ and the identities $\boldsymbol{id}_A$, $\boldsymbol{id}_B$, and $\boldsymbol{id}_C$.

Fig. 5.   The Only Consistent Merge Function for the Connector Application of Fig. 3

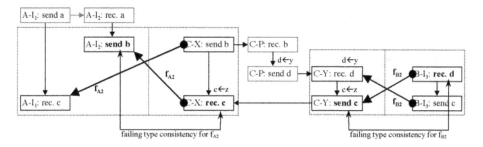

Fig. 6. Two External Event Mappings that Cause Inconsistency in a Merge Function

nal connector events. Thus, in our example we construct four merge functions by combining the f_{Ai} with f_{Bj} and the identities id_A, id_B, and id_C, $i,j \in \{1,2\}$ (see again Fig. 5).

Message type consistency means that the message types of the message events identified by an external event mapping coincide: the identified message events in the connector and in the MSC construct refer to the same action by showing the same message name and the same input/output indication.[4] Obviously, f_{A2} and f_{B2} do not fulfil this requirement (see Fig. 6), so a merge function in which they are involved is not message type consistent.

Ordering consistency simply requires that the merge function, which actually produces the union of the ordering relations of the MSC connector and the connected MSC constructs, yields a relation which is, together with its transitive closure, again an ordering relation. This holds for the only merge function in our example which is message type consistent and hence, we have shown that the connector application of Fig. 3 defines the overall behavior as shown in Fig. 7.

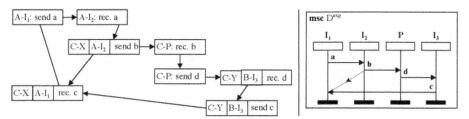

LPO representation of the behavior of the connector application in Fig. 3, derived through the consistent merge function given in Fig. 5. MSC D^{exp} is the result of the merge procedure, rewritten as MSC.

Fig. 7. Labeled Partial Ordering Representation: Connector Application

---

[4] If we take into account message parameters and timing constraints this rule will be slightly modified. To elaborate the full details is however still part of our future work.

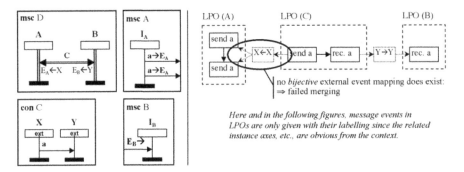

Fig. 8. Failing Connector Application due to a not Covered Message to Instance E_A

Multiple Connector Applications to an MSC Construct The merge procedure is very sensitive to the number of events that are identified by the external event mappings. Because they have to be bijective, it is evident that the number of the thereby associated external and connected events has to be the same. Otherwise, there is no valid merge function. If no other merge function proves to be consistent, as it is the case in Fig. 8, the connector application fails.

To consider the connector application in Fig. 8 as failed is justified. Applying connector C to A via the environmental instance E_A "binds" this environmental instance: it is no longer part of the "environment", that is, part of the system boundary. The connector application made it internal (actually, E_A is going to disappear) and a leftover message to E_A does not make any sense.

This observation makes it obvious that (1) the *application scope* of a connector application has to be determined unambiguously, and (2) the connector

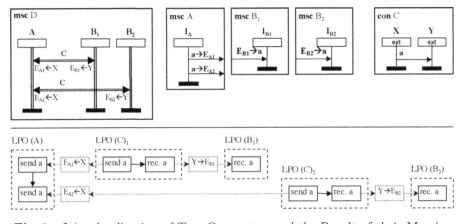

Fig. 9. Joint Application of Two Connectors and the Result of their Merging

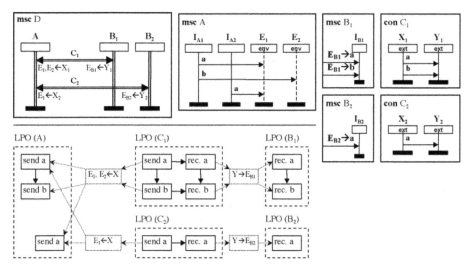

Fig. 10. Application of Connectors C_1 and C_2 (their application cannot be ordered)

semantics has to be adjusted to multiple connector applications to the same MSC construct.

The application scope of a connector application is basically given by the entire MSC construct. Only for plain instances and the like constructs, a "point-like" application (such as a message event) is defined. The application scope will be discussed in greater detail in Sect. 3.

The application of two or more connectors to an MSC construct can be done in arbitrary order, as long as the sets of environmental instances that are associated with the respective external connector instances are mutually disjoint (see Fig. 9). In this case, the respective connected events are uniquely related to one connector only and thus, no conflict arises when the bijective external event mappings are determined.

If connector applications, however, share environmental instances in their external instance mappings, then connectors very likely have to share connected message events. In this situation, we can no longer require independent bijective external event mappings as basis for the merge function but we have to consider those external event mappings with disjoint images that together form a bijection.

In Fig. 10, the external instance mappings E_1, $E_2 \leftarrow X_1$ for C_1 and $E_1 \leftarrow X_2$ for C_2 share the environmental instance E_1 in A. The respective external message events for C_1 and C_2 are $M_{X1} = \{C_1\text{-}X_1\colon \text{send } a,\ C_1\text{-}X_1\colon \text{send } b\}$ and $M_{X2} = \{C_2\text{-}X_2\colon \text{send } a\}$. Corresponding connected message events are $M_{E1/E2} = \{A\text{-}I_{A1}\colon \text{send } a,\ A\text{-}I_{A1}\colon \text{send } b,\ A\text{-}I_{A2}\colon \text{send } a\}$ and $M_{E1} = \{A\text{-}I_{A1}\colon \text{send } a,\ A\text{-}I_{A2}\colon \text{send } a\}$. Since $M_{E1/E2} \cap M_{E1}$ is not-empty, we have to prevent the joint association of both connectors with the same message event. To achieve this, we must not consider the individual external event mappings

$F \equiv \{ f: M_{X1} \rightarrow M_{E1/E2} \}$ and $G \equiv \{ g: M_{X2} \rightarrow M_{E1} \}$

in isolation, but we have to find external event mappings $f \in F$ and $g \in G$, such that $(f,g): M_{X1} \cup M_{X2} \rightarrow M_{E1/E2} \cup M_{E1}$ is a bijection. As a further requirement, of course, f and g have still to be message type consistent. In our example, we can find two such pairs: (f_1, g_1) with f_1 identifying the "send a" events on X_1 and I_{A1} and the "send b" events on the same pair of instances, and g_1 mapping the "send a" of X_2 onto the "send a" on I_{A2}. In the other pair (f_2, g_2), "send a" on X_2 is identified with the "send a" on I_{A1} by g_2 and f_2 identifies the remaining "send a" events on X_1 and I_{A2} (the mapping of the "send b" events is the same as for f_1).

As it can be seen in Fig. 10, there is no distinction made with respect to the placement of the connector application symbol when it comes to determining the merge function. Actually, the example was chosen in a way that any strict ordering of the connector applications does not make sense: the two "send a" events are unordered themselves. Starting the connector application C_1 with one of them (regardless which one) does not give it precedence over the C_2 application. However, things can be different. If we look at Fig. 11 (which presents a slight variant of the connector application in Fig. 9), we see that MSC D_1 actually resembles an alternative with respect to the order in which the message a is sent to the decomposed instances B_1 and B_2. This may very well be wanted (there are many ways to uniquely express the desired ordering of this message exchange, one is shown in Fig. 9, where the distinct environmental instances ensure the "correct delivery"; another possibility would be to define the message exchange with *one* connector which preserves the ordering of the sent events). To avoid any ambiguities, we propose an explicit *connector application ordering* which optionally may be added to a connector application. It is expressed by a natural number placed in parentheses above the arrow head of the connector application symbol (see MSC D_2 in Fig. 11).

To define an ordering among connector applications only makes sense if their external instance mappings share some environmental instances. The respective external event mappings can be considered as a tuple of mappings that together form a message type consistent bijection. We assume, that these external event mappings are numbered according to the respective application ordering. If LPO^{T} is the transitive closure of the labeled partial ordering of the MSC construct to which the connectors are applied, and λ the respective labeling function, we can define:

A tuple $(f_1, \ldots, f_n)$ of external event mappings as characterized above is application ordering preserving, if and only if for any message event e and e' holds:

$$\lambda(f_i(e)) = \lambda(f_j(e')) \wedge (f_i(e), f_j(e')))\in\mathrm{LPO}^{\mathrm{T}} \Rightarrow i{<}j.$$

This means, that if two external event mappings identify two connected events with the same message type, and if these connected events are in an

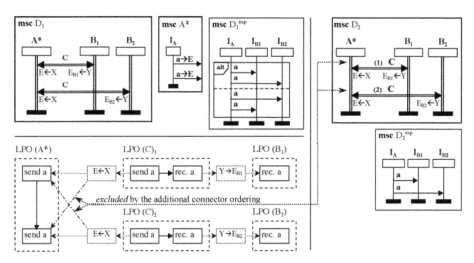

Fig. 11. Connector Application Variant with and without Ordering the Applications. (Definitions of the connector C and the decomposed instances B_1 and B_2 are in Fig. 9.)

ordering relation due to the ordering of the MSC construct, then this ordering corresponds to the ordering defined for the connector application.

The definition of the merge function consistency has to be adapted accordingly.

Connector application ordering is only relevant in the rather marginal case where multiple connector applications are intertwined due to common environmental instances in the external instance mappings. We defined the application order preservation mechanism to have a consistent treatment and an unambiguous definition, but we do not advocate its usage. Application guidelines for MSC connectors may discuss whether it should be allowed to occur in a reasonable design or not.

Failing Connector Applications Connectors describe the potential interactions of the connected MSC constructs. This implicitly implies, that not all possible interactions are necessarily realized. However, a connector application defines an interaction and thus, at least one of the thereby determined interaction patterns has to be accomplished.

Which behavior alternatives of the connected MSC constructs can be combined with which alternatives of the connector behavior, is determined by identifying the consistent merge functions. If no behavior combination with consistent merge functions can be found, then the connector application fails.

The failing of a connector application may not be confused with a connector application resulting in an empty behavior (that is, an LPO set containing only $(\emptyset,\emptyset,\emptyset)$, the empty LPO): the failing of the connector application is an irregu-

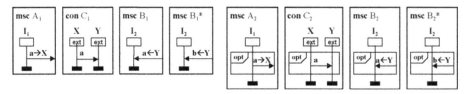

Fig. 12. Definitions of MSC connectors and decomposed instances, used in Figures 13-15

larity; the empty behavior may be an acceptable behavior (not to interact is a possible interaction pattern) – if specified within the connector.

Figures 13-15 exemplify the subtle differences between a plain message exchange via a connector, the empty connector behavior and a connector application failure and how connectors and MSC constructs have to be built in mutual dependency to achieve (or avoid) the respective effect. The figures are based upon a very simple scenario: a message a should be sent from the decomposed instance A to decomposed instance B via connector C.

Fig. 13a reflects this situation exactly: A_1 sends message a to the environmental instance X, B_1 receives a message a from its environmental instance Y, and the connector C_1 conveys a message a from external instance X to external instance Y. The exchange of message a between A_1 and B_1 is achieved. In Fig. 13b, C_1 is replaced by connector C_2 which offers two behavior alternatives: (1) "sending a (on X), then receiving a (on Y)" and (2) the empty behavior. A_1 and B_1 however "insist" on the message exchange (that is, there is no merge function for the empty behavior of C_2) and the potential optionality in C_2 is not exploited.

In Fig. 14a, sending and receiving a is declared optional in A_2 and B_2, respectively. Without connection between both entities, we obviously have four possible behavior combinations: A_2 either sends or sends not, and B_2 either receives or receives not message a. Without connector, of course, any exchange of message a is only done with the respective environments X in A_2 and Y in B_2. Applying connector C_1, any optionality of the message exchange disappears. This connector actually insists on a message exchange. If we however allow an optional exchange of message a between the external instances X and Y, as is done in C_2 (see Fig. 14b), the optionality can be exploited. A_2 and B_2 have of course to opt in the same way.

In Fig. 15b, in which A optionally sends a message a, but B optionally expects a message b, it is obvious that the established connection can only result in neither sending a nor receiving b. The connector applications in Fig. 15a fail completely due to message incompatibility between A_1 and B_1 * or the exclusion of the empty behavior by C_1.

Figures 13-15 stress the difference between failing connector applications and connector applications without interaction. If connector applications fail in these examples, it is always due to the impossibility of finding the necessary consis-

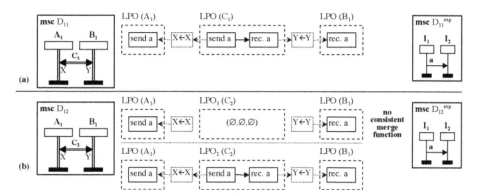

Fig. 13. Connector application variants I (definitions of A_1, B_1, C_1 and C_2 in Fig. 12)

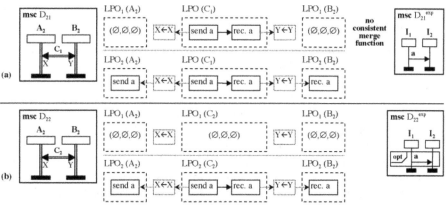

(a) no cons. merge functions for $\mathrm{LPO}_i(A_2), \mathrm{LPO}(C_1), \mathrm{LPO}_k(B_2)$ $1 \leq i, k \leq 2, i \neq k$.
(b) no cons. merge functions for $\mathrm{LPO}_i(A_2), \mathrm{LPO}_j(C_2), \mathrm{LPO}_k(B_2)$ $1 \leq i, k \leq 2, i \neq k$.

Fig. 14. Connector Application Variants II (defs. of A_2, B_2, C_1 and C_2 in Fig. 12)

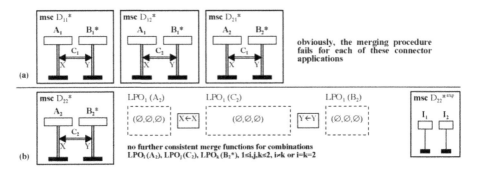

Fig. 15. Connector Application Variants III (A_1, A_2, B_1*, B_2*, C_1 and C_2 in Fig. 12)

tent merge functions. However, particularly in the context of multiple connector applications, unwanted results may occur which are not ruled out through the impossibility of finding consistent merge functions. To exclude such cases, additional rules will be defined. But this is still ongoing work and will be presented later.

3   Applying MSC Connectors to MSC Constructs

The previous section described the general rules for the connector application. This section discusses particular properties of the connector applications for respective "connectable" MSC constructs. Thereby, it suggests itself to form the following four groups:

- *Connector applications to MSC references, MSC reference expressions and decomposed instances.* The main principles for these kind of connector applications are already described in the general connector application definition in Sect.2.3. A few additions are discussed.
- *Connectors applied to plain instances.* Connector applications to the general environment or to environmental instances also belong in this group as well as the application of a connector to a co-region.
- *Connectors applied to inline operator expressions.* This comprises the connector applications to **seq**, **alt**, **par**, **loop**, **opt** and **exc** operators.
- *Connectors applied within connectors to external instances.* This provides for the possibility of composing connectors out of other interaction patterns (of course, themselves defined as connectors).

3.1   Connecting Decomposed Instances, MSC References and MSC Reference Expressions

The examples illustrating the MSC connector concept in Sect. 2 are based upon decomposed instances. We could have chosen MSC references as well. For both

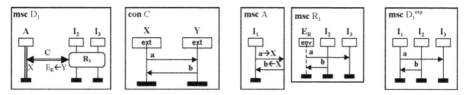

Fig. 16. A Typical Connector Application to an MSC Reference. D_1 expands to $D_1{}^{exp}$

constructs, the connector application presents itself completely alike. For decomposed instances, the application scope is the entire instance; the application scope of MSC references and MSC reference expressions is also the entire entity.

MSC D_1 in Fig. 16 shows the application of connector C to the MSC reference R_1. Thereby, the external instance Y in C is associated with the environmental instance E_R which is "local" to R_1 and not visible in D_1. Environmental instances defined "globally" in D_1 cannot be used for a connector application to R_1 – even if they pass R_1, since they represent the interface of D_1 to its outside. Such a situation is reflected in Fig. 17: The MSC reference R_2 connects R_1 to the environmental instance E which is global in R_2 (for the application of connectors to environmental instances, see Sect. 3.2). The MSC reference $R_2{}^*$ presents a variant: the environmental instance E_R, which is globally defined in $R_2{}^*$, also passes R_1; thus, the message exchange in R_1 with the environment E_R becomes now a message exchange with the environment of $R_2{}^*$ and is therefore visible in the application of connector C in $D_2{}^*$.

For MSC reference expressions, connector applications are handled analogously to MSC reference applications, since MSC reference expressions can immediately be transformed into corresponding MSC references, describing the behavior by the respective inline expressions.

3.2 Connecting Plain Instance Axes and the Environment

The semantics definition in Sect. 2.4 describes the application of an MSC connector to an MSC construct as merging message events on external connector

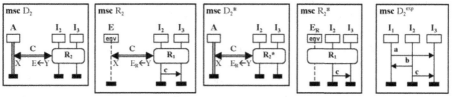

Two variants for the interaction of a "global" environmental instance and the MSC reference R_1. MSC D_2 and MSC $D_2{}^*$ both expand to MSC $D_2{}^{exp}$.

Fig. 17. Example of Fig. 16 Continued

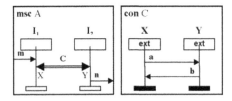 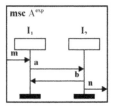

Fig. 18. MSC Connector C Applied to Plain Instances I_1 and I_2. A expands to A^{exp}

instances with corresponding events on connected instances in the MSC construct. Which events are to be merged and which instances are the connected instances is determined by the external instance mapping and the environmental instances of the MSC construct.

With plain instances, connector application is different. There is no additional environment and there are no connected message events to be matched with those in the connector. But if we recall that connectors serve as an interaction abstraction – that is they represent a possibly complex exchange of messages – it becomes obvious that the application of a connector to a plain instance can only mean to insert exactly that behavior into the plain instance that is specified for this endpoint by the connector. The insertion point is the point where the connector is attached to the instance axis. All the events of the plain instance above the insertion point are before the inserted events, all events below are after them.

In Fig. 18, the external instance X in the MSC connector C is identified with the plain instance I_1 and thus, after reception of message m, message a is sent and afterwards, message b is received at this instance. On I_2, the external instance Y is inserted, thus establishing the event sequence receiving a, sending b, and sending n for this instance.

The formalism for the external instance mapping is slightly modified: it only lists the external connector instances that are inserted into the plain instance. If two or more external instances are listed, then the behavior to be inserted is not totally ordered; consequently, the "insertion point" is altered to a co-region with a generalized ordering that reflects the ordering defined by the external instances on their respective message events.

Figure 19 provides an example for this. The application of connector C^* inserts the two external instances X_1 and X_2 into the plain instance I_1. The insertion is order preserving, thus, sending message a and receiving message c remains ordered on I_1, whereas the reception of message b is not ordered.

The application of a connector to a co-region is also rather simple: The connector application as a whole is not ordered with respect to the other events within the co-region, however, the ordering of the external instance events specified by the connector has to be preserved by adding the necessary general ordering. An existing general ordering between the events in the co-region that are

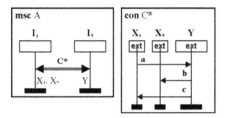 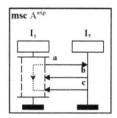

Fig. 19. Two External Instances Mapped into a Plain Instance. A expands to A^{exp}

not related to the connector application is not influenced at all. For an example see Fig. 20.

Environmental instances and the general environment are treated like plain instances. A connector application simply means the insertion of the respective connector events on the environment. Because the events are not ordered on the environment, we need not care about keeping ordering relations defined by the connector. An example is given in Fig. 21.

3.3 Connecting Inline Operator Expressions

The connector application scope of inline operator expressions is the entire operator expression, including all operands. This means, that a connector is applied to all alternatives defined for an **alt** operation or to all executions of a **loop** construct, etc. The environmental instances are treated in the same way as they were treated in MSC references. An environmental instance that starts and ends outside the operator expression is considered global (in particular, if there is a message exchange with parts of the MSC outside the operator expression). Global environmental instances cannot be used for connector applications to the inline operator expression, as, for instance, the instance E in Fig. 22. Only

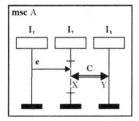 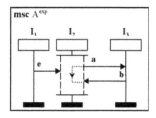

MSC connector C (as defined in Fig. 18), connecting a co-region on instance I_2 with the plain instance I_3. MSC A expands to MSC A^{exp}. The general ordering relation within the co-region establishes the ordering of the two connector events "sending a" and "receiving b"; the reception of message e remains unordered.

Fig. 20. Connecting a Co-region and Plain Instance

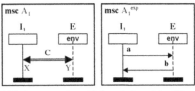
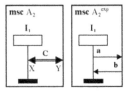

MSC connector C (as defined in Fig. 18) connecting the plain instance I_1 with either the environmental instance E (in MSC A_1) or the general environment (in MSC A_2). MSC A_1 and MSC A_2 expand to MSCs A_1^{exp} and A_2^{exp}, respectively.

Fig. 21. Connecting a Plain Instance to an Environment

environmental instances restricted to the operator expression itself are acceptable for this purpose (which are, again in Fig. 22, expressed using the "arrow mechanism" $a \rightarrow X$ for messages a to the environment X).

If a connector application should be restricted to only one operand (for instance, for the **alt** or the **par** operator expression), then it is necessary to restrict the environment involved in the connector application to this operand, too (see Fig. 23).

Connectors can be defined as "concrete connectors" with a particular connector application in mind. In this case, they will specify exactly the required interaction. Or they are defined as an interaction pattern applicable in many cases after adaptation to the concrete situation by an appropriate message mapping. Figure 24 demonstrates this variability. The two connectors in Fig. 24 actually are quite different. C_1 allows the alternation of the two messages a and b and thus corresponds exactly to the behavior specified by the connected alternative construct in MSC A_1. Connector C_2 describes only the exchange of one message between the external instances. Not until the connector is applied, can it be seen that an alternative is involved. The message mapping, that defines the substitution of the external connector message x with either a or b makes the alternative possible. The resulting MSC behavior is in both cases the expected alternative sending of message a and message b.

Figure 25 presents the connection of a **loop** construct to an MSC reference with a slightly differently structured loop. The connector itself specifies the re-

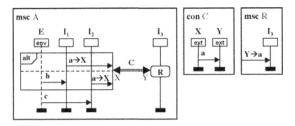
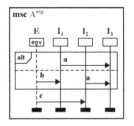

Fig. 22. MSC Connectors C Applied to an **alt** Operation. (A expands to A^{exp})

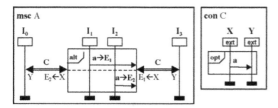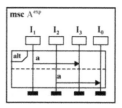

Fig. 23. MSC Connectors C Applied to each Operand of an **alt** Operation Separately (A expands to A^{exp})

peated exchange of a message from external instance X to external instance Y. The message mapping identifies the messages a and b as being exchanged. Due to the loop parameters given in MSC R, also the number of loops becomes restricted for the connected **loop** construct in MSC A, as is shown in A^{exp}.

The connector C in Fig. 25 can be seen as a very "universal" connector, because it may apply in many cases. It will be part of our future work to identify interaction structures that can serve as the most useful connectors between MSC constructs and to analyze their properties.

3.4 MSC Connector Applications in MSC Connector Definitions

Also external instances in connector definitions can be associated with (other) connectors. The external instances are treated like plain instances (see Sect. 3.2 and Fig. 26).

4 Conclusion and Outlook

Within this paper, a further elaborated semantics for the connector concept and rules for the connector applications to the "connectable" MSC constructs have been presented. The enhancement of the semantics applies to both areas of envisaged connector application, that is, to the field of component oriented development and interface engineering where connectors serve as specifications

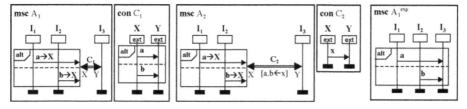

Fig. 24. Variants of the Representation of Alternative Behavior by Connectors

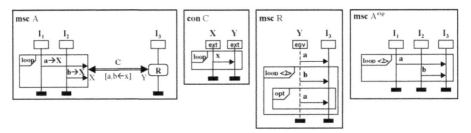

Fig. 25. Connecting a **loop** Construct

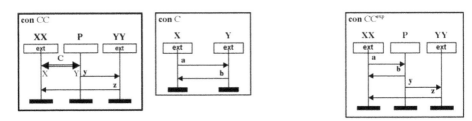

Fig. 26. MSC Connector C Applied to an External Instance in the Connector CC

of interaction protocols for components, as well as to the modularization and abstraction of the message exchange on the MSC construct level where connectors are intended to provide an easier approach than the gate concept [11].

Further semantics extensions are needed to include message parameters and the MSC timing concepts. Both extensions seem to be straightforward and will be provided as a next step.

Deriving static rules for connector applications with certain properties and the definition of MSC connectors as interaction patterns for MSC constructs is also still ongoing work. In the context of system family engineering where connectors are considered as a specification means for interface protocols, they are used as a methodical approach to analysis and evolution of component interactions with variation points, which is crucial for product derivation and product line development.

Acknowledgments

I would like to thank Ekkart Rudolph with whom I have worked together very closely on the subject of this paper and whose untimely death has interrupted a personal friendship and a very fruitful co-operation.

The work presented here was performed within the Eureka Σ Programme, ITEA Project ip00004 CAFÉ, and funded by the German BMBF.

References

[1] J. Grabowski, P. Graubmann, E. Rudolph: HyperMSCs with Connectors for Advanced Visual System Modelling and Testing. SDL 2001: Meeting UML, 10th Int. SDL Forum, Copenhagen, Denmark, Springer, LNCS 2078, 2001. 77, 78

[2] P. Graubmann: Describing Interactions between MSC Constructs – The MSC Connectors. To appear in: Computer Networks, Special Edition on ITU-T Languages, Elsevier 2003. 77, 78, 79, 81, 83

[3] P. Graubmann, E. Rudolph: MSC Connectors – The Philosopher's Stone. In: SAM 2002, 3rd Workshop of the SDL Forum Society on SDL and MSC, Aberystwyth, Wales, E. Sherratt, editor, Springer, LNCS 2599, 2003. 77, 78, 79, 83

[4] P. Graubmann, E. Rudolph, J. Grabowski: Component Interface Descriptions using HyperMSCs and MSC Connectors. IEEE Visual Languages and Formal Methods, Stresa, Italy, September 5-7, 2001. 77, 80

[5] ITU-T. Recommendation Z.120 (10/96): Message Sequence Chart (MSC) – Known as "MSC-96", Superseded (see [6, 7]). International Telecommunication Union, Geneva, 1996. 77

[6] ITU-T. Recommendation Z.120 (11/99): Message Sequence Chart (MSC) – Known as "MSC-2000" (See also [7]). International Telecommunication Union, Geneva, 2001. 77, 79, 84, 101

[7] ITU-T Recommendation Z.120 Corrigendum 1 (12/01): Message Sequence Chart (MSC) – Corrections and modifications to "MSC-2000". International Telecommunication Union, Geneva, 2002. 77, 79, 84, 101

[8] P. Baker, E. Rudolph, I. Schieferdecker: Graphical Test Specification – The Graphical Format of TTCN-3. SDL 2001: Meeting UML, 10th Int. SDL Forum, Copenhagen, Denmark, Springer, LNCS 2078, 2001. 78

[9] E. Rudolph, I. Schieferdecker, J. Grabowski: HyperMSC – A Graphical Representation of TTCN. SAM 2000, 2nd Workshop of the SDL Forum Society on SDL and MSC, Grenoble, France, 26-28 June 2000, LNCS 2599, Springer 2003. 78

[10] J.P. Katoen, L. Lambert: Pomsets for Message Sequence Charts. SAM 1998, 1st Workshop of the SDL Forum Society on SDL and MSC, Berlin, Germany, June 1998. 84

[11] S. Loidl, E. Rudolph, U. Hinkel: MSC'96 and Beyond – A Critical Look. SDL '97 Time for Testing – SDL, MSC and Trends, 8th Int. SDL Forum, Evry, France, North Holland, Sept. 1997. 100

Industrial Application of the SDL-Pattern Approach in UMTS Call Processing Development – Experience and Quantitative Assessment – [*]

Rüdiger Grammes[1], Reinhard Gotzhein[1], Christian Mahr[2], Philipp Schaible[1], and Helmut Schleiffer[2]

[1] Computer Science Department, University of Kaiserslautern
Postfach 3049, D-67653 Kaiserslautern, Germany
{grammes,gotzhein,schaible}@informatik.uni-kl.de
[2] Siemens AG
Lise-Meitner-Str. 7/2, D-89081 Ulm, Germany
{Christian.Mahr,Helmut.Schleiffer}@siemens.com

Abstract. In 1997, the SDL-pattern approach was introduced to the scientific community. Since then, the approach has been improved in many ways. In particular, the pattern pool has been extended to cover a variety of distributed systems and communication protocols, a notation to define patterns has been added, and the methodology for pattern-based system design has been refined. Based on the results of more recent case studies, the approach has been assessed as consolidated, and is currently being transferred to industry. In this paper, we present our experience of applying the SDL-pattern approach in an industrial environment, the development of a UMTS call processing system, a part of the Radio Network Controller (RNC). Furthermore, the benefits of applying the approach are evaluated in this context and quantified.

1 Introduction

Design patterns [1] are a well-known approach for the reuse of design decisions. In [2], a specialization of the design pattern concept for the development of communication protocols, called *SDL patterns*, has been introduced. SDL patterns combine the traditional advantages of design patterns – reduced development effort, quality improvements, and orthogonal documentation – with the precision of a formal design language for pattern definition and pattern application.

Usually, a number of advantages are associated with design patterns, such as reduced development effort and improved design quality. This, however, remains a theoretical claim unless practical evidence is provided. For industry, it is essential to have an evaluation that quantifies both costs and benefits of a new

---

[*] This work has been partially supported by Deutsche Forschungsgemeinschaft (DFG) as part of Sonderforschungsbereich 501, *Development of Large Systems with Generic Methods*.

R. Reed (Ed.): SDL 2003, LNCS 2708, pp. 102–117, 2003.

approach before applying it in a project. In an industrial cooperation, we have
done this kind of evaluation, and for the first time can present strong evidence
that the SDL pattern approach has the potential of improving design quality
by a significant reduction of design errors. This in turn leads to a reduction of
rework, therefore cutting development costs and shortening time-to-market.

In Sect. 2 we briefly survey the SDL pattern approach. We describe our
strategy for transferring the approach to industry in Sect. 3. In Sect. 4, an excerpt
of the RNC-pattern pool, a proprietary pool consisting of project-specific SDL
patterns, is presented. Section 5 presents the evaluation of the RNC-pattern
pool and assesses its potential impact on the RNC project. We summarize our
experience in Sect. 6.

2   The SDL-Pattern Approach

The SDL-pattern approach [3, 4] consists of the *SDL-pattern design process*,
a notation for the description of generic SDL fragments called *PA-SDL* (*Pattern
Annotated SDL*), a *template* and *rules* for the definition of SDL patterns, and
an *SDL-pattern pool* for the communication systems domain.[1] The approach has
been applied successfully to the engineering and re-engineering of several communication systems, including the Internet Stream Protocol ST2+ [5], a quality-
of-service management and application functionality for CAN (Controller Area
Network) [6], and the customized communication system of the light control in
a building [7]. Applications in industry are in progress (for example see [8]).

An *SDL pattern* [2, 3] is a reusable software artifact that represents a generic
solution for a recurring design problem with SDL as the design language. The
main argument for this choice is that SDL [9] is one of the few formal description techniques that are widely used in industry. One reason for this success is
certainly the graphical notation, which supports the intuitive understanding of
specifications. Furthermore, the availability of excellent commercial tool environments has contributed to the wide distribution of SDL in industry.

The SDL-pattern design process is part of an overall system development
process, as shown in the left graph of Fig. 1. The starting point for the communication system design activity is a set of communication requirements, which
is decomposed into a sequence of subsets (middle part of Fig. 1). The objective
of this decomposition is to incrementally develop the SDL design specification
by taking the subsets of the sequence into account one by one. Experience has
shown that such a decomposition is usually feasible, with the length of the sequence (and thus the granularity of the design activity) varying according to the
complexity of the communication requirements and the assumptions concerning the underlying communication service. The communication system design
activity in Fig. 1 is based on this sequence, starting with the first subset and

---

[1] Although the SDL-pattern pool has been developed in the communication systems
    domain, many of its patterns are of a more general nature, and can be applied in the
    design of distributed applications, too. For this reason and in order to emphasize the
    close relationship to the formal design language SDL, we call them *SDL patterns*.

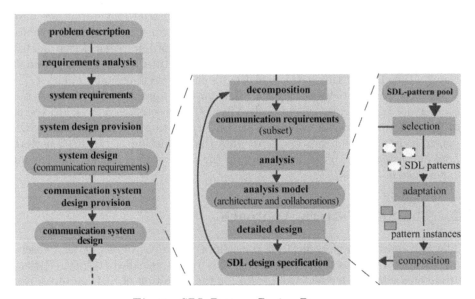

Fig. 1. SDL-Pattern Design Process

taking additional communication requirements into account only after a solution for this subset in the form of an SDL design specification has been found. As a consequence, the design process is incremental, and finally leads to a complete SDL design specification.

For each subset of communication requirements, several steps are performed. Firstly, an analysis of the requirements is performed. This leads to an *analysis model*, consisting of an architectural part described in terms of a UML object model and a set of collaborations described by message scenarios using MSC [10]. Note that each time additional requirements are taken into account, the analysis starts from the analysis model obtained so far, which is extended and/or modified. Based on the analysis model, an SDL design specification that meets the communication requirements is developed, which can in turn be refined into a sequence of steps. As with the analysis model, the SDL specification obtained for a given subset of communication requirements forms the context specification when the next subset is taken into account.

It is in the detailed design activity where SDL patterns are applied. Based on the analysis model, the designer searches the SDL-pattern pool for suitable SDL patterns, which he then selects, adapts, and composes (see right part of Fig. 1). The definition of SDL patterns supports the selection step based on UML class models and MSC use cases, which can be related to the analysis model. Next, the selected SDL patterns are adapted to fit the embedding context, yielding a pattern *instance*. Adaptation is restricted by constraints on the SDL context, and by renaming and refinement rules in the pattern definition, such that with each pattern application, certain properties are preserved. Finally, the pattern instance is embedded into the context specification, leading to a modified SDL specification. Note that several SDL patterns may be applied simultaneously. Also, patterns can be applied sequentially. If, for some requirements, the pattern pool does not contain an adequate solution, the corresponding parts of the SDL design are developed in the conventional way.

3   Transfer to Industry

Currently, the SDL-pattern approach is being transferred to industry [8]. As it has already turned out, it is possible to phase-in the approach even into running projects. We have developed a strategy with short term and strategic objectives:
Short Term Objectives:

- Analyze existing SDL designs and develop a project-specific, proprietary SDL-pattern pool. This pool will contain modified versions of already existing SDL patterns and/or a number of new SDL patterns, and be built up gradually.
- Evaluate the project-specific SDL-pattern pool on the basis of existing trouble reports, and quantify the benefits of pattern-based development in terms of saved rework and shortened release times.
- Define problem-specific, pattern-based developer guidelines, and train an initial team of system developers.
- Gradually integrate SDL-pattern-based design into the ongoing development project (starting with the design review).

These first steps are scalable and can be taken with a small investment. Steps 1 and 2 will reveal whether the approach is useful in a given project, but have no influence on the running project whatsoever. Steps 3 and 4 are taken only if the results of steps 1 and 2 show evidence for a positive impact. Once the benefits are clearly visible, further objectives, in particular the reuse aspect, should be envisaged.
Strategic Objectives:

- Apply SDL patterns and pattern-specific checklists in further projects to reduce the number of defects. This will reduce rework and shorten release times.
- Build up a full-scale, evolutionary product-line experience base, containing SDL patterns, experience reports, and developer guidelines. This will minimize the loss of know-how inflicted by staff fluctuation.
- Use the product-line experience base, in particular by training project staff, fully incorporating developer guidelines into projects, and by integrating the SDL-pattern approach into projects. This will maximize the degree of reuse and lead to high-quality designs.

Further industrial transfer activities in progress address graphical tool support for the documentation and application of SDL patterns. This will further enhance productivity of developers as well as quality of system design.

4   The RNC-Pattern Pool

The RNC-pattern pool is a proprietary pattern pool, containing project-specific SDL patterns that represent experience from the RNC-project. It has been derived by analyzing the results of the ongoing UMTS call processing development of a RNC (Radio Network Controller), and packaging them into 8 SDL patterns. The patterns we have identified so far can be classified into 5 categories:

Architecture Patterns capture generic architectures and their refinements.
> Example: RNCCLIENTSERVER. This pattern captures a client/server architecture of a distributed system.

Interaction Patterns capture the interaction among peers, e.g., a set of application agents, or a set of clients with a server.
> Example: RNCSYNCHRONOUSINQUIRY. This pattern introduces a confirmed interaction (called *inquiry*) between two peers. After a trigger from the embedding context, an agent sends an inquiry and is blocked until receiving a response from the second agent.

Control Patterns deal with the detection and handling of errors that may result from the loss, delay, or corruption of messages, or from agent failures.
> Example: RNCBLOCKINGCONTROL. Some procedures contain wait states that block a process until certain responses. If - due to design errors or message loss, for instance - a response releasing the process from a wait state is missing, the process will remain in that wait state, blocking resources as well as further functionality. This pattern introduces a timer-based mechanism that releases the process from its wait state.

Management Patterns deal with local management issues, such as buffer creation or message addressing.
> Example: RNCBUFFERMANAGEMENT. When a signal is passed between two processes, the signal parameters are stored into a buffer, and a buffer reference is sent instead. This reduces memory consumption and the number of data copies. This pattern addresses the correct management of buffers such that memory leaks, for instance, are avoided.

Interfacing Patterns replace the interaction between peers by interaction via a basic service provider. This may include segmentation and reassembly, lower layer connection management, and routing.
> Example: RNCATMADAPTATIONLAYER5. A Radio Network Controller (RNC) communicates with other nodes (RNCs, Node Bs etc.) using various protocols (e.g., RNSAP, NBAP, RANAP) on top of ATM Adaptation Layer 5. This pattern provides a generic solution for encoding service data units (SDUs) and interface control information into protocol data units, the exchange of PDUs among specific protocol entities, and the decoding and forwarding of SDUs.

The definition of SDL patterns supports their selection during the protocol design. The result of the object-oriented analysis of requirements is an analysis model consisting of a UML class model and an MSC use case model (see below).

Comparing the structure and the message scenarios of SDL patterns against this analysis model strongly supports the selection of suitable patterns. As the number of patterns in a typical pattern pool is relatively small (10-30 patterns), and with additional information contained in the pattern pool (for instance, on cooperative usage) this should be sufficient for a proper selection.

The following excerpt from the SDL pattern pool illustrates how SDL patterns are defined. Items of the pattern definition template are underlined. Statements in [*brackets*] provide additional explanation.

RNCBLOCKINGCONTROL [*Each pattern is identified by a pattern name, which serves as a handle to describe a protocol design problem, its solution, and its consequences. The name raises the vocabulary of the protocol engineer to a higher level.*]

Intent [*provides a short informal description of the design problem and its solution*]: Some procedures contain wait states, blocking the process until certain signals arrive and meanwhile suspending other functionality. This happens for example every time the RNCSYNCHRONOUSINQUIRY pattern is applied inside a procedure. If, because of communication, hardware or design errors, a signal releasing the process from the wait state is lost or never sent, the process may be trapped in this state forever, blocking resources and possibly blocking other processes that wait for responses from this process. RNCBLOCKINGCONTROL introduces a timer-based mechanism that terminates the procedure when the timer expires, releasing the process from the wait state.

Motivation [*gives an example for the pattern usage*]: ...

Structure [*is a graphical representation of the involved design components and their relations. Structural aspects before and after the application of the pattern are covered.*]: The following UML class diagram shows the structural aspects of the design solution. Both the calling *Automaton_A* and the called *Blocking-Procedure* are refined when applying the pattern. Procedures called directly or indirectly by *BlockingProcedure* are also refined.

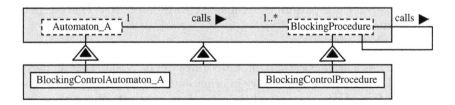

Message Scenarios [*illustrate typical behavior related to this pattern and thus complement the structural part.*]: The following MSCs show generic usage scenarios addressed by this pattern:

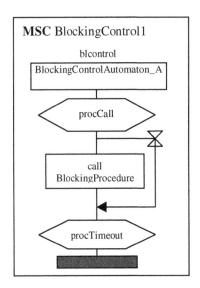

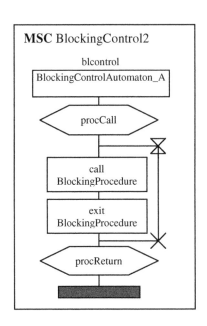

<u>SDL Fragment</u> [*describes the syntactical part of the design solution, which is adapted and composed when the pattern is applied. The notation used here is called PA-SDL (Pattern Annotated SDL), it defines the context in which the pattern is applicable, the permitted adaptations, and the embedding into the context specification.*]: Timer *ResetTimer* is set before calling the blocking procedure and reset after the procedure returns. The procedure is refined by adding a transition triggered by timer signal *ResetTimer* to every state, terminating the procedure. The timeout case (timer signal consumed before procedure returns) is considered when deciding the next state of the automaton.

NOTE: If a timeout occurs but the timer-signal is not consumed inside the procedure (this can happen, if the timer signal is queued after a controlled signal), it is deleted from the queue immediately when the procedure returns by resetting the timer. Thus it cannot happen that a following instance of the RNCBLOCKINGCONTROL pattern is terminated early by a *ResetTimer* signal remaining in the queue.

Syntactical Variants:

- *Procedures:* As a syntactical variant, procedures can be used to contain parts of the SDL Fragment. All necessary information must be passed to the procedure via formal parameters and the procedure must return necessary information via formal IN/OUT parameters or a return value.
- *Synonyms:* ResetTimerDuration can also be a synonym for a duration.
- *Inheritance:* The *ResetTimer* transition can be defined inside a different procedure that is inherited by every procedure containing a wait state. Making

the transition virtual allows redefining it inside these procedures, if more precise error handling is necessary.

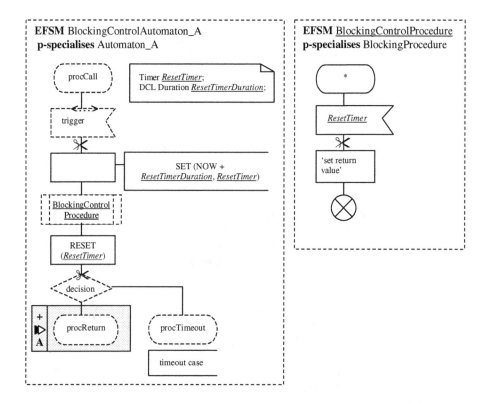

Syntactical Embedding Rules [*constrain the application of the pattern such that certain desirable properties are added or preserved.*]: Assign a duration to *ResetTimerDuration*.

Semantic Properties [*resulting from the correct application of the pattern.*]: Under the Assumption that . . .

(A-1) *ResetTimer* is not set or reset in any branch of procedure *BlockingProcedure*.

(A-2) Every blocking procedure called directly or indirectly by *BlockingProcedure* is p-specialized like *BlockingProcedure*.
Sufficient condition: Every procedure containing a state is p-specialized like *BlockingProcedure*.

. . . the following Commitment holds:

(C-1) Procedure *BlockingProcedure* eventually returns.

Refinement [*states rules for further redefining an applied pattern in accordance with the patterns intent.*]: Normally, the pattern instance needs further refinement, e.g., error handling in case of a timeout. The following properties determine refinements of the RNCBLOCKINGCONTROL pattern that are considered to be safe:

(R-1) Additional statements do not disrupt or bypass the thread of control from predefined input to predefined output statements.
(R-2) *ResetTimer* is not set or reset in any branch of procedure *BlockingProcedure*.

Additionally, if calls to new procedures with blocking states are introduced into *BlockingProcedure* or any procedure called by *BlockingProcedure*, these must be refined by adding a *ResetTimer* transition to each state according to the SDL Fragment.

Cooperative Usage [*describes the usage together with other patterns of the pool.*]:

- With RNCSYNCHRONOUSINQUIRY:
  Application of the RNCSYNCHRONOUSINQUIRY pattern inside a procedure introduces a wait state and makes it a blocking procedure. Such a procedure can be controlled by application of the RNCBLOCKINGCONTROL pattern.
  Correct application of the RNCSYNCHRONOUSINQUIRY pattern should assure that the response arrives and the wait state is left, however for several reasons it can still happen that the response won't arrive:
    - *Hardware Error*: When two RNCs participate in a synchronous inquiry and the RNC sending the response crashes, the inquiring RNC is blocked in a wait state.
    - *Communication Error*: Especially in case of RRC connections, the assumption that the basic service is reliable does not always hold. When the user moves into an area with no reception, the mobile phone cannot send or receive a response and the inquirer is blocked in a wait state.
  There is also the possibility of an incorrect pattern application (i.e. a design error).
- With RNCSYNCHRONOUSGROUPINQUIRY:
  The statements made above also apply to the RNCSYNCHRONOUSGROUPINQUIRY pattern.

Known Uses [*documents where the pattern has been applied so far.*]:

- UMTS RNC CP

Checklist [*documents the items to be checked during the design review. There is some overlap with the assumptions listed in Semantic Properties, which is intentional. Furthermore, the checklist is extended based on problems occurring during usage of this pattern.*]:

- BlockingControlAutomaton_A
  - ⋆ *ResetTimer* is set directly before calling *BlockingControlProcedure* and reset directly after the procedure returns.

⋆ All procedures in *BlockingControlAutomaton_A* containing a wait state
are pattern-specialized as described in the SDL Fragment.
− BlockingControlProcedure
  ⋆ *ResetTimer* is not set or reset inside any branch of procedure *Blocking-
    ControlProcedure* (this includes any procedure called by the procedure).
  ⋆ An appropriate return value indicating an error is set in the *ResetTimer*
    transition.

---

5   Quantitative Assessment of the RNC Pattern Pool

The classical approach for a quantitative assessment of the RNC-pattern pool
would be to conduct a controlled experiment, with two groups of developers
designing the same system features, where one group applies RNC-patterns, and
the other group proceeds in the traditional way. During the development, the
design errors are recorded and assessed with regard to the required rework and
their impact on release time.

Since controlled experiments require a substantial amount of resources, we
propose a different approach to assess the benefits of RNC-patterns. The approach is based on the assumption that the past enables a sufficiently precise
prediction of the future. In this particular case, the past manifests itself to some
extent in the form of trouble reports, which are filed by the tester after detecting
a defect. The proposed approach is to analyze these trouble reports and decide
whether certain problems would most likely have been avoided, given the RNC-
pattern pool. Based on an estimate of required rework, the benefits of RNC
pattern usage are quantified.

In order to determine if a problem could have been avoided by applying the
RNC-pattern pool, the checklists supplied with each pattern are used. For example, one of the evaluated trouble reports describes the following scenario (see
Fig. 5): an inquiry is sent, and the sender waits for the response of the receiver.
The receiver receives the inquiry in a state where it is neither saved nor explicitly
consumed. According to the SDL semantics, the inquiry will be discarded, and
no response will be returned to the sender. As a result, the sender will be dead-
locked. This type of interaction is captured by the RNCSYNCHRONOUSINQUIRY
pattern. The checklist of this pattern contains an item stating that "*the inquiry
is saved in all states of the response automaton that do not explicitly consume
the signal*", which is a sufficient condition to avoid the problem.

Therefore, this kind of defect should be found in a design review using the
checklist supplied with the appropriate RNC-pattern.

To perform the analysis, a subset of the available trouble reports against
a specific part of the SDL design is selected. First, the scope of the trouble
reports is restricted to a subset of the UMTS call processing system, where
SDL has been used for the system design. Second, the time period the trouble
reports were raised is limited to a certain time span. Finally, only those trouble

reports related to design errors are selected. In our evaluation, this has led to a reasonably large set of trouble reports suited for the analysis (76 relevant trouble reports recorded over a period of one year).

For a defect, there are three important points in time: The time the defect was introduced, the earliest time the defect could have been discovered, and the time of actual defect discovery (see Fig. 5). We examine defects introduced during SDL design and SDL coding. Defects introduced during feature specification cannot be avoided by applying SDL patterns, and are therefore excluded.

The amount of rework needed to correct a defect described by a trouble report depends on the project phase in which the defect is discovered (see Fig. 5). Project experience shows that the amount of rework increases significantly the later the problem is found. In the UMTS call processing project, after the SDL design of a feature is complete, the SDL specification goes through different test stages, testing the feature itself and the integration of the feature at first on the development machine and later on the target machine. The amount of rework for defects found during the target machine tests is estimated to be twice as high as for defects found during tests on the development machine.

During the evaluation, we sort the trouble reports into three categories:

- *covered*: trouble reports that can be avoided by applying the checklists of the RNC patterns,
- *coverable*: trouble reports for which a RNC pattern that would make the described defects avoidable can be defined, and
- *not coverable*: trouble reports that can not be avoided by defining a RNC pattern.

The covered trouble reports are a subset of the coverable trouble reports.

The evaluation of the trouble reports yields the following results (see Fig. 5): 37% of the evaluated trouble reports were classified as "covered", 47% were classified as "coverable". This means, given a sufficiently large RNC-pattern pool, almost half of the trouble reports can be avoided. Even if we assume that a certain percentage of these defects would not be discovered in a checklist-

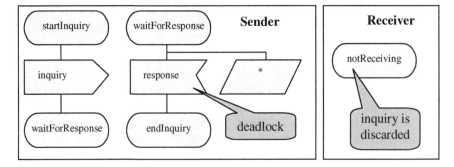

Fig. 2. Defect described by a trouble report

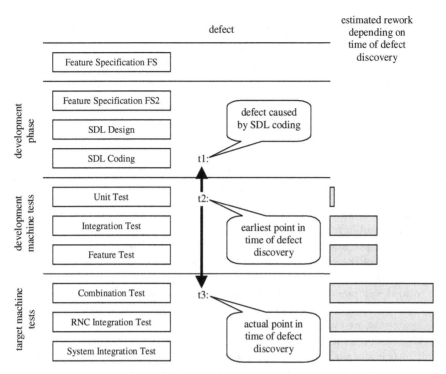

Fig. 3. Defect and defect discovery

based review, this would still be a significant reduction of defects, and thus an improvement of the quality of the design.

Of the trouble reports coverable by RNC patterns, the RNC-pattern pool covers 78%, despite its relatively small size. A closer look shows that the three most frequently used patterns cover already 61%. This indicates that the most important RNC patterns have already been discovered, and that the checklists supplied with these patterns are sufficiently complete. Also, it becomes evident that an extension of the RNC-pattern pool will only have a limited effect on coverability, as the remaining trouble reports are of quite different nature.

$$
\text{est. saved rework} = \frac{\sum_{\text{trouble reports}} ((\text{correct. effort} \times \#\text{release}) + \text{retesting})}{\text{total project effort (all phases)}} \tag{1}
$$

After having identified the trouble reports that can be avoided by RNC patterns, we are going to estimate the amount of rework that can be saved by avoiding these trouble reports. In order to achieve this, we assign, based on project experience, an estimated amount of rework to each of these trouble reports. This amount depends on the time of defect discovery, as well as on the number of product releases affected by this trouble report. The estimated

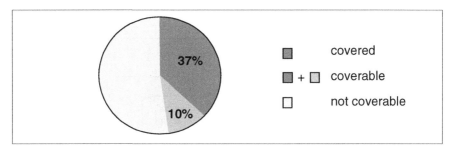

Fig. 4. Classification of the evaluated trouble reports

total amount of saved rework is the sum of the estimated saved rework of the individual trouble reports.

Based on project data, an estimation of the total amount of work for the development of the evaluated part of the project can be obtained. By comparing this value to the estimated amount of saved rework, we can find out how much the total development effort could have been reduced by using a pattern-based development approach (see Equation 1). Based on the trouble reports covered by RNC patterns, we estimate the potential for saved rework to be 4,7% of the total development effort (6% based on coverable trouble reports). This is a remarkable result, especially for a large project like the UMTS call processing system.

The project effort in Equation 1 is the combined effort of the different development phases (analysis, several design and testing phases). The improvement

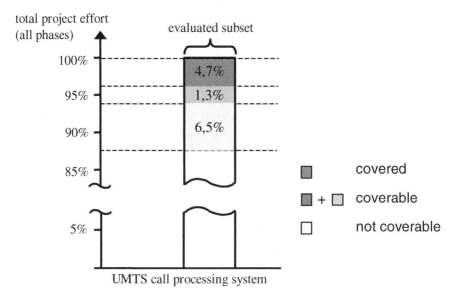

Fig. 5. Estimated Saved Rework

Table 1. Trouble reports and estimated savings by category

Category	Coverable Trouble Reports	Covered Trouble Reports	Potential Savings (man-days)	Realized Savings (man-days)	Savings per Trouble Report
Interaction Patterns	15	15	60	60	4,0
Management Patterns	9	8	42	37	4,6
Control Patterns	3	2	17	12	6,0
Interfacing Patterns	9	3	40	16	5,3

by SDL patterns is related to design and testing. No improvements are made and no additional effort is needed in the analysis phase.

Table 1 shows the results of the evaluation by pattern category. Most trouble reports are covered by interaction patterns, potentially saving up to 60 man-days with respect to the analyzed part of the UMTS call processing system. Control patterns have the highest savings per trouble report, implying that trouble reports covered by these patterns were raised later in the project, and thus were more expensive.

At the time of the evaluation, no trouble reports raised after deployment, i.e., during operation of the system, have been available. It can be safely assumed that defects discovered during operation are particularly expensive. Therefore, the given estimate is conservative in the sense that the actual savings in terms of rework may even be higher.

Additional effort is needed for introducing RNC patterns, e.g. for developer training and design review. However, this effort is small compared to the benefits of applying RNC patterns.

6   Experience and Conclusions

We have analyzed the results of an ongoing UMTS call processing project, and have defined a proprietary SDL-pattern pool, containing 8 SDL patterns. Several of them are sufficiently generic and can therefore be used in a wide range of projects. For example, RNCCLIENTSERVER is a generic pattern that captures the architecture of a client-server system. Other patterns, e.g., RNCATMADAP-TATIONLAYER5, are project-specific and therefore not applicable outside the RNC-CP project. In some cases, SDL patterns of the pattern pool of the Computer Networks Group, e.g., RNCSYNCHRONOUSINQUIRY, have been adapted with little effort.

The benefits of this pattern pool have been assessed by evaluating trouble reports raised during project development and maintenance. We found out that 37% of these trouble reports could have been avoided with the pattern pool, and that up to 47% of the trouble reports could be avoided with patterns. This would lead to a reduction of the development effort of 4,7% up to 6%. This is a conservative estimation, since defects discovered after deployment that would further increase the development effort and thus the potential for a reduction could not be evaluated.

So far, the assessment of the industrial application of the SDL-pattern approach in the UMTS call processing development has shown very positive results. With the definition of an RNC-specific pattern pool, the quantification of the benefits of pattern-based development, and the introduction of RNC patterns into a branch of the running project, most of the short-term objectives have been achieved with favorable results. The training of an initial team of system developers has been approved. In a first step, it is planned to use the pattern-specific checklists in the design review.

To fully exploit the benefits of the SDL-pattern approach, graphical tool support for the definition, application, and documentation of SDL patterns will be needed. This will further enhance productivity of developers as well as quality of system design. Currently, we are preparing a tool prototype to demonstrate the feasibility of this kind of support.

References

[1] E. Gamma, R. Helm, R. Johnson, J. Vlissides. Design Patterns: Elements of Reusable Object-Oriented Software. Addison-Wesley, Reading, Massachusetts (1995)   102

[2] B. Geppert, R. Gotzhein, F. Rößler. Configuring Communication Protocols Using SDL Patterns. In Cavalli, A., Sarma, A., eds.: SDL'97 - Time for Testing, Proceedings of the 8th SDL Forum, Amsterdam, Elsevier (1997) pp. 523–538   102, 103

[3] B. Geppert. The SDL-Pattern Approach - A Reuse-Driven SDL Methodology for Designing Communication Software Systems. PhD thesis, University of Kaiserslautern, Germany (2000)   103

[4] R. Gotzhein. Consolidating and Applying the SDL-Pattern Approach: A Detailed Case Study. Information and Software Technology (2003) Elsevier Sciences (in print)   103

[5] F. Rößler,B. Geppert, P. Schaible. Re-Engineering of the Internet Stream Protocol ST2+ with Formalized Design Patterns. Proceedings of the 5th International Conference on Software Reuse (ICSR5), Victoria, Canada (1998)   103

[6] B. Geppert, A. Kühlmeyer, F. Rößler, M. Schneider. SDL-Pattern based Development of a Communication Subsystem for CAN. Formal Description Techniques and Protocol Specification, Testing, and Verification, Proceedings of FORTE/PSTV'99, Boston, Kluwer Academic Publishers (1998) pp. 197–212   103

[7] P. Schaible, R. Gotzhein. View-based Animation of Communication Protocols in Design and in Operation. Computer Networks **40** (2002) pp. 621–638   103

[8] R. Gotzhein, p. Schaible. Evaluation and Application of the SDL-Pattern Approach in the Telecommunications Domain based on the UMTS-RNC-System. Technical Report Project Report UKL-020522, University of Kaiserslautern (2002)   103, 105

[9] International Telecommunication Union (ITU): ITU-T Recommendation Z.100 (11/99): Specification and Description Language (SDL) (1999)   103

[10] International Telecommunication Union (ITU): ITU-T Recommendation Z.120 (11/99): Message Sequence Chart (MSC) (1999)   104

Synthesizing SDL from Use Case Maps: An Experiment

Yong He, Daniel Amyot, and Alan W. Williams

School of Information Technology and Engineering, University of Ottawa
Ottawa, ON K1N 6N5, Canada
{yonghe,damyot,awilliam}@site.uottawa.ca

Abstract. The Use Case Map (UCM) notation is part of the User Requirements Notation (URN), the most recent addition to ITU-T's family
of languages. UCM models describe functional requirements and high-
level designs with causal scenarios, superimposed on structures of components. It has been shown that UCMs can be transformed into more detailed MSC scenarios. However, UCMs are not executable as such. Early
validation and exploration of requirements could benefit from a transformation to a formal, executable language. This paper presents the results
of an experiment combining existing tool-supported techniques for the
generation of MSCs from UCMs and for the synthesis of SDL from MSCs.
In particular, this experiment provides useful results on the current interworking of such techniques and on requirements for future generations of
tools. Through a simple case study, this paper also highlights questions
and partial answers on the complementariness of these languages, on the
usefulness of the resulting SDL models, and on potential improvements
on the approach and on the languages themselves.

1 Introduction

Generating designs and implementations automatically from requirements is an
old dream of many system developers. However, for particular types of systems,
notations, and purposes, this dream may be very close to becoming reality. This
paper explores the potential for automated generation of SDL models from Use
Case Map (UCM) requirements scenarios in the context of early validation of
distributed systems.

The Use Case Map notation is one of the latest additions to the ITU-T
family of languages. It is being standardized as a scenario notation part of the
User Requirements Notation in the Z.150 series [1, 2]. UCM graphical models
describe functional requirements and high-level designs with causal scenarios,
superimposed on structures of components [3, 4]. UCMs are suitable for many
requirements engineering activities and for dealing with abstract and intuitive
representations of complex distributed systems. SDL is a well-established specification and design language that enables the execution and formal validation
of models described as communicating state machines [5]. One of our goals is to
combine the strengths of both languages.

R. Reed (Ed.): SDL 2003, LNCS 2708, pp. 117–136, 2003.

In the scenario-driven development of distributed systems and services, it is important to leverage the investment in scenarios in order to generate systems rapidly, at low cost, and with a high quality. Constructing state-based behavioral models from scenarios that span multiple components is beneficial because this helps developers move from requirements to design in a systematic way. Such construction, whether analytic (i.e. manual, build-and-test approach) or synthetic (i.e. partially or fully automated), however raises many issues similar to those observed in the protocol engineering community [6]. The level of completeness, consistency, and formality of the source scenarios will influence what type of technique will be more suitable, e.g., analytic approaches are often more tolerant about the quality of the scenarios than synthetic approaches. On the other hand, synthetic approaches offer fast and deterministic transformations that are "correct" according to properties ensured by their construction algorithm, at the cost of less flexibility (e.g. non-functional requirements such as maintainability can hardly be considered during the conversion).

In the past ten years, many scenario-based construction techniques have been proposed (a recent survey of which is available in [7]). Most start from a scenario language that specifies component communication, such as Message Sequence Charts (MSCs) [8] or UML sequence diagrams [9]. The automated construction of design models from more abstract scenario notations such as UCMs or UML activity diagrams proved to be more challenging because communication detail is not explicit and must be inferred during the construction.

This paper does not introduce a new synthesis technique based on UCMs. Rather, it reports on experiments that combine existing work on the generation of MSCs from UCMs, and on the synthesis of SDL models from MSCs. Both parts are automated, and together they provide a continuous transition from requirements to design. For instance, the second release of the UCM Navigator tool (UCMNav 2, [10]) provides MSC generation capabilities while Telelogic Tau 4.4 integrates KLOCwork's MSC2SDL synthesizer [11, 12].

Results from a case study (simple telephone system) will help us illustrate several problems faced during UCM→MSC→SDL transformations, in terms of existing practices and tool interworking. Section 2 first describes our source UCM specification, which contains a number of scenario definitions. The latter are used to produce individual MSCs (Sect. 3), which can be combined in various ways with a High-Level MSC (HMSC). Section 4 presents SDL models synthesized from these (H)MSCs. Several strategies aiming to solve language and tool interworking problems are explored along the way. Our main observations and recommendations regarding several concrete and important questions are found in Sect. 5, followed by related work and conclusions.

2   Source Use Case Map Model

The following UCM model describes the connection request phase in an agent-based telephony system with user-subscribed features. It was selected for this experiment because it covers most path constructs in the UCM notation, and

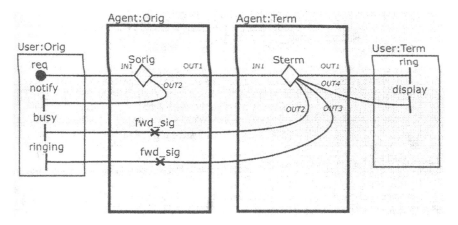

Fig. 1. Simple Telephony System: ROOT UCM

because it already contained a set of scenario definitions covering all the paths (see [10]).

2.1 Simple Telephony System

The root map in Fig. 1 gives an overview of the requirement scenarios that our system must support. Upon the request of an originating user (req), the originating agent will select the appropriate user feature (in stub Sorig) which could result in some feedback (notify). This may also cause the terminating agent to select another feature (in stub Sterm) which in turn can cause a number of results in the originating and terminating users.

The feature UCMs (see Fig. 2) are found two levels down. Stub Sorig contains the ORIGINATING plug-in whereas stub Sterm contains the TERMINATING plug-in. These sub-UCMs have their own stubs, whose plug-ins are user-subscribed features. In stub Sscreen we have:

- **OCS** (Originating Call Screening): blocks calls to people on the OCS filtering list.
- **TeenLine**: restricts call attempts during a specific period of the day (the active period). Callers with a valid PIN (if entered in a timely manner) have no restriction.
- **Default**: used when not subscribed to any other originating feature.

And in stub Sdisplay we have:

- **CND** (Call Name Delivery): displays the caller's number on the callee's device.
- **Default**: used when not subscribed to any other terminating feature.

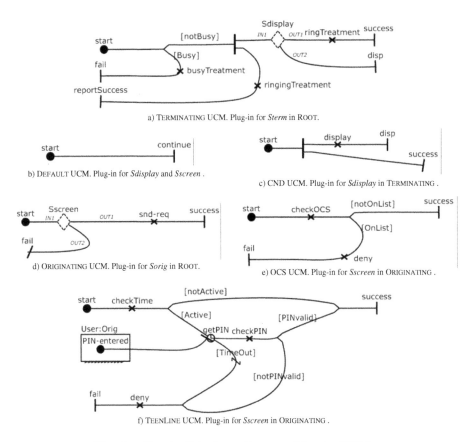

Fig. 2. Simple Telephony System: Plug-in UCMs

Note that many plug-ins contain guarded alternative paths. The TERMINAT-ING and CND plug-ins also use AND-forks, for concurrent paths. TEENLINE contains a timer (getPIN), reset by PIN-entered, and a timeout path. Each plug-in is also bound properly to its parent stub, i.e. stub input/output segments (*IN1*, *OUT1*, etc.) are connected to the plug-ins' start/end points, as specified in Fig. 3. In addition, note that a plug-in can be reused in multiple stubs (e.g. DEFAULT), so the labels of the start/end points may differ from those of the stub input/output segments.

A component can contain nested sub-components, and plug-in UCMs can also contain components. The semantics is that the components and path elements in a plug-in UCM are allocated to the component containing the parent stub. For example, snd-req in Fig. 2d, which is a plug-in bound to stub Sorig in Fig. 1, is therefore allocated to component Agent:Orig. This is applicable at any level of nesting: checktime in Fig. 2f also belongs to component Agent:Orig (TEENLINE belongs to Sscreen, and ORIGINATING to Sorig).

ROOT UCM
  Sorig Stub
    ORIGINATING UCM. Condition: *True*. Binding: {*<IN1*, start>, *<OUT1*, success>, *<OUT2*, fail>}
    Sscreen Stub
      TEENLINE UCM. Condition: *subTL*. Binding: {*<IN1*, start>, *<OUT1*, success>, *<OUT2*, fail>}
      OCS UCM. Condition: *subOCS*. Binding: {*<IN1*, start>, *<OUT1*, success>, *<OUT2*, fail>}
      DEFAULT UCM. Condition: ¬(*subOCS* ∨ *subTL*). Binding: {*<IN1*, start>, *<OUT1*, continue>}
  Sterm Stub
    TERMINATING UCM. Condition: *True*. Binding: {*<IN1*, start>, *<OUT1*, success>, *<OUT2*, fail>,
                                                     <OUT3, reportSuccess>, *<OUT2*, disp>}
    Sdisplay Stub
      CND UCM. Condition: *subCND*. Binding: {*<IN1*, start>, *<OUT1*, success>, *<OUT2*, disp>}
      DEFAULT UCM. Condition: ¬*subCND*. Binding: {*<IN1*, start>, *<OUT1*, continue>}

Fig. 3. Selection Policies and Binding Relationships for Plug-in UCMs

Anchored components, which are shown with small diagonal lines (shadow) under the component, are handled differently. These are references to components existing outside the current scope. For instance, User:Orig in Fig. 2f makes reference to a component at the same nesting level as Agent:Orig (see Fig. 1), i.e. User:Orig is not contained inside Agent:Orig.

2.2 Scenario Definitions

UCMs integrate many individual scenarios. *Scenario definitions* are used to record and highlight particular scenarios represented as partial orders of UCM elements (i.e. sequence and concurrency are preserved, but alternatives are resolved). They make use of a *path data model* composed of global (Boolean) variables used on guarding conditions. A scenario definition contains an identifier, a name, initial values for the global variables, a list of start points, and (optionally) post-conditions expressed using the global variables.

Fifteen scenario definitions are summarized in Fig. 4. The first four variables are used to guard the various OR-forks found in the plug-ins (see Fig. 2a, e, and f), *getPIN_timeout* is used to force a timeout at the getPIN timer, and the last three are used to define the selection policies found in the dynamic stubs (i.e. they indicate whether a user is currently subscribed to a feature, see the conditions in Fig. 3). Four scenarios use two start points (req and then PIN-entered). No post-conditions are necessary here.

Together, these scenarios cover all the paths found in our UCM model. The next section discusses how they are used in the generation of MSCs.

3   Generation of (H)MSCs from UCMs

A tool-supported procedure for generating MSCs from UCMs was described by Miga *et al.* in [10]. This section presents the results of its application to our example UCM. We also discuss two potential HMSCs that can be used to combine the individual MSCs during the synthesis of the SDL model.

Number	Scenario Name	Variables								Start Points	
		Busy	*OnOCSList*	*PINvalid*	*TLactive*	*getPIN_timeout*	*subCND*	*subOCS*	*subTL*	*req*	*PIN-entered*
01	BCbusy	T	-	-	-	-	F	F	F	X	
02	BCsuccess	F	-	-	-	-	F	F	F	X	
03	OCSbusy	T	F	-	-	-	F	T	F	X	
04	OCSdenied	F	T	-	-	-	F	T	F	X	
05	OCSsuccess	F	F	-	-	-	F	T	F	X	
06	CNDdisplay	F	-	-	-	-	T	F	F	X	
07	OCS_CNDdisplay	F	F	-	-	-	T	T	F	X	
08	TL_CNDActiveBusy	T	-	T	T	F	T	F	T	X	X
09	TL_CNDActiveDisplay	F	-	T	T	F	T	F	T	X	X
10	TL_CNDnotActiveBusy	T	-	-	F	-	T	F	T	X	
11	TL_CNDPINInvalid	-	-	F	T	F	T	F	T	X	X
12	TL_CNDTimeOut	-	-	-	T	T	T	F	T	X	
13	TL_CNDnotActiveDisplay	F	-	-	F	-	T	F	T	X	
14	TLnotActiveSuccess	F	-	-	F	-	F	F	T	X	
15	TLActiveSuccess	F	-	T	T	F	F	F	T	X	X

Fig. 4. Simple Telephony System: Scenario Definitions

3.1 MSC Generation with UCMNAV

The generation of MSCs from UCMs requires that the paths be allocated to components (this is the case in our example), that scenario definitions be provided, and that a traversal mechanism be used. The latest version of UCMNAV (2.1.1) improves upon the mechanism used in [10] by supporting scenario definitions with multiple start points and post-conditions. Responsibilities can now also modify the values of the global variables using Boolean expressions; however there is no need in our particular UCM model for responsibilities to modify these variables. The traversal mechanism is also more in line what the path traversal guidelines proposed in the draft Z.152 document [4].

For each scenario definition in Fig. 4, UCMNAV produces an individual MSC by traversing the UCM from the specified start point and selecting alternative branches and plug-ins in dynamic stubs according to their guarding conditions. At a branching point, if more than one condition evaluates to true (non-determinism), or if all conditions evaluate to false (deadlock), then the traversal stops with an appropriate error message. This validation step and the fixes needed to solve such problems are done prior to the generation of MSCs (in our example, we start from an UCM without such errors). The traversal also preserves the concurrency introduced by UCM AND-forks, as well as synchronizations of concurrent paths.

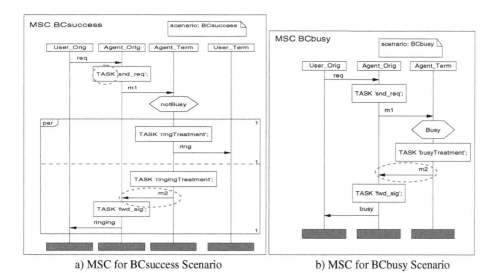

a) MSC for BCsuccess Scenario   b) MSC for BCbusy Scenario

Fig. 5. Two MSCs Generated by UCMNAV (#02 and #01)

Fig. 5 shows two of the fifteen scenarios generated with UCMNAV. UCM start points and end points are converted to messages, responsibilities to actions, components to instances, and guarding condition labels to MSC conditions. These MSCs show a flattened view of the scenarios, and the hierarchical structure of UCMs with stubs and plug-ins disappears. Concurrent path segments in UCMs are captured explicitly using the PAR in-line expression. The conversion from UCMs to MSCs also ensures that names are preserved, but they may be slightly modified to satisfy Z.120 syntax rules (e.g., User:Orig becomes User_Orig).

Abstract messages (m1, m2, ...) are added by the converter to preserve the causal relationship expressed by UCM paths that span multiple components. These messages could be refined with more descriptive names and details during design, but they are sufficient as is for early validation purposes. Partial ordering (dashed arrows in MSCs) could have been used instead of messages in order to refine inter-component causality, however the resulting MSCs would be useful simply as requirements scenarios, not as design artifacts used in the synthesis of communicating systems. Also, we are not aware of synthesis tools that can use partial ordering in lieu of messages.

The information highlighted in dashed ellipses will be discussed in Sect. 4.

3.2   Two Strategies for the Generation of HMSCs

The MSC2SDL synthesizer embedded in Telelogic TAU accepts HMSCs as input, and we would like to explore the impact of different strategies providing such models from UCMs. Our first strategy consists in constructing a default HMSC that integrates all the MSCs as independent alternatives (Fig. 6a). This is easily automatable.

124   Yong He et al.

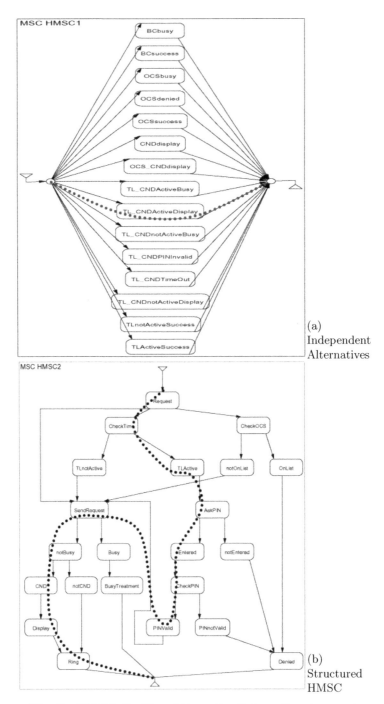

Fig. 6. HMSCs for Two Alternative Integration Approaches

The HMSC in Fig. 6b illustrates our second strategy, where the individual MSCs have been manually analyzed to extract common parts and to compose them. The first messages of any two sibling MSCs (who share the same predecessor) are different. Each path from the start to the end point corresponds to a scenario specified by an original MSC (for instance, the scenario #09 is highlighted in both HMSCs). The rationale for considering the second strategy is that the source UCM model already integrates the scenarios, and this integration is lost during the conversion to individual MSCs. The HMSC Fig. 6b will be used to assess the need for and worth of a labor-intensive integration of MSCs before the synthesis. Other potentially valid HMSCs exist, but we felt that these two extremes (unstructured and structured with no overlap) would be sufficient to study the impact of integration and structuring aspects.

4   Synthesis of SDL Model from HMSCs

The MSC2SDL synthesizer used in this experiment (previously known as the MOST tool [13, 12]) has several constraints on the type of MSCs acceptable as input, and consistency among the MSCs produced by UCMNAV needs to be improved. Manual modifications of our MSCs are hence discussed in Sect. 4.1. A series of SDL models synthesized according to different strategies is then presented in Sect. 4.2. Remarks on the impact of the various strategies explored are given in Sect. 5.

4.1   Modifications to Input MSCs

Several modifications to our input MSCs appeared to be required in order to enable the synthesis of SDL models. The first two categories are mainly syntactical whereas the last three are mainly concerned with semantic aspects of the MSCs produced by UCMNAV:

- All action names in the MSCs must start with the *TASK* keyword. UCMNAV does not generate them, as they are not required by Z.120 or by Telelogic TAU. However, the synthesis does not seem to work without their presence (see Fig. 5a).
- UCMNAV transforms UCM timers into MSC timers, but it uses the syntax of MSC2000, which seems to cause some incompatibility with TAU and with MSC2SDL. The TAU syntax for timers was hence used (and is now supported in UCMNAV 2.1.1).
- Each abstract message generated by UCMNAV is unique within one MSC, and the identification number (m1, m2, ...) is incremented by one for each message. However, these messages are used inconsistently across a set of related MSCs. For instance, message m2 is used in the two MSCs of Fig. 5 for two very different purposes: one leads to the sending of a busy signal whereas the other causes a ringing signal. Such inconsistent use of message names is confusing for any type of synthesis, and UCMNAV should in fact

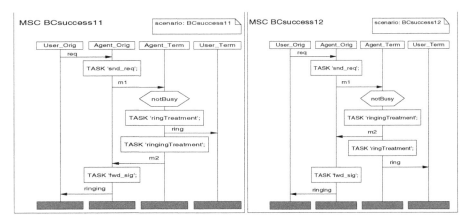

Fig. 7. Sequential MSCs Resulting from the Removal of the PAR in Fig. 5a

ensure that message names are used consistently across the scenarios. In our example, m2 in Fig. 5b had to be renamed m3. There were many other such updates required in our fifteen MSCs.

- Although an appropriate MSC condition is generated each time a branch is selected in a UCM (to preserve traceability), conditions capturing the selection of particular plug-in maps in a dynamic stub were never generated in the MSCs. For instance, when the CND plug-in is selected in stub Sdisplay, there should be a CDN condition added to the Agent_Term instance in the corresponding MSC scenario. These conditions proved to be useful in avoiding the synthesis of SDL models that are unnecessarily more non-deterministic than the initial UCMs.
- KLOCwork's MSC2SDL synthesizer does not support the PAR in-line expression, which is used extensively by UCMNAV when converting concurrent paths. Consequently, we removed the PAR statements from our MSCs. Many such MSCs can result from the interleaving of actions and messages in parallel sections of a PAR statement. In this study, we limited our synthesis experiment to cases where only one sequential refinement is used (top part followed by the bottom part), and then where two such refinements are used (by swapping the bottom part of the PAR statement with the top part, see Fig. 7). We imposed this limitation on ourselves in order to avoid a combinatorial explosion in the number of MSCs so generated (note that this is not a language issue).

4.2   SDL Synthesis with MSC2SDL

Several synthesizing strategies were experimented in order to investigate their impacts on the final SDL models. The first system synthesized was from the independent alternative HMSC (see Fig. 6a). In the process of extracting the common parts of the scenarios to produce the structured HMSC found in Fig. 6b,

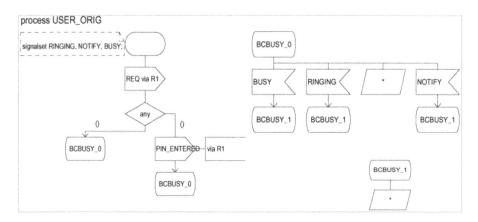

Fig. 8. Description of the USER_ORIG Process in the First Synthesized SDL Model

it was discovered that a condition (indicating that the CND plug-in was selected) was missing from an original scenario and this was retroactively added. With the two consistent sets of HMSCs and MSCs, two SDL systems were generated. As an example, Fig. 8 shows an SDL process generated by this mechanism (with the message and process names traceable to the UCM). Surprisingly, the two resulting SDL systems turned out to be identical.

The synthesizer did not take into consideration the values of the variables used by the selection policies or by the OR-forks and expressed as conditions in our MSCs. After the experiment, we found out that conditions with values need to be provided in a very explicit and specific way to the synthesizer for them to be converted to suitable SDL code. However, even without values, the conditions are used to match MSC segments in the synthesizer.

After analysis, the SDL systems were shown to have the potential to produce what the TAU validator called a "deadlock," although it is more properly identified as livelock blocking since there may be messages in the queue. The cause is an SDL state (BCSUCCESS_1) that accepts no inputs, and saves all signals (see Fig. 9). This results in continuous preservation (without discarding) of the signal(s) in the SDL input queue. This state was reached via an "any" non-deterministic branch from the initial state. The MSC2SDL synthesizer generates such states in many situations, and this is not related to the semantics of UCMs.

The next iteration was to include two sequential MSCs with different interleaving of messages for each MSC with a PAR in-line expression generated by UCMNAV (as discussed in the previous section). Eight such MSCs were hence added to our initial set of fifteen, and the HMSC in Fig. 6a was updated accordingly. Our goal here was to evaluate the impact of the removal of the PAR statements from the original MSCs. It turned out that the resulting SDL system no longer had the "any" problem in the process AGENT_TERM. The effect can

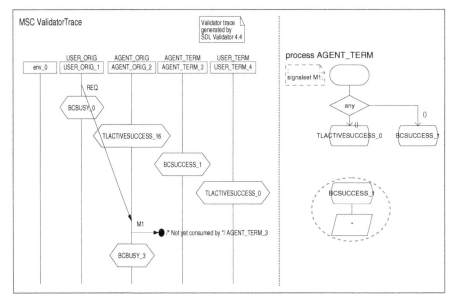

Fig. 9. Problematic State in First SDL System

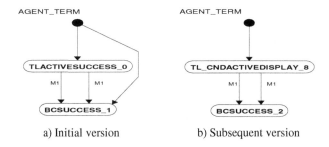

a) Initial version   b) Subsequent version

Fig. 10. State Diagram Overviews of Two Generated SDL Processes for Terminating Agent

be seen in the two state diagram overviews in Fig. 10, where the extra transition from the initial has disappeared (being generated automatically by the synthesizer, the names of the states are usually different).

The next iteration involved adding a transition in the independent alternative HMSC from the end of the scenarios back to the start, to simulate a system that runs continuously. This led to the discovery of an unspecified reception, as a message (PIN_entered) that was not accepted accumulated enough copies in an SDL input queue to cause an overflow (Fig. 11, left). This problem was then fixed by adding an additional message (enter_PIN) to the input MSCs covering TEEN-LINE scenarios (e.g. right MSC in Fig. 11). This message constrained the input of PIN_entered, which could have been received by the originating agent before the connection request (req). This solution should in fact be also reflected in the TEENLINE UCM (Fig. 2), where the PIN_entered start point is not constrained.

We also experimented with the synthesis of an SDL model without any HMSC. Curiously, despite warning messages that the conditions in the MSCs would be ignored, this result was the removal of the problem of the "any" branch in the initial state seen in Fig. 9.

In summary, the "best" SDL model for our example was produced with the initial set of fifteen MSCs with no HMSC and where the enter_PIN message was added.

5 Observations and Recommendations

5.1 Impact of the Different HMSCs

It appears that, at least in this case study, taking the effort to construct a structured HMSC, both in terms of extracting the common elements of the original scenarios and then producing the structured HMSC diagram, is not needed for the purposes of the MSC2SDL synthesizer. Indeed, there is no new information added in this construction process in our example. In fact, not including an HMSC at all seemed to produce the best result. Because the tool gives warning messages that the conditions in individual scenarios are being ignored, this would seem to imply that there is an inconsistency in the MSC conditions that is producing the extra unwanted branch in the SDL diagram in Fig. 9.

Also interesting is that including an HMSC with independent alternatives and omitting the HMSC altogether result in slightly different SDL systems. Aside from the conditions, it is possible that there is an ordering effect among the various scenarios. The HMSC in Fig. 6a may be traversed in the order in which the scenarios appear in the diagram, while omitting the diagram may result in some other ordering, such as alphabetically by file name (although our experiments later showed that alphabetical ordering was not used by the tool). This is still under investigation.

The conclusion that it is not worth the effort to produce a structured HMSC has several positive points. First, the independent alternative approach is consistent with "typical" manual construction of MSCs, where a single MSC describes a standalone scenario. Most users do not then manually analyze their collection of MSCs to isolate common elements. The second positive point is that the independent alternative approach is also consistent with the automated generation of MSCs from UCMNAV.

5.2 Impact of Interleaving Strategies

In a UCM, a similar construction is used to indicate responsibilities that can truly be considered concurrent, as opposed to responsibilities where the order does not matter from the requirements point of view, and can be fixed by a designer at design time. Both of these situations are shown with parallel paths.

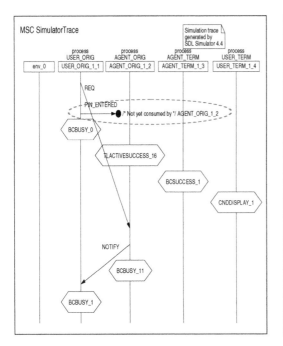 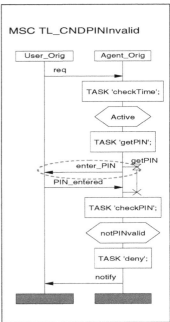

Fig. 11. Unspecified Reception and its Resolution with the Addition of an enter_PIN Message

For example, consider the situation in a normal phone call just after the terminating agent determines the called party is not busy (see Fig. 5). At this point, the terminating user should hear a ring, and the ringing tone should be heard by the originating user. From the overall system point of view, it is not significant as to which event occurs first. As long as both events occur within a reasonable interval after the notBusy condition, the system is considered to be functioning correctly. It may be a case of over-specification to decide to which user the ringing notification should be sent first. This decision should properly be left to the designer, who could then choose an ordering that would optimize internal constraints and considerations.

The MSC2SDL synthesizer does not currently handle the MSC "PAR" construct, so the MSC in Fig. 5 was manually replaced with the two MSCs shown in Fig. 7 that describe two obvious orderings of the messages. Note that only message interleaving was considered here, not task interleaving. Using interleaving in this example did not result in significant benefits in the synthesized SDL model.

So what is the nature of the parallelism implied by UCMs with AND-forks? Assuming that multiple sequential MSCs can be extracted, the resulting SDL model will contain "any" non-deterministic branches where each possible ordering appears on a different branch. When running such an SDL system using the Telelogic TAU simulator, the simulation stops and asks the user to choose one of the branches. Unless one is performing an SDL trace, the location of the "any" construct is not apparent, and as the branches are not labelled, there is not a convenient reference name for the user to identify a branch to select.

The sequential nature of an SDL transition forces a design decision regarding the choice of an ordering of the output actions. A mechanism is needed at this point to indicate to the MSC2SDL synthesizer that it is permitted to choose an ordering for us, as a designer would do. This information has to come from the methodology used to describe the requirements.

There are implications at later stages of the development process if test cases are derived from scenarios described by UCMs and/or MSCs. The test case should represent the requirements, namely any one of the orderings may have been implemented. The test cases should not assume the ordering chosen by the designer, nor should there be test cases checking that all orderings can be produced by the system.

Also, if we are to demonstrate conformance for unspecified ordering, we need to use a conformance relation that permits implementation behaviour that is a reduction of the behaviour described in the requirements. On the other hand, in cases where true interleaving is present, the conformance relation should not allow such reduction.

A clear distinction between "interleaving required" and "unspecified ordering" is therefore needed in the requirements capture method.

5.3   The SDL Environment Instance

By default, the model we obtain from the synthesizer is a closed system that has no connection to the environment. This creates difficulties in showing the interactions between external actors and the system. This tool limitation contrasts with, for example, UML tools that allow different external actors to interact with a system. While MSCs can be constructed so that all messages from outside a system emanate from a single instance of an "environment" process, most users of MSCs would prefer to show a time line for each external system actor.

Two approaches could be used, although neither is completely satisfactory. The first approach, and the one that we used in this experiment, is that users are considered to be part of the SDL system. In the MSCs, this means that each external actor has its own process timeline. When an SDL model is synthesized from this approach, the result is a *closed SDL system* with no connection to the environment. Each "external" actor, now part of the SDL system, becomes a non-deterministic process that spontaneously decides to send signals to the implementation parts of the system.

There are several disadvantages to this approach. The first is that when running an SDL simulation, the simulation operator directs the behaviour of the external actors by choosing any branches in the processes modelling those actors. The operator has to be aware of the structure of these processes, which are generally set up to be a mirror image of the implementation, in order to select the execution path. This does not fit well with the usual concept of choosing an input event to stimulate the system; instead, one has to locate the SDL transition branch containing the desired stimulus.

More importantly, the user process is synthesized to contain inputs to the implementation which were described in the set of MSCs. This makes it more difficult to stimulate the system with other events for testing purposes, particularly unexpected or inappropriate events.

The second approach consists in keeping the single SDL environment instance at the MSC stage, but then the MSCs themselves become less natural and more difficult to interpret. One has to look at the other end of a message to or from the environment and infer from the source of the message to which external actor the message is associated. In some cases, this may be less obvious if the source or destination is contained as a message parameter, as opposed to being apparent from the process handling the message. Also, the concept of a single environment is not contained at the UCM stage, and is not required by MSCs as well.

5.4   Summary of Recommendations

Our experiment demonstrated that the automated generation of SDL models from UCMs is possible, but it also motivated several recommendations for the various languages involved, for transformations, and for tool support.

- For UCMNAV: The generation of MSCs from UCM models must ensure that abstract message identifiers are used in a consistent way across scenarios.
- For UCMNAV: MSCs generated from UCM models should include conditions expressing the selection of plug-in maps.
- For UCMNAV, MSC2SDL, or TAU: The resulting MSCs must satisfy the syntactic requirements of the synthesizer tool. In our case, the syntax of timers, action names, and labels in general requires particular attention. UCMNAV could automatically generate MSCs usable by the other tools, but MSC2SDL could also support plain actions (and insert the *TASK* automatically), and TAU could support the latest syntax for MSC timers.
- For MSC2SDL and TAU: The MSC models should not be limited one environment instance.
- The generation of HMSCs from UCMs does not appear to be essential. However, further investigation is needed to establish this as a fact.
- For UCMNAV or MSC2SDL: Since the PAR statement is currently not supported by the synthesizer, the conversion should permit one to generate purely sequential MSC or a collection of such MSCs representing the interleaved PAR sections. Alternatively, the MSC2SDL synthesizer could accept MSCs with PAR statements and do the conversion itself.
- For UCM, MSC, and SDL: Ways of distinguishing between required "interleaving/concurrency required" and "unspecified ordering" that can be made more sequential are needed. These should be taken into account during transformations as well.

- For UCM and UCMNav: The generation of MSCs from UCM models should permit the description of closed systems (where users are independent instances and may lead to non-deterministic SDL processes) and of open systems (where the user instances are grouped into a single environment instance). The latter requires a better identification of actors in the UCM.

Note that most of these recommendations are valid in a context where MSCs are used as an intermediate step. It may be possible to go directly from UCMs to SDL, and then the scenario integration information in the UCMs could be taken into account during the synthesis process.

6   Related Work

Automated generation of SDL models from UCM scenarios is an original contribution of this paper. However, other alternatives to our UCM→MSC→SDL transformation could be explored.

There exist several other solutions to the synthesis of SDL from MSCs, although KLOCwork's seems to be the only one commercially available at the moment. Khendek and Vincent proposed an approach for the incremental construction of an SDL model given an existing SDL model, whose properties need to be preserved (an extension relation is provided), and a set of new MSC scenarios [14]. Using their MSC2SDL tool, old MSCs and new ones can also be integrated to produce a brand new SDL model. Dulz et al. present an approach where performance prediction models (throwaway prototypes in SDL) are also automatically synthesized from MSC scenarios, but this time supplemented with performance annotations [15].

Bordeleau explored the manual generation of communicating state machines from UCMs and HMSCs [16]. No construction algorithm is proposed, but transformation patterns are provided for mapping UCMs to HMSC, and for the construction of ROOMCHARTS from HMSCs. The manual construction of SDL models from UCMs was also explored by Sales in his thesis [17]. He demonstrated his approach with the description and analysis of IETF's Open Shortest Path First routing protocol. Both Bordeleau and Sales target the manual construction of usable design models rather than fast prototypes for early validation of requirements and scenarios.

Guan provides a synthesizer for the generation of LOTOS models [18] from UCM scenarios [19]. Her goals are related to ours in that she attempts to quickly generate executable prototypes useful for exploration and formal validation of the UCM scenarios. Her work automates many of the construction rules proposed in Amyot's SPEC-VALUE approach [20] in a Java tool called UCM2LOTOSSPEC, which uses as input the UCM files (in XML) saved by UCMNav. Since LOTOS is an algebraic language that does not require the existence of components (unlike MSCs and SDL), input scenarios do not have to be bound to components, which is more general than the approach suggested here. These scenarios must be expressed using a subset of the UCM notation (e.g. timers are not supported).

Her algorithm translates the whole UCM model at once, without using scenario definitions or conditions that involve the global variables. As a result, many invalid scenarios can emerge in the target LOTOS model.

Many other scenario-based construction techniques are discussed in [7]. These approaches use different source scenario models (including Petri Nets and UML sequence, collaboration, and activity diagrams) and generate manually or automatically various types of target models (e.g. UML state diagrams, SDL, communicating state machines, etc.). This opens the door to many potential strategies for generating executable state-based models from UCMs.

7 Conclusions

This paper presented the results of an experiment that combined existing tools and techniques to enable the automated synthesis of SDL models from Use Case Maps scenarios. UCMs and their scenario definitions are first used by UCM-NAV to generate individual MSCs, which can then be input to KLOCwork's MSC2SDL synthesizer in order to produce an executable SDL model. Analysis of this model with tools such as the Telelogic TAU validator can help finding requirements problems (whose symptoms are unspecified receptions, deadlocks, livelocks, etc.) very early in the development process. These steps were illustrates with a simple telephony system example.

The various problems we faced along the way resulted in a set of recommendations for improving tools interworking and for producing more useful models. Many of these suggestions are related to UCMNAV and can be implemented using a very recent addition to the tool. UCMNAV now decouples the traversal of UCM models according to scenario definitions from the generation of target models. The result of the traversal can be stored in an XML file, which can then be postprocessed (e.g. with XSLT) to produce MSCs while taking into consideration the constraints of the tool that will use these MSCs. Interworking with the MSC2SDL synthesizer is hence simplified. We plan to experiment with this approach in the near future.

The availability of such XML files also enables the generation of scenarios in other target languages, such as UML sequence and activity diagrams. This opens the door to the use of many other synthesizers that could be used for constructing models in UML state diagrams or other such languages. We also have plans to explore this path in the future.

Acknowledgements

This work was supported financially by NSERC and by the University of Ottawa (Canada). We also thank our colleagues and industrial partners on the RDA research project, including Telelogic and KLOCwork (with special thanks to Dr. Nikolai Mansurov for his tutorial on the MSC2SDL synthesizer), as well as the anonymous referees who provided many useful comments.

References

[1] D. Amyot. Introduction to the User Requirements Notation: Learning by Example. To appear in: Communication Networks, 2003. 117

[2] ITU-T. Recommendation Z.150, User Requirements Notation (URN) - Language Requirements and Framework. Geneva, Switzerland, 2003.
http://www.UseCaseMaps.org/urn/   117

[3] R. J. A. Buhr, (1998) Use Case Maps as Architectural Entities for Complex Systems. IEEE Transactions on Software Engineering. Vol. 24, No. 12, December 1998, 1131-1155. 117

[4] ITU-T, URN Focus Group. Draft Rec. Z.152 - UCM: Use Case Map Notation (UCM). Geneva, Switzerland, 2002. 117, 122

[5] ITU-T. Recommendation Z.100, Specification and Description Language (SDL). Geneva, Switzerland, 2000. 117

[6] K. Saleh. Synthesis of communications protocols: an annotated bibliography. ACM SIGCOMM Computer Communications Review, Vol.26, No.5, October 1996, 40-59. 118

[7] D. Amyot, A. Eberlein. An Evaluation of Scenario Notations and Construction Approaches for Telecommunication Systems Development. To appear in Telecommunication Systems Journal, 2003. 118, 134

[8] ITU-T. Recommendation Z. 120, Message Sequence Chart (MSC). Geneva, Switzerland, 2001. 118

[9] OMG. Unified Modeling Language Specification, Version 1.5. March 2003.
http://www.omg.org   118

[10] A. Miga, D. Amyot, F. Bordeleau, C. Cameron, M. Woodside. Deriving Message Sequence Charts from Use Case Maps Scenario Specifications. Tenth SDL Forum (SDL'01), Copenhagen, Denmark, June 2001.
http://www.UseCaseMaps.org/tools/ucmnav/   118, 119, 121, 122

[11] KLOCwork Corporation. KLOCwork MSC to SDL Synthesizer Tutorial, Version 1.0, 2002. 118

[12] N. Mansurov, D. Zhukov. Automatic synthesis of SDL models in use case methodology. Ninth SDL Forum (SDL'99), Montréal, Canada, 1999. 118, 125

[13] N. Mansurov, D. Campara. Using Message Sequence Charts to Accelerate Maintenance of Existing Systems. Tenth SDL Forum (SDL'01), Copenhagen, Denmark, June 2001. 125

[14] F. Khendek, D. Vincent. Enriching SDL Specifications with MSCs. 2nd Workshop of the SDL Forum Society on SDL and MSC (SAM2000), Grenoble, France, June 2000. 133

[15] J. W. Dulz, S. Gruhl, L. Lambert, M. Söllner. Early performance prediction of SDL/MSC specified systems by automated synthetic code generation. Ninth SDL Forum (SDL'99), Montréal, Canada, 1999. 133

[16] F. Bordeleau. A Systematic and Traceable Progression from Scenario Models to Communicating Hierarchical Finite State Machines. Ph.D. thesis, School of Computer Science, Carleton University, Ottawa, Canada, 1999. 133

[17] I. Sales. A Bridging Methodology for Internet Protocols Standards Development. M.Sc. thesis, SITE, Univ. of Ottawa, Canada, August 2001. 133

[18] ISO. Information Processing Systems, Open Systems Interconnection, LOTOS - A Formal Description Technique Based on the Temporal Ordering of Observational Behaviour, IS 8807. Geneva, Switzerland, 1989. 133

[19] R. Guan. From Requirements to Scenarios through Specifications: A Translation
     Procedure from Use Case Maps to LOTOS, M.Sc. thesis, University of Ottawa,
     Canada, September 2002. 133
[20] D. Amyot. Specification and Validation of Telecommunications Systems with Use
     Case Maps and LOTOS. Ph.D. thesis, SITE, University of Ottawa, Canada, 2001.
     133

Enhanced SDL Subset
for the Design and Implementation
of Java-Enabled Embedded Signalling Systems[*]

Christoforos Kavadias[1][**], Bernard Perrin[2],
Vangelis Kollias[1], and Michael Loupis[3]

[1] TELETEL SA; 124, Kifissias Avenue, Athens, Greece
C.Kavadias@teletel.gr V.Kollias@teletel.gr
[2] CSEM: Centre Suisse d'Electronique et de Microtechnique
Rue Jaquet-Droz 1, CH-2007 Neuchâtel
bernard.perrin@csem.ch
[3] SOLINET GmbH Solutions for Innovative Networks
Mittlerer Pfad 26, 70499 Stuttgart, Germany M.Loupis@SOLINET.com

Abstract. This paper proposes an enhanced SDL subset for the implementation of embedded signalling systems and describes a novel methodology for its translation to Java based applications. Although SDL is widely used in the telecommunications field, it is also now being applied to a diverse number of other areas ranging over aircraft, train control, medical and adaptive systems. Embedded signalling systems form a class of applications in the telecommunications field with specific requirements within the SDL domain. Although SDL is commonly used to specify embedded signalling systems, typically it is only a subset of the SDL language that is relevant. Within this contribution the key requirements of embedded signalling systems are identified and an enhanced subset of SDL 2000 is proposed for their specification and implementation. Additionally, this paper proposes a methodology for the translation of SDL systems based on this enhanced SDL subset, to Java applications using an SDL to Java Translator for supporting emerging Java based applications. The current proposal does not contradict with any SDL specification, but instead it is complementary to current SDL standards considering together design and implementation requirements of embedded signalling systems.

1 Introduction

Nowadays, we are experiencing a technology revolution in the telecommunications field. Modern telecommunication systems (including embedded signalling systems) are characterized by dynamic expansion and heterogeneous nature due to the interconnection of components having diverse technical characteristics.

---

[*] This work is partially supported by the EC under the IST-65002 REMUNE project.
[**] Correspondence author.

R. Reed (Ed.): SDL 2003, LNCS 2708, pp. 137–149, 2003.

With this level of continuous technical evolution it is essential that simple, efficient and highly reliable telecommunications systems are required before network operators offer new services to the users.

Currently in the market, there are various tools available for the specification of event based embedded signalling systems based on ITU-T SDL[1, 2, 3]. Although SDL is widely used in the telecommunications field, it is also now being applied to a diverse number of other areas ranging over aircraft, train control, medical and packaging systems. The expansion of SDL beyond the telecommunications field has led to the development of complex SDL based tools, supporting numerous of SDL features and keywords. Thus, the more complex the design of a signalling system is, the more complex is its implementation. Although SDL is commonly used to specify embedded signalling systems, typically it is only a subset of the SDL language that is relevant. From an implementation point of view and concerning platforms that support the execution of SDL based systems, simplicity is required in order to provide higher reliability and efficiency.

On the other hand, Java technology has become a significant force stimulating the evolution of embedded systems. The simplicity and platform-independence of the language attracted developers who struggled with portability issues and project deadlines. Since that time, developers in the embedded device market have come to understand and appreciate the benefits of the Java platform.

Sect. 2 of this paper defines a meaningful SDL subset for the support of embedded signalling systems design and implementation and Sect. 3 proposes the necessary enhancements to this SDL subset in order to satisfy the requirements of embedded signalling systems design and implementation. The aim of the enhanced SDL subset proposed in this paper is to provide simplicity and efficiency at the design level, something that leads to the implementation of robust and highly reliable telecommunication systems. Because Java is widely used in the implementation of embedded telecommunications system, Sect. 4 provides a methodology for the translation of SDL systems based on this enhanced SDL subset, to Java applications using an SDL to Java Translator for supporting emerging Java based applications.

2   Definition of a Meaningful SDL Subset for the Support of Embedded Signalling Systems Design and Implementation

Embedded signalling systems have the general characteristics mentioned in the introduction. User demands in terms of improved service quality, high-reliability, efficiency, increased bandwidth and advanced telecommunication services are gradually growing. As new technologies are integrated, customers expect and demand that personal communications will be capable of managing and delivering a much wider range of information services to the global market.

Given the speed and efficiency of evolution of new technologies and the continually growth of user requirements, in terms of improved service quality, high-reliability, efficiency and unlimited bandwidth, the rapid increase of the existing telecommunication networks' size and complexity is unavoidable. New requirements abound, driven by a large and diverse user population and the progress of technology. Furthermore, the convergence of various networks for the provision of advanced network services and applications is growing rapidly.

With this level of continuous technical evolution it is essential that simple, efficient and highly reliable telecommunications systems are required before network operators offer new services to the users.

Embedded signalling telecommunication systems have specific characteristics and address areas with unique requirements. They are based on Finite State Machines (FSMs), which means that they have defined states from where they can receive and send signals. Additionally, they consist of processes that send signals to each other based on a peer architecture. When waiting for an input signal a process is idle, which is a key difference to other (batch) applications. Such systems have specific requirements within the SDL domain and commonly only a subset of SDL is relevant.

In the work presented in this paper we have identified the requirements of embedded signalling systems ranging from embedded telecommunication protocols (SS7, V5, ISDN etc.) to other industrial systems. This work is a part of the work that is being performed within the context of the REMUNE IST project [5, 6]. The key features required from the current version of SDL to support the design and implementation of embedded signalling systems are:

- Data types, constants, variables
- Signals
- Connections between FSMs
- Decisions
- Procedures
- FSMs
- Timers
- Assignments

New features that have been added in the latest versions of SDL (including object-oriented features) are not of great importance for signalling systems, because no added value capabilities are provided for the design and implementation of such systems.

3   Enhancements to the SDL Subset

The current version of SDL provides the features that support design and implementation of embedded signalling systems. However, there is a set of requirements that are not directly satisfied by the current SDL features.[1] These requirements are classified in three main areas:

---

[1] Editorial note: In the editor's opinion the issue is mainly the current lack of tool support: an issue which the REMUNE project is addressing.

- Efficient management of resources: such as CPUs, memory especially in embedded systems, simple memory operations for dynamic memory allocation;
- Design in SDL to map the implementation constraints: such as the ability to assign to a variable a specific value centrally (at a system level) without having to assign the desired values "hard-coded";
- Need for more modularity: such as the ability to define substates within states in order to provide more simplicity and maintainability.

The following paragraphs analyze this set of requirements and propose a set of additional SDL keywords to support these concepts within the SDL domain. The current proposal does not contradict with any SDL specification, but instead it is complementary to current SDL standards considering together design and implementation requirements of embedded signalling systems.

3.1   Enhancements of SDL for Efficient Resource Management

As far as the efficient resource management is concerned, telecommunication systems and especially embedded systems are characterized by limited resources including CPU and memory. Although SDL can be used as a specification and description language for embedded signalling systems, there are tools that support the execution of SDL based systems directly to the target. The efficient resource management is not a main requirement for the description and design of systems using SDL, but in the case of SDL based implementations this is no longer true.

Currently, SDL supports arrays for the declaration of variables that belong to a specific group of variables of the same type. However, arrays are not applicable in areas such as embedded systems, where the resources are limited and efficient memory management is required. Therefore, simple memory operations for dynamic memory allocation are needed.

This contribution proposes some additional SDL keywords that can be used for the efficient memory management in embedded signalling systems. The proposed concepts are coming directly from other programming languages such as ANSI C, which supports a set of memory operations for efficient memory handling. The proposed SDL keywords and a short description for each one is provided below:

- PUSH - Handling Lists' variables. The PUSH function is used in order to add elements to a list.
- POP - Handling Lists' variables. The PUSH function is used in order to read and remove elements from a list.
- PUSH_FRONT - Handling Lists' variables. Same operation as PUSH.
- PUSH_BACK - Handling Lists' variables. The PUSH_BACK function is used in order to add elements to the end of a list.
- POP_FRONT - Handling Lists' variables. Same operation as POP
- POP_BACK - Handling Lists' variables. The POP_BACK function is used in order to read and remove elements from the end of a list.

- ELEMENT_FRONT - Handling Lists' variables. The ELEMENT_FRONT function is used in order to read elements (without removing them) at a given index in a list (start counting from the beginning of a list).
- ELEMENT_BACK - Handling Lists' variables. The ELEMENT_BACK function is used in order to read elements (without removing them) at a given index in a list (start counting from the end of a list).
- REMOVE_FRONT - Handling Lists' variables. The REMOVE_FRONT function is used in order to delete elements from the beginning of a list.
- REMOVE_BACK - Handling Lists' variables. The REMOVE_BACK function is used in order to delete elements from the end of a list.

3.2 Enhancements of SDL to Map Implementation Constraints

As far as the design in SDL to map the implementation constraints is concerned, embedded signalling systems and especially switching systems require a mechanism for the management of variables that the system behavior depends on. A specific scenario, for example, may be for a protocol layer to be dynamically changed from user to network mode. Such a mechanism will allow the changes of specific variables within SDL based systems to be performed centrally, even during runtime (for executable SDL based systems).

The concept for addressing this requirement is based on the Management Information Bases (MIBs), which are a collection of definitions, which define the properties of the managed object within the device to be managed. Every managed device keeps a database of values for each of the definitions written in the MIB. It is not the actual database itself - it is implementation dependent.

The current version of SDL does not support a keyword that allows the efficient management and configuration of significant SDL variables in SDL based implementations that may affect the behavior of an SDL based system. The proposed SDL keyword as well as a short description and an example is provided below:

- MIB - Variables' update declaration. This special variables' declaration is used in order to allow the user to have the ability of assigning a different value to a variable, even during the systems' execution. From the standard value assignment, the MIB assignment differs only at the end of the assignment where the keyword MIB is added.

3.3 Enhancements of SDL for more Modularity

As far as the need for more modularity is concerned, most of embedded signalling systems in the telecommunications world are of high complexity and therefore the difficulty in the maintenance of their implementations increases, having as a result the increase of costs. Although SDL is a modular language, the telecommunication industry asks for special features that will allow advanced modularity of SDL based systems. Within this contribution, the concept of nested states is proposed. The proposed SDL keywords that will allow this are as follows:

- SUBSTATE – Begin of nested state
- ENDSUBSTATE – End of nested state

These keywords are used for nesting states into other states. This concept is mostly covered by SDL 2000, which provides the concept of composite states. However, the composite states concept is more complex than the one proposed in this paper, since it incorporates additional functionality. The current proposal does not contradict with the composite states concept, but instead it is used to serve as the part of the composite state functionality that has to do only with nesting of states in other states.

The reason for introducing these keywords is again that of simplicity.

The paragraphs above provide a description of the enhancements that should be performed to the current SDL keywords for satisfying the requirements that derived directly from the telecommunications world for the design and implementation of embedded signalling systems. The following section provides a methodology for the translation of the enhanced SDL subset to Java using an SDL to Java Translator for supporting emerging Java based applications.

4   Mapping SDL Designs to Implementation Platforms (SDL to Java Translator)

Java technology has become a significant force stimulating the evolution of embedded systems. The simplicity and platform-independence of the language attracted developers who struggled with portability issues and project deadlines. Since that time, developers in the embedded device market have come to understand and appreciate the benefits of the Java platform.

The aim of the enhanced SDL subset proposed in this paper is to provide simplicity and efficiency at the design level, something that leads to the implementation of robust and highly reliable telecommunication systems. Because Java is widely used in the implementation of embedded telecommunications system, this section proposes a methodology for the translation of SDL systems based on this enhanced SDL subset, to Java applications using an SDL to Java Translator.

4.1   Working Assumptions

Today, there are more and more small-embedded systems supporting a Java Virtual Machine (JVM). The Sdl2Java translator has been designed for such systems. So we considered as an important constraint to keep the Java generated code as simple as possible. Although tempted, we avoided using complex enhancements such as Java Beans or Enterprise Java Beans (EJB).

A second advantage coming with this simplicity is the production of fast code, having a short response time and prepared for real-time (RT) applications. Java is usually considered slow. However, this is only true when we use the above enhancements or (for a GUI) the Abstract Windowing Toolkit (AWT).

Another important aspect we considered prior to our developments is the portability of the translator itself. Portability confers an evident added value to one tool when you can use it on diverse platforms.

4.2   Tools Choice

The choice was made between two families of tools:

- lex/yacc (flex/bison)
- JavaCC[7]/JJTree-JTB[8]

The first one produces C-code, which can be considered as portable. The second one generates Java code, which by the very essence of Java is portable at an executable level. We found the following advantages to the second family and therefore selected it:

1. JJTree or JTB (Java Tree Builder) are automatically adding the parse tree building actions.
2. The generated parser is in the same language as the code to be produced by the translator. It is certainly an advantage to think in a single language (Java) rather than two (C+Java).

4.3   The SDL Package

In order to keep the generated code as short as possible, we based it on an existing and hand-written package, the SDL package. All the base classes instantiated within the generated code are defined in this package. Some of them are represented in Fig. 1. The generated code always instantiates two classes: an SdlSystem class and an Engine class. The last step in the generated code of the main() method is to invoke the exec() method of the Engine class with a reference to the SdlSystem.

As shown below, there are two kinds of engines, both derived from the Engine class. A basic method of this ancestor class is OneTickExecute() and differently called by the child engines. The SimulatorEngine children invokes this method each time the user would like to execute a step or repeatedly when after a run command is issued. The RealTimeEngine invokes the OneTickExecute() method at a given timer period. If the previous call is not returned before the timer expires, the system will stop and display an error (tick time interval is too short).

The SimulatorEngine class includes a very primitive user interface supporting commands such as:

- go [ticks]: run the simulator for a given number of ticks (no given value means forever)
- step: run the simulator for 1 tick (equivalent to "go 1")

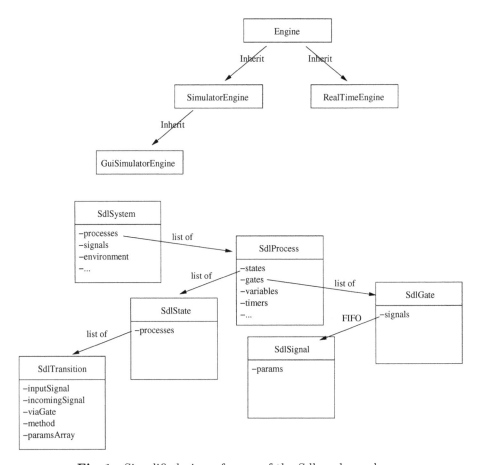

Fig. 1. Simplified view of some of the Sdl package classes

- batch file: execute one file in batch mode. The file must end with <exit> to return to the normal mode
- output <sig> <proc> <gate> : send a signal <sig> from the environment to process <proc> via gate <gate>
- var: display all variables of all processes
- gate: display gates in each process and their contents
- state: display the current state of each process
- trace [value]: display or set the trace level (higher -> more debug messages)
- time [value]: display or set the current time in number of ticks
- exit | quit: quit the simulator

The GuiSimulatorEngine redirects the IO stream to a socket server, where the GUI is located. A web based GUI has been built and is shown below in Fig. 2.

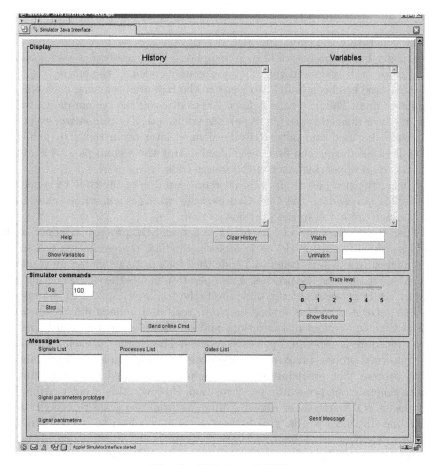

Fig. 2. Web based GUI

As shown in Fig. 1, an SDL system is constituted from a list of SdlProcess (java LinkedList). Each SdlProcess holds among others a list of SdlState, where each one is defined by a list of SdlTransition. Each transition is characterized by the conditions able to start it and the associated methods to run, with their parameters.

The timers are not shown but are simple entities, decremented, when running, after each tick. A timer occurrence is managed in the same way as a sent signal.

OneTickExecute() calls the SubTickExecute() method as long as transitions are occurring. This last method is the kernel of the Engine: its basic task is to look through all gates in all processes and extract the queued signals, if any, to start the necessary transitions.

4.4   The Generated Code

Before generating the code, the SDL description is parsed. A parse tree is automatically built, thanks to JTB. A template visitor method is also generated by JTB for each node and this allows a recursive visit of the entire tree. After the parse tree has been built, two visits to the tree are necessary, each one with a different goal. The first pass is dedicated to discover the system name, the signals, the user defined types (syntype), the states, etc. To summarize, everything that could be used and potentially be defined later on in the SDL pr file has to be detected during the first pass. Then during the second pass, it is already known even if appearing later in the source code.

During the two passes, an internal representation of the code to generate is built. This is based on the CodeGen package, which is sometimes close to the Sdl package presented in the previous section.

Then the design has to be flattened. When an SDL process is defined within a block, which in turn could be in a block, the final representation will just be one process. In the Java generated code the block instance hierarchy is used for the name preamble of the process. This operation makes the signal routing much simpler. Only processes at the same level (the top level) appear in the system.

The generated code is rather simple to read and understand. It consists of Sdl package component instantiations and by the relations between them. One Java procedure is generated per each process. The Engine at each transition of the concerned process invokes it. The process initialization is the first transition of any process. The procedure returns a pointer to the next state. Our first idea was to generate one procedure per transition. However, this is not possible since SDL has a JOIN statement allowing jumping from one transition body to any other one. In other words, this SDL statement can lead to a non structured program. On the other hand, a Java program is, by its language definition, always structured. Introducing a switch statement in an infinite loop with break statements has solved this problem.

We also considered the solution of starting one thread per process, and to realize the signal communication through channels via message queues. However, we were soon convinced that this solution would not require less overhead and will be more difficult to control in order to be compliant with the SDL specification (same signal scheduling leading to the same potential deadlocks).

4.5   The Enhanced SDL Subset for Sdl2Java

We enhanced the SDL subset with the following keywords:

- #JAVA_CODE, #JAVA_ENDCODE
- #JAVA_HEADING, #JAVA_ENDHEADING
- #SDL()

The first two statements allow the possibility to introduce Java code directly in the SDL specification. This is particularly useful to call an already developed and tested Java method. The next two statements are mainly used to be able to include the package reference where the above used methods reside. The last keyword is used to pass an SDL variable to this Java code.

Example of usage of these keywords
```
SYSTEM SBus1;
    #JAVA_HEADING import my_package.* #JAVA_ENDHEADING
    Process TYPE Client_PT;
        #JAVA_CODE
        Arith arith = new Arith();
        #JAVA_ENDCODE
        GATE Master_G WITH SBUS_SL;
        TIMER Reactivate_T:=2000;
        START;
        ...
        STATE Begin_Data;
        INPUT PH_Act_Ind VIA Master_G;
        TASK i:=#JAVA_CODE arith.incr(#SDL(i),#SDL(k)) #JAVA_ENDCODE;
        OUTPUT PH_Data_Req VIA Master_G;
        NEXTSTATE Finish_Data;
        ENDSTATE Begin_Data;

        . . .
    ENDPROCESS TYPE;
ENDSYSTEM;
```

4.6   The Trials and the TINI^{TM}

We used for our first trials the same machine to run the Sdl2Java translator and the generated code.

We first tried it on the following platforms:

- Sun/Solaris
- Mac/OsX
- PC/Windows
- PC/Linux

We had the same expected and correct results for all the 4 platforms. The test vehicle was a door access control. This small system is composed of two main instances: a door access controller, presenting the interface to the user, and a central controller, storing and checking to/from a database the access right of the different users presenting at the door.

We then decided to try the generated code on a small-embedded platform, the TINI^{TM} board (see Fig. 3) from Dallas Semiconductors. Such a board is shown below. The Java generated & compiled code and the Sdl package classes have to

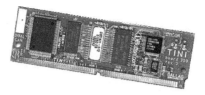

Fig. 3. TINI^{TM} board at SIMM card format

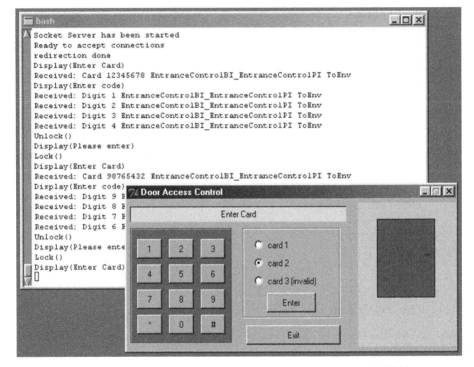

Fig. 4. Door Access Control GUI and log window on the TINI^{TM} board

be translated through a Dallas utility (TINIConvertor) before an execution on the TINI^{TM} JVM.

Until now, the classes' conversion works without any error and the tested system runs correctly. We had to rewrite the LinkedList class, which is not supported and find a workaround to a known bug of the TINI^{TM}: an invoke with a NULL argument produces a "null pointer exception" even if it works correctly on the other platforms.

Figure 4 shows a log window on the TINI^{TM} where the Door Access Control System has been run. A Tcl/Tk GUI has been built on a PC to converse with the above system environment. The closed door on the right symbolizes the door to open with the right code associated with a known card (card 1 or 2).

5   Conclusions

The enhanced SDL 2000 subset proposed in this paper is relevant for the implementation of embedded signalling systems. With the selected subset and extensions proposed in this contribution, most signalling or embedded systems can be modeled, thus there is no need for further complexity to be introduced in the overall SDL specification, which is targeting additional domains as well. Additionally, the proposed SDL subset and the extensions provide simplicity and efficiency at the design level, something that leads to the implementation of robust and highly reliable telecommunication systems. The current proposal does not contradict any SDL specification, but instead it is complementary to current SDL standards considering together design and implementation requirements of embedded signalling systems.

Because Java is widely used in the implementation of embedded telecommunications system, this paper proposes a methodology for the translation of SDL systems based on this enhanced SDL subset, to Java applications using an SDL to Java Translator. The choices and assumptions made for the Sdl2Java development has now revealed their correctness. This tool is still under development and is not yet compatible with the proposed enhanced SDL subset. However, there is no intrinsic limitation in the existing software structure which would inhibit its introduction.

References

[1] ITU-T Recommendation Z.100: Specification and Description Language   138
[2] ITU-T Recommendation Z.105: SDL combined with ASN.1 modules   138
[3] ITU-T Recommendation Z.107: SDL with embedded ASN.1   138
[4] Study Group 17 web site:
    http://www.itu.int/ITU-T/studygroups/com17/languages
[5] IST-65002 REMUNE project deliverable D21 "Industrial Requirements Analysis"
    139
[6] IST-65002 REMUNE project deliverable D22 "REMUNE Functional Specifications and Validation Scenarios"   139
[7] JavaCC web site: http://www.webgain.com/products/java_cc/   143
[8] JTB web site: http://www.cs.purdue.edu/jtb/   143

Generating a Compiler for SDL
from the Formal Language Definition

Andreas Prinz[1] and Martin v. Löwis[2]

[1] DResearch Digital Media Systems GmbH
Otto-Schmirgal-Str. 3, 10319, Berlin, Germany
`prinz@dresearch.de`
[2] Humboldt-Universität zu Berlin
Unter den Linden 6, 10099, Berlin, Germany
`loewis@informatik.hu-berlin.de`

Abstract. The Specification and Description Language (SDL-2000) has formal definitions for syntax, well-formedness, and dynamic semantics. While these definitions have well-understood mathematical foundations, engineers prefer to execute formal definitions, instead of studying them on paper. We present a tool chain which starts with the formal definition, and translates that into a compiler. The resulting compiler starts with a textual representation of the specification, and produces a program in the underlying formal calculus (Abstract State Machines, ASM). The ASM program, when executed, produces a trace of the SDL specification according to the formal language definition. In the process of developing this compiler, a number of errors were found in the formal semantics, which have been corrected.

1 Introduction

Defining the formal semantics of programming languages is an area of ongoing research. While formalizing the syntax of the language by means of grammars is well-understood, various techniques have been studied to define other properties of the language. We think that a language is sufficiently formalized if the following aspects are defined [1]:

1. The lexis: How is the input sequence of bytes transformed into a sequence of tokens?
2. The syntax: Given a sequence of tokens, is that a sentence of the language?
3. The well-formedness rules (static semantics): Given a sentence of the language, does that meet certain additional constraints?
4. The run-time (or dynamic) semantics: What does the program do when executed?

Not all of these aspects apply to all computer languages. For example, declarative languages may not have an execution semantics.

In this paper, we discuss these aspects of the language definition for the ITU-T Specification and Description Language [2]. For each of these aspects,

R. Reed (Ed.): SDL 2003, LNCS 2708, pp. 150–165, 2003.

we elaborate how the language has been formalized, and what tools we use to generate a real compiler from the formal definition.

We started this work as we believed that writing down a formal language definition is not enough, even if it is theoretically executable. With the formal definition alone, it is unclear whether

a) the formal definition is correct (that is, without contradictions within itself),
b) matches the informal definition, and
c) can be used by SDL practitioners.

With the development of tools, we can not only claim theoretical executability of the formal definition, but we can watch example SDL specifications being executed on a computer. We can then use these tools to experiment with the formal definition: for example to validate whether certain aspects match the informal definition, or whether an implementation conforms (in some specific aspect) to the language definition. This goes beyond reading an informal or formal language definition on paper, since a human interpreter of the standard may always overlook errors and ambiguities, whereas an automatic tool allows independent verification of an analysis.

Section 2 gives an overview over the formal methods used in defining the SDL formal semantics, and the tools used to implement them. The choice of methods is further elaborated in [6]; the choice of tools is discussed in Sect. 5. Section 3 gives examples for the issues we encountered when attempting to execute the formal definition. Section 4 provides a quantitative analysis of our results.

2   The Formal Semantics Definition

SDL is intended for "unambiguous specification and description of telecommunications systems" [2, Scope-objective]. It is used for the specification of telecommunication protocols in other ITU-T recommendations, for the documentation of protocol implementations, and for deriving protocol implementations themselves.

For these applications, it is important that the semantics of a system specification is undebatable; this requires that language specification itself is unambiguous. Defining the language in plain English is not sufficient. Therefore, SDL has had a formal definition of both static and dynamic semantics since 1988. While this definition has helped to clarify the language semantics in the past, it also became clear that a mathematical definition alone can be used by experts for the underlying calculus only.

For the most recent revision of SDL (SDL-2000), we attempted to develop a compiler alongside with developing the language definition. This compiler is not a reference implementation in the traditional sense; instead, it is mechanically derived from the formal language definition, so that changes in this definition are automatically reflected in the compiler.

The formal language definition describes static and dynamic aspects of SDL. The static aspects are outlined in figure 1, and consist of the processing steps for:

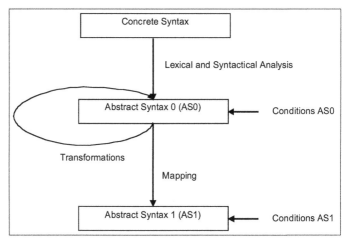

Fig. 1. Static Aspects of SDL

- the lexical rules;
- the syntactical rules;
- the abstract syntax AS0;
- well-formedness conditions on AS0 and AS1;
- the transformations;
- the abstract syntax AS1.

The following paragraphs outline the process of converting an input SDL specification to the abstract syntax AS1.

2.1   The Lexis

In SDL-2000, the lexis is specified using the Backus-Naur Form, and assuming the International Reference Alphabet [3] as the character set. Unfortunately, the specification using this calculus is incomplete, as additional "informal"[1] constraints apply – among others:

- Lexical units extend in a "greedy" fashion; the lexical unit extends up to the first character that cannot be part of lexical unit anymore;
- Sequences of letters are identifiers only if they are not keywords;
- Spaces and comments may be inserted between arbitrary tokens.

From the definition of the lexis, a GNU flex input file is generated.

   To provide the precise meaning of the lexical rules, the following ad-hoc knowledge was taken into account:

- Pattern matching in flex always finds the longest possible match, implementing the intended semantics of SDL lexical rules.

---

[1] Constraints expressed rigorously in natural language.

- The generator knows that the production <keyword> specifies the list of keywords, and emits the rule for keywords before the rule for identifiers.
- The generator creating the flex input is given a list of non-essential tokens (spaces and comments), and emits flex rules to ignore those tokens.

With these special cases, it is possible to automatically generate a lexical analysis from the language definition: no manual intervention is necessary here.

2.2   The Syntax

The syntax of SDL is also given using the Backus-Naur Form. As printed in the standard, it is meant for presentation, not necessarily to derive parsers. For example, the production <signal list item> reads

```
<signal list item> ::= <signal identifier>
         | ( <signal list identifier> )
         | <timer identifier>
         | [ procedure ] <remote procedure identifier>
         | [ interface ] <interface identifier>
         | [ remote ] <remote variable identifier>
```

Here, the underlined words denote semantic categories, rather than merely names of non-terminals: Using this technique, the grammar definition can already impose additional semantical constraints, limiting the set of identifiers that can occur as a signal list item. For syntactical analysis, these semantic categories are not available, and must be ignored. As a result, the grammar becomes ambiguous, with disambiguation becoming necessary on the semantic level. In the example, reading an <identifier> would match 5 of the 6 right-hand sides

Nevertheless, it can be used to automatically derive a Bison grammar, using the various techniques, including:

- Expand BNF constructs not supported by bison: for example, optional fragments;
- Combine duplicate productions into one: for the example, the right-hand sides <signal identifier> and <timer identifier> will be merged.

In the example, this gives the Bison fragment (leaving out semantic actions)

```
signal_list_item:
    identifier
  | signal_list_item_gen_identifier
  | signal_list_item_gen_procedure
  | signal_list_item_gen_interface
  | signal_list_item_gen_remote
signal_list_item_gen_identifier:
    '(' identifier ')'
```

```
signal_list_item_gen_procedure:
  PROCEDURE identifier
signal_list_item_gen_interface:
  INTERFACE identifier
signal_list_item_gen_remote:
  REMOTE identifier
```

Even with these transformations, the resulting grammar would still produce many conflicts in Bison's LALR(1) algorithm. Many of these conflicts could be removed by manual editing of the grammar; the remaining conflicts have been documented for further study. It is likely that those conflicts will be resolved by having the parser accept a more general language, and disambiguate ambiguous cases on the level of semantical analysis.

In the current state, the bison parser is handcrafted starting from the automatically produced version. It is not feasible for us to generate it automatically due to the bad structure of the SDL grammar.

2.3   The Abstract Syntax AS0

SDL-2000 defines two abstract syntaxes: The Abstract Syntax 0 (AS0) is closely related to the concrete syntax. While it was originally derived automatically from the concrete grammar, the definition of the AS0 is now a normative part of SDL-2000. The abstract syntax AS0 mainly serves the purpose of unifying the differences between the two concrete syntax forms of SDL, a textual one and a graphical one. Because of the close relationship between the concrete syntax forms and the abstract syntax AS0, the mapping between them is straightforward, and has not been formalized further. For the example, the abstract syntax reads

```
<signal list item> ::=(::)
   [ signal | signallist | timer | remote procedure |
      interface | remote variable ] <identifier>
```

Each non-terminal of the abstract syntax defines a new domain; in this case a tuple domain. The tokens (signal, signallist, etc.) form a set domain {*signal, signallist, timer, remote procedure, interface, remote variable*}. <identifier> is a domain on its own, defined in the production for <identifier> (not shown here). In turn, the resulting domain is

$$\{signal, signallist, timer, remote\ procedure, interface, remote\ variable\} \times <identifier>$$

The language Kimwitu++ [4, 8] is used to represent the abstract syntax in the compiler. In Kimwitu++, all AS0 domains are processed as operators of the AS0_rule phylum. For the example, the resulting operator definition is

```
ASO_signal_list_item(ASO_rule ASO_rule)
```

To construct the abstract syntax, the Bison grammar is augmented with calls to Kimwitu++ operators. Taking one alternative of the signal list item as an example, the resulting Bison production reads:

```
signal_list_item_gen_procedure:
    PROCEDURE identifier
       { $$=ASO_signal_list_item( ASO_TOKEN(
         mkcasestring("REMOTE PROCEDURE")), $2 ); }
```

The semantic rules can also be generated automatically. However, some of them will not be correct with respect to the AS0. Using the generated (and manually corrected) Bison parser, we get a representation of the input in AS0.

Unfortunately, the relation between AS0 and concrete syntax is not formal enough to be used for an automatic generation of the parser.

2.4   Well-Formedness Conditions

The standard imposes a number of constraints on any correct SDL specification. Those constraints are formulated as predicates both on the abstract syntax AS0, and the abstract syntax AS1 (presented later).

To continue the example, there is a requirement for <signal list definition>, which is given in plain English as

> The <signal list definition> <signal list definition> must not contain the <signal list identifier> defined by the <signal list definition> <signal list definition> either directly or indirectly (via another <signal list identifier>).

In the formal language definition, this is formulated as a predicate in predicate calculus:

$\forall siglistDef \in$ <signal list definition>$:\neg isSiglistContaining_0(siglistDef, siglistDef)$

This definition, in turn, uses an auxiliary function:

$isSiglistContaining_0$
$\quad (sld1$:<signal list definition>$,sld2$:<signal list definition>$)$:BOOLEAN$=_{def}$
$\quad \exists sid \in$ <identifier>$:sid.parentASO.parentASO=sld1 \wedge sid.idKind_0 =$ **signallist**
$\quad\quad \wedge (getEntityDefinition_0(sid, \textbf{signallist}) = sld2$
$\quad\quad\quad \vee (\exists\ sld3 \in$ <signal list definition>:
$\quad\quad\quad\quad isSiglistContaining_0(sld1, sld3) \wedge isSiglistContaining_0(sld3, sld2)))$

These definitions are compiled into Kimwitu++ code. Quantifications are compiled into iterations, because the base domains are always finite. A predicate amounts to a boolean-valued function. It is possible to do this compilation automatically. However, currently the static conditions are not handled by the tool set.

2.5   Transformations

In SDL, a number of transformations are applied to the abstract syntax AS0, to simplify the definition of the dynamic semantics. These transformations are defined as rewrite rules. For the example, a transformation is described in English text as

> *Every <signal list identifier> is replaced by the list of signals of its definition.*

In the formal language definition, this rule is expressed as

< <signal list item>(*kind*, *id*) > **provided** *id.refersto$_0$* $\in$ <signal list definition> =8=> *id.refersto$_0$*.**s**-<signal list item>-**seq**

This transformation uses a number of auxiliary constructs (such as the function *refersto$_0$*) which are defined in a similar manner as used for the functions in the previous section. The operator =8=> indicates that, in transformation step 8, a node of the AS0 that matches the left-hand side is transformed to the right-hand side. The left-hand side term is a pattern, possibly augmented with an additional predicate.

The transformations are compiled into Kimwitu++ rewrite rules. The example then becomes

```
ASO_CONS(ASO_signal_list_item(v_kind, v_id), ASO_NIL())
provided (in_signal_list_definition(refersto0(v_id)))
-><trans_8: RETURN(Select(1, "<signal list item>-seq",
   refersto0(v_id))) >;
```

The transformation into kimwitu++ is completely automatic and does not require any manual intervention. As long as new or changed transformations do not go beyond the expressiveness of the current ones, this will not change.

2.6   Mapping to Abstract Syntax 1

The dynamic semantics of SDL is based on another abstract syntax, called Abstract Syntax 1 (AS1). For example, in AS0, a gate definition is described as

<textual gate definition> ::
        <gate> <gate constraint> [<gate constraint>]
<gate constraint> ::
     { **out** | **in** } [<textual endpoint constraint>] <signal list item>*

In the abstract syntax AS1, this construct is simplified as

Gate-definition	::	*Gate-name*
		In-signal-identifier-**set**
		Out-signal-identifier-**set**
In-signal-identifier	=	*Signal-identifier*
Out-signal-identifier	=	*Signal-identifier*

This example demonstrates a number of simplifications, for example:

- In the concrete syntax, and AS0, the signal list items are ordered. In AS1, the order is ignored.
- Various alternatives for signal list items have been simplified. For example, identifiers referring to signal lists have been converted into the individual elements of the signal list.

As a result, not all constructs of the AS0 are still relevant in the AS1. The transformation from AS0 to AS1 is defined through a function named *Mapping*, which uses pattern matching to create AS1 for a given AS0 pattern. For the AS0 domains from the signal list example, the formal semantics defines the following patterns

```
| < <signal list definition>(*,*) > => empty
| < <signal list item>(*, id) > => Mapping(id)
| <signal list item>(*, id) => Mapping(id)
```

The *Mapping* function is translated into a Kimwitu++ with statement, where the fragment dealing with signal lists gets translated into

```
ASO_CONS(ASO_signal_list_definition(*, *), ASO_NIL()):
    { AS1_rule result = AS1_NIL(); RETURN; }
ASO_CONS(ASO_signal_list_item(*, v_id), ASO_NIL()):
    { AS1_rule result = Mapping(v_id); RETURN; }
ASO_signal_list_item(*, v_id):
    { AS1_rule result = Mapping(v_id); RETURN; }
```

This translation into kimwitu++ is completely automatic without manual intervention.

2.7   The Dynamic Semantics

The dynamic semantics is defined by means of Abstract State Machines (ASM) [5]. We will give only an overview of the structure of the dynamic semantics here, for details, the reader is referred to [6]. Figure 2 summarizes the aspects of the dynamic semantics:

- Starting point of the dynamic semantics is the abstract syntax (AS1), which defines the structure of the SDL system, the behavior of individual agents, and the data types used.
- The behavior is compiled into a set of primitives of the SDL Virtual Machine (SVM).
- The structure is executed by means of a initialization process, which recursively unfolds the system, traversing the abstract syntax.
- A number of control programs are provided in the SVM which determine the agent performing the next transition, the transition being fired, and the step-by-step execution of the transition. Within the transition, data expressions are computed based on the previous state of the agent, yielding the next state.

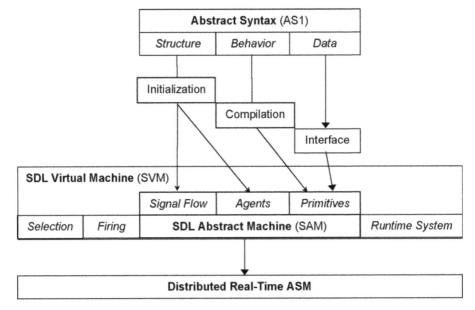

Fig. 2. Dynamic Aspects of SDL

The dynamic semantics is transformed into AsmL code, which amounts to slight syntactic changes. It is performed completely automatically.

3   Studying Specific Aspects

With the tool chain available for experiments, it becomes possible to analyze specific systems, and to study the formal semantics in action. In doing so, we found that a number of errors had to be corrected, and we found that the formal semantics sometimes showed a surprising interaction of its various parts. In this section, we want to give an example for such an interaction.

3.1   Signal Transport

In SDL-2000, both blocks and processes (SDL agents) can receive signals. In the ASM model, signals are transmitted by means of links, which are ASM agents that copy signals from one end of the link to the other. Copying of signals is not immediate, but may be delayed by the channel delay. While "in transit", signals are kept in a queue of the target gate. The ASM program of a link is defined through the rule

FORWARDSIGNAL ≡
    if *Self.from.queue* ≠ *empty* **then**
        let *si = Self.from.queue.head* **in**
            if *Applicable*(*si.signalType,si.toArg,si.viaArg,Self.from,Self*) **then**
               DELETE(*si,Self.from*)
               INSERT(*si,now+Self.delay,Self.to*)
               if *Self.channelAS1* ≠ *undefined* **then** // not for implicit Links
               si.viaArg := *si.viaArg* \
                    {*Self.from.gateAS1.nodeAS1ToId,*
                        Self.channelAS1.nodeAS1ToId}
               endif
            endif
        endlet
    endif

In this ASM rule, the function *Self* indicates the current link (the one executing this rule). Two functions *from* and *to* return the gates which the link connects. The function *queue* returns the list of signals currently pending in this gate.

So this rule first checks whether a signal is pending in the *from* gate of the link. If there are signals, the first signal is retrieved from the queue, and a test is performed whether this link should transmit the signal: that is, whether the link is capable of transmitting the signal and whether the receiver of the signal can be reached through this link. This entire test is performed in the predicate *Applicable*.

If the signal is applicable for this link, it is deleted from the *from* gate, and inserted into the *to* gate, considering a possible delay. If the signal was sent with an **output via** specification, the link just passed must be deleted from the via list of the signal.

This entire computation is an ASM agent step: it can only entirely succeed, or entirely fail.

3.2   Receiving Signals at the SDL Agent

As links connect gates, we found that a mechanism is needed to eventually put signals into the input port of an SDL agent. Gates are, most of all, associated with the agent type: each gate belongs to an agent type, rather than to an agent instances (i.e. there are no gate instances in SDL-2000). Accordingly, the formal semantics definition creates gates only for each agent instance set, rather than for each agent. The channels connecting to the agent set are defined by a pair of links between gates on agent sets.

However, the agent set is not capable of ultimately processing the signals. Therefore, links are created between each SDL agent's input port, and each gate of the agent set. These links are established through the following rules:

CREATEALLLINKS(ow:AGENT) $\equiv$
    do forall g: $g \in ow.ingates$
        CREATELINK (ow, g, $ow.inport$, **NODELAY**,
            $g.gateAS1$.**s-**In-$signal$-$identifier$-**set**, $undefined$)
    enddo
CREATELINK(ow:AGENT, $fromGate$:GATE, $toGate$:GATE, nd:**NODELAY**,
        w:In-$signal$-$identifier$-**set**,
    cd:[$Channel$-$definition$]) $\equiv$
    extend LINK **with** l
        $l.channelAS1$:= cd
        $l.owner$:= ow
        $l.from$:= $fromGate$
        $l.to$:= $toGate$
        $l.noDelay$:= nd
        $l.with$:= w
        $l.program$:= LINK-PROGRAM
    endextend
LINK-PROGRAM:

FORWARDSIGNAL

The rule CREATEALLLINKS invokes the rule CREATELINK for all input gates of the agent (the function *ingates* is a derived function, looking at the gates of the agent set). The rule CREATELINK adds a new link, establishes the from and to gates of the link, and initiates the execution of FORWARDSIGNAL for the new link. As a result, the links will simultaneously look at all of the input gates, determine which signals are targeted at the agent, and put those signals into its input port. This models the semantics of the input port of the SDL agent.

3.3   Behavior of the Agent Instance Set

While considering signal processing, we had to consider the question of how signals get discarded when the receiver of the signal stops. To adequately represent this behavior, an activity was defined for the agent set:

EXECAGENTSET $\equiv$
        DELIVERSIGNALS
   DELIVERSIGNALS $\equiv$
      choose g: $g \in Self.ingates \land g.queue \neq empty$
      let $si = g.queue.head$ **in**
        DELETE(si,g)
        if $si.toArg \in$ PID $\land si.toArg \neq undefined$ **then**
           choose
               sa: $sa \in$ SDLAGENT $\land sa.owner = Self \land sa.self = si.toArg$
               INSERT(si, $si.arrival$, $sa.inport$)
           endchoose
        else

choose sa: $sa \in \text{SDLAGENT} \wedge sa.owner = \textit{Self}$
      $\text{INSERT}(si,\ si.arrival,\ sa.inport)$
   endchoose
  endif
 endlet
endchoose

In this rule, the agent set continuously inspects its gates, and determines which gates have signals pending. It chooses an arbitrary one of these gates, and removes the first signal from that gate's queue. It then checks whether the signal has a receiver Pid defined. If it does, that receiver is computed, and the signal put into its input port. Otherwise, an arbitrary receiver is chosen, and the signal delivered to that agent. When an agent is stopped, it is deleted together with its implicit connection, such that no further signal is transmitted to it.

3.4 Putting It All Together

Looking at these two mechanisms combined, it turns out that there are now two ways in which a signal can reach its target process: either through the link between the gate and the input port, or through the copying that the agent instance set does. This leads to an ambiguity (which of these routes is taken) which wasn't found before a system was actually executed.

Further analysis shows that the ambiguity is shallow, and doesn't constitute an error, in the sense of an incorrect definition of the SDL language: as ASM actions are atomic, there is a guarantee that only one or the other paths will be taken. It cannot happen that both a link and the instance set read the same signal from the gate's queue, in which case the signal would get duplicated. Since the copying takes no delay, this ambiguity doesn't affect the overall system behavior. In fact, the second rule (DELIVERSIGNALS) adds behavior, because it will also attempt to transmit signals whose receiver is already dead. In this case, the signal is simply deleted.

4 Correcting Errors

Each time the tools showed unexpected results, an analysis was necessary to determine precisely what the problem was. In some cases, we found that simply the expectations were wrong, and that the observed behavior is really a possible interpretation of the SDL system. For example, with the introduction of user-defined operators, the order of evaluation of decision answers may affect the meaning of the SDL system: comparing a decision answer with the question value may raise an exception, or fail to terminate due to an infinite loop. In the standardization process, it was then clarified that this is the intended

Table 1. Errors found in the formal semantics

Category	Error count in F.2	Error count in F.3
Syntax errors	352	189
Spelling Errors	115	80
Missing or superfluous parameters	159	34
Type errors	88	314
Incorrect usage of abstract syntax	144	83
Minor semantic errors	57	227
Major semantic errors	12	3
Undefined functions		32
Insufficient abstract syntax 0	4	

behavior of SDL-2000, and that the order of evaluation of decision answers is non-deterministic.[2]

In other cases, we traced the error to a bug in the tool chain. In many cases it was easy to find errors in the tool chain simply because the tool chain did the wrong transformations. In the case of runtime errors, this was harder to detect and required a long analysis. We assumed that the compiler construction meta tools used work correctly and in our case, they did.

If the problem turned out to be an error in the formal semantics, this error was corrected. For this latter category, we counted all errors we corrected, and classified them further. The result of this classification is shown in Table 1. The document F.2 is part 2 of the formal semantics definition; it defines the static semantics of SDL. Part F.3 describes the dynamic semantics.

The categories of errors were invented ad-hoc after a first quick overview of the errors present. "Syntax errors" refers to errors by the parser. Static semantics errors are split into the categories spelling errors, parameter errors, typing errors and abstract syntax errors.

The next kind of errors refers to the dynamic semantics with minor semantic errors (e.g. wrong index accessed) and major semantic errors. The major semantic errors required a structural change to the semantics.

Moreover, sometimes there was insufficient information in the abstract syntax 0, meaning that important information was not present in the AS0: for example, the optional identifier after the closing keyword.

In interpreting these numbers, we made the following observations:

- Syntax errors: Those errors arise from incorrect usage of the notations for the formulae. As F.2 has roughly twice as many pages as F.3, it appears that the density of such errors is constant within the entire text. The same analysis applies to the incorrect usage of abstract syntax; those were primarily caused

---

[2] Editorial note: Decision answers have ranges defined by constant expressions. It is allowed (but to be avoided — tools should flag a warning) for the ranges of different answers to overlap.

by changes made to the definition of the abstract syntax after it was already used in formulae.

- Type errors: Such errors originate from a violation of the typing system. That we found more such errors in F.3 probably originates from the tools used to perform the type check: The AsmL tool performs a much stricter type check than the C++ compiler, as many of the ASM domains map to the same C++ class. It is likely that a stricter type check will find many more such errors.
- Minor semantic errors: They were detected when executing the formal semantics. The large number of such errors found in F.3 results from a few systematic errors that had to be corrected in many similar places.
- Undefined functions: In the definition of the dynamic semantics of data types, a number of calls to functions where made that were nowhere defined. Defining these functions properly was more than a simple textual correction, so we counted them separately.
- Insufficient abstract syntax 0: Since the abstract syntax 0 is only used in the definition of the static semantics, obviously no such errors can be present in part F.3.

5 Related Work

For the comparison of the SDL formal semantics with other formal semantics definitions, see [6]. In the scope of this paper, we only want to have a look at the executable formal semantics work and compiler construction tools.

It is not a completely new idea to define a formal semantics for a language. There were several other attempts to define programming language semantics formally. However, the direction for the formal semantics was different most of the time. The formal semantics started from the abstract grammar, and was hence used to prove certain properties of the language (good ones and bad ones). It was not really possible to derive a real compiler from the formal language description, because the front-end properties of the language (the compiler-related part) was not formalized. In addition, many of these attempts to formalize a language only targeted a subset of the language. For example, attempts to provide a formal semantics for the C and C++ programming languages ([11], [12]) ignore (among other things) the semantics of the pre-processor.

There have also been lots of attempts to define tools that generate compilers including the semantics of the languages: examples are kimwitu [9], Eli (Paderborn) [10], and Cocktail (Karlsruhe) [13]. Our choice of tools was based on prior experience with these tools. We have not performed an extensive comparison of these tools, but we found that tool limitations are not obvious at first, and will only become visible at a late stage. At this point, efforts are typically better spent on overcoming the limitations of the tool chosen, instead of switching to a different tool – which may have a different set of limitations.

From our experience with the tools we have chosen, it is likely that an advanced parser generator might help to solve the problems we encountered with bison, in particular to eliminate parser conflicts by using a more powerful parsing algorithm. Unfortunately, such advanced compiler generators are often limited in the integration of a given abstract syntax; for this project, we cannot accept that the tool defines an abstract syntax for us, but we must use the abstract syntax mandated by the formal SDL definition.

Compiler toolkits such as Cocktail also offer powerful attribution mechanisms for syntax trees, and use those to simplify the implementation of static semantics of a language. While such techniques are useful for a production compiler, they don't simplify the execution of the formal semantics, where the well-formedness conditions are given in predicate calculus quantifying the entire structure of the syntax tree, instead of referring to specific attributes of certain syntax nodes. Cocktail also provides a transformation tool to implement rewriting systems, which appears to be equivalent in expressiveness to Kimwitu++.

6   Summary and Conclusions

With the formal definition of SDL-2000, it is possible to derive an executable program that implements the formal semantics of SDL. This process is nearly automatic, requiring only minimal manual adjustment of the generation process, in particular on the lexical and syntactical level.

While it is a significant effort to first produce a formal language definition, and then produce a generator that automatically derives an executable reference implementation, we believe that it is feasible to apply such techniques to other programming languages as well. In the process of doing so, we found numerous errors in the formal definition, and in our conversion tools, which helps to improve the rigor of the language definition. Having tools available also helps practitioners of the language to really understand the language definition.

Moreover, it turns out that writing a formal semantics is an engineering activity similar to writing a compiler. In particular it is necessary to make extensive use of tools to assure that the resulting formalization is correct.

Acknowledgments

We would like to thank the SDL Forum Society and Microsoft Research for funding this research, and providing access to both the SDL standard, and beta versions of the AsmL compiler.

References

[1] A. Prinz. Formal Semantics for SDL – Definition and Implementation. Humboldt-Universität zu Berlin, 2001.   150
[2] ITU-T. Recommendation Z.100 (08/02), Specification and Description Language (SDL). International Telecommunication Union, Geneva.   150, 151

[3] ITU-T. Recommendation T.50 (1992)International Reference Alphabet (IRA) (Formerly International Alphabet No. 5 or IA5) - Information technology - 7-bit coded character set for information interchange. International Telecommunication Union, Geneva. 152

[4] M. Piefel. Kimwitu++. http://site.informatik.hu-berlin.de/kimwitu++. 154

[5] Y. Gurevich. Evolving Algebras 1993: Lipari Guide. Specification and Validation Methods, pages 9-36, Oxford University Press, 1995   157

[6] R. Eschbach,U. Glässer, R. Gotzhein, M. von Löwis, A. Prinz. Formal Definition of SDL-2000 – Compiling and Running SDL Specifications as ASM Models. Journal of Universal Computer Science 7 (11), 2001, Springer, pp. 1025-1050   151, 157, 163

[7] Microsoft Research. AsmL. http://research.microsoft.com/foundations/AsmL/

[8] M. von Löwis, M. Piefel. The Term Processor Kimwitu++. Proceedings of the 6th World Conference on Systemics, Cybernetics, and Informatics, Orlando, 2002. 154

[9] P. van Eÿk. Tools for LOTOS, a Lotosphere overview. Tutorial proceedings of 11th Symposium on Protocol Specification, Testing and Verification, Sydney, 1991. 163

[10] U. Kastens. Executable Specifications for Language Implementation. Fifth International Symposium on Programming Language Implementations and Logic Programming, Tallinn, 1993, Springer LNCS 714, pp. 1-11.   163

[11] Y. Gurevich, J. K. Huggins. The Semantics of the C Programming Language. Springer LNCS 702, Springer, 1993.   163

[12] C. Wallace. The Semantics of the C++ Programming Language. Specification and Validation Methods, Oxford University Press, 1995.   163

[13] J. Grosch, H. Emmelmann. Werkzeuge für den Übersetzerbau. Achern, 1995.   163

Modelling and Evaluation of a Network on Chip Architecture Using SDL

Rickard Holsmark, Magnus Högberg, and Shashi Kumar

Embedded System Group, Department of Electronics and Computer Engineering
School of Engineering, Jönköping University, Sweden
{rickard.holsmark,ef01homa,Shashi.Kumar}@ing.hj.se

Abstract. Network on Chip (NoC) is a new paradigm for designing large and complex systems on chips (SoCs). In this paradigm, a packet switched network is provided for on-chip communication. The NoC paradigm provides the required scalability and reusability to reduce design time of SoCs. A NoC simulator is an important tool required to support development of designs based on a NoC architecture. In this paper, we describe the design of such a simulator using the ITU-T Specification Description Language (SDL). Features of SDL for representing structural hierarchy using blocks, concurrent processes and dynamic generation of processes, communication channels, user defined data types and timers are useful for modelling a NoC architecture at various levels of communication protocols. We use an event driven SDL simulator to carry out interesting experiments to evaluate various architectural options such as buffer size in switches, and their effect on the performance such as delay and packet loss.

1 Introduction

It is predicted that semiconductor technology will continue to advance according to Moore's law for at least another ten years. In a few years time, it will become possible for designers to integrate more than fifty cores, each the size of a small processor along with many memory blocks of different types on a single chip. Network on Chip (NoC) is a new paradigm for designing such future systems on chips [1, 2].

NoC adapts the idea of a router-based network from computer networks and uses it for packet switched on-chip communication among cores. A NoC architecture provides a scalable communication infrastructure for interconnecting cores. Because the communication infrastructure as well as the cores from one design can be easily reused for a new product, NoC provides the maximum possibility for reuse.

Recently many research groups have proposed specific NoC architectures. The NoC architectures differ in the switch network topology, communication protocols and access of the network by the cores [3, 4, 5, 6]. NoC architectures being general purpose provide a lot of programmability and flexibility. But we

R. Reed (Ed.): SDL 2003, LNCS 2708, pp. 166–182, 2003.

have to pay the price of this flexibility and reusability by loosing some communication performance, especially critical in real time applications.

NoC research is still in its infancy. There is a need to evaluate various architectural features of NoC. Designing a network for on-chip communication is similar to the problem of designing a local area computer network with some computing and communication requirements. Therefore, it is necessary to evaluate the performance of these networks to make sure that they provide the required performance for the intended applications.

The purpose of evaluation could be either to decide parameters of the network for an application, or to estimate the performance of the network for a set of applications having certain on-chip communication traffic. In the absence of availability of actual network and real applications which are going to be run on NoC systems, the only choice available for the evaluation is to use models of networks and applications. Network and applications can be modelled using a set of parameters relevant to the evaluation task.

Researchers have borrowed ideas and tools used for the evaluation of general computer networks to evaluate on-chip networks. Yi-Ran et. al. [7] have used the network simulator **ns-2** developed at the University of Berkeley, for evaluation of the KTH-VTT NoC proposal. Researchers are also building dedicated simulators from scratch for studying NoC architecture and on-chip packet switched communication [8]. Because **ns-2** was not developed for on-chip networks, it does not provide facilities for modelling the detailed architecture of switches and does not allow accurate measurement of delays in the network. Developing a dedicated simulator is a very time consuming activity.

In this paper, we describe our experience of designing an SDL based simulator for a specific NoC architecture. In the next section we give a brief introduction to the KTH-VTT NoC architecture. In Sect. 3, we discuss the modelling of various components of a NoC architecture using SDL. Section 4 discusses parameters related to NoC architecture, application and NoC performance related to NoC architectural evaluation. Section 5 describes a few, among a large number, of the simulation experiments and their results carried out by us. At the end we give some general conclusions.

2 KTH-VTT NoC Architecture [1]

The Royal Institute of Technology (KTH), Stockholm and VTT Electronics, Oulu Finland have jointly developed a NoC platform for developing large and complex SoCs. The NoC architecture consists of a two-dimensional mesh of switches or micro-routers. Cores (called resources) are placed in the slots formed by the switches. A direct 2D layout of switches and resources is assumed providing physical-architectural design integration.

Each switch can be connected to one resource and four neighboring switches, and each resource is connected to one of the surrounding switches. Figure 1 shows a comparison between a bus based SoC and a 3 x 3 NoC. The resources in NoC could be memory blocks, DSPs or special purpose ASICs. A resource

Traditional SoC using
shared buses

Proposed SoC using NoC
(3*3 Resources)

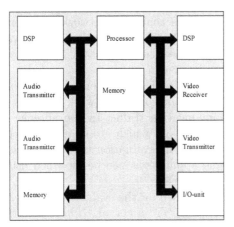

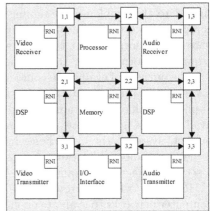

Fig. 1. A Traditional SoC and a 3 x 3 NoC Platform

is connected to the network through a special interface called resource-network interface (RNI).

The network of switches supports datagram based as well as virtual path based communication. A five-layered protocol stack has been proposed for layered communication among resources. These layers have been adapted from the OSI reference model which can be studied from any book on computer networks, for example [9].

The lower three layers, namely physical, data-link and network layers are compulsory layers and are implemented by each switch as well as each resource. A transport layer is also defined to establish and maintain communication between source and destination resources. The lower three layers put together provide the service of delivering a packet of data from one resource to any other resource in the network.

The switch network is called the communication backbone of NoC. The performance of a NoC architecture is highly dependent on the design of the switch. The switch has the functionality of transferring packets from one of its input ports to one or more of its output ports. The time gap between when the packet enters the switch and when it leaves the switch is called switch delay. The switch may have buffers to receive incoming packets and buffers to store packets before they are put on the output port.

Figure 2 shows a schematic diagram of a generic NoC switch. Another feature of a switch, which affects NoC performance, is the routing algorithm that is implemented in the switch control. The cost of the switch depends on the size of the buffers as well as the complexity of the routing algorithm. For our modelling purpose, we have assumed a switch having small input and output buffers.

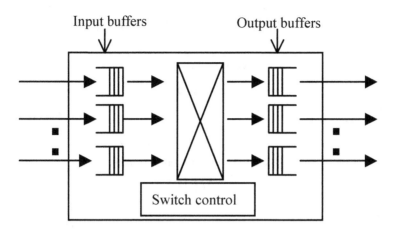

Fig. 2. A Generic NoC Switch

3   Modelling of NoC in SDL

One of the motivations for using SDL for modelling NoC was to support a design process where a specification at a higher level of abstraction can systematically be transformed to an implementation at a lower level of abstraction. This means that we have a possibility of getting a RTL level VHDL design from block level SDL behavior of NoC. It is also possible to generate very simple models of resources in NoC using the programming language-like control constructs in SDL.

3.1   NoC Design Flow

We envisage that it is possible to develop a NoC using the design flow shown in Fig. 3. The flow consists of three stages ordered from system level down to implementation. The network behavior is modelled at the system level in SDL. Certain descriptions of the system behavior will come out from the VHDL design. Since the VHDL model will be clock synchronous, the number of clock cycles a function takes, will be used in the SDL model to get a more realistic timing behavior. The meaning of Fig. 3 is that the design will be refined and information from a lower level will be used to improve the model at a higher level.

3.2   SDL Model of NoC

SDL was used since it is suited to model reactive data communication systems [10, 11]. We model the layered packet switched communication in a 2D mesh of switches (micro-routers). To have flexibility as well as efficiency of simulation, we provide a mode switch in our model so that it is possible to simulate the model either at data-link layer or at the network layer.

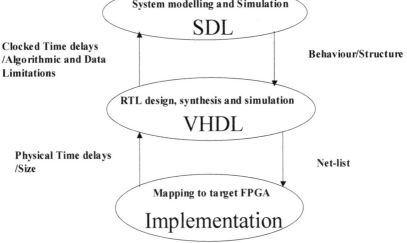

Fig. 3. Design Refinement for NoC Design

Because data-link layer does not add information on how the routing and buffers work, it would be possible to leave this layer out when making evaluations of network performance at network layer level. The physical layer defines the actual physical connections that are the basis for a network. Because our implementation is intended for an FPGA platform and it is difficult to model the placement and routing process of FPGA design tools, currently we do not have a model at the physical layer level.

Model Overview. At the top level in the design the type definitions, signals and configuration constants (synonyms) are set. As an example, the simulation can be performed on the network layer by setting the synonym DLS to 0. If the behavior of the data link layer also is to be simulated, DLS should be set to 1. We also provide a facility for setting the behavior of each resource at system level using synonyms as parameters.

The major decision for the block division is that a block should encapsulate a specific function of the network. To some extent they should also reflect the physical units that form the network. The design makes frequent use of type definitions, in order to make components easy to reuse. Because the model is to be used for simulation purposes the network size is an important parameter.

For modelling purposes, we group a switch, a resource, and a resource network interface as a single block and call it a NoC node. Figure 4 shows the SDL model of a NoC node. Before a simulation the number of nodes that are the product of

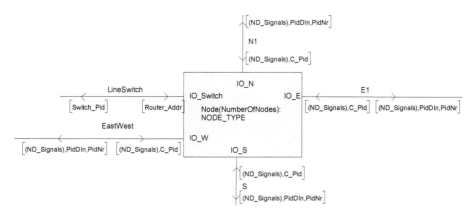

Fig. 4. SDL Model of a Node in the NoC Architecture

the values assigned to row size*column size are created. The connections between the nodes in the network are then automatically set up.

The internal structure of the Node block is shown in Fig. 5. It is divided into three blocks namely Router, Resource and RNI. The IO_Switch is a channel that is only used in the initialization of the simulation in order to get all the created routers connected appropriately. We briefly discuss SDL modelling of various components of the NoC architecture in the next sub-sections. More details are available in [12].

Micro-router. A micro-router is built using the layered design, which provides the ability to change the service on one layer without affecting the other. Figure 6 shows the network layer block of the Router, consisting of one switch/routing block, four in/out buffers, and one RNI in/out buffer.

The routing function in the micro-routers decides the transfer of data between any arbitrary nodes in the network. The block SWITCH_CONTROL contains the processes Switch and Route_Control. The Switch receives packets from the in-buffers and sends information about the packet's desired destination to the Route_Control. The Route_Control has information about the state of the out-buffers and makes a decision about the route for the packet.

We use a very simple dynamic routing algorithm for making routing decisions. For every input packet we first try to send it in a direction (north or south) leading to the shortest path. If that is not possible we investigate the next best direction (west or east). If buffers in the preferred direction are not available, it will be sent to any direction with a free buffer. If there is no free input buffer in a particular direction, the switch, which can send a packet to it, is informed about this. If it is not possible to route a packet out of a switch for some specified number of time units (timeout time), the packet is dropped.

This strategy is chosen because when the network is heavily loaded, the resources should not send a packet that will most likely be dropped. This brings the

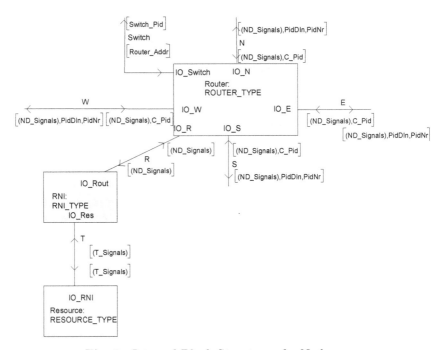

Fig. 5. Internal Block Structure of a Node

information regarding the network traffic closer to the source, and the decision on how to react is made by the resource.

The buffers use the BUFFER_TYPE block and handle all communication in one direction (North, South, West, and East). To make it possible to set a different configuration for the buffer connecting to RNI this is of a special type called RNI_BUFFER_TYPE. These blocks are also able to communicate with the neighboring router or RNI, both directly on the network layer and via the data-link layer.

The data-link layer is divided into a separate block, D_IO_TYPE that connects to the buffers and performs services of the data-link layer.

Model of Resource Network Interface. The purpose of the Resource Network Interface (RNI) is to be a link between a micro-router in the network and the resource connected to it. The idea of having a RNI is that there is no need

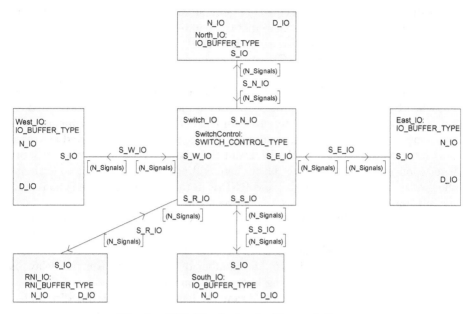

Fig. 6. SDL Blocks in the Network Layer

for a resource to implement the network layer. Thus, some complexity of the resource will be removed.

In the model it is assumed that the transport layer is implemented in the resource part of the interface between the RNI and resource. This is because there is a possibility that every resource will not have identical use of this layer's service. As a result the RNI will receive transport layer packets, perform network layer services such as adding the address of the desired destination node for transporting the packet.

It encapsulates the block type N_LAYER with processes that perform the network layer services in the RNI. It contains one RNI service block and one in/out-buffer towards the micro-router. There is also a possibility to use a data-link layer block. The block RNI_SERVICE is responsible for the transformation of data between the resource and the network. In this design the resource sends transport layer packets.

In the process RNI_OUT, T_Layer packets are attached with network layer information and sent out on the network. In the process RNI_IN the N_layer packets are unpacked to transport layer and sent to the resource.

The N_BUFFER_TYPE is used to handle the communication with the network router on the network layer or via the data-link layer. It is similar to the BUFFER_TYPE in the router except that it is of an own type for configuration options.

In the block D_LAYER there is one sub-block of the type D_IO_TYPE.

Resource. Because of the need to get good simulation results, the resources in the model should mimic the behavior of the real resources. There can be different kinds of resources in a real system, such as DSPs, general-purpose processors or memory. The block RESOURCE is a container of the type of resource that is connected.

For our simulation purposes a resource is a generator of packets. A resource is modelled by two concurrent processes, sender and receiver. The process Sender simulates the behavior of the resource. In this model the resource simulates the transport layer service, which results in that data is sent and received as transport layer packets. Between the RNI and the resource there is only a transport layer connection. Adding lower layers here will not give any benefit to evaluate the model. Because the resource and RNI sit in the same node there is no reason for implementing the network layer between these.

There is a possibility to choose between bursty and continuous base behavior. Bursty behavior means that a certain number of packets are put out with a maximum rate, called burst, and after that there is a delay called burst gap before the process repeats itself. The number of packets between the delays is selected around a mean according to the Poisson distribution.

The burst gap is calculated from a random delay that is uniformly distributed between a minimum and a maximum value. The length of the burst gap is weighted with the number of packets in the burst, which results in a longer burst gap if the number of packets to be sent is big.

The selection of addresses can be random within the limits of the network, and addresses situated next to the sender have double probability to be chosen because this is the most likely scenario for communication. With the continuous behavior it is possible to set the delay between two packets transmitted which gives the output frequency.

In the Receiver process the time of arrival of the packet is noted and the packet information is written to a file. It is now possible to compare the logged information from the receiver with other values. We can get a lot of information from these logs, for instance the number of packets sent/received, transfer time and many other interesting figures.

Data-Link Layer Block. The data-link layer deals with how the transfer of data between two micro-routers can be reliable. Data is grouped into frames that may consist of a header, payload and checksum. The D_IO_TYPE block type contains processes to perform the data-link layer services. The processes in this block will not be active during network layer simulation.

The process N_D_TYPE is consuming network layer data packets from the network layer, framing them with data link layer information and error check. After that it passes them to the data-link when the receiver is ready to receive. If there is an error introduced in the transmission there will be a retransmission of the failing message.

Process D_N_TYPE receives data-link layer data packets from the data link, unframes the data-link layer information and checks for errors. After that it passes them to the network layer. If there is an error in the transmission the packet will be trashed and a signal will be sent to the sender.

3.3 Design Tool

The programming tool that was available and used was Tau 4.3 from Telelogic [13]. This package contains an SDL suite that fully supports SDL-92 and partially SDL-96. The design has been done with the graphical notation of SDL. The tool automatically generates a C/C++ code equivalent to the SDL model behavior and the generated program can be used for discrete event simulation of the modelled system.

It is possible to include a Graphical User Interface (GUI) library during the design phase of the model. This library makes it possible to use a built-in GUI, where the systems execution could be viewed both in text and MSC diagrams. But simulation speed with this set up is very slow.

Another library, called the performance simulation library, helps to produce compact C/C++ code which runs much faster. With this library the produced executable code for the NoC model was approximately 400 Kbyte. A simulation run in this configuration took only a few minutes for simulation of NoC architecture for 10000 clocks. In this case the simulation results were recorded to a file and were analyzed and graphs were generated using Microsoft Excel.

4 NoC Evaluation Parameters

The parameters could be divided into three categories, namely, architectural parameters, application parameters and performance parameters.

4.1 Architectural Parameters

These parameters include the topology and size of the network. Packet buffer size used in every switch of the network will be an important parameter. It also includes various parameters used at various layers in the protocol stack used for communication. Important parameters in this category include the routing algorithm, packet priority scheme at network layer level and error control at data link layer level. Packet formats at various levels will also fall in this category.

4.2 Application Parameters

For the evaluation of the network, the relevant feature of an application can be modelled by the communication behavior of various resources running the application. The communication requirement of various resources will determine the traffic in the network. Therefore, the following parameters are useful for specifying traffic:

Rate of Packet Generation: The packet could be generated at random intervals or could be generated periodically. The packets generation could be bursty or have uniform time gaps.

Destination Address of Packets: The destination address of a packet originating from a resource may have a fixed set of destinations, random destination or may have bias towards neighboring resources.

4.3   Performance Parameters

As discussed earlier, the purpose of network evaluation could be for finding the best architecture for an application or a set of applications, or for checking the suitability of a specific on-chip network for an application. Therefore, the chosen performance parameters should help in the above task. The following are a set of generic parameters. There could be other parameters, which could be network specific or application specific.

Spread: This parameter measures the percentage of packets, which take a route longer that the shortest in the network.

Packet Delay: This refers to the time it takes for a packet to go from source to destination. Depending on the context, average packet delay or maximum packet delay may be important.

Packet Drop Probability: It defines the probability of a packet being lost in the network due to heavy traffic and limited buffer capacity in the switches. This could be due to defects/errors from various layers in the network.

The packet delay and drop probability will depend on the network load and buffer sizes in the switches. These will also depend on the routing algorithm and priority schemes used.

5   Simulation Experiments and Results

We have evaluated how the performance of the network is affected by different buffer configurations. Other factors that have an impact on network performance are the delays in the different components that packets will pass through.

The performance measures used are packet loss probability in terms of packet drops/100 packets and mean packet delay regarding all packets sent and received in the network. One thing that must be considered is what kind of traffic load should be offered to the network. The following parameters are varied for various simulation experiments.

Burstiness – Bursty traffic can be generated by specifying gaps between bursts, number of packets/burst and average packet rate.

Network Clock Speed – This changes the delays in the network components.

Network Load – This is controlled by changing the number of resources putting packets on the network.

For simulation purposes we used a 4*4 node network. This size is chosen because a smaller size will not test the routing thoroughly and a larger size would take too much time to simulate and analyze. For a SoC it also seems a size that could be realistic in a near future. After studying some simulations the following set-ups were used for experiments:

- A mixed set-up with one continuous and 15 bursty resources. The positions of the resources will be same for all simulations in order to make a fair comparison.
- Set up all sending resources as bursty.

We carried out a very large number of experiments. Below we describe a very small representative subset of these experiments.

5.1   Simulations with Equal Delay of Switch and Buffer

The following simulations were made with equal delay of the buffers and the switch. In this case the minimum period of the micro-router is 3 clock cycles. For example, if the network clock period is 0.5 ns, this results in a maximum bandwidth of $1/(3*0,5*10-9)=667$ Mpackets/s.

Simulations with 1 Continuous and 15 Bursty Resources. In this simulation experiment, 15 of the resources are set to bursty sources, and one to continuous behavior. Every bursty resource communicates with one other resource, and has a mean packet rate at 100 Mps (Mpackets/s), the burst rate is at 384 Mps. The resource that sends continuously communicates with six other resources. The communication rate is 64 Mps with each resource, the total communication from the continuous resource will then be 384 Mps. The mean distance that a packet travels is three switches, both for bursty and continuous resources.

When evaluating what happens to the sent packets we have divided the packets into three different categories, namely Transferred, Cancelled and Dropped.

Transferred packets are those that have been sent on time, that is when the resource wants to put it to the network, and reached their destination.

Cancelled packets are those that have not been sent on time because the buffers are full. These packets will be dropped by the transmitting resource.

Dropped packets are those that are sent on time but later got dropped by a micro-router because the required buffers are full.

The results show that a network that works with 0.5 time units per clock cycle gets no dropped packets and only a few cancelled packets. The network is so fast that the buffer configuration [in-buffer:out-buffer] has no or very little influence on the performance. Increasing the period to 0.8 time units, reveals that the single out-buffer configurations does not perform very well, as can be seen in Fig. 7.

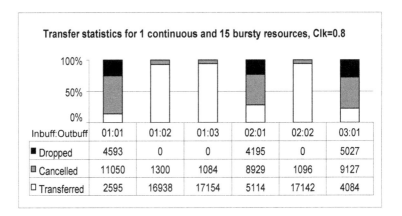

Fig. 7. Transfer Statistics for 1 Continuous and 15 Bursty

We experimented with different input buffer and output buffer sizes to see their effect on packet delay. The mean transfer time in Fig. 8 shows that the configuration with 02:02 (two input buffers and two output buffers) is slightly faster than 01:02 and 01:03 on networks working on 0.5-0.6 time units. When the period time is increased further, the configurations with one input buffer does not increase their mean transfer time as much as 02:02 does.

We wanted to know what lays behind the differences in performance of the different buffer configurations. This measurement we called spreading as shown in Fig. 9. It is defined as the percentage of packets in their optimal path compared to packets out of their optimal path.

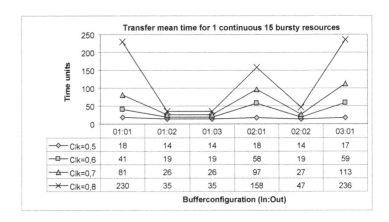

Fig. 8. Transfer Mean Time for 1 Continuous 15 Bursty Resources

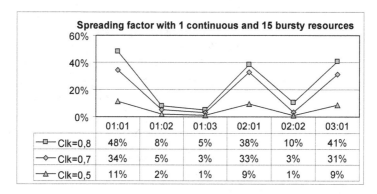

Fig. 9. Spreading Factor with 1 Continuous and 15 Bursty Resources

For example a 60% spreading shows that out of one hundred packet switchings, switches that reside out of the packets optimal path switch 60 of them. Switches that lay in the packets optimal path make 40 switchings. If a packet does not travel the shortest possible path the number of switchings will increase rapidly, and may cause drops if there is heavy traffic.

The buffer configuration 01:02 has a slightly higher spreading than 02:02 and 01:03 at a high frequency, that is when the network clock=(0.5;0.7). This can be explained by the fact that this configuration only has three buffers compared to four in the other two. The probability that all buffers are full is higher when there are fewer buffers, and the router then has to find an optional route.

When the network-clock is set to 0.8 the configuration 02:02 suddenly begins to spread the packets more than 01:02, which seems rather odd because more buffers should give better result in most situations. One reason for this could be that the router is now able to route the second packet in the input queue before there is any space in the desired output buffer, and this causes the router to send the packet into a non-optimal route.

Simulation with 16 Bursty Resources versus 14 Bursty Resources.
Simulation Set-up: Every bursty resource communicates with one other resource, and has a mean packet rate at 100 Mps (Mpackets/s), the burst rate is at 384 Mps. The average number of switches each has to go through is three.

When comparing the number of packets transferred in Fig. 10 we can once again see that the network that runs with a period of 0.5 time units is so fast that the buffers have a very small influence on the behavior of the network.

There are no drops and the numbers of cancelled packets are also very small using this configuration. When increasing the period time to 0.7 time we can see that the influence of the buffers starts to increase. The simulations made with more than one output buffer is significantly better than the ones with only one output buffer. The results from All Burst and clk=0.9 shows that the combination of two input- and two output-buffers falls back as the load increases.

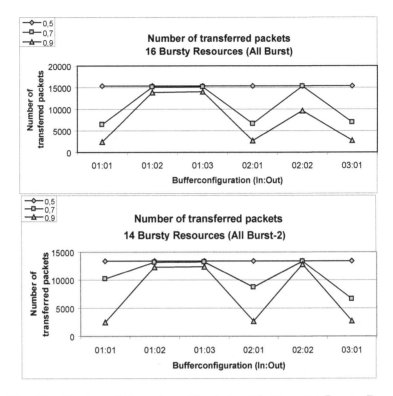

Fig. 10. The Number of Transferred Packets with 16 vs. 14 Bursty Resources

When looking at the mean transfer time it is observed that the results from all the configurations with one output buffer increase their transfer time much faster than the other configurations, see Fig. 11. The configurations with more than one output buffer have almost the same performance as long as the load is not too high. When the load gets higher the 02:02 set-up falls back and the set-ups 01:02 and 01:03 are by no doubt the fastest.

As mentioned earlier, we have done many other simulation experiments, for example with different degrees of burstiness and also unequal speed of switches and buffers. More results are given in [12].

6   Conclusions

Our experience in modelling a specific NoC architecture shows that SDL is well suited to make models and simulate complex electronic systems. The block type and process type features are very useful to describe structural and functional hierarchy; timers are useful for measuring time; user defined data types are useful for modelling protocols. The following conclusions can be drawn from the results of the simulation experiments that we have carried out.

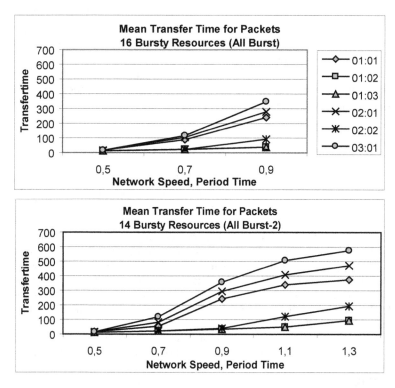

Fig. 11. Mean Transfer Time with 16 vs. 14 Bursty Resources

– The performance of the network improves with the size of the output buffer
  more than the input buffer. A buffer size configuration of 1:2 or 1:3 seems
  to provide good performance for most of traffic situations.
– It also seems that adding more input-buffers only makes the network performance worse.
– A longer burst-length does not benefit from larger buffers as compared to
  the shorter burst-length.

We have successfully carried the design process described in Figure 3 from an
SDL specification of NoC to a prototype implementation on an FPGA board [12].
We feel that it is quite easy to incorporate changes in our SDL model to model
other NoC architectures. After this study, one thing that seems important is to
include some special mechanisms for getting higher communication performance,
especially for hard real-time systems.

Some researchers have proposed that a mixed packet switched and circuit
switched network could be the solution for this [6]. A circuit switched network
makes it possible to transfer data very fast as soon as the data path has been
locked.

Another solution for increased real-time performance is to give packets in the NoC different priorities. Packets that are given high priority can overtake the packets with lower priority in the network. We are planning to extend our model to include application specific cores as resources.

We are quite sure that the NoC paradigm will soon become available as an important option for developing complex SoCs. Modelling and evaluation tools will need to be developed for this purpose.

References

[1] S. Kumar, A. Jantsch, J-P. Soininen, M. Forsell, M. Millberg, J. Öberg, K. Tiensyrjä, A. Hemani. A network on chip architecture and design methodology. Proceedings of IEEE Computer Society Annual Symposium on VLSI (April 2002) 166, 167

[2] S. Kumar. On Packet Switched Networks for On-Chip Commincation. Book chapter in a forthcoming book entitled Network on Chip (Editors Axel Jantsch and Hannu Tenhunen), Pulblishers Kluwer Publication (March 2003) 166

[3] E. Rijpkema, K. Goossens, P. Wielage. A Router Architecture for Networks on Silicon. Proceedings of Rogress, 2nd Workshop on Embedded Systems (2001) 166

[4] L. Benini, G. De Micheli. Networks on Chips: A New SoC Paradigm. IEEE Computer Society (2002) 166

[5] P. Wielage, K. Goosens. Networks on Silicon: Blessing or Nightmare?. Euromicro Symposium On Digital System Design (DSD 2002), Dortmund, Germany (Sep. 2002) 166

[6] D. Wiklund, D. Liu. SoCBUS: The solution of high communication bandwidth on chip and short TTM. Proc. of the Real-Time and Embedded Computing Conference, Gothenburg, Sweden (Sep. 2002) 166, 181

[7] Y. Sun, S. Kumar, A. Jantsch. Simulation and Evaluation for a network on chip architecture using NS-2. Proceedings 20th NORCHIP conference, Copenhagen (Nov. 2002) 167

[8] R. Thid. A Time Driven Network on Chip Simulator Implemented in C++. Master of Science Thesis, Laboratory of Electronic and Computer Systems, Royal Institute of Technology (KTH), Stockholm, Sweden (2002) 167

[9] G. N. Higginbottom. Performance Evaluation of Communication Networks. Artech House (1998) 168

[10] A. Olsen, O. Færgemand, B. Møller-Pedersen, R. Reed, J. R. W. Smith. System Engineering Using SDL-92. North-Holland (1994) 169

[11] J. Ellsberger, D. Hogrefe, A. Sarma. SDL Formal Object-oriented Language for Communicating Systems. Prentice Hall (1997) 169

[12] R. Holsmark, M. Högberg. Modelling and prototyping of a Network on Chip. Master of Science Thesis, Embedded Systems, Department of Electronics and Computer Engineering, School of Engineering, Jönköping University, Sweden (2002) 171, 180, 181

[13] "Telelogic Tau 4.3" Telelogic AB (2001) 175

Formalizing Graphical Service Descriptions Using SDL

Kenneth J. Turner

Computing Science and Mathematics, University of Stirling, Scotland FK9 4LA
kjt@cs.stir.ac.uk

Abstract. It is convenient to describe telecomms services using a graphical notation that is accessible to non-specialists. However, the notation should also have a formal interpretation for rigorous analysis. CRESS (Chisel Representation Employing Systematic Specification) has been developed for this purpose. A brief overview of CRESS is given. It is explained how features (additional services) can be defined in a modular fashion, and automatically combined with a base service. Brief case studies illustrate how the approach has been used to describe services in the IN (Intelligent Network), SIP (Session Initiation Protocol), and IVR (Interactive Voice Response). Finally, it is shown how CRESS diagrams are translated into SDL for automated simulation, validation and implementation.

1 Introduction

A telecomms service is a set of capabilities packaged and sold to end-users, while a telecomms feature is a self-contained aspect of a service. However, the terms 'service' and 'feature' tend to be used interchangeably. It is costly and time-consuming to develop a new telecomms service. It is therefore desirable to have a precise description of what is to be built. A critical lesson from telephony is that services often interfere with each other in unexpected and undesirable ways – so-called feature interaction [1].

A formal description can be used for automated analysis of service incompatibilities. However, both technical and non-technical people must cooperate in defining a service. A formal description is likely to be understood only by specially trained engineers. It is therefore desirable that service descriptions be meaningful to the non-specialist, such as a manager or a marketing person. The ideal service description should be graphical (accessible to non-technical staff), abstract (permitting a variety of implementations), and precise (automatically translated into a formal language)

The representation of services has been well investigated for traditional telephony and the IN (Intelligent Network). Feature interaction in these domains is also well researched. However the world of communications services has moved rapidly beyond these into new applications such as mobile communication, web services, Internet telephony, and interactive voice services.

R. Reed (Ed.): SDL 2003, LNCS 2708, pp. 183–202, 2003.

The author's approach to defining and analyzing services is a graphical notation called CRESS (Chisel Representation Employing Systematic Specification). CRESS is a significant extension of the original Chisel notation developed by BellCore [2]. The author was attracted by the simplicity, graphical form, and industrial orientation of Chisel. Although it has mainly been used in telecomms, CRESS is not tied to this. Indeed, CRESS supports plug-in application domains that define the vocabulary used to describe services. Applying CRESS to a new application mainly requires the definition of a new vocabulary for events, types and system variables.

CRESS is neutral with respect to the target language. It can, for example, be compiled into SDL (Specification and Description Language [3]) and LOTOS (Language Of Temporal Ordering Specification [4]). This gives formal meaning to services defined in CRESS, and allows rigorous analysis of services. The semantics of a CRESS diagram is thus defined by the target language. In principle, this risks inconsistency. In practice, CRESS diagrams are sufficiently simple that they can be given the same interpretation in different languages.

For direct implementation in certain domains, CRESS can also be compiled into SIP CPL (Call Processing Language), SIP CGI (Common Gateway Interface, realized in Perl) and VoiceXML. CRESS is thus a front-end for defining, analyzing and implementing services. It is not in itself an approach for detecting feature interactions.

This paper explains how SDL is used to support CRESS. The general approach is illustrated with examples taken from telephony with the IN (Intelligent Network [5]), Internet telephony with SIP (Session Initiation Protocol [6]), and IVR (Interactive Voice Response) using VoiceXML (Voice Extended Markup Language [7]).

Several graphical representations are used to describe communications services. SDL is the main formal language used in telecomms. Although it has a graphical form, SDL is a general-purpose language that was not especially designed to represent services. SDL service descriptions are not accessible to non-specialists as they tend to be low-level and rather technical. MSCs (Message Sequence Charts [8]) are higher-level and more straightforward in their representation of services. However neither SDL nor MSCs can readily describe the notions of feature and feature composition that are important in defining services. CRESS was designed to fill this gap.

Because CRESS can be translated to SDL, the same services could (of course) be described directly in SDL. This is not done for a variety of reasons:

- The CRESS diagrams are much more compact than their SDL equivalent. CRESS diagrams also require less technical knowledge than SDL. As shown by BellCore [2], even non-technical people can understand diagrams in the style of CRESS.
- CRESS service descriptions are more abstract than their equivalent in SDL. Although UML could be used, services do not usually lend themselves to an object-oriented treatment. (This is a reflection on typical services, not UML.)

- CRESS has explicit support for features and feature composition. Only approximations to these exist in UML or SDL. As a result, it would be necessary to re-invent the support – which CRESS provides natively.
- CRESS is *language-independent*. The same diagrams can be translated to different target languages. This is very powerful, because the same diagrams can then be used for different purposes. Consider, for example, an IVR service. This can be formulated in CRESS for discussion among technical and non-technical staff. It can then be translated into SDL, where reachability analysis and MSC-based validation are very convenient. It can also be translated into LOTOS, where model-checking, theorem-proving and test generation algorithms are available. Finally, it can be translated into VoiceXML for actual implementation.
- CRESS provides domain-specific frameworks. For example, the IN framework has built-in support for SCPs (Service Control Points), user profiles and billing. These would all need to be devised and specified using a plain SDL approach.

The paper aims to show that CRESS, supported by SDL, can be used with a variety of kinds of services. Section 2 provides a brief overview of the CRESS diagrammatic notation. It is not feasible to provide a tutorial on CRESS here, but more information can be found in [9, 10]. Sections 3, 4 and 5 show how CRESS can be applied to services in the IN, SIP and VoiceXML; some knowledge of these areas is assumed. Finally, Sect. 6 discusses how CRESS diagrams are turned into SDL and then analyzed.

2   The Cress Notation

This section gives a compact overview of the CRESS notation used in this paper. For concreteness, examples are taken from diagrams that appear later in the paper.

2.1   Diagram Elements

A CRESS diagram is a directed, possibly cyclic graph. Oval nodes contain events and their parameters (such as *StartRing A B*). Events may also occur in parallel ($\|\|$). Events may be signals (input or output messages) or actions (like programming language statements). An event may be followed by assignments optionally separated by '/'. A *NoEvent* (or empty) node, meaning no event occurs, can be useful as a connector. It may join a number of preceding and following nodes as a more compact way of linking all the nodes.

Nodes are identified by a number, which may be followed by a symbol to indicate the kind of node. For example, '<' denotes an input node, while '>' denotes an output node. A feature start node is marked '+' or '−', depending on whether it is appended or prefixed to the matching node that triggers it. Sometimes it is necessary to prevent a node from matching a feature template by appending '!' to its node number.

As an example of a node, the following appears in Fig. 6:

2> Ack Q P / P <− ForwardBusy P

This output node, numbered 2, sends a SIP acknowledgment from caller Q to callee P. The callee address P is then replaced by the one used for forwarding on busy. Parentheses are often omitted in CRESS if there is no ambiguity, so *Ack Q P* for example means *Ack(Q,P)* and *ForwardBusy P* means *ForwardBusy(P)*.

A directed arc between nodes links them in sequence. Branching is permitted if there is a choice of events. The arcs between nodes may be labeled by guards. These are either value expressions (imposing a condition on the behavior) or event triggers (that are activated by dynamic occurrence of a condition). Event triggers are distinguished by their names. Examples of guards appear in Figs. 2 and 8:

Free A B in the IN means that B is free for a call from A
Filled in VoiceXML triggers the behavior for correct user input.

A CRESS diagram can contain a rule box (a rounded rectangle) that defines things such as the diagram variables, parent diagrams, macros, and configuration information like subscriber profiles. Sample rule boxes appear in Figs. 2 and 3:

Uses Address *A,B* defines diagram variables A and B of type **Address**
Uses */ POTS* says the parent diagram is that for *POTS*
Off-hook P / Busy P <- **True** is triggered by signal *Off-hook* with parameter P; it notes the status of phone P as busy when it goes off-hook.

Ultimately, CRESS deals with a single diagram. However it is convenient to construct diagrams from smaller pieces. A multi-page diagram, for example, is linked through connectors. More usefully, features are defined in separate diagrams that are automatically included by either copy-and-paste or by triggering.

2.2   Services and Features

CRESS diagrams are interpreted in the context of a specification framework that defines a domain-specific infrastructure. For example, IN billing is handled by a separate subsystem that cooperates with call control. Similarly, call processing in the IN collaborates with an SCP (Service Control Point). It is therefore normal for CRESS to define a framework for each application domain. Such a framework is specified using the same target language as the one to which diagrams are compiled (for example, LOTOS, SDL, VoiceXML). Although the framework is specific to a domain and a target language, it is independent of the particular services or features deployed.

The framework includes macro calls that are handled by the CRESS preprocessor. For SDL, the macro call *Cress(Types)* generates **Signal**, **SignalList** and **Type** definitions appropriate to the application domain. This information is determined by the plug-in vocabulary. Feature diagrams are automatically combined with the root diagram by the macro call *Cress(Features)*. If there are several root diagrams, each root and its features are combined by a macro call such as *Cress(Features/Proxy)* for a SIP Proxy Server. Finally, the macro call *Cress(Profiles)* automatically generates configuration-specific details and the subscriber profiles. This information is defined by a special CRESS configuration diagram.

A main CRESS diagram defines the root (or basic) behavior. Although this may be the only diagram, CRESS also supports feature diagrams that modify the root diagram (or other features), augmenting basic behavior with new or modified capabilities.

A spliced (plug-in) feature adds to a root diagram by copy-and-paste. The feature indicates how it is linked into the original diagram by giving the insertion point and how it flows back into the root diagram. This may lead to nodes and guards being inserted, existing nodes and guard being replaced, and portions of the root diagram being deleted. This style of feature is appropriate for a one-off change to the original diagram.

A template (macro) feature is triggered by some event in the root diagram. The triggering event is given in the first node of the feature. Feature execution stops at a **Finish** (or empty) node. At this point, behavior resumes from the triggering node in the original diagram. A template feature is realized statically, instantiating it with the parameters of the triggering event. The instantiated feature may be appended or prefixed to the triggering node. As it is common for features to be triggered by the same event, feature activations may be chained. In such a situation, CRESS defines priorities for features to control their order of application. Some features are cyclic, for example call forwarding may yield a new address that is itself subject to call forwarding (see Fig. 6). A loop back to the beginning of a feature is treated as a return to the start of the feature chain.

Although CRESS is mainly concerned with user services, it also supports ancillary aspects such as subscriber profiles and billing (dependent on the application domain). Profiles define the services chosen by each subscriber. CRESS also has explicit support for billing features such as credit card calling and independent billing for each call leg.

2.3   Tool Support

The CRESS toolset has the form of a conventional compiler but is unusual in some respects. For portability it is written in Perl, comprising about 13,000 lines of code. Java would also have been a possibility, but Perl is just as portable and is very convenient for CRESS purposes. A traditional compiler deals with textual languages. However CRESS is a graphical language, and this creates interesting challenges such as compiling cyclic rather than hierarchical constructs.

The CRESS toolset consists of five main tools. Including test scenarios, there are about 600 supporting files for all domains and target languages. Internally the CRESS toolset comprises a preprocessor (that instantiates the specification framework), a lexical analyzer (that deals with various diagram formats), a parser (that performs syntactic analysis), and several code generators (including one for SDL). CRESS has been designed to work with a number of diagram formats. Currently, diagrams are drawn with the *Diagram!* tool that runs on five different platforms. However a platform-independent diagram editor is currently being implemented using the open-source *jGraphPad*.

CRESS supports the IN, SIP and VoiceXML domains. For formal analysis, SDL and LOTOS are the target languages. For SIP, the primary target language is a specialized use of Perl for CGI scripts. Preliminary work has been undertaken on compiling into SIP CPL, but this is possible for only very limited forms of feature diagram. For interactive voice services, VoiceXML is the obvious target language for implementation.

The CRESS user draws root and feature diagrams using an appropriate graphical editor. A single button-click retrieves all the diagrams, combines them with the appropriate specification framework, and translates them to SDL. Validation and verification may use any standard SDL mechanism such as reachability analysis. However it is often most convenient to use MSC validation. Each feature is characterized by a set of use-case scenarios expressed as MSCs. These may be created manually, or may be derived from simulation of the feature. Validating a feature then means validating these MSCs. Features can be validated in isolation. This is useful to gain confidence in the feature description. More usefully, features can be validated in combination – the most complete test being when all features are deployed simultaneously.

In fact, the CRESS design procedure already eliminates a number of feature interactions. For example, CRESS requires the specifier to prioritize features so that they are applied in an appropriate order. A common interpretation of feature interaction is that a feature operates correctly on its own but not in combination with other features. Feature interaction shows up as failure to validate an MSC. Once characteristic MSCs have been defined, the validation process is completely automated. This is particularly valuable when new features are added to a system. The existing MSCs can be used as regression tests to check that existing features still behave correctly.

3   Case Study: IN Services

The IN (Intelligent Network [5]) defines an architecture for flexible support of services in telephony. A key contribution is the separation of call switching in SSPs (Service Switching points) from service handling in SCPs (Service Control Points). The IN has been used to implement a wide variety of services such as various forms of billing (e.g. as split charging), busy handling (e.g. call waiting), call forwarding (e.g. on no answer), call screening (e.g. on caller identification), and conferencing (e.g. three-way calls).

The goals of using CRESS with the IN are:

– to define features in a comprehensible way
– to allow features to be validated in isolation
– to validate features in combination, checking for feature interactions.

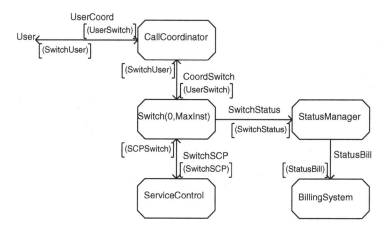

Fig. 1. CRESS SDL Structure for the IN

The CRESS specification framework for the IN occupies 15 pages of SDL/GR, so only the top level can be given here; more detail can be found in [9]. The main block structure is shown in Fig. 1. Telephone users communicate with the network via the *User* channel. This allows users to send signals such as *Off-hook*, *Dial* and *On-hook*. The network can send the user signals such as *DialTone*, *Disconnect* and *StartRinging*. The internal structure of the network is hidden from the users. It comprises the following processes whose behavior is fixed, except for that of *Switch*:

Switch is multiply instantiated up to the concurrent call limit *MaxInst*. It describes the operation of a switch (SSP) provisioned with features. The switch behavior is that of the POTS root service defined in CRESS, modified by the features described in separate CRESS diagrams.

CallCoordinator is responsible for linking users and their calls. For example if a user goes off-hook, it is necessary to create an instance of the *Switch* process and send it the *Off-hook* signal. The *CallCoordinator* process therefore acts as a distributor of user signals.

StatusManager maintains the status and profiles of all users. The dynamic status (whether busy or the number of the last caller) of each user is maintained. The profiles define the user's telephone number, which features have been selected, and the parameters of these features (such as a forwarding address). Subscriber profiles are provided by the CRESS configuration diagram.

BillingSystem logs all billing information. Because SDL does not directly support external files, this process merely absorbs the raw billing data (caller and callee, paying party, start and finish times of call). However this information can be used in (say) simulation or validation output.

ServiceControl describes the operation of an SCP. It provides the support expected of an IN SCP. It also retrieves user statuses and profiles from the *StatusManager*.

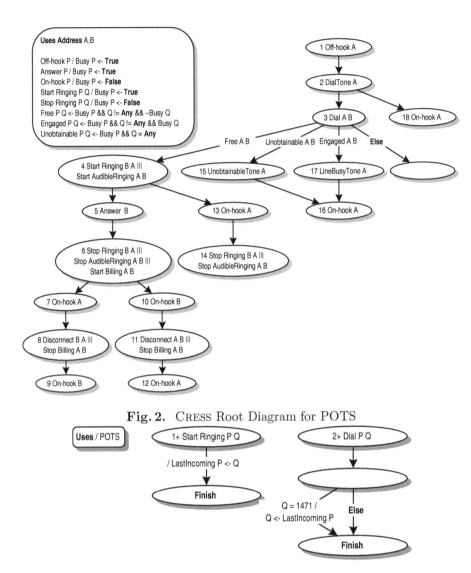

Fig. 2. CRESS Root Diagram for POTS

Fig. 3. CRESS Feature Diagram for Return Call

Figure 2 shows the CRESS root diagram for POTS. This (plus features) is used to generate the body of the *Switch* process in Fig. 1. The IN model deals with complete (caller plus callee behavior) calls, and not just one side of a call. CRESS diagrams have also been created for 11 typical IN features, based on descriptions in the first feature interaction contest [11]. Most features are switch-based, but those designated as IN features make use of SCP capabilities. The features occupy about 10 pages of CRESS diagrams, and include billing, busy handling, call forwarding, call screening and conferencing. As a sample feature,

Fig. 3 shows the template for Return Call. This is triggered when a phone starts ringing, storing the caller's number. It is also triggered by dialing. If the dialed number is 1471 (the UK code for Caller Return), it is replaced by the last caller.

The features are combined with POTS and the IN specification framework to yield about 2500 lines of SDL/PR. Depending on complexity, each feature has between 2 and 23 MSCs as use-case scenarios. The CRESS validation demonstrates well-known interactions among typical features. For example, Call Forwarding may interact with Call Screening: a caller may be forwarded to an undesirable number. Call Forwarding also interact with itself by causing a forwarding loop. However, CRESS is most valuable when analyzing novel features for compatibility with existing ones.

4   Case Study: SIP Services

SIP (Session Initiation Protocol [6]) is an Internet standard for controlling sessions. In the context of Internet telephony, SIP is used to control voice calls. However SIP is a general-purpose protocol that can be used to establish multimedia sessions such as video-conferences. SIP has also been adopted for use in call control for 3G (third generation mobile communication).

The goals of using CRESS with SIP include those for the IN. However SIP services are not yet so well understood, and SIP can support new kinds of services. Additional goals are therefore:

- to clarify what SIP services mean, and where they can be deployed
- to provide an architecture for defining SIP services
- to define a base of 'typical' SIP services.

SIP services can be deployed in three places: User Agents (which support the user interface to SIP), Proxy Servers (which relay and may manipulate requests), and Redirect Servers (which indicate how calls should be redirected to reach a user). As a consequence, the CRESS model of services exposes all three elements. Unlike the IN, CRESS has to define models for SIP of half-calls (the behavior of the caller or callee in isolation). For familiarity, service primitives follow telephony terminology. Thus a user is said to go *Off-hook* or *On-hook*, even though an actual phone may not be in use.

Ideally, SIP services would be described without internal protocol details. However SIP services are closely related to the protocol. CRESS is therefore obliged to include some aspects of this when describing features. This is not entirely desirable because it is then necessary to give the mapping between user actions and protocol actions. A reasonable compromise has been reached by mapping to an abstract view of SIP. This high-level interface is easily mapped onto the actual protocol.

The SIP specification framework resembles that for the IN. As it occupies 22 pages of SDL/GR, only the top level can be given here; more detail can be found in [10]. The main block structure is shown in Fig. 4. Internet telephony users communicate with the network via the *User* channel. The internal structure of

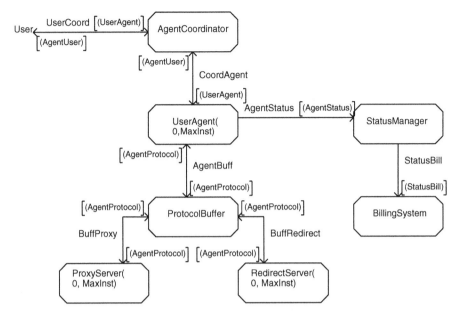

Fig. 4. CRESS SDL Structure for SIP

the network comprises the following processes. In the SIP framework the *UserAgent*, *ProxyServer* and *RedirectServer* processes are all generated automatically; the other processes are fixed.

UserAgent consists of multiple instances up to the concurrent session limit *MaxInst*. The relevant CRESS diagrams define the root behavior and features of a User Agent. It uses the abstract SIP interface to communicate with a *ProxyServer* or *RedirectServer* via the *ProtocolBuffer*.

ProxyServer consists of multiple instances up to the *MaxInst* limit. The relevant CRESS diagrams define the root behavior and features of a Proxy Server.

RedirectServer consists of multiple instances up to the *MaxInst* limit. The relevant CRESS diagrams define the root behavior and features of a Redirect Server.

AgentCoordinator creates *UserAgent* instances and distributes user signals – much as the IN *CallCoordinator* does.

ProtocolBuffer distributes User Agent signals to Servers, and vice versa. It also creates instances of *ProxyServer* and *RedirectServer* as required. A Redirect Server is used if the called User Agent has call forwarding, otherwise a Proxy Server.

StatusManager maintains the status and profiles of all users (like its IN equivalent).

BillingSystem logs all billing information (like its IN equivalent).

Figure 5 is the CRESS root diagram for a Redirect Server. A sample feature appears in Fig. 6. This is triggered when a SIP response message *M* from callee

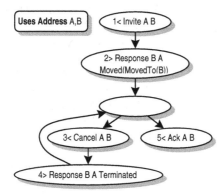

Fig. 5. CRESS Root Diagram for SIP Redirect Server

P to caller Q is received by a Proxy Server. If the response is 'Busy Here', it is checked whether P has a forwarding address. If so an acknowledgment is sent from Q to P, and a fresh Invite is sent to the forwarding address of P. The new response message $M3$ is also subject to a forward-on-busy check.

The kinds of SIP features described using CRESS are a subset of those for the IN. This is partly because SCP-based features are, of course, irrelevant for SIP: there are no centralized services. Because features may be deployed in three places (User Agent, Proxy Server, Redirect Server), there are variants of each feature. For example, call forwarding differs according to where it is deployed. Many IN features focus on handling busy conditions. In fact a SIP user may never be busy because there is no single telephone line/instrument that becomes

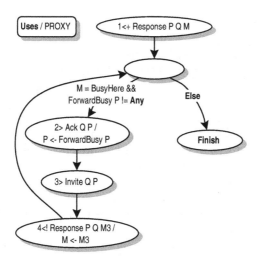

Fig. 6. CRESS Feature Diagram for Proxy Server Call Forwarding on Busy Line

occupied. For this reason, the notion of 'busy' is *defined* in CRESS. It may simply be as in the IN, only one call at a time is permitted. However it may be defined in a more complex manner to depend on the time of day, the caller, and the subject of the call.

As for the IN, root and feature diagrams for SIP are automatically combined and validated. A difference is that there are separate diagrams for User Agents, Proxy Servers and Redirect Servers. SIP features are characterized by MSCs and validated in the same way as for the IN. When standard IN features such as call forwarding and call screening are reformulated for SIP, similar kinds of interactions are discovered. However, SIP lends itself to new kinds of features not found in the IN [12]. CRESS is useful to investigate new interactions arising from these.

5   Case Study: VoiceXML Services

VoiceXML (Voice Extended Markup Language [7]) draws on earlier scripting languages for interactive voice services. The underlying model of VoiceXML is that the user completes fields in forms (or menus) by speaking in response to prompts. Each field is associated with a variable that is set to the user's input. Some actions may be governed by a condition or a count that specifies when the action is permitted. A script may throw an event, aborting current behavior and activating a matching event handler.

The goals of CRESS for IVR (Interactive Voice Response) services differ somewhat from use with the IN or SIP:

– to explore the concepts of feature and feature interaction in an IVR setting
– to represent and analyze a range of generic and application-specific features
– to automate discovery of flaws in IVR applications.

VoiceXML is a large language embedded in an even larger framework. For example, VoiceXML includes support for EcmaScript (JavaScript). It also supports complex grammars for speech recognition and markup for speech synthesis. VoiceXML is integrated with other technologies such as databases and web servers. It is not feasible to represent the entirety of such voice-based services. Instead, CRESS concentrates on the essential aspects of VoiceXML control. In the main, this means that a number of additional parameters may be given in a CRESS diagram at the end of an action. They are copied literally when CRESS is converted to VoiceXML, but are ignored for translation to other target languages.

VoiceXML applications are often written as a number of documents containing a number of forms. However a VoiceXML application can be considered as a single document with a single form, and this is how it is ultimately represented in CRESS. The fields of a form can be mimicked as separate sections or pages of a CRESS diagram, using connectors to join them. However, fields are deliberately not prominent in CRESS and are instead introduced implicitly.

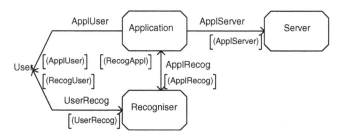

Fig. 7. CRESS SDL Structure for VoiceXML

The VoiceXML specification framework is much simpler than for the IN or SIP. The top-level structure is shown in Fig. 7. Telephone users communicate with the system via the *User* channel. Prompts and audio are 'spoken' to user, who 'speaks' in response. When using SDL, the goal is analysis and simulation so voice messages are represented by character strings. When using VoiceXML, voice messages indeed use audio.

Application is the main VoiceXML behavior, created from the CRESS root and feature diagrams. The application may output **Audio** messages to the user. When a VoiceXML field needs to be filled in, the application sends information to the *Recognizer*: the required prompt and the grammar defining a valid response. The application may also submit information to the *Server*. The application may receive events from itself (**Throw**) or from the Recognizer. It therefore contains event dispatcher code that is generated statically from the service description.

Recognizer deals with the completion of fields. It issues a prompt and awaits a user response. This is checked according to the grammar, causing an application event like **Filled** (valid response), **NoMatch** (invalid response) or **NoInput** (input timeout).

Server represents a server supporting web and database access. Often the server just "absorbs" the results: that is, it writes them to a database. However, the server may return VoiceXML created on-the-fly. This cannot be handled except when VoiceXML is the target language. For SDL, CRESS handles the commonest cases of server scripts that produce no result (**Submit**), and scripts that compute some results (**Subdialogue**). Limited support is provided for the latter using a web adaptor written in C that links to the generated SDL.

IVR is quite different from the IN and SIP in having no unique root service. Rather, this depends entirely on the particular application. As a concrete example, Fig. 8 shows a quarry ordering application. It allows users to place telephone orders for a product (sand, gravel, cement) and the required weight. This information is then submitted for further processing to *order.jsp*, a Java servlet in the server. If the user requests help or says nothing, an explanation is given and the user is re-prompted.

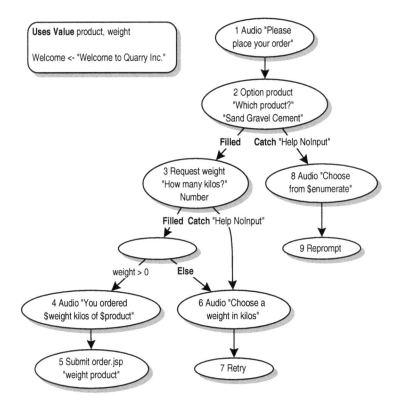

Fig. 8. CRESS Root Diagram for Quarry Ordering Application

VoiceXML was not defined with features in mind, though subdialogues act in a roughly similar manner. CRESS has been used to introduce a feature concept to VoiceXML. Generic CRESS features can be defined for use in a number of VoiceXML applications. Examples include defining VoiceXML behavior (such as timeouts), asking for positive confirmation of an action (such as charging an account), and collecting customer identification (for an order). CRESS can also be used to define application-specific features. For example, a common 'welcome' feature has been defined for all quarry applications (ordering, checking delivery status, etc.).

Feature diagrams are combined with the root diagram for the basic application (the quarry ordering). VoiceXML is not as prone to feature interaction as the IN or SIP. Nonetheless, the CRESS approach allows interactions to be discovered in the same way. Perhaps more importantly, CRESS allows other kinds of service flaws to be identified through simulation. For example VoiceXML services may unintentionally loop, or there may be part of an application that it is not possible to execute. CRESS allows such problems to be discovered through reachability analysis of the generated SDL.

6   Supporting Cress with SDL

This section gives an overview of how CRESS diagrams are translated into SDL. The translation strategy is designed for generality, even though a manual translation could be more straightforward in some cases. However the benefits of automated translation outweigh the occasionally indirect approach. CRESS is currently targeted at SDL 96 as this assures the widest tool support; small changes are required for SDL 2000.

6.1   Cress Expressions

CRESS types are defined by the domain vocabulary. In the IN for example, they are **Address** (phone number), **Boolean, Message** (service announcement) and **Time. Boolean** and **Time** translate to the same types in SDL. **Address** translates to a digit string (including '#' and '*'), while **Message** translates to a set of literals such as *EnterPIN*.

CRESS supports temporary variables, diagram variables and status variables. Temporary variables are declared for each type; for example $M0$ to $M9$ are available for message values. Variables may also be explicitly declared for use in a diagram: for example, Fig. 8 declares *product* and *weight*. Temporary variables and diagram variables translate into ordinary SDL variables belonging to the corresponding process. Such variables are used directly in an expression, and are assigned in an SDL **Task**.

Status variables are used to hold global information about a user, such as dynamic status or profile information. For example, SIP status includes whether the user is busy and the address of the user paying for the call. SIP profile information includes the user's forwarding number and the PIN used for charging a call to the user's account. Status variables are owned by a separate *StatusManager* process in the specification framework. They are **Revealed** by this process, and read elsewhere using **View**.[1] Status variables are arrays of values with the same index and result types. For example, *StatusAB* is indexed by user address (A) to yield a boolean (B) result. Status is accessed by giving the variable name and indexes. For example, the CRESS expression *Busy A* is translated into the SDL expression **View(StatusAB)((. Busy,A .))**. Updating a status variable requires a signal to be sent to the status manager. This gives the variable name, indexes and new value. The CRESS assignment *Busy A <- **True***, for example, is translated into **Output** *UpdateAB(Busy,A,True)*.

Expressions are otherwise translated in a straight forward way into SDL. Most CRESS operators have direct equivalents in SDL. A few (such as *After*, which removes a prefix from a string) are defined in the specification framework. The generic value **Any** is translated to a special value of the corresponding SDL type (such as *AnyAddress*). **Time** in CRESS means the current time, and corresponds to **Now** in SDL.

---

[1] This is the only case that code generation differs for SDL 2000, which requires status variables to be read by a remote procedure call.

6.2 Signals

A CRESS event node may contain parallel signals and also assignments. Although the CRESS translator has an option to deal with parallelism, for SDL this would have to explicitly unfold concurrency. (Sub-states in SDL 2000 might be an alternative.) The complex translation would hardly be worthwhile compared to the small increase in expressiveness. Concurrent inputs would also be very awkward to handle. Parallel signals as therefore translated as consecutive signals.

Assignments may be explicit in event nodes, or may be implied by the rules given in a rule box. For example in the IN, whenever phone P goes on-hook then the assignment *Busy P <- **False*** is implied (see the rule box in Fig. 2). Event assignments are handled like ordinary assignments.

Output events are reasonably straightforward. For example in node 2 of Fig. 2, the CRESS event *DialTone A* is translated as the SDL signal ***Output** DialTone(A)*. A complication arises because CRESS diagrams may contain cycles. Because another node may loop back to the one containing an output, each output is preceded by a label constructed from the diagram name and node number. For node 2 in Fig. 2, the label is *POTS.2*. A loop back to this would then be translated as ***Join** POTS.2*. Sometimes CRESS has to generate two labels for the same SDL statement. This is unfortunately not allowed by SDL syntax, so the labels are separated by a dummy statement ***Task** "*.

Input events can be awkward to translate. In a simple case such as node 5 of Fig. 2, the CRESS event *Answer B* is translated into the SDL ***Input** Answer(B)*. Because inputs must occur only at the start of a new state, this input is preceded with ***State** POTS.5*. If there are alternative inputs (see nodes 7 and 10 of Fig. 2), one is used to label the new state but the transitions are individually labeled.

A CRESS diagram may also loop back to an input. The transition that follows this input is therefore labeled with *POTS.5*. A loop back to this must be translated as a repeated ***Input*** and then ***Join** POTS.5*. It might seem that this could simply be translated as ***NextState** POTS.5*. Unfortunately this does not work in general because loops are to individual inputs in a state. It is therefore necessary to branch to these inputs.

CRESS parameters like A and B are fixed when they are first input. However, SDL is prepared to input a completely different value. The CRESS translator therefore has an option to check if the parameter input is the same as the value expected. This is achieved by performing a data flow analysis of the CRESS diagram. If an input parameter is already fixed, an error occurs (***Stop***) if the actual parameter differs.

CRESS permits alternative branches to input the same signal. For example, nodes 7 and 10 of Fig. 2 both refer to *On-hook*. SDL does not permit alternative inputs to carry the same signal. The CRESS translator must therefore look at all alternative inputs and group those with the same signal. A single SDL ***Input*** then reads this signal. The signal parameter is checked, and the appropriate branch is taken (for A or B in this example).

The CRESS parser optimizes diagrams before they are passed to a code generator. For example ***NoEvent*** nodes are removed where possible, and ***Else*** branches are moved to the end of the guard list. However it is not possible to remove a **NoEvent** node if it appears in loop (see Fig. 5). In such a case the **NoEvent** does not translate to any SDL, but the loop results in the same input being reached by different routes. A more complex state name must therefore be used. For example when node 5 is entered from node 4 in Fig. 5, the state label is *REDIRECT.5.REDIRECT.4*.

6.3   Actions and Guards

Application domains such as the IN and SIP require only inputs and outputs. However VoiceXML requires actions such as **Clear** (clear form fields) or **Throw** (cause an event). These do not input or output and so are classed as actions. Actions are domain-specific, so their translation into SDL is also domain-specific. A **Clear** translates into a **Task** that sets field variables to undefined (initial) values. A **Throw** transfers control to the event dispatcher code. As for output, an action is preceded by a label in case some other part of a diagram loops back to it.

Expression guards are straightforward to translate. For example, *Free A B* in Fig. 2 translates to a **Decision** in SDL. As noted earlier, *Free* is macro-expanded to a check of *Busy*. Because this is a status variable, it is accessed using **View**. An **Else** guard as in Fig. 2 corresponds to the *False* branch of a **Decision** in SDL.

An event guard is translated into an SDL **Input** of the corresponding signal. In VoiceXML, for example, this signal may come from the *Recognizer* process following the parsing of user input. An event guard may also be activated by a **Throw** within the application itself. A complication in VoiceXML is that event guards may be written at several levels: application, document, form and field. An event is handled at the closest enclosing level. In addition, events may have a hierarchical structure. Suppose that the quarry ordering application throws the *quarry.order.stock* event. If there is no event handler for this specific event, it may be caught by a handler for *quarry.order* or (failing that) *quarry* events. The CRESS translator manages this by maintaining the hierarchy of event handlers that apply at each level. (The hierarchy can be statically determined.) Events are interpreted by the event dispatcher according to the context, and may invoke platform, form or field handlers.

6.4   Sample Translation

Now that the basis of the SDL translation has been explained, it will be instructive to see what the generated code looks like. The following is the code created for Fig. 5. CRESS produces extensive comments that link the SDL back to the original diagrams. This is important because any flaw discovered in the SDL (such as an unreachable state) needs to be readily related to the original CRESS.

As mentioned earlier, state *REDIRECT.5.REDIRECT.4* is introduced because node 5 may be entered from node 4 via the empty node. As it happens, all the following inputs are available due to this loop. In this particular case,

NextState REDIRECT.5 could be the translation. But as explained previously, this is not always appropriate because only some inputs in a state may be repeated. The more indirect, but more general, solution is to handle the repeated *Input* signals and then *Join* the corresponding transitions.

```
Dcl A, A_0, B, B_0 Address;                                    /* call parameters */
Dcl A0, A1, A2, A3, A4, A5, A6, A7, A8, A9 Address;      /* temporary addresses */
Dcl M0, M1, M2, M3, M4, M5, M6, M7, M8, M9 Message; /* temporary messages */
Dcl T0, T1, T2, T3, T4, T5, T6, T7, T8, T9 Time;           /* temporary times */

Start;                                                   /* start call instance */
  NextState REDIRECT.1;                                     /* for next input */

State REDIRECT.1;                                            /* ready for input */
  Input Invite(A,B);                                    /* REDIRECT input 1 */
    REDIRECT.1:
    Task ";                                        /* dummy label separator */
    REDIRECT.2:                                       /* REDIRECT output 2 */
    Output Response(B,A,Moved(View(StatusAA)((. MovedTo,B .))));
    NextState REDIRECT.5;                                  /* for next input */

State REDIRECT.5;                                            /* ready for input */
  Input Ack(A,B);                                       /* REDIRECT input 5 */
    REDIRECT.5:
    Stop;                                               /* end of behavior */
  Input Cancel(A,B);                                    /* REDIRECT input 3 */
    REDIRECT.3:
    Task ";                                        /* dummy label separator */
    REDIRECT.4:                                       /* REDIRECT output 4 */
    Output Response(B,A,Terminated);
    NextState REDIRECT.5.REDIRECT.4;                      /* for next input */

State REDIRECT.5.REDIRECT.4;                                 /* ready for input */
  Input Ack(A,B);                                   /* REDIRECT input 5 (again) */
    Join REDIRECT.5;
  Input Cancel(A,B);                                /* REDIRECT input 3 (again) */
    Join REDIRECT.3;
```

7   Conclusion

The CRESS notation has been briefly presented. CRESS offers the following benefits:

- CRESS applies to a variety of domains using plug-in vocabularies. The application of CRESS to IN, SIP and IVR have been briefly overviewed in this paper. Although these are all examples of voice services, the approach is generic and should be relevant to non-voice applications such as web services. For example, it is hoped in future to apply CRESS to services for WSDL (Web

Service Description Language). It is advantageous to have a single notation that can be used in a number of domains.

- CRESS is graphical, therefore it is more accessible to non-specialists. The diagrams are also more compact than their translations into various languages.
- CRESS is language-independent. So the same diagrams can be used for verification, validation and implementation. CRESS can be translated into formal languages for rigorous analysis, as well as into programming languages for realization of services.
- CRESS explicitly supports features and feature composition. CRESS also provides domain-specific frameworks: for example, user profiles and billing. All these aspects would have to be re-specified if just a standard language were used.
- The CRESS tools are portable, and can be deployed on a variety of systems. CRESS can therefore be regarded as a platform-independent service creation toolset.

Although CRESS can be used in domains where features are not applicable, the most benefit is gained if this applies. CRESS should therefore be considered where a system can be thought of as having basic functionality plus additional features. CRESS has a simple notion of time as a monotonically increasing value. Any more realistic notion of time would require a target language with a concept of real time. CRESS therefore does not have explicit support for real-time systems.

CRESS itself is mainly a front-end for describing services. It is deliberately decoupled from analytic techniques. CRESS can therefore be used with any available technique, whether formal or informal. When used with SDL, reachability analysis and MSC validation are the most obvious techniques. But other techniques such as model-checking and theorem-proving are possible – limited only by the target language and its tool support.

References

[1] E. J. Cameron, N. D. Griffeth, Y.-J. Lin, M. E. Nilson, W. K. Schnure, and H. Velthuijsen. A feature-interaction benchmark for IN and beyond. IEEE Communications Magazine, pages 64–69, Mar. 1993. 183

[2] A. V. Aho, S. Gallagher, N. D. Griffeth, C. R. Schell, and D. F. Swayne. SCF3/Sculptor with Chisel: Requirements engineering for communications services. *Proc. 5th. Feature Interactions in Telecommunications and Software Systems*, pages 45–63. IOS Press, Amsterdam, Netherlands, Sept. 1998. 184

[3] ITU. Specification and Description Language. ITU-T Z.100. International Telecommunications Union, Geneva, Switzerland, 2000. 184

[4] ISO/IEC. Information Processing Systems – Open Systems Interconnection – *LOTOS* – A Formal Description Technique based on the Temporal Ordering of Observational Behavior. ISO/IEC 8807. International Organization for Standardization, Geneva, Switzerland, 1989. 184

[5] ITU. Intelligent Network – Q.120x Series Intelligent Network Recommendation Structure. ITU-T Q.1200 Series. International Telecommunications Union, Geneva, Switzerland, 1993. 184, 188

[6] J. Rosenberg, H. Schulzrinne, G. Camarillo, A. Johnson, J. Peterson, R. Sparks, M. Handley, and E. Schooler, editors. SIP: Session Initiation Protocol. RFC 3261. The Internet Society, New York, USA, June 2002. 184, 191

[7] V. Forum. Voice eXtensible Markup Language. VoiceXML Version 1.0. VoiceXML Forum, Mar. 2000. 184, 194

[8] ITU. Message Sequence Chart (MSC). ITU-T Z.120. International Telecommunications Union, Geneva, Switzerland, 2000. 184

[9] K. J. Turner. Formalizing the CHISEL feature notation. Proc. 6th. Feature Interactions in Telecommunications and Software Systems, pages 241–256, Amsterdam, Netherlands, May 2000. IOS Press. 185, 189

[10] K. J. Turner. Modelling SIP services using CRESS. In D. A. Peled and M. Y. Vardi, editors, Proc. Formal Techniques for Networked and Distributed Systems (FORTE XV), number 2529 in Lecture Notes in Computer Science, pages 162–177. Springer-Verlag, Berlin, Germany, Nov. 2002. 185, 191

[11] N. D. Griffeth, R. B. Blumenthal, J.-C. Gregoire, and T. Ohta. Feature interaction detection contest. Proc. 5th. Feature Interactions in Telecommunications and Software Systems, pages 327–359. IOS Press, Amsterdam, Netherlands, Sept. 1998. 190

[12] J. Lennox and H. Schulzrinne. Feature interaction in internet telephony. Proc. 6th. Feature Interactions in Telecommunications and Software Systems, pages 38–50, Amsterdam, Netherlands, May 2000. IOS Press. 194

Specification and Simulation of Real Time Concurrent Systems Using Standard SDL Tools

Giacomo Bucci, Andrea Fedeli, and Enrico Vicario

Dipartimento Sistemi e Informatica, Università di Firenze, Italy
{bucci,fedeli,vicario}@dsi.unifi.it

Abstract. The Specification and Description Language (SDL) and its supporting CASE tools have a major potential for the development of real-time systems. Unfortunately, SDL does not capture either duration properties of computations or policies of pre-emptive scheduling which are commonly employed to coordinate the execution of multiple concurrent tasks. We propose an extension of SDL expressivity which can capture both the aspects through annotations in the body of comments of a standard SDL model. The annotated model, that we call *modeling view* can be automatically translated into a *simulation view*, still expressed in standard SDL, which can be composed with an SDL model of the real-time microkernel that is supposed to be employed in the target environment. Simulation of the composed model through any SDL tool reproduces a behavior which is compliant with timing and resource constraints expressed in the comments of the initial modeling view. This permits specification, documentation, and simulation of real time systems to be kept within the limits of standardized SDL capabilities.

1 Introduction

SDL (Specification and Description Language) was originally conceived and standardized as a formal language to specify and validate protocols and telecommunication systems [1]. In the course of the years, usage of SDL has spread into a variety of different application contexts, due to a number of good reasons including the rigorous formalism coupled with a graphical and intuitive notation, and the availability of mature industrial tools supporting development throughout the different phases of the software lifecycle [2, 3].

In particular, usage of SDL has often been advocated in the context of real-time systems. In fact, language characteristics, such as the neat structuring scheme, the concept of communicating finite state machine (FSM), as well as object orientation, permit easy modeling of relevant aspects addressed in the design of real-time systems. However, in this context, SDL shows some major limitations in capturing common design schema of real time systems. The support of time in the language does not include the association of actions in a state transition with a predicted duration, which would possibly need to be delimited within a minimum and a maximum time. In fact, SDL makes no assumption on time progress: actions take an indeterminate time to execute, and a process may

R. Reed (Ed.): SDL 2003, LNCS 2708, pp. 203–217, 2003.

stay an indeterminate amount of time in a given state before taking the next transition [4]. Moreover, SDL assumes an "infinite resource" execution model which does not account for execution suspensions due to pre-emptive scheduling in the case of concurrent execution. Both aspects play a major role in determining sequencing and timing correctness in practice for real-time systems [5].

A lot of work has been done to overcome both limitations [6]. On the one hand, the timing semantics of the language can be extended, either through new constructs and new data structures [7], or through annotations expressed in the body of comments [4, 8, 9, 10]. In [4] and [8], a timed extension is proposed which adds *urgencies* to the semantics of SDL, so as to handle deadlines and time flow in the style of timed automata [11]. In [9] and [10], timing constraints are expressed as annotations in comment symbols and then used to translate the model into a different formalism, such as a timed automaton or a Time Petri Net [12, 13, 14].

On the other hand, extensions have been proposed include in the model the representation of pre-emptable resources: primarily the CPU in the case of a single processor applications. In [15] and [16], an annotation language is proposed which permits the definition of timing constraints and resource requirements in comments to capture both timing and concurrency aspects. In [17] and [18], the execution model is extended and implemented within non-standard simulation engines, which can reproduce the behavior of a timed model under a pre-emptive scheduling policy. In [19], an analysis of schedulability using earliest deadline first is carried out on an SDL model automatically transformed into an analyzable task network.

A common trait, in all these extensions is that the intended semantics of the model cannot be directly interpreted by existing industrial tools, either in the simulation stage or in the automated code generation. This lowers the value of the SDL.

In this paper, we propose a approach which aims at reconciling the need for augmented expressivity in the language with the capability to simulate models within consolidated industrial tools. To this end, timing properties of the model are expressed in the body of comments, along with resource requirements, scheduling priorities, and release policies. This annotated model, that we call *modeling view*, represents complex tasking sets according to the way in which these are usually conceived in the practice of concurrent and real-time programming. This facilitates specification and documentation, and opens the way to automated code generation.

The modeling view can be automatically translated into a *simulation view*, still expressed in standard SDL, which can be composed with an SDL model of the real-time microkernel that will be employed in the target environment.

Simulation of the composed model is carried out through an industrial simulation tool [2]. Usually, industrial tools fire transitions as soon as they are enabled, without letting time progress, therefore simulation is not compromised by the time indeterminacy of SDL semantics. As a result, simulation of the composed model reproduces a behavior which is compliant with timing and resource constraints expressed in the comments of the initial modeling view.

The rest of the paper is organized as follows. Section 2 describes the characteristics of tasking sets addressed in the model and defines the modeling view. Section 3 explains the translation of the modeling view into a simulation view and describes the model of a microkernel implementing a scheduling by priority. Conclusions are drawn in Sect. 4.

2   Modeling Tasking Sets

We address the case of a tasking set comprised of a number of processes, each characterized by a task *release policy* and by a sequence of *computation steps*. The release policy can be: periodic; sporadic (task instances are released repetitively, in asynchronous manner, with a minimum interarrival time); or one-shot (only one instance of the task is released, within a predefined time interval). Computation steps are characterized by a minimum and maximum computation time and by a priority level in the access to the CPU. Furthermore, computation steps belonging to different tasks can synchronize on mutual exclusion semaphores and on exchanged messages. The minimum and maximum values for computation time are usually employed to specify a non-deterministic duration. In a different perspective, fitting the model of imprecise computations of [20], they can also be interpreted so as to specify a mandatory and an optional part of the computation [21].

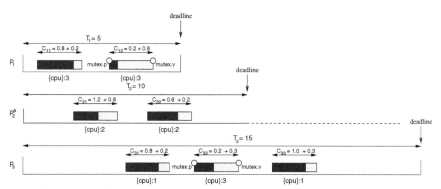

P_1 and P_3 are periodic with period 5 and 15 time units, respectively, while P_2^s is sporadic with minimum interarrival time of 10 time units. A mutual exclusion semaphore *mutex* rules access to a critical section for P_1 and P_3. Deadline is assumed equal to the period for processes P_1 and P_3 and equal to the minimum interarrival time for the sporadic process P_2^s.

Fig. 1. A Tasking Set with Three Processes

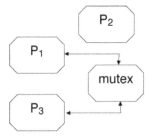

Fig. 2. The Block Diagram Representing the Tasking set of Fig. 1

A system with three processes is schematized in Fig. 1 using an intuitive baseline representation. Process P_1 periodically releases a task every 5 time units. The task is comprised of two steps; the first step has a minimum and a maximum computation time of 0.8 and 1 time units, respectively. Process P_2^s is sporadic with minimum interarrival time of 10 time units. Process P_3 is also periodic, with period of 15 time units, and releases a task made of three steps. Processes P_1 and P_3 synchronize through the mutual exclusion semaphore $mutex$. In Fig. 1 each step of any process is associated with a priority level.

A typical representation such as that of Fig. 1 is said to be a *baseline* model.

2.1 Modeling View

A baseline model such as that of Fig. 1 can be cast through a disciplined approach into an SDL model, that we call *modeling view*, which extends SDL expressivity with constraints annotated in the body of comments.

The modeling view is composed of an SDL-block-diagram and a set of SDL-process-graphs. The SDL-block-diagram represents the tasking set, counting each process as an SDL-process (see Fig. 2). Messages exchanged between processes are represented as SDL-signals. The diagram also includes an SDL-process for each semaphore used in the tasking set.

The SDL-process-graph of each process is annotated with comments specifying the following characteristics:

1. The *release policy* is defined through an annotation in the comment associated with the start symbol of the SDL-process-graph as seen either in Fig. 3(a) or in Fig. 3(b), depending on whether the process is repetitive or one-shot.
2. Each *computation step* is represented as a function in an action, annotated with a comment defining temporal parameters and priority, as in Fig. 3(c).
3. The *acquisition of a semaphore* sem is modeled in two steps (see Fig. 3(d)): a message to sem is first sent, then a wait state is entered until a grant is received from sem itself.
4. The *release of semaphore* sem is simply modeled as a message to sem itself.

Fig. 4 shows the modeling view obtained for the process P_1 in the tasking set of Fig. 1. As we mentioned, the representation is still intuitive and direct.

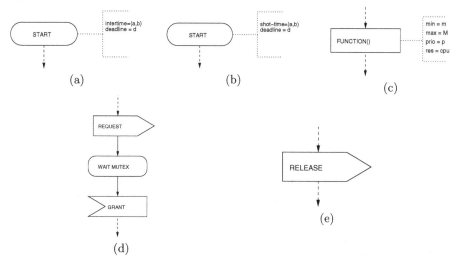

(a) Annotation to **START** state expressing the release policy of a periodic or sporadic task. The keyword **intertime** accepts a pair (a, b) representing the minimum and the maximum intertime between subsequent releases, respectively; keyword **deadline** specifies the deadline, relative to the task release time. **(b)** Representation of one-shot release process: keyword **shot-time** specifies a pair (a, b) representing a time interval within the absolute release time is sampled; keyword **deadline** specifies the deadline, relative to task release time. **(c)** Annotation of an SDL-function expressing a computation step. Annotation **res = cpu** indicates the computation requires the use of *cpu*; keyword **prio** the priority; keyword **min** and keyword **max** the minimum and the maximum computation time. **(d)** The SDL fragment expressing the acquisition of a semaphore composed by an SDL-signal to request it and the wait state for the grant. **(e)** The SDL-signal with the keyword **RELEASE** expresses the issuing of a signal to another process or to a semaphore to release it.

Fig. 3. Timing Additions and Semaphores

3 An Architecture for Simulating Specification Models

The modeling view comprises an unambiguous yet intuitive representation of the tasking set that serves for the purposes of design documentation and possibly for automatic target code generation. However, the modeling view is not suited to support a timed simulation of a model reproducing the actual timing and sequencing of execution, as it would occur under the control of a pre-emptive scheduler ruling concurrent execution on a single CPU. In fact comments are ignored by SDL simulation engines thus removing the intended meaning of annotations about expected duration of computation steps and about their sequencing under a pre-emptive scheduler.

To overcome this limitation, the modeling view is translated into a *simulation view* which modifies the SDL representation of the tasking set and integrates it with additional SDL-process-graphs representing the microkernel of a pre-

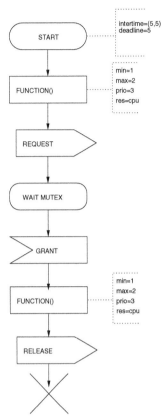

The two FUNCTION actions correspond to the two computation steps.

Fig. 4. Modeling View of Process P_1

emptive (real-time) operating system. While loosing the intuitive aspect and the direct correspondence with code, this opens the way to the exploitation of simulation tools that are commonly supported by SDL CASE environments.

As previously noted, to adhere to the semantics of SDL a simulator should make no assumption on the progress of time. This may lead to any possible combination of execution times, timer expirations and timer consumptions [4]. For instance, if a timer is set to now + t, the timer can be consumed at any time beyond now + t, even though consumption is specified to immediately follow the setting of the timer itself. However, industrial simulation tools handle progress of time by introducing a negligible delay in firing transitions that are enabled, resembling a semantics of time in which transitions are fired as soon as possible. This behavior ensures predictability of time as long as the delays introduced by the simulator are negligible with respect to temporal parameters specified in the annotated SDL model.

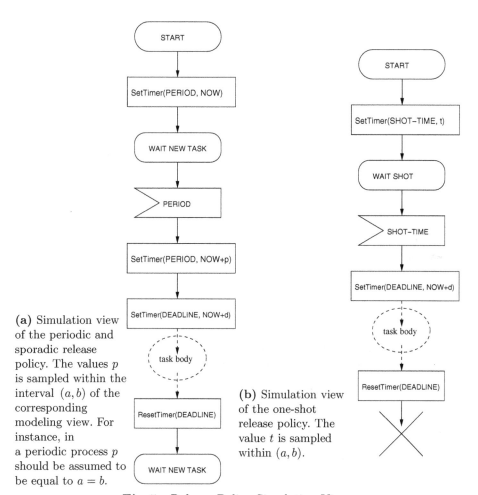

(a) Simulation view of the periodic and sporadic release policy. The values p is sampled within the interval (a, b) of the corresponding modeling view. For instance, in a periodic process p should be assumed to be equal to $a = b$.

(b) Simulation view of the one-shot release policy. The value t is sampled within (a, b).

Fig. 5. Release Policy Simulation Views

3.1 Simulation View of User Defined Tasks

The derivation of the simulation view from the modeling view is obtained through a one-to-one correspondence between each of the five modeling fragments enlisted in Fig. 3 and a corresponding simulation fragment.

1. The release policy of Fig. 3(a) is translated into the fragment of Fig. 5(a). This embeds the task execution (denoted as *task body*) within two clauses which enforce repetitive release of the task and set a deadline timer on each release.
2. In a similar manner, for one-shot tasks, the release policy of Fig. 3(b) is translated into the fragment of Fig. 5(b).
3. Any step computation action (Fig. 3(c)) is translated into a fragment as shown in Fig. 6. Value e, representing the actual computation time, is sam-

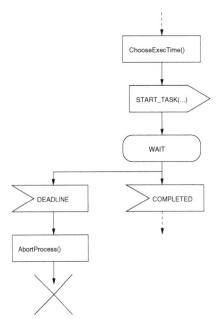

A computation step chooses at random an actual execution time through the function ChooseExecTime(), sends its parameters to the scheduler and waits for the signal COMPLETED from the scheduler. Alternatively, execution is forced to terminate by expiration of the deadline.

Fig. 6. A Computation Step in the Simulation View

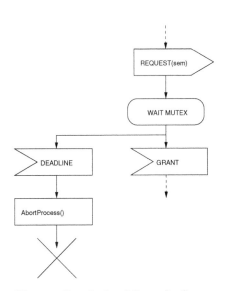

Fig. 7. Simulation View of a Semaphore Acquisition

pled in the interval [m, M] and sent to the SDL-process modeling the microkernel scheduler along with the priority level of the computation step(see Sect.3.2). In turn, the microkernel process has the responsibility to send back the COMPLETED signal after a time equal to e plus the additional delay due to possible suspensions. In case the completed signal is overtaken by the DEADLINE timer (that was set in the initialization clause), the task leaves the WAIT state and aborts.

4. The semaphore acquisition fragment of Fig. 3(d) is translated into the fragment of Fig. 7. In this case, a message with the identifier of the requested semaphore is sent to an SDL-process modeling the semaphore manager, which has the duty to send back a GRANT signal when the semaphore is assigned to the task. As in the above case, if the GRANT is not received within the deadline, the task leaves the wait state and aborts.

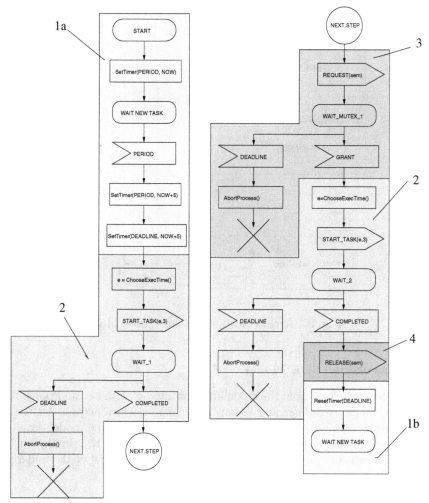

This view is obtained by one-to-one replacement of the modeling view (see Fig. 4). Different shading and numbering is used to make evident such correspondence.

Fig. 8. Simulation View of Process P_1

5. The semaphore release is simply an SDL-signal sent to the semaphore manager.

Fig. 8 shows the simulation view for the process P_1 derived from the modeling view in Fig. 4.

Note that, in the translation from modeling to simulation view, semaphores are embodied within the SDL-process representing the microkernel (see 3.2).

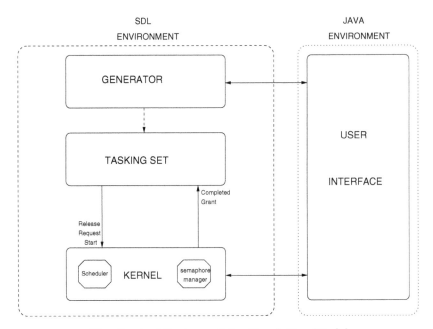

Fig. 9. Architecture of the Simulation Model

3.2 Microkernel SDL Model

SDL-processes derived from the modeling view interact with two additional SDL-processes, named *scheduler* and *semaphore manager* which account for the real time microkernel. Fig. 9 shows the overall architecture of the model developed for simulation purposes. The symbol *tasking set* represents the simulation view of the tasking set, while the symbol *kernel* is the SDL model of the underlying kernel.

Scheduler. The scheduler process is responsible for simulating the scheduling algorithm of the kernel so as to determine the time at which each computation step terminates its execution, according to the expected duration, the priority level, and the possible suspensions due to pre-emptive scheduling.

This functionality is supported through a *scheduling table* which keeps track of pending computation steps and through an UPDATE timer which indicates the time at which the running computation step will be completed.

In the table, each pending computation step is described by a process control block (*PCB*), which includes the Pid, the priority level, and the time to complete the step, as measured at the last operation on the table. PCBs are sorted on the basis of the scheduling policy (fixed priority or earliest deadline first) that is assumed for the target environment. In particular, the first row in the table always contains the PCB of the running computation step.

The scheduler process dwells in a wait state in which it can receive either the UPDATE timer or a START_TASK signal which indicates the release of a new computation step by a task of some user defined process.

When the UPDATE timer is received, the scheduler updates the table so as to represent the advancement of time marked by the arrival of the timer itself. According to this, the first PCB is removed from the table and a completed signal is sent to the computation step that was in the first row of the table. Afterwards, the scheduler sets the UPDATE timer equal to NOW+c where c is the time to completion associated with the first PCB in the table. Before entering the dwelling state again, the current time is saved.

Reception of a START_TASK signal indicates that a new computation step has been started before the running task has completed its execution. In this case, the UPDATE timer is reset and the scheduling table is updated: the time to completion of the running step is reduced by the value of time elapsed since the last operation on the table (the difference $NOW - LASTUPDATE$); the new computation step is inserted in the table in its proper position, according to its priority and to the scheduling policy. Finally, the UPDATE timer is started again, set equal to the time to completion of the first PCB in the table.

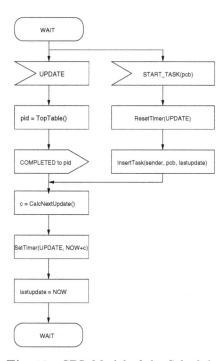

Fig. 10. SDL Model of the Scheduler

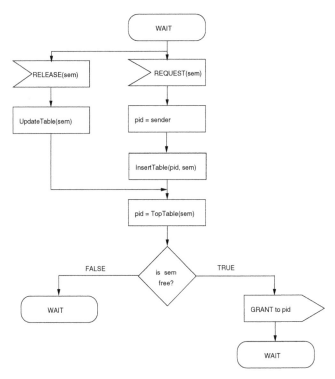

Fig. 11. SDL Model of the Semaphore Manager

Semaphore Manager. Figure 11 represents the SDL-process-graph of the semaphore manager. For each semaphore, the manager keeps a queue with the PID of requesting processes. In the state WAIT, the semaphore manager can receive a REQUEST or a RELEASE signal from a user task.

In the former case, the semaphore manager inserts the requesting task in the queue and sends back a GRANT signal if the new task has taken the top position in the queue (that is, if the queue was empty). In the latter case, the releasing task is removed from the queue and a GRANT signal is sent to the task which comes to the top of the queue.

User Interface. The architecture of the simulation system shown in Fig. 9 also includes a *generator* and a *user interface*.

The user interface supports user control over the simulation process. It allows the user to dynamically activate processes described through a process graph which must be created off-line, but which can be activated with parameters (time durations and priority levels) determined during the simulation itself. This is obtained through an SDL process named GENERATOR which exchanges messages with the user interface: first, the generator sends information about the process graphs that can be instantiated to the user interface, and then,

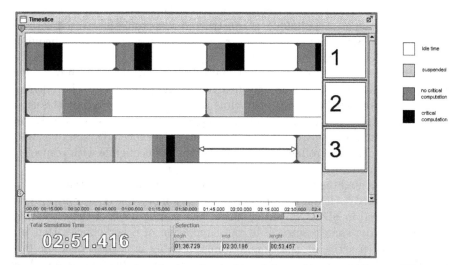

Screen of the user interface during simulation of the tasking set of Fig. 1. White color represents idle time; light gray represents suspended processes; dark gray represents computations without mutual exclusion resource; and, finally, black represents computations in a critical section.

Fig. 12.   User Interface

waits until it receives the requests and the correct parameters to instantiate them. During the simulation process, the user interface also allows the user to observe a visual timeline of ongoing simulated computations which augments conventional logging capabilities of simulation engines (see Fig. 9).

The interface is implemented in JAVA and communicates with the SDL simulator using a library based on the Java Native Interface technology: the library allows the basic communication between the SDL-environment and the JAVA application.

Fig. 12 shows the timing behavior observed through the aid of the user interface, when simulation of tasking set of Fig. 1 is performed.

4   Conclusion

A solution has been presented which permits use of a conventional SDL CASE tool to simulate timed and sequenced behavior of an SDL model with augmented semantics capturing timing and resource constraints expressed in the body of comments. The solution relies on the usage of two distinct SDL models, that we call modeling and simulation view.

The modeling view reflects the perspective of the designer, allowing natural and direct representation of temporal parameters and resource usage constraints. This supports design and documentation and enables automated code generation taking into account the presence of a specific scheduling environment.

The simulation view, which is derived from the modeling view through a one-by-one replacement technique, is constructed so as to be integrated with an additional set of SDL components which represent the behavior of the scheduling kernel and which support interaction with an external user interface. Simulation of the integrated model reproduces the behavior of the model, taking into account timing and resource constraints specified in the modeling view. The inherent indeterminacy of SDL with respect to time progress is neutralized by the usual implementation of simulation engines, which perform transitions as soon as they can be fired. More precisely, simulation reproduces the expected system behavior as long as the delays introduced by the simulator are negligible with respect to temporal parameters specified in the modeling view.

We experimented the entire system in the design of real time systems running under fixed priority scheduling. However, adaptation of a few details in C procedures (embedded in SDL) which implement the management of the scheduling table permits the same approach in the simulation of other policies that are relevant in the practice of real time systems: notably in earliest deadline first scheduling [5]. This enables a two-level design process to be devised, in which a system designer produces the model of the target environment according to the characteristics of a specific microkernel, and an application designer can restrain its activity to the creation of models which reflect the common perspective of real time concurrent programming.

The integration of the simulation environment with analysis techniques based on extension of Petri Nets that we call pre-emptive Time Petri Nets is ongoing with the aim of supporting exhaustive verification of reachability and timeliness analysis [14].

References

[1] ITU-T. Recommendation Z.100 (08/02), Specification and Description Language (SDL). International Telecommunication Union, Geneva. 203
[2] Telelogic SDT 4.3 manuals, 2002. 203, 204
[3] Cinderella SDL 1.2 manuals, 2002. 203
[4] M. Bozga, S. Graf, L. Mounier, I. Ober, J.-L. Roux, D. Vincent. Timed extensions for SDL. Proceedings of SDL Forum 2001, 2001. 204, 208
[5] G. Buttazzo. Hard Real-Time Computing Systems. Kluwer Academic Publishers, January 1997. 204, 216
[6] S. Graf. Expression of time and duration constraints in SDL. Proc. of SAM-2002, LNCS 2599, 2003. 204
[7] R. Gotzhein, U. Glässer, A. Prinz. Towards a new formal SDL semantics based on abstract state machines. SDL '99 - The Next Millennium, 9th SDL Forum Proceedings, pages 171-190, Elsevier, 1999. 204
[8] S. Bornot, J. Sifakis, S. Tripakis. Modeling urgency in timed systems. LNCS 1536, 1998. 204
[9] H. Fleischhack, B. Grahlmann. A compositional petri net semantics for SDL. Int. Conf. on Application and Theory of Petri Nets, 1998. 204
[10] M. Bozga, J.-C. Fernandez, L. Ghirvu, S. Graf, J.-P. Krimm, L. Mounier. IF: An intermediate representation and validation environment for timed asynchronous systems. World Congress on Formal Methods (1), pages 307-327, 1999. 204

[11] R. Alur, D. L. Dill. Automata for modeling real-time systems. Proceedings of 17th ICALP, 1990. 204

[12] B. Berthomieu, M. Diaz. Modeling and verification of time dependent systems using time petri nets. IEEE Transactions on Software Engineering, 17, 1991. 204

[13] E. Vicario. Static analysis and dynamic steering of time dependent systems using time petri nets. IEEE Transactions on Software Engineering, 2001. 204

[14] G. Bucci, A. Fedeli, E. Vicario. Timed state space analysis of fixed priority pre-emptive systems. Technical report, Dipartimento Sistemi e Informatica, Firenze, Italy, December 2002. also submitted to IEEE Transactions on Software Engineering, September 2002. 204, 216

[15] S. Spitz, F. Slomka, M. Dörfel. SDL* an annotated specification language for engineering multimedia communication systems. Sixth Open Workshop on High Speed Networks, 1997. 204

[16] R. Munzenberger, F. Slomka, M. Dörfel, R. Hofmann. A general approach for specification of real-time systems with SDL. Proceedings of 10th SDL Forum., LNCS 2078, Springer, 2001. 204

[17] J. M. Alvarez, M. Diaz, L. Llopis, E. Pimentel, J. M. Troya. Integrating schedula-bility analysis and SDL in an object-oriented methodology for embedded real-time systems. Proceedings of 9th SDL Forum., Elsevier, 1999. 204

[18] J. M. Alvarez, M. Diaz, L. Llopis, E. Pimentel, J. M. Troya. Integrating schedula-bility analysis and design techniques in SDL. IEEE Real Time Systems Journal, 2001. 204

[19] T. Kolloch, G. Farber. Mapping an embedded hard real-time systems SDL spec-ification to an analizable task network: a case study. Proceedings of the ACM SIGPLAN Workshop on Languages, Compilers and Tools for Embedded Systems (LCTES'98), LNCS, Springer-Verlag, June 1998. 204

[20] J.-Y. Chung, J. W. S. Liu, K.-J. Lin. Scheduling periodic jobs that allow imprecise results. IEEE Transactions on Computers, 1990. 205

[21] G. Bucci, A. Fedeli, E. Vicario. Predicting timeliness of reactive systems under flexible scheduling. Proceedings of Int.Symph. on Autonomous Decentralized Systems, April 2003. 205

RMTP2:
Validating the Interval Timed Extension for SDL with an Industrial-Size Multicast Protocol

Benoît Parreaux, Daniel Vincent, and Gérard Babonneau

France Telecom R&D
2 avenue Pierre Marzin, 22307 Lannion Cedex, France
{benoit.parreaux,daniel.vincent,gerard.babonneau}@franctetelecom.com

Abstract. The European IST project Interval (1999-2002) focused on coherent timed extensions for the ITU-T modeling languages SDL, MSC, TTCN. In the case of SDL, a set of extensions were defined and proposed to ITU-T in order to be a basis for a new recommendation. This paper gives a short overview of these extensions, and describes which enhancements were achieved on an SDL prototype tool in order to make it possible to use these extensions. For a more detailed description of these extensions see [1]. Finally we present an industrial-size experiment on an IETF protocol with the purpose of validating three things: accuracy of SDL time extensions, usefulness of the enhanced tool, and correctness of the protocol itself.

1   Introduction

Management of time and time constraints is one of the hardest things an engineer has to face during complex software systems development. Among these, telecom systems are really an everlasting challenge because they gather together most of the possible difficulties in software design: distribution, heterogeneity of communication means (speed, delays, reliability), synchronicity (or asynchronicity), fault tolerance, dynamic reconfiguration with or without mobility. . . All of these difficulties imply – more or less directly – time. Thus time constraints have to be managed in all phases of a software system development: initial requirements capture, analysis and model verification, performance evaluation, implementation, deployment, and testing.

While it is obvious that time is an important parameter of usability or even reliability of telecom systems, no definitive industrial-size methodologies or languages cover this aspect together with the complete cycle of functional design. For a modeling language such as the ITU-T Specification and Description Language (SDL) [2] claims to cover the development of various telecom and real-time systems, it not only has to allow the user to express time constraints or requirements on his system, but also to verify these constraints during validation, to keep these constraints in the code generation, and to perform the corresponding tests on an implementation.

R. Reed (Ed.): SDL 2003, LNCS 2708, pp. 218–233, 2003.

Launched at the end of 1999 and ended in June 2002, the European IST project INTERVAL tried to gather existing material (see chapter 2) and to draw up a set of rules in order to extend the possibilities of time handling for ITU-T languages SDL, MSC and TTCN. In Sect. 2, we briefly present the INTERVAL proposals for SDL. To validate these extensions, we need an industrial-size example: such as the IETF Reliable Multicast Transfer Protocol 2 (RMTP2) described in Sect. 3. To evaluate their usefulness and accuracy of the INTERVAL extensions, we now have to examine a tool implementing some of then. The extensions implemented in the ObjectGeode Interval prototype are therefore described in Sect. 4. Section 5 presents how we performed some experiments in simulating the RMTP2 protocol with the ObjectGeode prototype. France Telecom R&D achieved this experiment with useful help from the Verimag laboratory in Grenoble. Finally, we conclude on the results of this experimentation.

2   SDL Timed Extensions

The semantics of SDL presented in Z.100 are very abstract and it allows no assumptions on time progress. More specifically, actions take an indeterminate amount of time to be executed, and a process may stay an indeterminate amount of time in the current state before taking one of the next fireable transitions. This notion is realistic for code generation but is not useable for simulation and verification. A simulator that would use these semantics of time creates many unrealistic executions in the reachability graph because it is impossible to make any assumption on the way time progresses. In practice, simulation and verification tools have foreseen means for limited control over time progress. For example, to progress time only when no more transitions are fireable.

Why is handling of time that difficult? Time constraints have (at least) three categories:

- **Functional Constraints:** not depending on design options or configuration or communication means. For example "if the user does not answer within 30 sec from now, then . . . ". Here, the time is incompressible. Changing the configuration of the system will not change the value of "30 sec". This kind of constraint should be represented directly in the core language as SDL constructs, and SDL already allows a good management of that with timers. Nevertheless, immediate handling of corresponding timeouts is not easy in a formal way.
- **Quality of Service Requirements:** this kind of constraint when regarding time and performance is really external to the SDL model. They are expressed on a more or less complex path in the model, involving several processes: for example Round Trip Time in a protocol, complete service delivering delay... This kind of requirement cannot be expressed easily (and should not be) in an SDL model. Languages like MSC or Properties observation [3] languages are better suited for this.
- **Unit Measurements:** this kind of data represents assessments on computing effort, task priority, transmission delays or channel reliability or policy

that you may attach to a single and well identified SDL construct (a channel, a block, a process, a task or a continuous piece of transition). Their
values depend on the system configuration, and therefore it is not desirable
to have them represented as core language constructs, but rather as formal
annotations (in a graphical comment for example).

Several very valuable papers have been published on extensions for SDL,
in order to model non-functional time and performance aspects. We mention
among them (and not exhaustively) the work around performance evaluation [4,
5, 6, 7, 8], around requirements expression [9, 3, 10] and finally on timed verification [11] and schedulability [12, 13, 14]. Other real time frameworks for SDL
were presented in [15] and [16, 1] and some tools propose to attach explicit timing information with SDL constructs such as tasks, and in this way provide some
minimal deployment information. For example, we can quote a time-enhanced
version of ObjectGeode [17] as presented in [6, 18] and the tool and methods
based on Queuing SDL [19, 7].

One of the results of the Interval Project is to make proposals for the extension of SDL in order to manage time in the specification. We introduce here the
following extensions:

- notion of urgency;
- interrupts;
- constraints on durations;
- more flexible signal consumption by priorities;
- clocks and enhanced timers;
- information on the deployment.

More information on these extensions is presented in: [20, 21].

2.1   A Notion of Urgency

The notion of urgency is necessary to force the triggering of transitions at given
points of time. It describes when a transition must be taken to fulfill timing
requirement. Unfortunately up until now, it is not possible to express urgency
using the actual SDL standard. Thus, this notion is introduced by the Interval
timed extensions to give the possibility to design and verify systems in which
transitions are triggered when allowed or required by time constraints and variable constraints. With urgency, it is possible to specify when a transition can
be executed (enabling condition) and by when a transition must be executed
(deadline condition). In the Interval proposal, the timed automata urgency [22]
was chosen to specify urgency. It is a simple means to specify urgency as one of
only three values:

- A *lazy* transition is never urgent, even if further waiting may disable it.
- An *eager* transition is always urgent. It must be triggered as soon as it is
  enabled.
- A *delayable* transition becomes urgent and must be triggered whenever it is
  enabled and any time progress would disable the transition.

2.2   Interrupts of Transitions

Some real-time systems need an interrupt construct that allows to cancellation of and exit from a transition in the case that it cannot be finished in time. Because timeouts can only be taken into account in control states, the notion of eager transition is not sufficient to cause the interruption of a transition. Then we need an additional *interrupt* or*watchdog* construct. This extension makes it possible to exit a transition when some point of time has been reached or when a special signal arrives. This feature can be added to SDL by the extension of the existing exception mechanism to allow a time condition or a signal reception to raise an exception.

2.3   Constraints on Durations

The previous extensions allow specification of when some transition has to be triggered. It is also important to express where the time is spent, and how long an activity takes before it terminates. Time constraints for both, design and validation of real time system, are at least:

- Communication delays (duration between the moment when a signal is sent and the moment when it enters in the recipient's input queue);
- Time constraints of the environment, such as frequency of requests;
- Time distances such as the duration of transitions or tasks.

2.4   More Flexible Signal Consumption through Priorities

There exist several mechanisms to deviate from the FIFO consumption of signals such as the *save* construct, enabling conditions or priority input signals. The priority signals allow, in each state, the division of the input queue in an ordinary and a priority queue giving at most two levels of priority.

Note: A priority type of construct for inputs was proposed as an extension by the Interval project, but this feature is not implemented in the prototype yet.

2.5   Introduction of Clocks

In SDL, timers are a predefined concept for triggering actions at a particular point of time. Another solution is to use time depending enabling conditions. But timers and time depending enabling conditions are not sufficient in all cases. The Interval project proposes to use clock constructs, in the sense used in timed automata, to make the expression of these time dependent conditions more convenient.

As opposed to time, clocks are part of the system. A clock always progresses with time, it can be set to any value (zero by default) and it can be read, dynamically created and deleted. Of course, it is also possible to specify a specific behavior pattern: for example a cyclic behavior will be obtained with clock and 'auto reset' activated by a specific value.

2.6   Information on Deployment and Scheduling

The minimal information on deployment needed for timed validation is: the set of resources of the system and which processes are executed on a given resource. Moreover it is important to know which tasks or resources are preemptible and which ones are not. SDL architectural views are very convenient for this information. The Interval project proposed to introduce two kinds of annotations: resource definition using the SDL block diagrams and priority levels between processes.

3   Short Description of the RMTP2 Protocol Case Study

The Reliable Multicast Transfer Protocol (RMTP2) over IP has been published as an IETF draft in 1998. RMTP2 provides a reliable transmission of data sequences for large groups of receivers. The objectives of RMTP2 are a guaranteed reliability, a high throughput, and a low end-to-end delay on any network topology, while providing the network manager with control over transmission traffic. In a lossy environment, reliability can be obtained if data packets are acknowledged. However, due to the large number of receivers for each data channel, direct acknowledgment of packets from each receiver to the source would result in immediate network congestion. For this reason, the network is organized as a tree.

Receivers are grouped in local regions, and in each region a special control node (Designated Receiver) is responsible for maintaining receiver membership, aggregating the acknowledgments from the receivers and forwarding them to the Top Node.

The descending network (in Fig. 1 the vertical line from Broadcasting services and horizontal lines to receivers) represents the way data items are sent using IP multicast to all members of the RMTP2 tree. Data items are received in the Source Node from a sending application, and are then multicast on the descending network data channels. Packets are aggregated for acknowledgment by multiple levels of control nodes, which forward information about missed packets to the Sender Node using the upward paths.

Control Nodes may be of two types: Aggregator Nodes, which only aggregate and forward information about missed packets to the upper level, and Designated Receiver Nodes, which can keep a copy of data packets, and retransmit missed data to their sub tree. Acknowledgments are aggregated at the top of the tree by a node called Top Node, which retransmits this information to the Sender Node. Each node in the tree provides multiple services such as data transmission, tree integrity control, and quality of service maintenance...

The mechanisms to ensure reliability in this protocol are very complex, and the resulting and working model is not less than 9000 lines of raw SDL/PR (without any CIF). Some features of this protocol are:

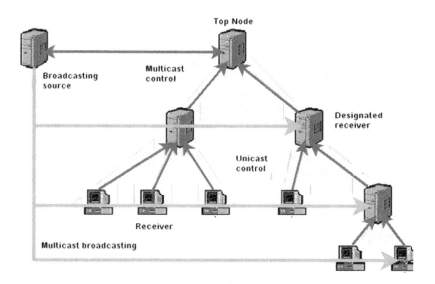

Fig. 1. RMTP2 protocol architecture

- Receivers can dynamically join or leave a stream in progress;
- A *heartbeat* mechanism ensures some life in the network when no data is currently under way (some timers working of course);
- Time bounded reliability with sliding window, aggregated acknowledgments (a lot of other timers and timing constraints)...
- Dynamically calculated speed of the source depending on previous observed Round Trip Times (RTT).

The last item above is a real challenge for exhaustive verification, because it uses time-stamping, and time-stamps need discrete values, thus breaking the symbolic handling of time constraints. This point was heavily discussed, but finally we chose to stay close to the IETF draft, and to keep time-stamps.

3.1 Purpose of the Experiments

A multicast protocol functions correctly, if the protocol is able in each case to reach a point where the transmission can still progress.

We should thus demonstrate that the protocol always continues until the end of the transmission, verifying that the last packet sent has been acknowledged, even if each particular receiver did not get all the packets. At least, we should verify that in each case, the last packet has been emitted once, and that the receivers had the possibility to claim for missing packets. Some interesting and more detailed test objectives were considered:

- Each lost packet or suite of lost packets is retransmitted at least once;
- Transmission always progresses towards the end: some specification problems (see chapter 5.7 of the IETF draft) could occur with insufficient RxMax (Maximum number of retransmissions allowed for a given data packet);
- Transmission always progresses when two receivers have very different RTTs due to difference of media (ADSL vs 100 Mbs);
- Adjust the Thack timer (Maximum time between successive acknowledgments transmissions for each receiver) value so that any lost packet will be asked for, even after transmission of the last packet;
- Verify that in stable working conditions, the RTT value is converging, and therefore the transmission speed of the source converges too.

4   Modeling Time Constraints with the ObjectGeode Interval Prototype

To verify these properties on the RMTP2 protocol with the ObjectGeode Interval prototype, we used the following timed extensions to enrich the model.

4.1   Architectural View

The simulator allows using constraints at the architectural level, namely available resources and channel characteristics (delays, quality...).

Resources Management. The #node() annotation gives the possibility to allocate the same resource for execution of all tasks included in the node (see Fig. 2). The behavior of the model becomes therefore closer to reality in a distributed system like RMTP2, as it is possible to indicate which processes execute concurrently on the same processor.

Process Priorities. Some processes like ChildFailure (see Fig. 3) have been given the highest priority 0 using the #priority(0) directive. Note that several processes may have the same priority level, and that those with no given priority have the lowest possible priority. High priorities were given to functionally important processes (for example DataTN has priority 1) or to processes that have to manage a timer (such as ChildFailure with 0).

Delaying Channels. Transmission delay can be annotated by the directives #pipeline or #delay (see Fig. 2). Each of these constructs allows for use of parameters configuring the channel delay (an integer or an integer interval). A transiting signal is only delivered in the queue of the target process after a certain transit delay that is calculated as follows:

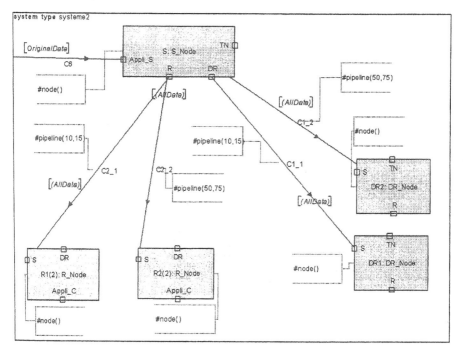

Fig. 2. Resources definition (only descending way represented)

- A signal sent through a channel marked with pipeline(A,B) at a moment T arrives at the receiving end at a moment between $T + A$ and $T + B$. The arrival time is further constrained by the fact that the order of the signals is preserved, so a signal may not arrive at the end of a channel before the signal preceding it in the channel queue.
- A signal sent through a channel marked with delay(A,B) at a moment T arrives at the receiving end at a moment between $T' + A$ and $T' + B$, where T' is the maximum between T and the arrival time of the previous signal transferred through the channel (a signal is not allowed to enter a channel as long as another signal is there).

These two constructs are particularly useful in the case of a very distributed (soft) real time system like the protocol RMTP2.

Lossy Channels. The #lossy() annotation allows specification of loss rates for the packets in a channel. This annotation may be used together with #Delay annotations. In the case of RMTP II, this annotation produced a lot of simplifications of the model, where (before) explicit losses were represented. This is shown in Figure : 4 :

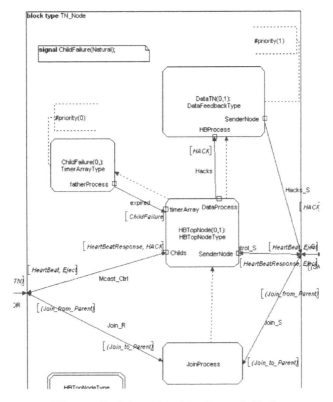

Fig. 3. Defining Priorities in each Node

- in the left definition of mcastData, we didn't use lossy channels and we had to specify a mechanism to simulate data losses;
- in the right definition of mcastData, we used lossy channels and the specification seems to be simpler.

Even if this construct is very useful, it should be enhanced with the possibility to express probability laws or special scenarios for losses: e.g. all the packets lost during a certain amount of time.

4.2   Process Diagrams: Functional Aspects

In the following sections, we describe the use of the extensions in the automata part of the specification. When possible, we compare a solution without extension and our solution using timed extensions.

Time Consuming Tasks. We used the directive #delay in some procedures (see SendPacket and Resendpacket) to represent consumption of time. Without

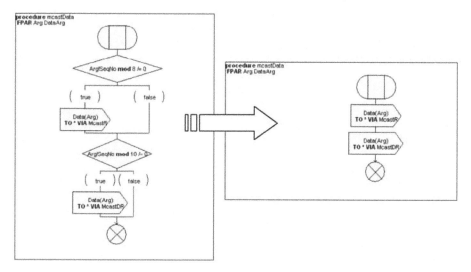

Fig. 4. Simplification of mcastData allowed by the #lossy Annotation

this directive we had to pollute the model with a timer construct whose role is to simulate time passing.

Time Variables, Timers and Clocks. Classical SDL allows time handling mainly through the use of timers, the time variable NOW and duration variables. With the new extensions, we use clocks and clock constraints that allow handling of a dense time. Discrete values of NOW should no more be used.

Nevertheless, a big problem with the RMTP2 protocol (and most of the IETF protocols) is the necessity to obtain the current time value, and to store it into a variable. More precisely, a mechanism to adjust dynamically the acknowledgment time-out needs to use these time values. A lot of significant properties of the protocol directly derive from this mechanism, and thus we had to keep it in the model just to conform to the draft. This solution implies storing discrete time values into a variable and is of course catastrophic for state explosion: we lose the possibility to make an exhaustive verification of the model.

Following our demand, and despite loss of exhaustivity, the #choiceclock directive was introduced in the Interval prototype. This directive forces the constraints to extract a possible value (min, max or random) for the associated clock variable.

To manage the current time value by using this directive, we had the choice between two solutions: use of an observer or use of an RPC function. The first solution is simpler than the RPC solution because we only need to define an observer that assigns the result of the #choiceclock directive to a set of variables in the model. With the RPC solution it is necessary to fire the RPC transition prior to all the other transitions. As a drawback, the observer solution is the

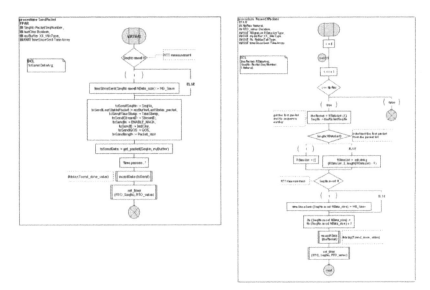

Fig. 5. Use of the #delay() Directive

worst solution for the verification because it is not easy to specify when a time value is really needed, and thus we must calculate a time value after each firing of a transition. With the RPC solution, we calculate a time value only when we need it, so it is a better solution. To realize our verification we started with the first solution, but we finally used the second one.

5 Validation

Different experiments with the RMTP2 protocol have been performed in order to validate the Interval timing approach on an industrial-size model. Special attention was given to problems whose analysis was not possible with untimed techniques. In addition, features still missing in the tools or features to be enhanced have been identified.

We first had to look closely at how the behavior of the protocol changes with a timed model. Some surprises came from the functioning of the simulation tool. For example, the very useful *feed* construct (an ObjectGeode facility for simulating the outside world) did not work in the timed model with a "reasonable" environment because, due to the heartbeat mechanism, time could always progress and thus normal transitions could be fired instead of feeds.

We were then forced to provide feeds in an unreasonable environment (that is, external events can occur at any time and with an unlimited frequency), and to suppress the effects of further feeds as long as the first one is not completely processed.

5.1   Isolated and Bursty Packet Losses

One of the unavoidable properties to verify is if the protocol is able to recover from packet losses. A next step is naturally to consider how the protocol reacts in bursty cases: when several consecutive packets are lost, known as storm effect for atmospheric transfer. The #lossy construct proposed in the prototype is not sufficient in this case, and we were forced to represent this kind of loss directly in the model. The #lossy annotation, to be useful has to be enhanced.

It was nevertheless possible to make the most of the intended simulation without too much trouble. The protocol has the expected behavior: it is able to ensure that every transmitted packet is either received or negatively acknowledged.

Figure 6 shows the case of very heavy losses, as packets a and b are totally lost, c and d are partially lost until e is sent normally. Variable Laststable only progresses to 1 after a has been retransmitted by an rdata message. The remaining of the sequence could not be reproduced here on the page, but in the simulation, all lost packets are successfully retransmitted. The time needed to reach the correct value of laststable is naturally increased in case of these heavy losses, but the protocol still seems to behave correctly as long as we do not put constraints for limiting the total time of transmission.

In conclusion, the protocol seems to behave correctly against isolated or bursty losses.

5.2   Experiments with Heterogeneous Channel Delays

We experimented on the protocol with heterogeneous delays on the different channels as in real life where, in a multicast protocol, receivers are reachable through different media (ADSL, 100 Mbs, ...) in Fig. 2 (where only descending flow is represented)

The fact that some channels are faster than other ones did not provoke any loss of packet (through a too fast transmitting window progress), or any failure in the acknowledgment mechanism, and no blocking of the protocol was detected. Note that this kind of result would not have been easily obtained without the Interval extensions for channel delays.

5.3   Experiment on RTO Timer Value

The RMTP2 mechanism involves a very important variable for the quality of transmission: the RTO (Retransmission TimeOut). This variable allows some upper bound limit to be given to the time that the protocol has to wait before resending a data item if it has not been acknowledged. The protocol is able to refine this value dynamically, taking into account the Round Trip Time (RTT) values needed for previous transmissions. The need for discrete time values to refine the values has led us to ask Telelogic to change the way of calculating time constraints in the prototype (see the #choiceclock directive above). Until then, elapsed time was treated as a set of constraints defining a set of possible intervals,

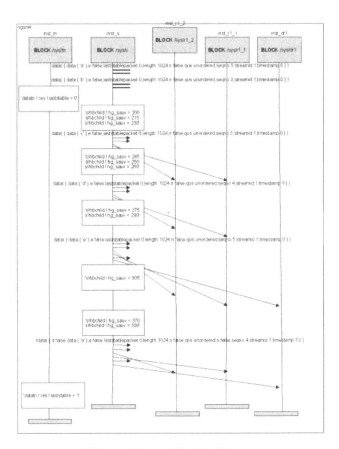

Fig. 6. Bursty Packet Losses

and this could not be handled by the refining function. The RTO variable is given an initial value (defined in the draft), and in the case of good stability of the network, this value should converge to an optimal time value close to the real communication time. It is important to verify this property, because divergence or periodicity of this variable would affect the overall adaptation capability of the protocol.

Figure 7 illustrates some of the results we obtained during verification of the RTO convergence property. The short dottted line represents the initial packet sending of the source (from packet 0 to packet 26). The value of RTO (long dotted line starting from 10000) decreases as the packets are acknowledged (Laststable is the plain line). In fact, the new value of RTO is calculated in the protocol each time the value of Laststable is updated. By continuing the simulation a very long time, we could find in the case of Fig. 7 that the RTO is converging close to 3400.

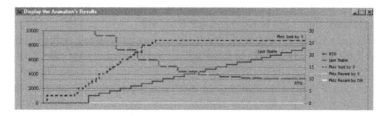

Fig. 7. Convergence of RTO (long dotted line) in the Case of Stable Environment

Of course, due to the necessity to get discrete time values for the RTT, we could no more achieve an exhaustive verification, which in fact was not even possible before, because each state in the accessibility graph was very big (hundreds of timing constraints) and the verification run very quickly out of memory. Nevertheless, all the simulations in different configurations showed no counterexample to the property.

More complete experiments are described in the Interval project deliverables.

6   Conclusion

In this paper, we presented the SDL timed extension results of the IST Interval project and we introduced an industrial case study. In this RMTP2 case study, three different results were expected:

- Validation of usefulness of the SDL extensions for managing time constraints;
- Evaluation of the tool implementation of the new features;
- Some results concerning the correctness of RMTP 2.

Concerning the two first points, we experimented on almost all proposed extensions (except explicit transition urgencies): resources (nodes), local time and clocks, process priorities, task delays, channel delays, lossy channels. For model validation purposes, all these extensions are needed for a protocol like RMTP2, and we could even verify that most of them have a promising implementation in the tool.

Some drawbacks were found in the use of clocks: a symbolic handling of time constraints does not allow easy use of actual time values, and in such a protocol these values are needed for time-stamping or for some calculation. A solution was proposed, but even if it works, it is not completely satisfactory because it prohibits any exhaustive verification.

In conclusion on this point, for verification purposes, the set of proposed extensions seems rather complete and useful. Some of these extensions modify the SDL semantics and others are just annotations. One of the most important semantic changes, the clock extension, was proposed in order to make exhaustive verification possible by symbolic handling of a dense time. But a condition for that is never to store actual time values in a variable (for example for time-stamping), and alas, this is required for RMTP2.

Concerning the protocol RMTP2 itself, some interesting results, concerning its reliability, were obtained, but we never could ensure that the protocol will work correctly in any configuration. The model could be made clearer with the extensions, since some non-functional modeling could be put as annotations.

From our point of view, the results of this experiment were positive. The time extensions allow us to specify non-functional aspects of this protocol and the influence of these aspects on the different executions. We have increased (a bit) our confidence in the RMTP2 protocol, even if no exhaustive verification was possible.

References

[1] M. Bozga, S. Graf, L. Mounier, I. Ober, J-L. Roux, D. Vincent. Timed Extensions for SDL. Proceedings of SDL Forum 2001, LNCS 2078, June 2001. 218, 220

[2] ITU-T. Recommendation Z.100 (08/02), Specification and Description Language (SDL). International Telecommunication Union, Geneva. 218

[3] B. Algayres, Y. Lejeune, F. Hugonnet. GOAL: Observing SDL behaviors with Geode. Proceedings of SDL Forum 95. 219, 220

[4] F. Bause, P. Buchholz. Qualitative and quantitative analysis of timed SDL specifications 220

[5] S. Spitz, F. Slomka, M. Dörfel. SDL - an annotated specification language for engineering multimedia communication systems" Workshop on high speed networks, Stuttgart, October 1999 220

[6] J.-L. Roux. SDL Performance analysis with ObjectGeode, Workshop on performance and time in SDL, 1998 220

[7] A. Mitschele-Thiel, F. Slomka. A methodology for hardware/software co-design of realtime systems with SDL/MSC. Computer Networks 31, 1999 220

[8] M. Malek. PerfSDL: Interface to protocol performance analysis by means of simulation. Proceedings of SDL Forum 99 220

[9] S. Leue. Specifying Real-time requirements for SDL specifications. Proceedings of PSTV'95 220

[10] M. Dörfel, W. Dulz, R. Hofmann, R. Münzenberger, SDL and non-functional requirement. Internal Report IMMD7 05/01, University of Erlangen-Nuremberg, Germany, August 20, 2001. 220

[11] I. Ober, B. Coulette, A. Kerbrat. Timed SDL Simulation and specification. Technical report: Telelogic Technologies Toulouse, 2000 220

[12] J-M Alvarez, M. Diaz, L. Llopis, E. Pimentel, J. M. Troya. Embedded Real-time Systems Development using SDL. IEEE Real-time Symposium, 1999 220

[13] J-M Alvarez, M. Diaz, L. Llopis, E. Pimentel, J. M. Troya. IntegratingSchedulability Analysis and Design Techniques in SDL. Real Time Systems Journal 220

[14] J.-M. Alvarez, M. Diaz, L. Llopis, E. Pimentel, J. M. Troya. Deriving Hard-Real Time Embedded Systems Implementations Directly from SDL Specifications. CODES'01: 9th International Symposium on Hardware/Software Codesign. 25-27 April 220

[15] F. Slomka, M. Dörfel, R. Münzenberger, R. Hofmann. Hardware/Software Codesign and Rapid-Prototyping of Embedded Systems. IEEE Design & Test of Computers, Special issue: Design Tools for Embedded Systems, Vol. 17, No. 2, April-June 2000. 220

[16] M. Bozga, S. Graf, A. Kerbrat, L. Mounier, I. Ober and D. Vincent. SDL for realtime: what is missing?. Proceedings of SDL & MSC Workshop. Grenoble, June 2000. 220

[17] ObjectGeode 4-1 Reference Manual. Telelogic Technologies Toulouse. See also http://www.telelogic.com/ 220

[18] I. Ober. Spécification et Validation de Systèmes Temporisés avec des Langages de description formelle: étude et mise en œuvre. Phd Thesis, (in english), Toulouse, 2001 220

[19] M. Diefenbruch, E. Heck, J. Hintelmann, B. Müller-Clostermann. Performance evaluation of SDL systems adjunct by queuing models. Proc. of SDL-Forum '95, 1995. 220

[20] IST Project Interval. Final Validation and Improvement Report. June 2002, see http://www-interval.imag.fr/ 220

[21] ITU-T. Delayed Document Q23/17, Q13/17: Timed extensions for SDL.. February 2002, Geneva meeting. 220

[22] S. Bornot, J. Sifakis, S. Tripakis. Modeling Urgency in Timed Systems. International Symposium: Compositionality - The Significant Difference, Malente (Holstein, Germany), 1998, LNCS Vol. 1536 220

Refining Timed MSCs

Tong Zheng[1], Ferhat Khendek[1], and Benoît Parreaux[2]

[1] Department of Electrical and Computer Engineering, Concordia University
1455 de Maisonneuve W., Montreal (P.Q.) Canada H3G 1M8
[2] France Telecom R&D, Lannion, France

Abstract. We propose an approach for refining high level specifications into design specifications using the MSC language. We have previously introduced such an approach for un-timed MSCs. In this paper, we focus on the timing features of MSC-2000. We propose a framework for adding time constraints and refining them further, while preserving the properties of the high-level specification during the refinement process. We introduce conformance relations between MSCs and algorithms for checking these relations.

1 Introduction

In traditional development processes, designers take as input a requirement specification and develop in one big step a design specification. This design specification is then validated against the requirement specification. When the design specification does not satisfy the requirements, it is reworked. The design and validation activities are repeated until the design satisfies the requirements. An alternative to this approach is stepwise refinement. Indeed, the requirement specification can be taken as input and enriched step by step. In this approach, we validate small design steps instead of a complete design activity.

In a previous work [1], we introduced a refinement approach for un-timed MSC specifications. In our approach, we consider the relationship between a system and its environment. The refinement approach is such that the environment should not distinguish between a given system and its refinement. In other words, a system in a given environment can be replaced by a refined version. We distinguish between horizontal and vertical refinements. They can be seen as structural and behavioral refinements. In a vertical refinement, a designer decomposes a given instance into multiple instances according to the SDL [2] target architecture. In a horizontal refinement, the MSC specification is enriched with messages. A process alternating between vertical and horizontal refinement has been defined. To ensure the preservation of the properties of the MSCs during the refinement (for instance the orders between the events), we introduced a conformance relation that must hold between MSC at stage i and MSC at stage $i+1$ of the refinement process.

The latest MSC standard, MSC-2000 [3], has introduced time constructs for the specification of real time systems with quantified time. In this paper, we tackle the challenging time features of MSC-2000 [3] and propose an approach

R. Reed (Ed.): SDL 2003, LNCS 2708, pp. 234–250, 2003.

for a stepwise refinement of timed MSC specifications. A refinement in this case, may consist of decomposing processes, adding messages, and changing or adding time constraints. We define and discuss time constraint refinement. To validate refinement steps, we need to compare timed MSCs. For that purpose, we define conformance relations between MSCs. We introduce algorithms for the validation of these conformance relations and discuss their complexity.

Refinement of real-time specifications has been tackled in [4, 5]. These approaches [4, 5] are based on equivalence relations between specifications. They do not allow for the refinement of time constraints. Our view is that a refinement approach should allow for strengthening time constraints on the system and relaxing assumptions on the environment. This way, the behavior of the system can still be accepted by the environment, or even other environments with weaker assumptions.

The rest of the paper is organized as follows. In Sect. 2, for the purpose of completeness, we briefly review the time constructs in MSC-2000, and briefly introduce a semantics for timed MSC. In Sect. 3 and Sect. 4, we introduce an approach for refining bMSCs and HMSCs, respectively. We also introduce conformance relations between MSCs and algorithms for checking these conformance relations. In Sect. 5, we discuss related work prior to concluding in Sect. 6.

2   A Semantics for Timed MSC

MSCs consist of plain MSCs and HMSCs. In a plain MSC, the behaviors of processes are described explicitly. For instance, the MSC in Fig. 1(a) specifies exchanges of messages *m1* and *m2* between processes *i* and *j*. In addition to message exchanges, a plain MSC may also contain internal actions, timer events, conditions, and some structures, such as references and coregions. In this paper, we consider plain MSCs containing message exchanges only. We refer to these MSCs as basic MSCs (bMSC). A bMSC specifies only a partial behavior or one scenario of a system. For a more complete specification, different scenarios have to be combined. HMSCs are used to describe the composition of MSCs. In an

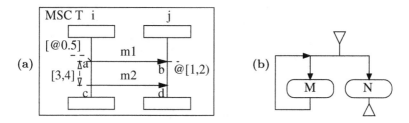

Fig. 1. bMSC and HMSC

HMSC, the component MSCs are connected process by process[1] according to the weak sequencing semantics. Alternatives are expressed by branches, while repetitions are expressed with loops. The HMSC in Fig. 1(b) specifies the execution sequences of MSC M and N. Either M is executed infinitely, or M is executed a finite number of times and then followed by N. In this paper, an HMSC refers only to bMSCs. In other words, the components in an HMSC are all bMSCs.

Time constraints have been introduced in MSC-2000 to describe real-time systems using quantified time. In the MSC standard, the time domain must be a total order with a least element. Time progress is the same for all processes as in an MSC. All events are instantaneous. They do not consume time. A time constraint can be used to specify a delay between two events (relative time constraint), or the occurrence time of an event (absolute time constraint). A time constraint is an interval of time with upper and lower bounds. For example, in Fig. 1(a), absolute time constraints are shown as @[1, 2) and [@0.5], which is a shortcut for @[0.5, 0.5]. Due to these absolute time constraints, event a (sending message $m1$) can occur only at time 0.5 and event b (receiving message $m1$) is allowed to occur between time 1 and 2. Delays between events are specified by relative time constraints. The delay between events a and c is at least 3 and at most 4.

2.1   A Semantics for bMSCs

Similar to [6, 7], we define the semantics of MSC using a non-interleaving model named timed lposets (labeled partially ordered sets) [8]. A partial order is a reflexive, transitive, and antisymmetric binary relation. For the definition of a timed lposet, we use *Time* to represent a time domain, which might be nonnegative real numbers or nonnegative integer numbers. $P(Time)$ is a set of time intervals. An interval could be open or closed.

Definition 1. *A timed lposet is a tuple* $(I, A, E, \leq, l, D, T)$, *in which*

- I *is a set of processes.*
- A *is a set of labels.*
- E *is a set of events.*
- $\leq \subseteq E \times E$ *is a partial order on E. It specifies causal orders between events.*
- $l\colon E \to A$ *is a labeling function, which associates an event to a label.*
- $D\colon E \to P(Time)$ *is a function that associates an event to a time interval. It defines a range within which an event should occur.*
- $T\colon E \times E \to P(Time)$ *is a function that associates a pair of events to a time interval. It defines the delay between two events.*

Labels in A represent the types of events. An event could be a message output, or a message input. Their corresponding labels are *send(i, j, m)* and *receive(i, j, m)*. The first label means that process i sends a message m to process j, and the second one means process i receives a message m from process j. Every event in

---

[1] Editorial note: The paper uses the term *process* for the MSC term *instance*.

an MSC is associated with a unique label. If a process sends a message m twice to another process, we re-label them as $m1$ and $m2$.

The semantics of a bMSC is defined as a timed lposet, which contains all the events in the bMSC and specifies their causal orders. The orders are determined by message exchanges and process axes in the bMSC. Along each process axis, events are ordered from top to bottom. Between different processes, a message output event happens before the corresponding message input event. The semantics of the bMSC T in Fig. 1(a), for instance, is $(I, A, E, \leq, l, D, T)$ where E includes events a, b, c, and d, $\leq$ is the transitive closure of $\{(a, b)\ (c, d)\ (a, c)\ (b, d)\}$. $D(a) = [0.5]$, $D(b) = [1, 2)$ and $T(a, c) = [3, 4]$.

2.2   A Semantics for HMSCs

An HMSC is a directed graph $(S,\ E,\ L)$, where S is a finite set of nodes, $E \subseteq S \times S$ is the set of directed edges, L is a function that maps each node in S to a bMSC. A path of an HMSC is a finite or infinite sequence of nodes $s_0 s_1 \ldots s_n \ldots$, in which s_0 is the start node, $(s_i, s_{i+1}) \in E$, $i \geq 0$.

To define the semantics of HMSC, we first define sequential composition of lposets. The sequential composition of two lposets p and q preserves the orders and the time constraints in p and q, and adds a new order and a relative time constraint between two events in the same process in p and q. For simplicity, we consider relative time constraints between two events in different MSCs as $(0, \infty)$. It means that there are no relative time constraints split between different bMSCs.

Formally, let $p = (I_p, A_p, E_p, \leq_p, l_p, D_p, T_p)$ and $q = (I_q, A_q, E_q, \leq_q, l_q, D_q, T_q)$ be two timed lposets in which A_p and A_q are disjoint; E_p and E_q are disjoint. We use S^+ to represent the transitive closure of a relation S. The sequential composition $(\cdot)$ of p and q is defined as:
$$p \cdot q = (I_p \cup I_q, A_p \cup A_q, E_p \cup E_q, (\leq_p \cup \leq_q \cup \leq)^+, l_p \cup l_q, D_p \cup D_q, T_p \cup T_q \cup T),$$
in which

- $\leq\ = \bigcup_i (E_p^i \times E_q^i)$, E_p^i and E_q^i are the sets of events that occur at process i, $E_p^i \subseteq E_p$, $E_q^i \subseteq E_q$,
- $T = \{((e, f), (0, \infty)) | e \in E_p^i, f \in E_q^i\}$.

The sequential composition is weak sequencing. In $p \cdot q$, an event in q may appear before some events in p, if they do not have causal orders.

When composing a timed lposet p with itself, we need to re-label the events in the second occurrence of p to make them different from the events in the first occurrence of p.

The semantics of an HMSC is defined as a set of timed lposets. For each path in the HMSC, there is a corresponding lposet, which is obtained by composing sequentially the bMSCs (i.e. nodes) along the path. A timed lposet may correspond to several paths. The set of lposets may be infinite when the HMSC contains loops. For example, the HMSC in Fig. 1(b) can be represented by an infinite set $\{q,\ p \cdot q,\ p \cdot p \cdot q,\ \ldots\}$, in which p represents the bMSC M and q represents the bMSC N.

The semantics of timed MSC presented in this section can also be used as a semantics for un-timed MSC. In an un-timed MSC, all the absolute and relative time constraints can be considered as $(0, \infty)$. So an un-timed MSC can also be represented by a timed lposet (or a set of timed lposets).

3   Refining bMSCs

3.1   Refinement Methodology

We defined vertical refinement and horizontal refinement in the previous work [1]. In the vertical refinement, a component of a system is decomposed into several sub-components according to the architecture of the system given as an SDL specification [2]. During a horizontal refinement, detailed communications can be added between the sub-components. Usually a vertical refinement is followed by a set of horizontal refinements. The refinement process can be repeated many times by alternating vertical refinements and horizontal refinements.

In this paper, we extend our approach for handling time constraints. Time constraints can be added after horizontal refinements and then refined. Our refinement approach now consists of vertical refinements, horizontal refinements and time constraint refinements.

Adding Time Constraints. In a horizontal refinement, designers may add performance requirements, such as the delay between two events, or the time when a process must send a message. These requirements can be represented by absolute and relative time constraints in timed MSC. For example, the bMSC in Fig. 2(a) describes a use case of a door controller [9]. A user inserts his card and enters a PIN, then the Door Controller (DC) opens the door and returns the card. In a vertical refinement, DC is decomposed into an Access Point (AP) and an Authorizer ($auth$) as shown in Fig. 2(b). In a following horizontal refinement, we specify the interactions between AP and $auth$. The AP sends the card ID and PIN to $auth$ for authorization. If they are valid, $auth$ sends back *approval*. Notice that in the bMSC *access2* we are only considering the partial behavior of authorization. After a horizontal refinement, we can add timing requirements, such as AP has to return the card within 10 time units after the user enters a PIN, or $auth$ has to response AP with a delay between 1 and 8 time units. They are represented by the relative time constraints shown in Fig. 2(b).

In our refinement approach, we allow relative time constraints to be added between causally ordered events only. Relative time constraints between un-ordered events are not allowed, because they cannot be guaranteed in a distributed system without further enrichment of the specification. For instances, in Fig. 2(b), either event a (returning card) in AP or event b (opening door) in *door* could occur first. If we add a relative time constraint [1, 2] between them, once one event occurs, the other one has to wait at least 1 and at most 2. Actually process AP does not know what happens in process *door*, and vice versa. This time requirement is at a high level of abstraction and cannot be satisfied without

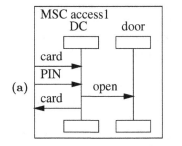 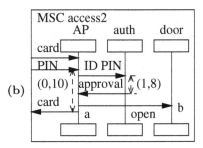

Fig. 2. Refining a door controller

adding other message exchanges between the processes to relate these events. If this kind of time constraint appears in the specification, designers are forced to make events causally ordered by adding messages. In our approach, we can check the existence of this kind of time constraint easily, and then notify designers.

Designers may not add time constraints for all the events in a bMSC in one refinement. If absolute or relative time constraints are not stated explicitly for some events, we assume them to be the whole time domain minus the least element. For example, if the time domain is nonnegative real numbers, then the time constraints are $(0, \infty)$. We reserve the absolute time constraint @[0] for a special event (the beginning of the world). A relative time constraint cannot be 0 because we allow for relative time constraints to appear between causally ordered events only, and these ordered events cannot occur at the same time.

Adding time constraints raises the issue of time consistency [10, 11, 12, 13]. For example, for events a and b such that a occurs before b, if the absolute time constraints for event a and b are @[2, 3] and @[5, 6] respectively, but the relative time constraint between them is [6, 7], then event b should occur between [8, 10], which contradicts its absolute time constraint (@[5, 6]). We consider that a bMSC is consistent if the lposet corresponding to the bMSC is consistent [13]. The time consistency of a bMSC can be checked in polynomial time.

If a bMSC is consistent, we can derive *reduced absolute time constraints* for its events, which are maximal intervals within the original absolute time constraints such that every value in the interval can be an occurrence time for the event without invalidating the consistency. A detailed discussion on reduced absolute time constraints can be found in [13]. Similarly, we can define *reduced relative time constraints* as maximal intervals within the original relative time constraints such that each value in the interval is a delay between two events when they occur within their reduced absolute time constraints. Reduced (absolute and relative) time constraints can be calculated using the Floyd-Warshall algorithm as done in [13].

Refining Time Constraints. When first adding a time constraint, a designer may not know how tight the constraint should be. He should be allowed to refine this time constraint later on. For example, for the bMSC in Fig. 2(b), the designer may find that the delay before AP returns the card (the relative time constraint $(0, 10)$) is too long. The designer may reduce this time constraint to $(0, 8)$, for instance. Note that changing a time constraint which is $(0, \infty)$ is considered as adding a time constraint to the associated event, because the event is actually not constrained.

To define rules of refining time constraints, we first consider the effects of time constraints on a system and its environment. From our point of view, time constraints specify requirements/constraints on a process in the system and assumptions on its environment. The environment of a process consists of all the processes in communication with the process within and outside the system under consideration. Adding an absolute time constraint on a sending event, adds a time requirement/constraint to the process executing the event. For instance, if the time constraint is @$[3, 5]$, then the process has to send the corresponding message at any time between time 3 and 5. If the event is a reception event, the time constraint not only adds a requirement/constraint to the process, but also implies an assumption on the environment. For example, if a time constraint is @$[3, 5]$ for a reception event, then the process has to consume a message from its channels at any time between 3 and 5. To ensure this, the environment has to send this message before time 5.

Similarly, relative time constraints also specify requirements and assumptions. We consider that a relative time constraint between two ordered events is associated with the second event. It constrains the occurrence of the second event, because it specifies how long after the occurrence of the first event, the second event can occur. If the second event is a sending event, the relative time constraint states a requirement for a delay on the process executing the event. The process has to send a message within the delay specified by the time constraint. If the second event is a reception event, the relative time constraint specifies a delay that the process has to wait for a message. In another word, the environment is expected to deliver the message within the time constraint. So relative time constraints on reception events specify assumptions on the environment.

For the refinement of time constraints, we require that constraints on a process become stronger, while assumptions on the environment become weaker. Specifically, we define the following rules.

– If an event is a sending event, the range of the absolute or relative time constraint associated to it can be reduced. The process executing the event is more constrained.
– If an event is a reception event, the range of the absolute or relative time constraint associated with it can be increased. This makes the assumptions on its environment weaker. (Note that the time constraint could be enlarged to $(0, \infty)$, which means the event is not constrained any more.)

With such rules, a refined process can still fit in the same environment. For example, in Fig. 2(b), the delay before AP returns the card is $(0, 10)$. The user expects to get his card within 10 time units after entering PIN. If we refine the time constraint to $(0, 8)$ as shown in Fig. 3, the user may get the card sooner

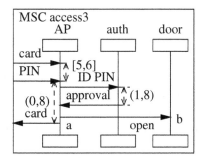

Fig. 3. Refining a door controller further

and his expectation is still met. A time refinement adds more constraints to the system, and reduces its non-determinism. On the other hand, assumptions on the environment can be relaxed by a refinement. For example, in Fig. 3, the relative time constraint [5, 6] specifies a delay between receiving card and PIN in *AP*. The user has to enter PIN within the time constraint. We may change it to [4, 7] in a refinement to relax the assumptions on the user.

3.2   Conformance of bMSCs

After a refinement step, we need to check if the resulting specification conforms to the previous one. In a refinement step, we may add new events to a bMSC and add or refine time constraints. The original events should be preserved and causal orders between them should not be violated. Time constraints can be added and refined only according to the rules defined in Sect. 3.1. Moreover, the time consistency of the new MSC specification has to be considered. If a consistent bMSC is refined into an inconsistent bMSC, then the relation between time constraints is changed from consistency to inconsistency. Semantic errors have been introduced during the refinement. The second bMSC cannot conform to the first one. On the other hand, we do not consider refining further inconsistent bMSCs, because they contain semantic errors.

To define the conformance relation between bMSCs formally, we first define it on lposets.

Definition 2. *Let* $p_1 = (I_1, A_1, E_1, \leq_1, l_1, D_1, T_1)$ *and* $p_2 = (I_2, A_2, E_2, \leq_2, l_2, D_2, T_2)$ *be two timed lposets, and time constraints in* D_i, T_i *($i = 1, 2$) are reduced time constraints. If* p_1 *is time consistent, then* p_2 *conforms to* p_1 *if and only if* p_2 *is time consistent, and there are two injective mappings* $m_e : E_1 \to E_2$*, and* $m_a : A_1 \to A_2$ *such that the following conditions are satisfied:*

- *For events* $e, f \in E_1$*, if* $e \leq_1 f$*, then* $m_e(e) \leq_2 m_e(f)$*.*
- *For an event* $e \in E_1$*,* $m_a(l_1(e)) = l_2(m_e(e))$*.*
- *For an event* $e \in E_1$ *such that* $D_1(e)$ *is not* $(0, \infty)$*, if* e *is a sending event, then* $D_1(e) \supseteq D_2(m_e(e))$*; if* e *is a reception event, then* $D_1(e) \subseteq D_2(m_e(e))$*.*

- For events $e, f \in E_1$ such that $e \leq_1 f$ and $T_1(e, f)$ is not $(0, \infty)$, if f is a sending event, then $T_1(e, f) \supseteq T_2(m_e(e), m_e(f))$; if f is a reception event, then $T_1(e, f) \subseteq T_2(m_e(e), m_e(f))$.

The first condition in Definition 2 means the causal order between two events has to be preserved, and the second condition specifies the relation between m_e and m_a. The last two conditions specify the relation between time constraints. We consider reduced time constraints because they represent the actual time that events could occur and actual delays between events. If a time constraint is $(0, \infty)$, it means the event associated with the constraint is not constrained in fact. Changing a time constraint that is $(0, \infty)$ corresponds to adding a time constraint in an MSC specification. However, once a time constraint is not $(0, \infty)$, changing it has to obey the rules specified in Sect. 3.1.

The conformance relation between bMSCs is defined as follows. Notice that in Definition 2, the set of events in an lposet could be infinite, while in Definition 3, a bMSC contains a finite number of events.

Definition 3. *A bMSC M_2 conforms to a consistent bMSC M_1 if and only if the lposet representing M_2 conforms to the lposet representing M_1.*

Definition 3 is applicable to both timed and un-timed bMSCs, because an un-timed bMSC can also be represented by a timed lposet, in which all the time constraints are $(0, \infty)$. An un-timed bMSC is always time consistent.

For example, the timed bMSC *access2* in Fig. 2(b) conforms to the un-timed bMSC *access1* in Fig. 2(a) because events and orders in *access1* are preserved in *access2* and *access2* is time consistent. The bMSC *access2* is refined further into the bMSC *access3* in Fig. 3. Events and orders are same in these two bMSCs and the time constraints satisfy the relation in Definition 2. The bMSC *access3* is also time consistent. So *access3* conforms to *access2*. However, if we have changed the time constraint $(0, 10)$ in Fig. 2 to $(0, 15)$, the constraint on AP for returning the card becomes weaker. With such a system, the user may get his card back 13 units of time after entering PIN, which was not allowed previously in *access2*. The resulting bMSC would not conform to *access2*.

Our conformance relation extends the matching (conformance) relations for un-timed MSCs defined in [1, 14, 15]. The conformance relation is reflexive, but it is not transitive in general. Let us assume an absolute time constraint @[2, 5] on a reception event. Following the rules, we can enlarge it to @$(0, \infty)$. It means that the constraint is relaxed to the maximum. In other words, there is no constraint any more for this event. Later on, a designer may see this event as an un-timed event and decide to add a constraint @[3, 4]. The time constraint @[3, 4] does not satisfy the relation with the original time constraint @[2, 5] as stated in Definition 2, and we cannot have conformance with the original MSC. To ensure transitivity, we do not allow for a time constraint associated with a reception event to be enlarged to $(0, \infty)$.

Proposition 1. *The conformance relation of bMSCs is reflexive. The conformance relation of bMSCs is transitive if time constraints associated with reception events are not enlarged to $(0, \infty)$ when they are not $(0, \infty)$.*

To check if a bMSC M_2 (represented by $(I_2, A_2, E_2, \leq_2, l_2, D_2, T_2)$) conforms to another bMSC M_1 (represented by $(I_1, A_1, E_1, \leq_1, l_1, D_1, T_1)$), we check the conditions in Definition 2. We first check the time consistency of M_1 and M_2. As discussed in [10, 11, 13], this can be done using the Floyd-Warshall algorithm in time $O(n^3)$, where n is the number of events.

Then we need to decide the mapping m_a between the label sets A_1 and A_2. To achieve this, we have to know which process in I_1 is vertically refined into which processes in I_2. That is, we need to have a surjective function $m_p : I_2 \to I_1$. Designers decide this mapping according to the architecture of the system. Then it is used as an input of our algorithm. For every label $a_1 = send(i_1, j_1, m)$ (or $a_1 = receive(i_1, j_1, m)$), $a_1 \in A_1$, if there is a label $a_2 = send(i_2, j_2, m)$ (or $a_2 = receive(i_2, j_2, m)$), $a_2 \in A_2$, such that $i_1 = m_p(i_2)$ and $j_1 = m_p(j_2)$, we say a_1 is mapped to a_2. If we can not find a mapping for a label in A_1, then two lposets do not conform. Because we need to compare each label A_1 with a label in A_2, the complexity of this step is $O(n^2)$.

According to m_a, we can get m_e between the event sets E_1 and E_2 through $l_1 : E_1 \to A_1$ and $l_2 : E_2 \to A_2$. Because every event is associated with a unique label, l_1 and l_2 are bijective functions. So we can always find m_e according to m_a. For every event $e_1 \in E_1$, we can find an event $e_2 \in E_2$, such that $m_a(l_1(e_1)) = l_2(e_2)$. Then we obtain the mapping m_e between E_1 and E_2. This step can be done in the complexity of $O(n)$.

After obtaining m_e, we check if the orders of events in $\leq_1$ are still preserved in $\leq_2$. In [1], we use event order tables (EOT) [16] to represent orders $\leq_1$ and $\leq_2$. If events e and f have an order, then the cell (e, f) in the EOT is marked as True, otherwise it is marked as False. We extend EOTs to include time constraints in cells. If two events e and f are constrained by a relative time constraint, we write it in the cell (e, f). We write the absolute time constraint of an event e in the cell (e, e). For every cell (e, f) in EOT1, if it is marked as True, we check if the cell $(m_e(e), m_e(f))$ in EOT2 is still marked as True. We also check if the time constraint associated with the cell (e, f) and the time constraint associated with the cell $(m_e(e), m_e(f))$ satisfy the relations defined in Definition 2. Since there are n^2 cells in an EOT, the complexity of this step is $O(n^2)$. Thus the complexity of the whole algorithm is $O(n^3)$.

4   Refining HMSCs

4.1   Refinement Methodology

A bMSC only specifies one scenario of a system. A more complete specification of a system is often given as an HMSC, in which different scenarios are combined. When refining an HMSC specification, we refine each bMSC referred by the HMSC in the way discussed before. Ideally, new bMSCs can be added into the HMSC. For example, if an HMSC specification of an Automatic Teller Machine (ATM) contains bMSCs *login* and *withdraw*, designers may add a bMSC *deposit* to enrich the specification. While this gives more flexibility to designers, it is very complex to check the conformance between HMSCs as discussed in the next subsection. Since the conformance is checked after each refinement procedure, it is important to have an efficient algorithm. A trade-off is to restrict the refinement of HMSCs. To reduce the complexity, we impose the following rules for HMSC refinement.

- Keep the road map of the HMSC unchanged;
- In vertical refinement, all bMSCs are refined at the same time so that each bMSC has the same set of processes;
- In horizontal refinement, each bMSC is refined such that there is at least one event in each process;
- Time constraints are added or changed within each bMSC such that the bMSC is time consistent;
- For each pair of adjacent bMSCs M and N in a path (M appears before N), in each common process of M and N, the upper bound of the reduced absolute time constraint for the first event in N is larger than the upper bound of the reduced absolute time constraint for the last event in M, or both upper bounds are infinity.

The first three rules are taken from our refinement approach of un-timed MSC [1]. Since the road map cannot be changed, the number of bMSCs has to be decided at the beginning, but the bMSCs can be at a very abstract level. The fourth rule requires the consistency of each bMSC and restricts the usage of relative time constraints within bMSCs. In other words, we do not allow for relative time constraints specified between events in different bMSCs. On one hand, a relative time constraint between events in different paths of an HMSC is not meaningful, because these events are alternative. On the other hand, a delay between events in the same path can be set implicitly by absolute time constraints on these events[2] and the relative time constraints within individual bMSCs. The fifth rule is based on the consistency of each bMSC as required by the fourth rule. Since each bMSC is consistent, reduced absolute time constraints exist for events in each bMSC.

For illustration purposes, let us consider the ATM specification in Fig. 4. We refine it according to these rules. We keep the road map unchanged and refine each bMSC. The process ATM_sys is decomposed into two processes ATM and $bank$ in every bMSC, and messages exchanged between them are added as shown in Fig. 5. Before refinement, a relative time constraint in bMSC $withdraw$ specifies the delay between obtaining the amount and delivering the money. It is reduced after refinement to constrain the ATM more. Moreover, the response delay of $bank$ is added in both bMSCs in Fig. 5.

4.2   Conformance of HMSCs

Each path in an HMSC defines an execution scenario of the system under consideration. We look at the conformance of HMSCs through the conformance

---

[2] Absolute time constraints in a loop may lead to inconsistency [13].

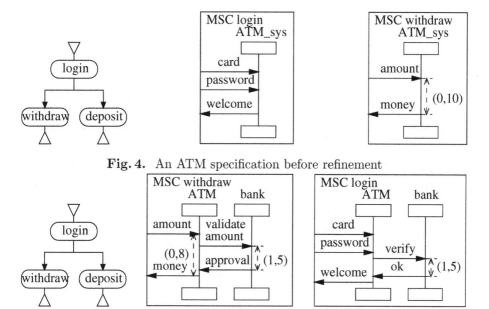

Fig. 4. An ATM specification before refinement

Fig. 5. An ATM specification after refinement

of paths. A path can be represented by a timed lposet obtained by composing sequentially all the bMSCs in the path.

Definition 4. *A path p_2 in an HMSC conforms to a path p_1 in another HMSC if and only if the lposet representing p_2 conforms to the lposet representing p_1.*

Notice that a path could be infinite. In such a case, the lposet contains an infinite number of events. From Definition 4, we define the conformance of HMSCs as follows.

Definition 5. *An HMSC H_2 conforms to another HMSC H_1 if and only if for every path p_1 in H_1, there exists a path p_2 in H_2 such that p_2 conforms to p_1.*

A path in an HMSC may be time consistent or inconsistent. This leads to the notions of strong consistency and weak consistency of HMSCs [13]. If all the scenarios in an HMSC are considered mandatory and must be implemented, then we require all the paths to be consistent. The HMSC must be strongly consistent. If the HMSC is seen as a set of possible behaviors to be implemented and implementing some of them only is sufficient, then the HMSC can be weakly consistent. Weak consistency allows for the inconsistency of some paths in the HMSC. In this paper, we consider strongly consistent HMSCs. Notice that Definition 5 is a general one and does not depend on the notions of consistency or on a specific refinement approach.

To check the conformance of HMSCs in general, we consider a related decision problem, that is, if a path exists in H_2 such that it conforms to a given path in H_1. Similar to the matching problem in un-timed MSC [15], this problem is NP-complete.

Proposition 2. *The problem of finding a path in an HMSC H_2 that conforms to a given (finite) path in H_1 is NP-complete.*

This result suggests a high complexity for checking conformance of HMSCs in general. In our setup and given the refinement rules, we consider a partial solution for checking the conformance as stated in the following proposition.

Proposition 3. *Given a strongly consistent HMSC H_1 and its refinement H_2 obtained following the refinement rules, if the following conditions are satisfied, then H_2 conforms to H_1.*

- *H_2 is strongly consistent,*
- *each bMSC in H_2 conforms to its corresponding bMSC in H_1,*
- *the lower bounds of reduced (absolute and relative) time constraints in each bMSC in H_1 are not changed in H_2, and*
- *in H_2, for each pair of bMSCs M_1' and M_2', such that $M_1' \cdot M_2'$ in H_2, and for each set of axes $\{A_{11}, \ldots, A_{1n}\}$ in M_1' and M_2' resulting from the decomposition of A_1 (in M_1 and M_2 in H_1), the order between the last event of A_1 in M_1 and the first event of A_1 in M_2 is preserved.*

This proposition extends Theorem 1 in [1] for timed MSC. The same applies for Theorem 1 in [1], the conditions in Proposition 3 are sufficient conditions only. If they are not satisfied, we cannot conclude that H_2 does not conform to H_1. For example, it is not necessary to keep the lower bounds of reduced time constraints unchanged. However, requiring this condition ensures that the relation between time constraints in corresponding bMSCs is preserved in HMSCs. Finding conditions that are both sufficient and necessary is currently under investigation.

The conditions in Proposition 3 are easy to check. First, because of the fourth and the fifth rules in our refinement methodology, the resulting HMSC H_2 is upper-bound-later as defined in [13]. The strong consistency of an upper-bound-later HMSC can be check in polynomial time [13]. For the second condition, the conformance of bMSCs can be checked in time $O(n^3)$ as discussed in Sect. 3. The third condition can be checked in linear time by checking each reduced time constraint. For the fourth condition, we need to check each pair of bMSCs and each process in a bMSC in the worst case. This can be done in time $O(m^2p)$, where m is the number of bMSCs and p is the number of processes. Therefore, checking all the conditions in Proposition 3 only requires polynomial time.

5   Related Works

Refinement of real time specifications based on true concurrency has been proposed in [4, 5]. In [4], an action refinement technique is developed using timed bundle event structures. Different equivalence relations have been defined for the purpose of action refinements. In [5], interval event structures are used as a model. An event can be refined into an event structure. Various notions of equivalence of interval event structures have been defined. In [4, 5], an event has a duration, which is different with the time concept in MSC. Moreover, these approaches do not allow for refinement of time constraints.

Besides our previous work [1], some work has been done on the refinement of un-timed MSC. Message refinement is discussed in [17]. A message can be replaced by an MSC, named protocol MSC. A protocol MSC can be unidirectional or bidirectional. Whether or not a message refinement can result in deadlocks in these two cases is investigated. In our refinement approach, we preserve the original messages and add new messages.

Refinement of interworkings is proposed in [14]. An interworking is similar to a bMSC, but the communication between processes is synchronous. When an interworking is refined, a process can be decomposed into constituents and internal messages can be added between these constituents. Using an operational semantics, a refinement relation is defined based on bisimulation. Our semantics is denotational, and our conformance relation can be seen as a combination of the refinement relation in [14] and the matching relation [15].

6   Conclusion

The specification of a system often begins with a description of functionalities at a high level of abstraction. This specification can be refined step by step into a design specification by adding details about the internal behavior, architecture, time constraints, etc. In a previous work [1], we introduced a refinement approach and conformance relations for un-timed MSC specifications. In this paper, we generalize them to timed MSCs to take into account the new time features in MSC. Our methodology allows for the refinement of an un-timed MSC into a timed MSC. The later can be refined further through the refinement of time constraints. Conformance relations have been defined, and algorithms for checking these relations have been developed and discussed.

In our refinement, we restrict the usage of relative time constraints. A relative time constraint can only be added on causally ordered events to ensure that a specification can be implemented. Alternatively, we may allow for relative time constraints between un-related events during design. However, to be implementable the final specification should not contain these relative time constraints. Moreover, we may allow a relative time constraint to be split between different bMSCs in an HMSC specification. Allowing for this kind of relative time constraints makes the conformance much harder to check. We will be investigating these issues in our future work.

When refining an HMSC, we impose refinement rules in order to reduce the complexity of checking the conformance. We will be investigating if some of the rules can be relaxed while the conformance relation between HMSCs can still be checked efficiently.

Acknowledgments

This work has been supported by France Telecom R&D through a contract between France Telecom and Concordia University. We also thank the reviewers for their helpful comments.

References

[1] F. Khendek, S. Bourduas, D. Vincent. Stepwise Design with Message Sequence Charts. Proceedings of FORTE'2001, Cheju Island, Korea, August 2001. 234, 238, 242, 243, 244, 246, 247, 249

[2] ITU-T. Recommendation Z.100 (08/02), Specification and Description Language (SDL). International Telecommunication Union, Geneva. 234, 238

[3] ITU-T. Recommendation Z.120 (11/99), Message Sequence Chart (MSC). International Telecommunication Union, Geneva. 234

[4] M. Majster-Cederbaum, J. Wu. Action Refinement for True Concurrent Real Time. Seventh International Conference on Engineering of Complex Computer Systems, Sweden, 2001. 235, 246, 247

[5] D. Murphy, D. Pitt. Real-timed Concurrent Refineable Behaviours, Proceedings of the 2nd International Symposium on Formal Techniques in Real-Time and Fault-Tolerant Systems, LNCS **571** (1992). 235, 246, 247

[6] S. Heymer. A Non-Interleaving Semantics for MSC. 1st Workshop on SDL and MSC(SAM'98), Germany, 1998. 236

[7] J.P. Katoen, L. Lambert. Pomsets for Message Sequence Charts. 1st Workshop on SDL and MSC(SAM'98), Germany, 1998. 236

[8] T. Zheng, F. Khendek, L. Helouët. A Semantics for Timed MSC, Validation and Implementation of Scenario-Based Specifications (VISS'02). ENTCS 65:7, 2002. 236

[9] Ø. Haugen. MSC-2000 Interaction Diagrams for the new Millennium. Computer Networks, 35 (2001) 721–732. 238

[10] R. Alur, G.J. Holzmann, D. Peled. An Analyzer for Message Sequence Charts. Proceedings of 2nd International Workshop on Tools and Algorithms for the construction and Analysis of Systems (TACAS'96). LNCS 1055, (1996) 35-48. 239, 243

[11] H. Ben-Abdallah, S. Leue. Expressing and Analyzing Timing Constraints in Message Sequence Chart Specifications. Department of Electrical and Computer Engineering, University of Waterloo. Technical Report 97-04, 1997. 239, 243

[12] X. Li,J. Lilius. Timing Analysis of UML Sequence Diagrams. Turku Centre for Computer Science. TUCS Technical Report **281** 1999. 239

[13] T. Zheng, F. Khendek. Time Consistency of MSC-2000 Specifications. to appear in Computer Networks, 2003. 239, 243, 244, 245, 246, 250

[14] S. Mauw, M.A. Reniers. Refinement in Interworkings. Proceedings of CONCUR'96, LNCS **1119**, (1996). 242, 247

[15] A. Muscholl, D. Peled, Z. Su. Deciding Properties for Message Sequence Charts. Proceedings of the 1st International Conference on Foundations of Software Science and Computation Structures, LNCS **1378** (1998). 242, 246, 247, 249

[16] M.M. Musa, F. Khendek, G. Butler. New Results on Deriving SDL Specification from MSCs. Proceedings of SDL Forum'99, Elsevier Science B. V., June 1999. 243

[17] A. Engels. Languages for Analysis and Testing of Event Sequences, Ph.D. thesis. Eindhoven University of Technology, 2001. 247

Appendix

Proof (Proposition 1). For a bMSC represented by $(I, A, E, \leq, l, D, T)$, we can build two mappings $m_e : E \to E$, and $m_a : A \to A$ such that Definition 3 is satisfied. So a bMSC conforms to itself.

For transitivity, if $M_2 = (I_2, A_2, E_2, \leq_2, l_2, D_2, T_2)$ conforms to $M_1 = (I_1, A_1, E_1, \leq_1, l_1, D_1, T_1)$, then there are two injective mappings $m_{e12} : E_1 \to E_2$, and $m_{a12} : A_1 \to A_2$ such that Definition 3 is satisfied. Similarly, for M_2 and M_3, if M_3 conforms to M_2, then there exist $m_{e23} : E_2 \to E_3$, and $m_{a23} : A_2 \to A_3$ such that Definition 3 is satisfied. We construct two functions, $m_e : E_1 \to E_3$ and $m_a : A_1 \to A_3$, which are the composition of m_{e23} and m_{e12}, m_{a23} and m_{a12} respectively. That is, $m_e = m_{e23} \cdot m_{e12}$, $m_a = m_{a23} \cdot m_{a12}$. Then for two events e and f in M_1, we have:

- If $e \leq_1 f$, since M_2 conforms to M_1, we get $m_{e12}(e) \leq_2 m_{e12}(f)$. Furthermore, because M_3 conforms to M_2, we get $m_{e23}(m_{e12}(e)) \leq_3 m_{e23}(m_{e12}(f))$. So $m_e(e) \leq_3 m_e(f)$.
- $m_a(l_1(e)) = m_{a23}(m_{a12}(l_1(e))) = m_{a23}(l_2(m_{e12}(e))) = l_3(m_{e23}(m_{e12}(e))) = l_3(m_e(e))$.
- If e is a sending event, and $D_1(e)$ is not $(0, \infty)$, we can get $D_1(e) \supseteq D_2(m_{e12}(e))$. Since $m_{e12}(e)$ is still a sending event, we get $D_2(m_{e12}(e)) \supseteq D_3(m_{e23}(m_{e12}(e))) = D_3(m_e(e))$. So $D_1(e) \supseteq D_3(m_e(e))$.
- If e is a reception event, and $D_1(e)$ is not $(0, \infty)$, we can get $D_1(e) \subseteq D_2(m_{e12}(e))$. Since $D_2(m_{e12}(e))$ is also not $(0, \infty)$ according to the condition of the proposition, we get $D_2(m_{e12}(e)) \subseteq D_3(m_{e23}(m_{e12}(e))) = D_3(m_e(e))$. So $D_1(e) \subseteq D_3(m_e(e))$.
- Similarly to absolute time constraints, we get $T_1(e, f) \supseteq T_2(m_e(e), m_e(f))$ if f is a sending event, and $T_1(e, f) \subseteq T_2(m_e(e), m_e(f))$ if f is a reception event.

So M_3 conforms to M_1. □

Proof (Proposition 2). For a given finite path in H_1, we can guess a path in H_2 which conforms to it. So the problem is NP. The Proposition 3.5 in [15] shows that matching an un-timed bMSC with an un-timed HMSC is NP-complete. We reduce the matching problem to our problem since a finite path can be seen as a bMSC. We add absolute and relative time constraints $(0, \infty)$ to events in an un-timed bMSC M and an un-timed HMSC H. Then they become a timed bMSC M' and a timed HMSC H'. M' conforms to H' if and only if M conforms to H. Then the problem is NP-complete. □

Proof (Proposition 3). Since we keep the road map unchanged, for each path p in H_1, there is a corresponding path p' in H_2. We prove p' conforms to p in the follows.

- Since H_2 is strongly consistent, p' is consistent.
- Due to the second and the third conditions of the proposition, according to Theorem 1 in [1], all the events and orders in p are preserved in p'.

- For a reduced absolute time constraint t in a bMSC in p, since each bMSC in p' conforms to its corresponding bMSC in p, the corresponding reduced absolute time constraint t' in the bMSC in p' satisfies the relation in Definition 2 with t. Because the HMSC is upper-bound-later, the upper bounds of t and t' are not changed in the lposets representing p and p' according to Proposition 11 in [13]. Since we do not change the lower bounds of reduced absolute and relative time constraints, the lower bounds of t and t' are same in the lposets representing p and p'. So reduced absolute time constraints in p and p' still satisfy the defined relation.
- For a reduced relative time constraint between events within a bMSC in p, since each bMSC in p' conforms to its corresponding bMSC in p, the corresponding reduced relative time constraint t' in a bMSC in p' satisfies the defined relation with t. Because the events are within one bMSC, the relation is still kept in the lposets representing p and p'.
- For a reduced relative time constraint t between events in different bMSCs (t is obtained implicitly from relative time constraints in the same bMSC and the delay between two bMSCs), since the delay between two bMSCs is assumed as $(0, \infty)$, the upper bound of t is always ∞. Because we do not change the lower bound of reduced relative time constraints when refining an HMSC, the lower bound of t is not changed. So t is not changed after refinement.

Thus p' conforms to p. ☐

Using Projections for the Detection of Anomalous Behaviors

Jacqueline Floch[1,2] and Rolv Bræk[2]

[1] SINTEF Telecom and Informatics
N-7465 Trondheim, Norway
jacqueline.floch@sintef.no
[2] Department of Telematics, Norwegian University of Science and Technology
(NTNU)
N-7491 Trondheim, Norway
{jacqueline.floch,rolv.braek}@item.ntnu.no

Abstract. A projection is a simplified system description or viewpoint that emphasizes some of the system properties while hiding others. In this paper, we describe a projection transformation that, when applied to SDL components, produces semantic interface descriptions. Contrary to traditional object interfaces that restrict the declaration of operation signatures, semantic interfaces describe dialogues and constraints between components, and can be exploited to build a system that behaves correctly. Using projections simplifies the validation analysis, and enables the designer to comprehend single interfaces. When following this approach, ambiguous and conflicting behaviors can be identified at design time.

1 Introduction

Building services that span across multiple network technologies at a pace and with a degree of harmonization that keeps up with user expectation requires new solutions and new engineering methods. Dynamic composition techniques are currently investigated at NTNU as a means to rapid service construction and deployment [1, 2]. Our work has addressed the following question:

How can we ensure that service components that are modified or added dynamically in a system interact consistently with other components of the system?

The dynamic composition of systems sets particular requirements on validation. The analysis should be restricted to the parts of the system affected by a modification. Furthermore, as components may be bound dynamically at runtime, the analysis should apply on types - not instances. We propose a validation approach that makes use of projections [3, 4]. The projection is an abstraction technique. A projection is a simplified system description or viewpoint that emphasizes some of the system properties while hiding others. Rather than analyzing the whole system, the projections are analyzed. This proves to be simpler, and also easier for the designer to understand.

R. Reed (Ed.): SDL 2003, LNCS 2708, pp. 251–268, 2003.

In this paper, we concentrate on the description of the projection transformation. We define a transformation that only retains the aspects significant for the purpose of validation of associations between components. The transformation applies to service components modeled as state machines using SDL [5]. The generated projections are also described as state machines, using a notation inspired by SDL. The objective of using the projection transformation is twofold. On one hand, it contributes to simplifying the validation analysis. On the other hand, it contributes to facilitating the comprehension of single interfaces, and it enables the designer to detect ambiguous and conflicting behaviors at design time.

We first introduce the modeling concepts of service roles (**s-roles**) and service association roles (**a-roles**). A-roles capture the interaction behavior of an s-role on an association between s-roles. They can be obtained by projection from s-roles. Sect 3 introduces the projection transformation and identifies the set of concepts needed for a-role modeling. In Sect. 4, three transformations are shortly described that can be applied on a-role state graphs in order to simplify the graphs and reduce their size. In Sect. 5, particular specification patterns are identified that may lead to ambiguous and conflicting behaviors. Ambiguous and conflicting behaviors are symptoms of errors. An interesting result in our approach is that these anomalous behaviors can already be identified during system design.

2   Actors, Roles and Collaborations

Service design is complex. Communication services normally require the coordinated effort of several distributed components, where some of the components may be involved in several services. In a dynamic context, this complexity increases further as services are designed to be dynamically adapted.

Our approach to service design makes use of roles [6]. A service is seen as a collaboration between s-roles, and service execution requires the assignment of roles to computational objects called actors. By using services roles (s-roles), we are able to better comprehend the collaborations between components involved in a service, and to break down the complexity of service specification. We are also able to compose s-roles to provide new services in a flexible way [7].

We describe service roles as state machines using SDL. As SDL does not define the concept of role, we select the SDL composite state concept to model s-roles. Both composite states and s-roles represent parts of behavior. SDL composite states support the structuring state machines, and thus also fit the modeling of s-role composition [7].

S-roles interact with other s-roles over associations. An association involves exactly two s-roles. An a-role (service **association role**) is the visible behavior of an s-role on an association (see Fig. 1). A-roles abstract the internal behavior of s-roles, and the interactions towards other s-roles. This abstraction facilitates the validation analysis, as we shall see.

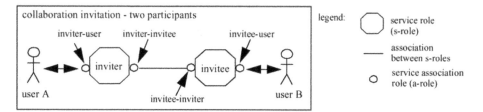

Fig. 1. S-roles and A-roles

An a-role describes an interface behavior. A-roles will be modeled as state machines (see Sect.3), and, in that way, they capture the semantics of interaction between s-roles. A-roles overcome the limitations of static object interfaces. In the current distributed processing approaches, computational objects are described by static interfaces limited to the declaration of operation signatures (see for example [8]). Such interface descriptions may facilitate the construction of a system by providing a means for retrieving objects that may potentially offer a function or feature, but they do not provide sufficient support for building a system that behaves correctly.

Architectures based on traditional object interfaces lack two main properties [9]. They only describe the functions provided by an object, and fail to describe the functions required by an object. This makes it difficult to determine the effects of changing an interface on other objects. Moreover, they do not describe the semantics of a connection between objects and the constraints on using the interfaces. For example, it is not possible to ensure that the interactions between objects will occur in a correct order.

Contrary to traditional object interfaces, a-roles describe dialogues between s-roles. The events that have previously occurred in the a-role are represented by states. Furthermore, two a-roles on an association complement each other. It is possible to determine the a-roles required by an s-role from the a-roles provided by this s-role.

3   A-roles as Projections of S-roles

A-roles are modeled as state machines using a notation inspired by SDL. As a-roles are restricted to the visible behavior of s-roles on associations, full SDL is not needed. Some extensions to the SDL notation are introduced to hide non-observable behaviors: the s-role behaviors not visible at the interface. The set of concepts needed for a-role modeling is identified by defining the projection transformation from s-roles to a-roles.

An important property of the projection transformation is that it maintains the observable behavior on associations between s-roles. In other words, a-roles exhibit the same behavior as the s-roles from which they are derived, on the association to which they are attached. This means that an s-role and the projected

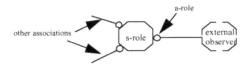

Fig. 2. A-role and External Observer

a-role *should be able* to generate the same sequence of outputs on an association when offered the same sequence of inputs on this association.

Note that the s-role and the projected a-role are not restricted to generate a single sequence of outputs for a given sequence of inputs; alternative sequences are allowed. The behavior determining the choice of a sequence is not visible at the association interface, and an a-role may appear to make non-deterministic choices. This non-determinism results from the abstraction of the s-roles internal decisions and the interactions on other associations.

The relation between an s-role and a projected a-role is a kind of equivalence relation. Several equivalence relations have been proposed [10]. These relations are based upon the concept of observable behavior: "two agents are equivalent, if they exhibit the same behavior", where several interpretations may be given as to what behavior is observable. In particular, the internal actions may be observable or not. In our approach, the observation is restricted to one association at a time, and the abstraction of internal actions is observed in terms of state changes, where each state represents different behavior events.

Definition: Observable Association Behavior.
The behavior provided by an s-role on an association is called the observable association behavior.

We will also use the term *external observer* to denote some external machine that interacts with the s-role on an association (see Fig. 2). An external observer perceives the signals sent by an s-role on an association. It can observe how an s-role reacts, or responds, to the reception of a signal or sequence of signals. An external observer does not observe s-role state changes directly, only indirectly when state changes lead to distinct responses.

The following sub-sections introduce the concepts of a-role modeling by defining the projection transformation from s-roles to a-roles. In our work, we have shown that the proposed projection transformation maintains the observable association behavior as s-roles. We omit presenting this proof in this paper.

3.1   Signals

We assume that all the communication between s-roles takes place by the exchange of signals, and that signals exchanged on an association between two s-roles are conveyed asynchronously on the same communication path. A communication path is constituted by a sequence of connected channels. With this

Fig. 3. Visible and Non-Visible Signals

assumption, we ensure that signal ordering is preserved during transport on an association. Communication through remote variables and remote procedure calls is not considered.

An association between two s-roles handles the signals that can be exchanged between these two s-roles, and does not contain any other signalling. For each s-role, the association includes the signals that can be received from the association, and the signals that can be sent on the association. We will use the terms *visible* signals and *non-visible* signals to denote signals that are respectively exchanged and not exchanged on the association where a projection is done (see Fig. 3).

An a-role state graph describes the exchange of visible signals :the sending and consumption of signals exchanged on the association too which the a-role is attached. The consumption of signals from other associations (that is, non-visible input signals) by the s-role may lead to state changes that influence the further behavior on the association to which the a-role is attached. These signals are abstracted in the a-role state graph and become SDL spontaneous inputs. Their accurate identification is not relevant: the state changes are. Spontaneous transitions are further explained in the next section. The signals sent on the other associations – the non-visible output signals – have no influence on the state changes, and are not represented in the a-role state graph at all.

3.2 States and Transitions

While a state in the state graph of an s-role represents a condition in which a signal may be consumed, a state in the state graph of an a-role represents a condition in which signals may be consumed or sent.

The s-role states that represent conditions for the consumption of visible signals are projected to states that also represent conditions for the consumption of these signals in the a-role. A simple projection is shown in Fig. 4. The behavior that is not visible at the interface, here sending signals "X" and "Y" on other associations, is represented by dashed symbols. This notation is also used in the subsequent figures.

The consumption of signals from other associations is projected to spontaneous transitions in the a-role. When modeling a-roles, a spontaneous transition indicates that some non-visible signal consumption has taken place that leads to a transition. To simplify the state graphs, we omit using the SDL spontaneous input designator "none". Signal sending, if any, is directly specified after the

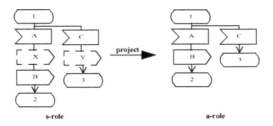

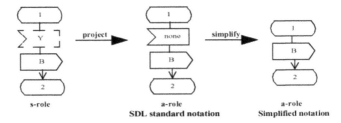

Fig. 4. State Projection: Condition for Signal Consumption

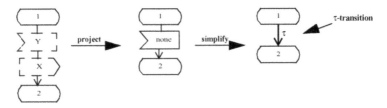

Fig. 5. Spontaneous Transition: Simplified Notation (extension to SDL)

Fig. 6. τ-Transition (extension to SDL)

state. Using this notation as in Fig. 5, the state appears as a condition for signal sending. This notation is an extension[1] to SDL.

When the transitions triggered by non-visible signals do not prescribe any visible signal sending, the simplified notation leads to empty transitions. We call such empty transitions τ-transitions. The transitions are marked using the symbol "τ" as in Fig. 6.

3.3   Implicit Transitions

We retain the SDL semantics for the interpretation of transitions between states. A signal received in a state that is not specified as input or save in that state, is implicitly consumed: it is discarded.

---

[1] Editorial note: The notation is the same as an unlabeled exit from a sub-state in SDL.

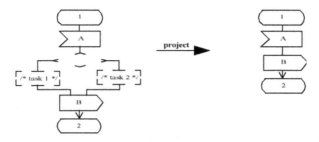

Fig. 7. Abstracting a Decision Node: Internal Behavior

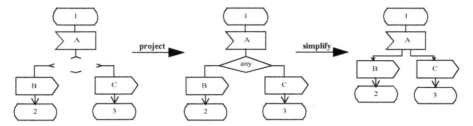

Fig. 8. Abstracting a Decision Node: Before Signal Sending (SDL extension)

3.4 Internal Actions

The internal actions of an s-role, such as tasks, agent instance creations or timer operations are not visible at the interface. They are not represented in the a-roles. Thus an a-role transition is either empty, or it describes the sending of a visible signal or a set of signals.

3.5 Decision

A decision consists of a question and a set of answers, where these answers lead to different behavior choices. The processing of the question is an internal action that is not visible at the interface. The answers also represent internal information. The choices, on the other hand, may result in visible behaviors, such as the sending of a signal or a transition to a new state. Such choices are described in the a-role.

In Fig. 7, the decision choices describe internal behaviors; they are not represented in the a-role.

In Fig. 8, the decision choices describe the sending of visible signals. The choices are represented in the a-role, but not the decision. The decision is abstracted to a non-deterministic choice. Note that we introduce an extension to the SDL notation: two transitions attached to the same input are not allowed in SDL.

A decision taking place within a transition that does not describe any visible signal consumption and sending is projected as described in the previous examples. The projection of decision may lead to multiple τ-transitions.

3.6   Initial States

S-roles initial states are projected to a-role initial states. An a-role initial state represents the start of interactions on an association. Initial states are modeled in the a-role state graph using SDL start nodes. S-role initial transitions are projected in a similar way as other transitions. Recall that the consumption of signals is not allowed in start nodes. An entry condition may be associated with an initial state. The projection maintains the entry conditions attached to the initial states.

3.7   Exit States

S-roles exit states are projected to a-role exit states. An a-role exit state represents the end of an interaction on an association. Exit states are modeled in the a-role state graph using SDL return nodes. An exit condition may be associated with an exit state. The projection maintains the exit conditions attached to the exit states.

3.8   Timer Signals

Timer signals are projected to SDL spontaneous inputs similarly as for signals received from other associations.

3.9   Save

The projection of save is complex. When the consumption of saved signals is combined with spontaneous transitions, the activation of spontaneous transitions may occur before the consumption of saved signals. The activation of a spontaneous transition may occur at any time, independently of the presence of signals in the input port. In order to define a simple projection of save that maintains the observable association behavior, we propose to constrain the use of save. Constraints will be expressed by design rules.

Save Projection: A Simple Definition. We would like to define the projection of save so that the saving of visible signals is maintained in the a-role graph, while the saving of other signals is not. Intuitively, this seems an acceptable definition. The information related to the saving of visible signals is of importance, as it influences the allowed ordering of signal sending on the association. On the other hand, only the knowledge about state changes triggered by the consumption of non-visible signals is relevant, not the identification of these signals, and not the moment of their arrival.

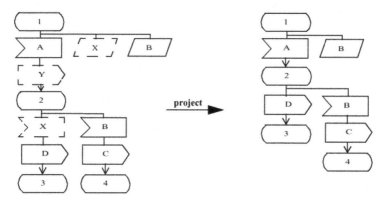

Fig. 9. Projection of Save Signals: a Simple Definition

Figure 9 illustrates this simple projection. Only the saving of the visible signal "B" is maintained in the a-role graph. An external observer may either send "A" before "B", or "B" before "A". In both cases, the two s-role behaviors described in state "2" can occur, depending on whether the saving of "X" has taken place before "B", after "B" or not at all[2]. An external observer either receives "C" or "D". The same two behaviors can also be observed when interacting with the a-role, depending on whether the spontaneous transition occurs immediately when entering state "2" or not.

Interference between Save and Spontaneous Transition. The save feature is often applied in order to enforce a strict ordering on the consumption of signals on an association. When this use of save is combined with interactions on other associations, the simple projection of save does not always maintain the observable association behavior. The activation of spontaneous transitions in the projected a-role may interfere with the retrieval of saved signals in an unintended way.

An example is shown in Fig. 10. Here the interaction on the association carrying "A" and "B" is combined with an interaction on another association. The visible signals "A" and "B" may be sent in various orders, and the s-role handles them in the fixed order "A" before "B". When "B" is sent before "A", "B" is necessarily the first signal in the input port when entering state "2". Thus the saving of "B" enforces the s-role to always handle "B" before "X". In that case, the s-role always sends "C". The a-role however, may either send "C" or "D" depending on the activation of the spontaneous transition that sends "D".

Similarly, the s-role described in case (a) in Fig. 11 and its derived a-role do not provide the same observable association behavior. While the s-role fails to interact consistently when "B" is sent before "A": "C" (and anything) never

---

[2] Editorial note: A "save" of "X" means "X" is not consumed in the state – there is no "saving" *action*: the *arrival* of "X" wrt. "B" determines the behavior.

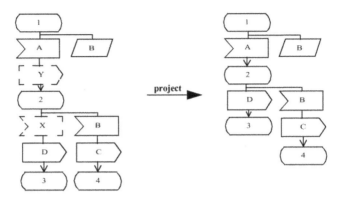

Fig. 10. Projection of a Save Signal: an Undesirable A-role Behavior (1)

happens, the a-role may sometimes send "C" depending on the activation of the spontaneous transition. We observe that the same a-role is obtained by projection of the s-role described in case (b). Here however, the s-role and its derived a-role behave similarly. The saving and retrieval of "X" occur independently from the saving and retrieval of "B". This is properly modeled by the spontaneous transition.

Of course, the behaviors described in Fig. 11 are not desirable. In both cases, "B" may be discarded in state "2". If the saving of "B" is introduced in state "2", we observe that the s-role and the projected a-role would provide an identical behavior.

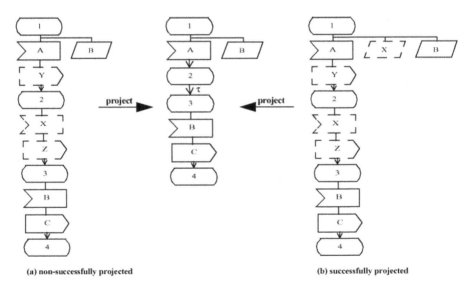

Fig. 11. Projection of Save Signals: an Undesirable A-role Behavior (2)

The interference between the spontaneous transitions and the retrieval of saved signals in the input port invalidate the proposed projection of save. The projection does not always maintain the observable association behavior. The previous examples illustrate two types of undesirable interferences:

- The spontaneous activation of a transition may prevent a saved signal from being discarded from the input port. In some way, the interference partially repairs an incorrect behavior specification. This was shown in case (a) of Fig. 11.
- The spontaneous activation of a transition may prevent a saved signal from being consumed when it is stored first in the input port. This was shown in Fig. 10.

While the first kind of interference is avoided by introducing a design rule enforcing a consistent use of save, the second may either be avoided by the redefinition of the projection of save, or by a design rule constraining how save should be used.

Save Consistency. The discarding of a saved signal from the input port is not desirable neither with respect to the projection of s-roles nor with respect to the consistency of interaction between s-roles. Therefore, we recommend the following design rule.

> **Design Rule: Save Consistency.** The saving of a signal should be repeated in the successor state(s) of the state where save is specified, until the consumption of the saved signal is specified. A successor state specified according to this rule is said to maintain save consistency, or to be save consistent with its predecessor state(s). An s-role specified according to this rule is said to be save consistent.

Using this rule, the two case examples shown in Fig. 11, should be redefined. "B" should be saved in state "2" in both cases. Then the projection of save faithfully maintains the observable association behavior.

Retrieval of Saved Signals. The design rule Save consistency' addresses the problem of the discarding of saved signals, but not that of retrieval as shown in Fig. 10. We may consider two kinds of solutions to the retrieval problem:

- One is to redefine the projection of the retrieval of a saved signal by adding control on the activation of the spontaneous transition.
- Another is to constrain the use of save. Save is a complicating feature and should not end up modeling both alternative orderings and concurrent association behaviors.

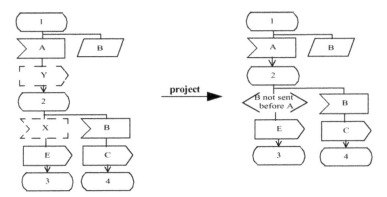

Fig. 12. Projection of a Save Signal: Using a Continuous Signal

Controlling the Activation of Spontaneous Transitions. Control can be set on the activation of a spontaneous transition by associating a precondition to the activation. In SDL, preconditions can be expressed using continuous signals. Figure 12 illustrates this approach. The precondition only depends on the inter- action on the association where the projection is done. "B not sent before A" means that B is not saved. Note that in the case where "B" is sent after "A", both transitions in state "2" of the projection may also occur. According to the SDL semantics, signals in the input port are retrieved before continuous signals are interpreted when entering a new state.

Preconditions should only be applied in the case where the non-visible signals projected to spontaneous inputs may interfere with the retrieval of a saved signal in an undesirable way. In the case where non-visible signals can be stored in the input port before the visible saved signal, preconditions should not be added. For example, in Fig. 9 the non-visible signal "X" may be saved before "B". Preconditions are not needed in that case.

Constraining the Use of Save. This refined projection of save is rather simple. However having in mind that the save concept introduces complexity, we propose to introduce constraints on using save.

Save serves two main purposes:

- It may be used to enable alternative signal sending orderings while a strict order on the consumption of signals is enforced. Seen from the complemen- tary a-role, the ordering of signal sending is relaxed.
- It may be used to facilitate the description of concurrent behaviors on mul- tiple associations. For example, save may be used to enable an interaction on an association not to be interrupted by the arrival of signals from other associations.

In order to limit the complexity of a design, we advise not to use save to re- lax the ordering of signal sending. Alternative orderings should only be specified when required for optimization purposes, or when constrained by external interfaces. Furthermore, we recommend not to combine the use of save for alternative orderings together with the description of concurrent behaviors. This constraint applies both when the modeling of concurrent behaviors involves save or not.

In Fig. 10, save is used to describe alternative sending orderings. This use of save overlaps with the description of a concurrent behavior: "X" can be received when "B" is retrieved. The s-role should be re-designed, avoiding the saving of "B".

In Fig. 9, save is used to describe alternative sending orderings and concurrent behaviors: both "X" and "B" are saved. The s-role should be re-designed. Although it is possible in that case to generate a projection that provides an identical observable association as the s-role, the s-role behaves in a non-deterministic manner.

> **Design Rule: Save and Ordering.** Using save for the modeling of alternative signal orderings on one association should be restricted to special cases, for example when required for optimization purposes, or when constrained by external interfaces.

Alternative orderings can easily be identified: a state that can both save and consume signals received from the same association models alternative orderings.

> **Design Rule: Ordering with Save and Concurrency.** Using save for the modeling of alternative signal orderings on one association should not overlap with the modeling of concurrent behaviors.

Overlapping can easily be identified: a signal saved in a state that can consume signals from the same association, should not be retrieved in a state that can consume signals from other associations. When this rule is enforced, the projected a-role does not describe any spontaneous transition in the state where the saved signal is retrieved. Thus interferences between spontaneous transitions and the retrieval of a saved signal do not occur.

3.10   Enabling Condition

We have assumed that communication between elementary s-roles take place through signal exchange. Thus enabling conditions are not used to describe any information exchange between s-roles. They represent local conditions that are set before entering the state to which the enabled conditions apply. The graph can be transformed by replacing the enabling condition with a decision before the projection transformation is applied.

4   A-role Graph Refinement

The state graph obtained by projection may be transformed in order to simplify the graphs and reduce their size. These transformations both contribute

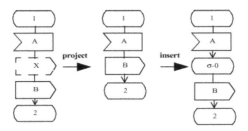

Fig. 13. σ-State Insertion

to facilitate interface validation and augment the comprehension of the interface behaviors by a designer. Three transformations are shortly introduced here. Similar to the projection transformation, they maintain the observable association behavior. We omit proving this property in this paper

4.1   Transformation to a Transition Chart

We first transform the a-role state graph to a transition chart. A transition chart is a particular state graph where each transition between states has just a single event: an input, an output or a silent event called the τ-event. τ-events trigger τ-transitions. σ-states are defined as a specialization of the SDL state: a σ-state implicitly saves all visible signals. Furthermore, at least one of the output events described in a σ-state always occurs. The transformation of an a-role state graph to a transition chart is performed by inserting a σ-state before the sending of a signal, when no state already precedes signal sending as in Fig. 13.

Using transition charts, reasoning about a-roles and their complementary a-roles (the provided and required a-roles) becomes easier.

4.2   Gathering

The transformation from s-roles to a-roles may lead to graphs where several states linked by τ-transitions take place successively. Gathering (see Fig. 14) is a transformation that replaces such states by a single state when the τ-transitions have no influence on the observable association behavior. Gathering can only be applied when:

– The τ-successor (the state triggered by the τ-event) and the τ-predecessor (the state preceding the τ-successor) define the same input behavior.
– The τ-successor and τ-predecessor define the same save behavior.

4.3   Minimization

Transition charts may contain equivalent states that exhibit the same observable association behavior and lead to states that also exhibit the same observable

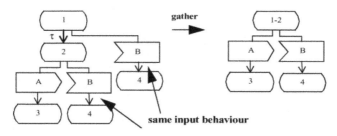

Fig. 14. Gathering

association behavior. In order to facilitate interface validation, such states are replaced by a single state. This replacement, called minimization, also reduces the size of the state graph.

Equivalence may be defined in different manners depending on whether τ-events are observed or not [10]. In our approach, gathering and minimization are combined. τ-events that contribute to state changes influencing the observable association behavior are retained.

We have defined equivalence in terms of triggering events such that it is possible to easily define an operational minimization algorithm, and we have proposed an algorithm based on the concept of partitions of k-equivalent states [11].

5 Ambiguous and Conflicting Behaviors

A-roles are simplified system descriptions that capture the component interface behaviors. A-role graphs are simpler that s-role graphs and thus easier to understand. The review of a-role graphs enables the designer to detect anomalous behaviors, such as ambiguous an conflicting behaviors. An ambiguous behavior takes place when an external observer is not able to determine which behavior is expected by an a-role. A conflict occurs when the behaviors of an a-role and its complementary a-role diverge. Ambiguous and conflicting behaviors are usually symptoms of errors. An interesting property is that they can be identified at system design - before validation analysis is applied. Ambiguous and conflicting behaviors are properties of state machine types - not instances.

We propose a classification of specification patterns that may lead to anomalous behaviors:

- Equivoque transitions and acute τ-transitions may lead to ambiguous behaviors.
- Mixed initiative states may lead to conflicting behaviors.

In our work, we have proposed validation solutions that handle anomalous behaviors and design rules that enable the designer to develop well-formed state machines. These techniques will be covered in a later article.

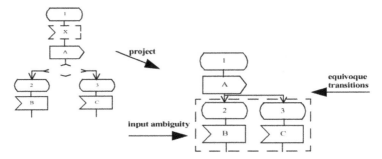

Fig. 15. Equivoque Transitions and Ambiguity

5.1 Equivoque Transitions

Two or more transitions are equivoque when they are defined for the same state and the same event (input, output or τ-event), and lead to distinct non-equivalent states. Equivoque transitions may lead to ambiguous behaviors (see Fig. 15).

We distinguish between several types of ambiguity:

– Strong input ambiguity occurs when at some stage of an interaction, an external observer is not able to determine which of the input(s) is expected by the a-role.
– Strong mixed ambiguity occurs when an external observer is not able to determine which of the input or output events is expected by the a-role.
– Weak input and mixed ambiguities are special forms of strong input and mixed ambiguities where some, but not all, events can be observed.
– Termination ambiguity occurs when at some stage of an interaction, an external observer is not able to determine whether the a-role has terminated, or is waiting for a triggering event to occur.
– Termination occurrence and condition ambiguities are special forms of termination ambiguity where termination is observed, but not its occurrence or its condition.

5.2 Mixed Initiatives

A mixed initiative state is a state where both signal consumption and sending can occur (see Fig. 16). As a-roles communicate asynchronously, they perceive the occurrence of communication at different moments of time. The reception of a signal is perceived some time after its sending. When an a-role and its complementary a-role are both enabled to send a signal during the same interaction step, the signals sent may cross each other. Such behavior may lead to unspecified signal reception, and deadlocks where each a-role state machine waits for the other machine's answer. A-roles and the s-roles from which they are derived, should be specified such that potential conflicts are detected and resolved, converging to a common behavior.

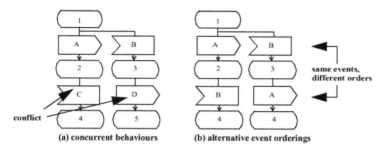

Fig. 16. Mixed Initiatives

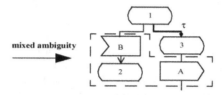

Fig. 17. Acute τ-Transitions and Ambiguity

5.3 Acute τ-Transitions

Acute τ-transitions are τ-transitions that are not removed from the a-role transition chart by gathering and minimization. Acute τ-transitions are usually symptoms of ambiguity (see Fig. 17). They may lead to ambiguous behaviors, either as triggers of equivoque transitions as explained in Sect.5.1, or when combined with other transitions.

6 Conclusion

This paper has described a projection transformation that can be used to generate semantic interface descriptions from SDL components. The transformation only retains the aspects significant for the purpose of validation of associations between components. Using this transformation, it is possible to detect - already at design time - anomalous behaviors that are symptoms of errors. The transformation contributes to identifying dynamic errors, which are often the most costly errors to find.

The projection transformation was initially defined as a simplification scheme in validation approaches. In a dynamic context where components are bound at run-time, projections are also interesting as they allow the validation of the interfaces to be bound. The projections overcome the limitations of static object interfaces that do not provide sufficient support for checking interaction correctness.

In our work, we have also proposed validation techniques for handling the various anomalous behaviors that can be identified by projection. These techniques have not presented here. They will be covered in a later article.

Acknowledgments

We would especially like to thank Richard Sanders for inspiring discussions and thorough comments. The work presented here has been supported by the Norwegian Foundation for Research (project grant no. 119395/431).

References

[1] F. A. Aagesen et.al. Towards a Plug and Play Architecture for Telecommunications. Fifth International Conference on Intelligence in Networks (1999). 251
[2] AVANTEL. Information at http://www.item.ntnu.no/avantel/avantel.html. 251
[3] S. S. Lam, A. U. Shankar. Protocol Verification via Projections. IEEE Transactions on Software Engineering, vol. 10, no. 4 (1984). 251
[4] R. Bræk, Ø. Haugen. Engineering Real Time Systems. Prentice Hall (1993). 251
[5] ITU-T. Recommendation Z.100 (08/02), Specification and Description Language (SDL). International Telecommunication Union, Geneva. 252
[6] T. Reenskaug and al. OORASS: Seamless support for the creation and maintenance of object oriented systems. Journal of O-O programming (1992). 252
[7] J. Floch, R. Bræk. Using SDL for Modeling Behavior Composition. 11th SDL Forum (2003), this volume. 252
[8] OMG. The Common Request Object Broker: Architecture and Specification. CORBA revision 2.5. September 2001. 253
[9] D. C. Luckham, J. Vera, S. Melda. Three Concepts of Architecture. Stanford University Technical Report CSL-TR-95-674 (1995). 253
[10] A. Milner. Communication and Concurrency. Prentice Hall. (1989) 254, 265
[11] F. C. Hennie. Finite-state models for logical machines. John Wiley & Sons (1968). 265

Applying Mutation Analysis to SDL Specifications*

Gábor Kovács, Zoltán Pap, Dung Le Viet,
Antal Wu-Hen-Chang, and Gyula Csopaki

Department of Telecommunications and Telematics
Budapest University of Technology and Economics
H-1117, Magyar tudósok körútja 2, Budapest, Hungary
{kovacsg,pap,csopaki}@ttt-atm.ttt.bme.hu
{lv202,wh201}@hszk.bme.hu

Abstract. Mutation analysis is a fault based testing method used initially for code based software testing, and lately for specification based testing and validation as well. In this paper, the method is applied to SDL (Specification and Description Language) specifications. It is used to automate the process of conformance test generation and selection for telecommunications protocols. We present two algorithms for automatic test generation and selection. These provide the basis of the Test Selector tool developed at the Budapest University of Technology and Economics. We present the results of an empirical study using the tool.

Keywords: Conformance Testing, MSC, Mutation Analysis, SDL, Test Generation, Test Selection

1 Introduction

One of the most important criteria that apply to telecommunications software is compatibility with systems from different vendors. This is usually achieved by the means of unambiguous[1] specifications defined by standardization organizations. Manufacturers develop actual products according to these specifications to ensure compatibility. Conformance testing provides the means to check whether systems operate correctly according to the standard. It is crucial to create adequate test sets to minimize the time spent with testing without sacrificing reliability. The test development process itself involves significant resources: it is very time consuming and requires the manual effort of many well-trained developers. Therefore, its automation is an important challenge.

Specifications may be defined in either a formal or an informal way, but typically, the specifications for telecommunications protocols are described using

---

* This research is supported by Inter-University Centre for Telecommunications and Informatics (ETIK).
[1] Editorial remark: Standards are often ambiguous – sometimes intentionally: testing is vital to assure interoperability.

R. Reed (Ed.): SDL 2003, LNCS 2708, pp. 269–284, 2003.

formal description techniques: SDL [1], Estelle .... The SDL specification of a system is an excellent starting point for both manual and automatic test case creation. It describes the behavior of the system in detail, its formal manner makes automation possible. Because SDL is widely accepted and used in the telecom industry, sophisticated tools support it.

Mutation analysis has initially been used for code based software verification and validation. Resent research has showed that it can be applied to various formalisms as well. Probert and Guo studied mutation analysis in the context of Estelle in [2]. Wang and Liu proposed a method for creating test cases that detect given faults in an EFSM (Extended Finite State Machine) specification specified by state transition graphs, and demonstrated their algorithms on the Alternating Bit Protocol [3]. Major research has been done by Fabbri et al in this field. For different formalisms, they defined mutation operator sets and presented case studies. The mutation analysis of Finite State Machines is introduced in [4]. They manually applied this technique to a transport protocol specification, using the method based on characterizing sets and the transition tour method [5]. They proposed the application of mutation testing for validating Estelle specifications [6]. They presented mutation analysis of Petri-Nets [7] and Statecharts [8] as well. Ammann and Black applied mutation analysis to model checking [9, 10, 11].

Our motivation is to investigate the applicability of mutation analysis in telecommunications protocol conformance testing. The main focus is the automation of the test selection process. We propose two algorithms based on mutation analysis for automatic test selection. The selection criteria are provided by the mutant systems generated by means of mutation operators.

A Test Selector tool has been developed at the Budapest University of Technology and Economics for automatic selection of test cases for telecommunications protocols given formally in SDL. We examine empirical data acquired from experiments on sample protocols.

The rest of the paper is organized as follows. In Sect. 2, a short summary is given on SDL. Section 3 recapitulates mutation analysis. Section 4 proposes mutation operators for SDL and two algorithms for automatic test selection. Section 5 summarizes the structure and operation of the tool. In Section 6, we present the results and findings of the empirical analysis of the presented method, and finally summarize our work in Sect. 7.

2   Specification and Description Language

SDL [1] is a formal language, widely used for specifying systems – especially in telecommunications. It has been standardized by ITU-T. One of the strengths of SDL is that it is a well-accepted world standard supported by the ITU-T and ISO. SDL is primarily used in the telecommunications industry for the description of telecommunication protocols, but it can be used in other fields as well. Typically complex, event-driven, real-time and communicating systems can be effectively described in SDL.

SDL specifies the dynamic behavior of a system by the means of processes communicating with signals. Each process is described by a CEFSM (Communicating Extended Finite State Machine). The state machines are labeled *extended*, because variables and timers can also be defined. All of the processes have their own memory for storing their variables and state information, and all of them contain a FIFO buffer of (theoretically) infinite length: a queue, for the incoming signals.

Formally, a CEFSM (an SDL agent: a process, block or system) can be described by an quintuple $CEFSM = (S, I, O, V, T)$ where S, I, O and T are the finite and nonempty set of states, inputs, outputs and transitions respectively, and V is the finite set of variables.

A transition $t \in T$ is a 6-tuple: $t = (s, i, P, A, o, s')$, where $s \in S$ is the start state, $i \in I$ is an input, $P : P(V)$ is a predicate on the variables, $A : V' := A(V)$ is an action on the variables, $o \in O$ is an output and $s' \in S$ is the next state.

Initially, the configuration of the machine is represented by the initial state $s_0 \in S$ and by the initial variable values.

Inputs $(i \in I)$ and outputs $(o \in O)$ are communication events. They may have parameters $(I \times V$ and $O \times V)$, and are realized by parameterized signals in SDL. A reception of a parameterized signal can be viewed simply as an input and a joint action assigning the new values. Inputs are stored in an infinite length queue — communication is asynchronous. The length of the queue increases by one as an input arrives and the input is added to the end of the queue. The length of the queue decreases by one as an input is processed. Henceforth, $i \in I$ denotes the input to be processed, which is not necessarily the first element. The SDL specific save mechanism means that if the specified input is the first element of the queue, then it is skipped and the next element is considered and so on until an input that is not saved is found.

Variables provide further details of the system's internal state. The reaction to a specified input depends on the actual value of some variables through predicates. Predicates are expressions built up from the actual subset variables at a given state. Actions represent the effect of a transition to a subset of the variables.

3 Mutation Analysis

The basic idea behind mutation analysis [12, 13] is that by applying small grammatically correct changes (or mutations) at atomic level to the specification exactly one at a time, faults are intentionally produced [14]. The rationale is that if a test set can distinguish a specification from its slight variations, the test set is exercising the specification adequately.

Mutation analysis is based on the knowledge of the internal logic of a system: it is a white box method. In this paper, mutation analysis is used to derive selection criteria to generate adequate black box test cases based on SDL specifications.

A mutation analysis system consists of three components: the original system, mutant systems and an oracle. A mutant system is a small syntactic element variation of the original. Applying mutation operators to the original system, where each operator represents a syntactic element change, creates mutant systems. The oracle is a person or – in our case – a program to distinguish the original from the mutant by their interaction with the environment. A mutation analysis system defines a set of mutation operators [15, 6]. Each operator is a type of an atomic syntactic element change. Using these operators is practical for two reasons. On the one hand, they enable the formal description of fault types. On the other hand, operators make automated mutant generation possible. By applying the operators systematically to the specification a set of mutants can be generated.

Traditional program-based mutation analysis assumes the competent programmer hypothesis [9] declaring that competent programmers tend to write nearly "correct" programs. That is, programs written by experienced programmers may not be correct, but they will differ from the corrected version by some relatively simple faults such as off-by-one fault. DeMilo's [12] "Coupling effect" proposes that a test data set that highlights simple faults in all programs is also sensitive enough to uncover more complex errors [16]. In the current work, we assume a similar hypothesis stating that the implementer of a system is likely to construct an implementation close to the specification. Therefore test data sets that distinguish all implementations differing from a correct one by only simple errors are so sensitive that they also implicitly distinguish more complex errors. In our recent work, we only apply first-order faults: that is we apply exactly one mutation at a time.

Test cases distinguish mutants from the original, if they produce different output. However, some of the mutants generated using the operators may be semantically equivalent to the original system. That is, a mutant and the original may compute the same function for all possible inputs. All equivalents should be ignored, but each non-equivalents should be considered during test selection.

4   Test Selection Method

4.1   Mutation Operators Proposed for SDL Systems

Much research has been done concerning mutation operators for different formalisms. In a recent paper, a very important additional consideration for the definition of operators is that they should allow of the automation of the mutation testing process. To automate the process, mutation operators have to be defined in a way that enables their application to any specification regardless of actual realization and data types. It is also essential to generate grammatically correct mutants. Static grammatical correctness is necessary to ensure that executable mutant systems are created.

According to these considerations, we use six types of mutation operators for the SDL model according to which part of the transition they are applied to, and additionally the properties of SDL were also taken into account:

- state modification operator,
- input modification operator,
- output modification operator,
- action modification operator,
- predicate modification operator,
- save missing operator.

Henceforth, let the $\Omega()$ function represent the syntactical change applied.

Operator 1 (State)   Modifying states. Here only exchange of inputs should be considered. Mutating the next state in transition
$$t \in T\colon t = (s, i, P(V), A(V), o, \Omega(s')).$$
In this case we replace the next state, that is we lead the system to a wrong state and induce incorrect operation. The mutation of the initial state is a special case of state mutation, where s_0 is modified: $\Omega(s_0)$.

Operator 2 (Input)   The input mutation in the transition
$$t \in T\colon t = (s, \Omega(i), P(V), A(V), o, s').$$

1. *Using $\Omega(i) := null$. This mutation is equivalent to the removal of a transition branch for an input at a given state.*
2. *Using $\Omega(i) := i_x$, where $i_x \in I'$, $I' \subseteq I$ is the set of inputs, that have transitions explicitly defined at the given s state.*
3. *Assigning the transition of input i_{inopp} ($i_{inopp} \in I$, but $i_{inopp} \notin I'$, where $I' \subseteq I$ is the set of inputs, that have explicit transitions defined at the given s) to the existing transition branch of input $i \in I$. This mutation means that we add a transition branch for the input i_{inopp}, that was implicitly consumed previously. Using this mutation, also the processing of inopportune (valid input arriving at wrong time) inputs can be inspected.*
4. *As mentioned previously, inputs and outputs may have parameters. If $i \in I \times V$, then we can mutate not only the input symbol, but the input parameter leaving the input symbol unchanged. This type of mutation is practically an action mutation, and can be viewed as the mutation of the implicit action assigning the new values. In this case, $\Omega(i) = i(\Omega(v))$, where $\Omega(v) := null$ – according to the action mutation (see below).*

Operator 3 (Output)   The mutation of an output event in the transition
$$t \in T \text{ is}\colon t = (s, i, P(V), A(V), \Omega(o), s').$$
If the output symbol has parameters ($o \in O \times V$), then we have the possibility to modify the parameter: $\Omega(o) = o(\Omega(v))$, where $\Omega(v) := null$.

Operator 4 (Action)   It is difficult to define a general mutation operator for actions, because of the presence of abstract data types. Only the $\Omega(A(V)) := null$ operator, that is the deletion of an action is suitable for this case. Missing action operator: $t = (s, i, P(V), \Omega(A(V)), o, s')$.

Operator 5 (Predicate)   The mutation of boolean predicates has similar effects as the mutation of inputs.

1. *Exchanging two branches of a decision in the transition $t \in T$ can be done simply negating the whole expression $t = (s, i, \Omega(P(V)), A(V), o, s'$, where $\Omega(P(V)) := not(P(V))$.*
2. *Setting the predicate to be stuck-at-true ($\Omega(P(V)) := true$) or stuck-at-false ($\Omega(P(V)) := false$) brings on the removal of the other branch.*

Operator 6 (Save) Because this paper considers SDL to be the specification language used, we have to take its specialties, such as the save mechanism, into account. Note that save is not part of the CEFSM model. This operator removes the save statement.

During test case generation, timeouts in the SDL systems are considered simple inputs, and accordingly, the input mutation operator mutates them. To be able to test timer transitions, timeout events are made controllable from the environment. That is, whenever a test case reaches a timeout, a corresponding "timeout" signal is sent directly to the owner process of the timer from the environment, and after its consumption the corresponding timer transition is executed. During the test execution, a timeout in the test case explicitly indicates that the tester will have to wait for the duration of the timer. This way, methods for test case generation in Sect. 4.2 become time independent.

It is important to note, that we replace non-boolean predicates with a sequence of boolean predicates, and apply the operators on them.

Table 1 demonstrates some examples of the application of the mutation operators on the INRES protocol.

Table 1. Mutation Operators for SDL

Operators	Original	Mutant
State	NEXTSTATE wait;	NEXTSTATE connected;
Input	INPUT ICONresp;	INPUT IDISreq;
Output	OUTPUT CC;	OUTPUT DT (number, d);
Action	TASK counter := 1;	/* Missing */
Predicate	DECISION sdu!id = CC;	DECISION NOT(sdu!id = CC);
Save	SAVE IDATreq (d);	/* Missing */

4.2 Algorithms for Test Selection

We defined two algorithms for automatic test selection. Although they are similar, and built on the same concept, they produce different resulting sets. Both procedures require the SDL specification of a system. There are practical and widely used tools, to assist the specification process: Telelogic Tau [17] is an example. After the specification is completed, in both cases processing can be automated. We represent test cases in MSC [18, 19]. The MSC test sets can be translated to different test description languages such as TTCN (Tree and Tabular Combined Notation). During generation [20], the system is stimulated using inputs or timeout signals from the environment, and the outputs to the environment are checked for inconsistency.

The input of the first algorithm is an SDL specification, which may also contain informal parts. As a result, we get a set of MSC test cases. This algorithm consists of the following steps.

Algorithm 1 (Derivation of test cases from a specification)

1. *First, a mutation operator is applied to the SDL specification, that is, a mutant specification is created.*
2. *The mutant is compared to the original system using a state space exploration algorithm, where timer signals are added to the input set ($\mathcal{I}$).*
3. *When the state space exploration algorithm finds an inconsistency, it generates a test case based on the set of stimuli (including timeout signals) sent from the environment and the outputs received until the inconsistency was discovered.*
4. *This procedure is repeated for all possible mutants.*

The algorithm must have break conditions: reaching a certain depth, exceeding a time limit . . . .

Figure 1 shows our second scenario. The second algorithm also requires the SDL specification of the system to be tested, and assumes that a finite size test set exists (for example in a form of a set of MSC test cases). These test sets are usually created by the means of state space exploration algorithms exploring the specification of the system, but could also be developed manually. This set is subject to optimization, meaning that a subset of test cases is selected with equivalent coverage (mutant detection ratio).

Let the matrix of criteria **C** be a two-dimensional matrix with boolean values.

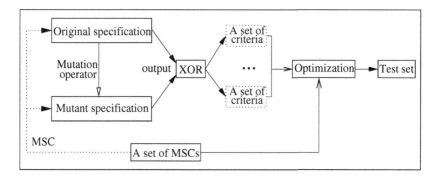

Fig. 1. Mutation Analysis of CEFSMs Based on an Existing Test Set

Algorithm 2 (Selecting test cases from an existing set)

0. Create a set of test cases.
1. Apply a mutation operator to the system, that is, create a mutant specification (the ith mutant).
2. Run the test set on the mutant specification and check for inconsistency.
3. Create a row vector $\mathbf{C}_i$ (the ith row of the C matrix).
   - Let $\mathbf{C}_{ij}$ be 0, if the jth test case is not able to detect the ith mutant.
   - Let $\mathbf{C}_{ij}$ be 1, if the jth test case is able to detect the ith mutant.

   In other words, select the test cases from the original set, which kill the given mutant.
4. Repeat steps 1-3 for i=1 to N, where N equals the number of all possible mutants that can be created from the given system using the mutation operators defined in Sect. 4.1.
5. Acquire the matrix of criteria, where rows represent the mutants and columns represent the test cases in the original set. This matrix describes for each test case the mutations the given test case is able to detect.
6. Apply some simplifications to the matrix of criteria (C):
   - If there is a column $\mathbf{C}_j$ in C, where $\forall i : \mathbf{C}_j[i] = 0$, it represents that the jth test case did not find any of the mutants. Therefore, the jth column can be omitted.
   - If there is a row C_i in C, where $\forall j : \mathbf{C}_i[j] = 0$, it represents either that the ith mutant is an equivalent, or that there was no test case in the original set that could find the difference (kill the mutant).
   - If there are rows $\mathbf{C}_m$ and $\mathbf{C}_n$ in $\mathbf{C}$, where $\forall j : \mathbf{C}_m[j] \leq \mathbf{C}_n[j]$, then the row $\mathbf{C}_m[j]$ is unnecessary.
7. Select an optimal test suite from the original set, using an integer programming method [21].

Both algorithms have their advantages and drawbacks. The first algorithm requires less computation and time than the second, but it does not provide enough data for any kind of optimization. To get good coverage, the initial test set of the second algorithm has to be large enough – the sufficient number of test cases varies from protocol to protocol. A major drawback of the second method is

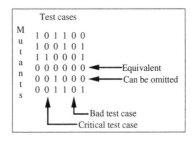

Fig. 2. A Sample Matrix of Criteria

that it is quite computation-intensive. The initial test set of the second algorithm may contain a number of inappropriate cases. Experience shows that there are permutation of Matrices of criteria that are rather block-structured. Certain faults are detected by many test cases. "Similar" test cases detect "similar" faults, that is, most of the true values in the matrix are in blocks. From the point of view of test selection the important criteria can be found in parts that are only rarely filled with true values.

5   The Test Selector Tool

To implement the automatic test selection procedure, a Test Selector tool has been developed in Java language based on the second algorithm. The main dialog can be seen in Fig. 3. The tool consists of several components indicated by rectangles in Fig. 4.

The mutant generator takes the SDL/PR (textual representation) description original specification as an input. It implements the mutation operators defined in Sect. 4.1 and shown in Table 1, and creates mutant specifications also in SDL/PR format.

The compiler generates Java code from the SDL/PR description. The specification is modified automatically before the code generation, so that timers are made controllable, and decisions with multiple branches are transformed to a series of boolean decisions. Though the timer transformations do change the

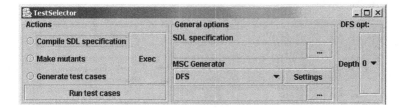

Fig. 3. The Main Dialog

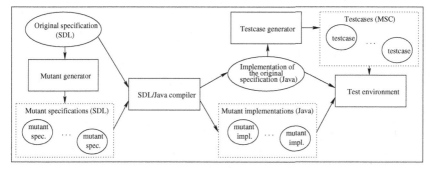

Fig. 4. Components of the Tool

behavior of the system, from the point of view of the presented method, however, they are invariant.

The MSC [18] generator module generates test cases in MSC form. The input and output signals and the timers are extracted from the SDL specification and a transition system is constructed from them [20]. The tree of the transition system is explored by different algorithms (depth-first-search – DFS, randomized, weighted DFS) until a certain depth is reached. Finally at the end of each branch it outputs an MSC sequence in textual form.

The test environment is the core of the tool (see Fig. 5). This component executes the test cases against the implementations, sends messages according to the MSC test cases, and evaluates the messages received. The test environment outputs a boolean matrix, which is the subject of optimization.

Several components – the mutant generator, the compiler, and the test environment – are based on a parser. To generate these parsers we used the lexical analyzer JLex [22] and the parser generator CUP [23] (Constructor of Useful Parsers).

For the compilation from SDL to Java we defined mappings between the two languages, and built a Java code generator on top of the parser. To keep the produced code small and clean, a run-time library has been created that provides a framework for the implementations. During the compilation the SDL specification goes through several stages. A preprocessor filters out timer actions

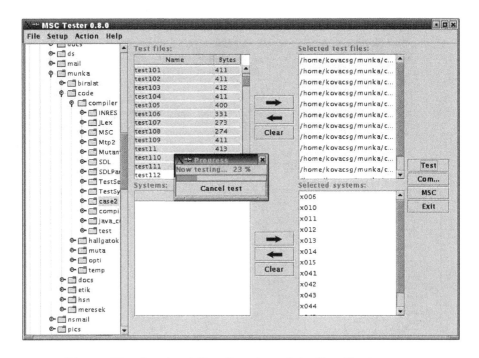

Fig. 5. The Graphical User Interface of the Test Environment

(set, reset), creates special channels to make them controllable, and also unfolds non-boolean decisions. The remaining parts are left untouched. This is followed by the code generation phase, when the parser processes the specification and the code generator exports Java source. In the last step the SDL compiler calls the Java compiler and transforms the sources to classes.

In contrast to the compiler, the test environment treats the MSC specifications as scripts and executes them without producing Java code. Generic script languages (for instance: perl, javascript . . .) operate this way. The structure of the MSC is sequential, and there are no conditions, therefore we can skip the code generation phase. During the test case execution, whenever a timeout is reached, a corresponding input signal is sent through the previously added timer channels.

Because the environment communicates with the implementation, we had to solve the problem of controllability. Thus an interface has been created which can be used to send signals to the examined system and to receive the outputs. The interface has built-in FIFO channels for by-passing messages and the most important control functions are available as well.

6   Empirical Analysis

6.1   Test Generation for the INRES Protocol

At first we used the well-known sample telecommunications system INRES [24] to investigate the method presented (see Fig. 6). We chose a sample protocol that includes all the typical properties of real life protocols, and is built on the OSI concept. INRES is a connection-oriented protocol that operates between two protocol entities Initiator and Responder. These protocol entities communicate over a Medium service. The SDL specification of the system was created using Telelogic Tau [17]. The structure of the system and the states of the processes are shown in Fig. 6. (The transitions of the processes are shown schematically, dots represent decisions. Inputs, outputs and actions are not represented. For more details see [24].)

For the creation of the initial MSC test case set we used the MSC generator module. Of course, by increasing the exploration depth, we get an exponentially growing number of test cases. In the case of the INRES protocol, depths of 3, 4 and 5 resulted in 29, 61 and 125 test cases respectively. We created mutant specifications for the INRES protocol, using the mutant generator module. It generated 125 mutant specifications (the number of mutants and test cases are only equal by chance). Using depth of 5 (meaning 125 initial test cases), the resulting test set contained only 23 test cases with equivalent mutant detection ratio. Some other information about the experiment is shown in Table 2.

As data entries in Table 2 indicate, state space exploration depth – and therefore the number of test cases – influences the mutant detection ratios. Using depth 3 – 29 test cases – provides less than 50 percent detected mutants (except the single save mutant). By increasing the depth to four – 61 test cases – we can

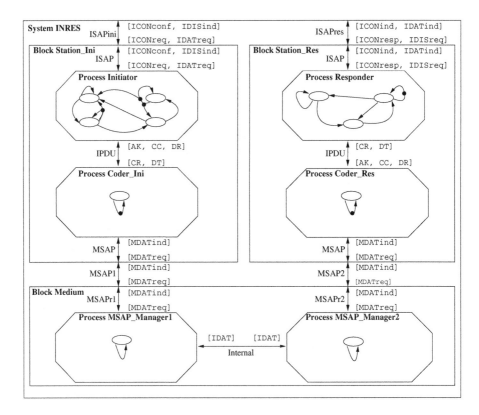

Fig. 6. The INRES System in SDL

notice a great increase in the detection ratio. By raising the exploration depth to five, we see another significant gain, but only in cases of input, output and predicate mutations. Another increase in the exploration depth, however, did not raise the detection ratio any further. There have been some mutations discovered by only one test case (critical mutants). The test cases detecting these critical mutants certainly have to be included in the resulting set. In the case of the INRES protocol we found 16 critical mutants. Most of the test cases detecting critical mutants were created using depth of 5, and the most critical mutants were created by state and predicate mutations.

6.2   Test Generation for the Conference Protocol

The conference protocol is a multicast chat box protocol [25]. A conference is a session of the protocol in which a group of users can participate by exchanging messages with other users that can change dynamically. A user is initially only allowed to perform a join to enter a conference. After performing a join, the user may send or receive a message. To stop participating in the conference, the user

Table 2. Data from the INRES Case Study

Mutation Operator	Generated Mutants	Detected Mutants (Depth of 3/4/5)	Detection Ratio (Depth of 3/4/5)
State	30	13/18/19	43%/60%/63%
Input	28	14/16/23	50%/57%/82%
Output	36	16/20/28	44%/55%/77%
Action	22	9/15/15	41%/68%/68%
Predicate	8	2/2/5	25%/25%/63%
Save	1	1/1/1	100%/100%/100%

can issue a leave at any time after a join. After that, another join primitive can be performed, starting a new participation in a conference. Different conferences can exist at the same time, but each user can only participate in at most one conference at a time. Messages may get lost or may be delivered out of sequence but are never corrupted.

We got similar results with the Conference Protocol experiment to those acquired for INRES. We used state space exploration depth 6, generating 217 test cases, and selected a subset of 29 tests. Table 3 shows detailed results of the experiment. An important difference is, that in case of the Conference Protocol we had more – 21 – mutants created using the Save operator. Thus, we got more realistic results concerning this kind of mutation than in the case of INRES, where we had only one save mutant. As the data shows, save mutants have the worst detection ratio.

There is another important observation we should notice, that the input and the output mutants were much easier to detect in both experiments. In the case of the output operator, this result is according to expectations, because it creates a fault in the system that is easy to observe and therefore to detect. The case of input operator is harder to explain. It indicates that input mutation results in very rough mutant systems. That is, they produce radical changes in the behavior of the system that can be detected by most of the test cases. State

Table 3. Data from the Conference Protocol Case Study

Mutation Operator	Generated Mutants	Detected Mutants	Detection Ratio
State	7	6	86%
Input	6	6	100%
Output	7	7	100%
Action	62	47	75%
Predicate	20	16	80%
Save	21	8	38%

mutation, on the other hand, produces errors that can be discovered by only a small percentage of the test cases.

6.3 Performance

Other fundamental questions of the empirical analysis are: topsep0pt

> How it is going to work out in real life in terms of performance?
> What kind of hardware we are going to need?
> How much time a test generation procedure will take?

The experiments were conducted under Windows 2000 OS, on a Pentium II Celeron 333 MHz PC with 192 MB of memory. Table 4 shows the running times of the individual modules. The two results in the Testing and Test Generation fields for the INRES protocol apply to test case depth of 3 and 5.

The generation of mutant systems and the initial test case set does not take much time. The most time was spent compiling the mutant systems to Java, because the javac compiler of the JDK is quite slow. The time required for the actual testing of the mutant systems depends on the number of mutant systems, on the number of test cases in the initial set, and on the complexity of the individual test cases. The memory requirement of the tool was considerable.

These performance results are acceptable considering the speed problems of the Java language, and the low-end testing hardware used. Based on these results, we can draw the conclusion, that using modern hardware and a faster performing programming language, the mutation analysis method and tool can be applied to complex, industrial size protocols.

Table 4. Execution Times on a Pentium II Celeron 333 MHz PC with 192 MB of Memory

Protocol	Mutant Generation	Code Generation & Compiling	Test Generation	Testing
INRES	1.5 min.	20 min.	0.5/2.2 min.	1.4/16 min.
Conference Protocol	1.5 min.	20 min.	0.5/2.2 min.	1.4/16 min.

7   Conclusions

Conformance testing is a vital part of the standard based telecommunications protocol development process. In the practice the creation of test suites is usually a very time consuming manual process, even though several computer aided test generation methods have already been developed. By means of the method proposed in this paper, it is possible to automate all steps of the test selection process.

In this paper we described how mutation analysis, a white box method, could be applied to formal SDL specifications. We used mutant systems as criteria to automate the selection of conformance test cases for black box testing. For this purpose we used a special set of mutation operators considering the requirements of automation and the specialties of SDL. We presented two algorithms for automatic test selection using the operators. Based on the method a Test Selector tool has been developed, and was used for case studies. Including the generation of the initial test sets and the optimization the whole procedure is all automatic.

A future goal is to reveal the effect of using different initial test and operator sets. An interesting possibility is the extension of our method to be adaptive. This means that we intend to make some experiments where the initial test and operator sets change on the fly.

References

[1] ITU-T. Recommendation Z.100 (08/02), Specification and Description Language (SDL). International Telecommunication Union, Geneva. 270

[2] R. L. Probert, F. Guo. Mutation Testing of Protocols: Principles and Preliminary Experimental Results. Proc. Protocol Test Systems, III., pages 57–76, 1991. 270

[3] C.-J. Wang and M. T. Liu. Generating Test Cases for EFSM with Given Fault Model. INFOCOM 93, volume 2, pages 774–781, 1993. 270

[4] S. C. P. F. Fabbri, J. C. Maldonado, M. E. Delamaro, P. C. Masiero Mutation Analysis Testing for Finite State Machine. Proc. ISSRE'94 - Fifth International Symposium on Software Reliability Engineering, pages 220–229, California, USA, 1994. 270

[5] D. Lee, M. Yiannakakis. Principles and Methods of Testing Finite State Machines – A Survey. Proc. of the IEEE, 43(3):1090–1123, 1996. 270

[6] S. R. S. Souza, J. C. Maldonado, S. C. P. F. Fabbri, W. Lopes De Souza. Mutation Testing Applied to Estelle Specifications. Software Quality Journal, 8(04), 2000. 270, 272

[7] S. C. P. F. Fabbri, J. C. Maldonado, P. C. Masiero, M. E. Delamaro, E. Wong. Mutation Testing Applied to Validate Specifications Based on Petri Nets. FORTE'95 - 8th International IFIP Conference on Formal Description Techniques for Distributed Systems and Communications Protocol, 1995. 270

[8] S. C. P. F. Fabbri, J. C. Maldonado, T. Sugeta T, P. C. Masiero. Mutation Testing Applied to Validate Specifications Based on Statecharts. Proc. ISSRE'99 - 10th International Symposium on Software Reliability Engineering, pages 210–219, Florida, USA, 1999. 270

[9] P. E. Ammann, P. E. Black, and W. Majurski. Using Model Checking to Generate Tests from Specifications. Second IEEE International Conference on Formal Engineering Methods, pages 46–54, 1998. 270, 272

[10] P. E. Black, V. Okun, Y. Yesha. Mutation Operators for Specifications. The Fifteenth IEEE International Conference on Automated Software Engineering, Proceedings ASE 2000, pages 81–88, 2000. 270

[11] P. E. Ammann and P. E. Black. A Specification-based Coverage Metric to Evaluate Test Sets. Proceedings of Fourth IEEE International High-Assurance Systems Engineering Symposium (HASE 99), pages 239–248, 1999. 270

[12] R. A. De Millo, R. J. Lipton, F. G. Sayward. Hints on Test Data Selection: Help for the Practicing Programmer. IEEE Computer, 11(4):34–41, April 1978. 271, 272

[13] P. G. Frankl, S. N. Weiss, C. Hu. All-uses versus mutation testing: An experimental comparison of effectiveness. Journal of Systems and Software, Sept 1997. 271

[14] D. R. Kuhn. A Technique for Analyzing the Effects of Changes in Formal Specifications. The Computer Journal, 35(6):574–578, 1992. 271

[15] D. R. Kuhn. Fault Classes and Error Detection in Specification Based Testing. ACM Transactions on Software Engineering Methodology, 8(4), October 1999. 272

[16] A. J. Offutt. Investigations of the software testing coupling effect. ACM Transactions on Software Engineering and Methodology, 1(1):5–20, January 1992. 272

[17] Telelogic Tau. http://www.telelogic.com. 274, 279

[18] ITU-T. Recommendation Z.120 (11/99), Message Sequence Chart (MSC). International Telecommunication Union, Geneva. 274, 278

[19] J. Grabowski, D. Hogrefe, R. Nahm. Test Case Generation with Test Purpose Specification by MSCs. North Holland, 1993. 274

[20] J. Tretmans. Specification Based Testing with Formal Methods: A Theory. FORTE / PSTV 2000 Tutorial Notes, October 10 2000. 275, 278

[21] T. Csvndes, B. Kotnyek. A mathematical programming method in test selection. EUROMICRO 97, pages 8–13, 1997. 276

[22] Jlex: A lexical analyzer generator for java. Princeton University, http://www.cs.princeton.edu/appel/modern/java/JLex/, 2000. 278

[23] Cup parser generator for java. Princeton University, http://www.cs.princeton.edu/appel/modern/java/CUP/, 2000. 278

[24] J. Ellsberger, D. Hogrefe, A. Sarma. SDL Formal Object-oriented Language for Communicating Systems. Prentice Hall, 1997. 279

[25] A. Belinfante, J. Feenstra, R. G. de Vries, J. Tretmans, N. Goga, L. Feijs, S. Mauw, L. Heerink. Formal test automation: A simple experiment. 12th Int. Workshop on Testing of Communicating Systems, pages 179–196. Kluwer Academic Publishers, 1999. 280

Automatic Formal Model Generation and Analysis of SDL*

Annikka Aalto[1], Nisse Husberg[2]**, and Kimmo Varpaaniemi[2]

[1] Yomi Solutions Oy, Finland
annikka.aalto@iki.fi
http://www.yomi.fi/eng/
[2] Helsinki University of Technology
Laboratory for Theoretical Computer Science (HUT-TCS)
P.O. Box 9205, FIN-02015 HUT, Espoo, Finland
{nisse.husberg,kimmo.varpaaniemi}@hut.fi
http://www.tcs.hut.fi/

Abstract. A tool for verification of distributed systems defined using standard SDL-96 is described. The SDL description is automatically translated into a high-level Petri net model which is analyzed using the Maria reachability analyzer. Compared to manual design of a formal model for the system this saves a lot of time and greatly reduces the human mistakes in creating the model. The design process is also considerably more efficient because it is possible to check that the system is correct at a very early stage. Methods to reduce the complexity of the analysis both at the modeling and at the analysis level are discussed.
Keywords: SDL, reachability analysis, high-level Petri nets, state space explosion problem

1 Introduction

Parallel and distributed systems are difficult to design and test. The difficulty of reproducing errors makes the use of special tools necessary. One possibility is to transform the system description into a *formal model* which is analyzed. There are many formal analysis methods, but *reachability analysis* is best suited for automatic analysis. In this method, all the reachable states of the system are created from the model, and usually the required properties are checked at creation time using *model checking*.

A major problem with reachability analysis is the so called *state space explosion*: even simple systems can generate a huge number of different states. To some extent, the explosion can be relieved using methods such as *abstraction*, *partial order reduction*, *symmetries*, and *modular state space generation*. For various reasons, commercial and academic tools tend to differ with respect to availability of such methods. Considering SDL, let us quote one of the VERILOG White Papers on OBJECTGEODE [1]:

---

* This work has been supported by the ETX program of The National Technology Agency of Finland and by Nokia Research Center.
** Corresponding author.

R. Reed (Ed.): SDL 2003, LNCS 2708, pp. 285–299, 2003.

Limitations in graph exploration come from the memory space available on your machine. Exhaustive simulation will stop when there is no more memory available. However, to allow for the evaluation of industrial-size models, the property checking facility implemented in the Simulator is performed on-the-fly.

The mere principle of on-the-fly verification alleviates state space explosion only when there is a counterexample/witness of a kind being looked for. So, something more is needed if we want to alleviate state space explosion regardless of the truth value of the property of interest. The differences between commercial and academic tools with respect to formal methods in general are discussed in the paper [2] that describes the IF toolset that contains an explicit verification back-end for OBJECTGEODE.

Another problem with reachability analysis is the *creation of the model*. Usually this is done manually and is the most time consuming and error-prone part of the complete analysis of a system. This problem can be relieved by performing *automatic translation* of the system description language into the input language of the reachability analyzer. After the analysis, the results should be *translated back* and presented in terms of the system description language to make them easier to understand [3, 4]. The Emma tool [5] works in this way. It uses the programming language TNSDL, a dialect of SDL-88, as a system description which is translated into the high-level Petri net description language of the reachability analysis tool PROD [6, 7].

The main problem with PROD, as with other traditional Petri net analyzers, is the *lack of data types* — only integers and enumerated symbolic constants are directly supported in all phases of analysis although indirect support is much wider because PROD allows an arc expression to call a function written in the C programming language. Even so, dealing with structured data types requires explicit encoding and decoding. This is especially problematic with SDL because it has a fairly large data type system. This led to the development of a new analyzer, Maria [8, 9], which has a very developed type system and makes the translation of SDL data types easy.

The possibility to define *data type constraints* is also important (even against state space explosion because some methods prefer types of small effective cardinality). Maria is *modular* because it is important to be able to easily add new analysis methods and new efficient algorithms. There is no analysis method which would be the "best" for all types of systems. The most efficient methods are good at analyzing only a narrow class of systems and therefore many different methods must be used by the analyzer.

The input language of Maria corresponds to *algebraic system nets* which are high-level Petri nets similar to the nets used in PROD. Considering storage of states and state transitions as vertices and edges in a reachability graph, Maria has a high degree of compression of information. Moreover, Maria is able to construct any reachability graph that has a few million vertices and edges such that a single vertex or edge requires at most a few thousand bits of storage space. This ability is almost independent of the amount of actual memory because the file system is utilized. The model checker [10] of Maria can handle requirement specifications written as linear time temporal logic formulas with *fairness constraints* incorporated in the model. An explicit interface to fairness constraints simplifies the overall verification process when compared to almost any indirect way of expressing such constraints.

The translation of the system description language into the input language of the analyzer is performed by a *front-end* of the analyzer. The Emma front-end was made for PROD but has been rewritten for Maria. However, it turned out to be less than feasible to revise the implementation in such a way that Emma would have taken advantage of all the features offered by Maria. It was thus decided to design a new front-end for standard SDL [11]. The new front-end, SDL2PN, uses the ideas of Emma but it has much more efficient translations which take advantage of the possibilities of Maria.

2   High-Level Petri Nets

A Petri net is a *directed bipartite graph* with two kinds of vertices, *places* and *net transitions*. The places and net transitions are connected by *arcs*. An arc can only connect a place to a net transition and vice versa — never a place to a place or a net transition to a net transition.

The places, net transitions and arcs are *annotated* with expressions. The annotations of the places are called *markings* (multisets of *tokens*) and are *changed dynamically*. A marking, mapping each place to the set of multisets of tokens, defines the *state* of the system. The net transitions have static annotations called *gates*: predicates using variables from the expressions on the arcs. The annotations on the arcs connected to a net transition are expressions with *variables* that are *local to the net transition*.

The labeled graph formed by a net and its gates and arc expressions is the *static part* of the net. The places have an *initial marking* which is the starting point for the *dynamic part* of the net: the *token game*. A binding of variables of a net transition *enables the net transition at a marking* if and only if the corresponding value of the gate predicate is true and the flow of tokens corresponding to the values of the arc expressions is realizable. Such a binding can (but does not have to) be *fired* which means that the flow in question is realized: multisets corresponding to the input arc expressions are removed from the respective input places, and multisets corresponding to the output arc expressions are inserted into the respective output places. Some of the inserted tokens can be among the removed tokens. This can be thought of as a mechanism of testing the presence of the token.

3   The SDL2PN Front-End

In Emma, the TNSDL compiler is used to parse the TNSDL program, and Emma is really only a model generator whereas the new SDL2PN front-end has its own SDL parser [12]. In a sense, it is an advantage in Emma that the TNSDL compiler is used because it is the same compiler which produces C code for the implementation. Thus the model is very close to the real system.

On the other hand, the standard SDL front-end should be used in a very early stage in the design process. Then possible errors are found already in the specification phase and are less expensive to correct than when the implementation is ready. It is also easier to analyze a specification before it has a lot of implementation details. The drawback is that errors may be introduced in the implementation stage.

3.1   Static Analysis

The front-ends Emma and SDL2PN perform a *static analysis* of the SDL system. This includes detection of potential receivers of a signal sent in an OUTPUT statement (cf. Sect. 4.3). From the point of view of overall efficiency of verification, it is obvious that static analysis should be developed to perform automatic abstraction of the model and to do data flow analysis as well as to automatically create data value range constraints.

3.2   Dominating Translation Principles at the Moment

In SDL2PN, queues are modeled using different places for different processes, but all instances of the same process use the same queue place. The *control places*, corresponding to the control points before (and after) each SDL statement, have been folded into one *program counter place*. In order to ensure straightforward translation of the flow of control, the SDL statements are identified by unique numbers.

3.3   Translating Data Types

Implementing all data types of SDL in a reachability analysis tool does not necessarily pay off. For example, there is no general discretization scheme for real numbers that would ensure feasible reachability analysis. Thus it is wise to perform discretization on the SDL level before using a reachability analysis tool.

One important data type which is supported by Maria is the *queue* type. In contrast to the approaches in [5, 13, 14], internal operations on a queue implemented with this data type do not create intermediate states. However, it is reasonable to have alternative ways for modeling a queue. For example, when some *low-level net method* is to be used for relieving the state space explosion problem, it is actually wise to generate intermediate states caused by internal operations of a queue. Moreover, it is possible to use *path compression* (cf. Sect. 6) by combining low-level net methods with on-the-fly elimination of intermediate states. Such a combination approximates the ideal that the reachability graph would not have such states at all.

In SDL2PN, simple types are translated first, then user-defined types and then the signal types. Last, the complex data types are generated. Maria has a strongly typed input language which is important in the analysis because type errors are detected when the reachability graph is generated. Typically this means that there are errors in the model.

4   Translating SDL Statements

SDL2PN usually does not need more than one net transition for modeling a single SDL statement. The statements are translated in such a way that a transition modeling a statement (see Fig. 1) updates the program counter field of the process instance in the *process control place* `Control X` (one for each process). All tokens in `Control X` are tagged with the PID of the process instance and the recursion level.

A full description of the translation principles can be found in the final version of [15], but a few examples are considered below. The expressions in the pictures below follow the syntax of Maria with the exception that Maria does not have any actual tuple delimiters ("⟨" and "⟩") and does not use "+" as a multiset union operator.

4.1   The TASK Statement

As an example of a simple SDL statement, the translation of the statement `task v(w) := w` is shown in Fig. 1. The net transition is enabled when the process control place `Control X` contains a token ⟨pid,rec,pc⟩. In a corresponding event of firing, this token is removed, and a new token ⟨pid,rec,newpc⟩, where `newpc` refers to the next SDL statement, is stored in `Control X`.

All the places representing SDL variables, here `Variable V` and `Variable W`, which are used in the assignment must be connected to the net transition. For the variables on the right-hand side of the assignment, the values are simply restored, whereas the value of the left-hand side variable is updated.

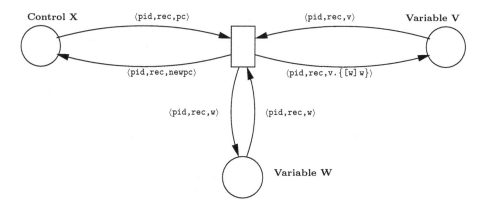

Fig. 1. The Net Transition Corresponding to the Statement `task v(w) := w`

If the expression to the right contains nested procedure calls, the assignment statement is divided into several statements with simple procedure calls.

4.2 INPUT Statements

Some SDL statements operate on the queue, e.g. the INPUT statement. Every process X has a queue place **Queue X**. As mentioned before, Maria has a built-in queue type. For example, the local net transition variable **buffer** in Fig. 2 represents a queue containing elements of type **signal_t**.

The Maria queue type has a unary "/"-operator for denoting the current number of elements in the queue, a unary "*"-operator for denoting the front-most element of the queue, and a unary "-"-operator for denoting the queue obtained by removing the frontmost element. In Fig. 2, these operators are used on the local variable **buffer**, and the gate expression checks that there is at least one element in the queue and that the frontmost signal is tagged by the tag **sig** of the "disjoint union type" **signal_t**.

There is a common **PID expression** place for all processes in the system. It contains tokens consisting of four PID values: the process identifier of the process instance and one for each special expression: SENDER, PARENT, and OFFSPRING. As one might guess, a net transition representing an INPUT statement updates the contents of the **PID expression** with SENDER. Due to the possibility of parameters in a signal, some variables of the process receiving the

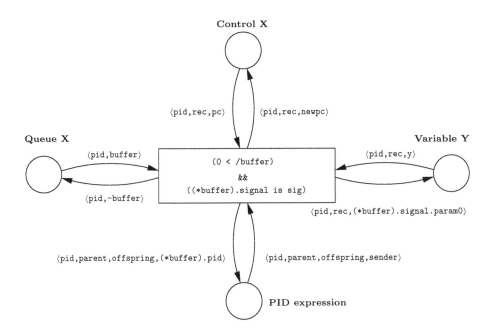

Fig. 2. The Structure of an INPUT Net Transition

signal may be updated in the INPUT statement. In Fig. 2, the value of variable Y is replaced by the value of **param0** of the signal.

4.3 OUTPUT Statements

The translation of OUTPUT statements is complicated in the general case. One reason for this is that SDL allows a situation where only one reception takes place but the receiver is chosen dynamically. Another reason is that there is the possibility of *broadcasting*: that is, a signal may be received by one of several receivers.

Fortunately, if the SDL description uses only basic structural components such as block, process, channel and signal route, it is straightforward to determine the set of potential receivers. Signal constraints and VIA restrictions are also easy to support.

4.4 Creating and Deleting Processes

Using high-level Petri nets, it is no problem to model dynamic constructs such as creating and destroying process instances. Some analysis tools (for example the version of the SPV tool described in [16]) exclude dynamic constructs, and so one might get the impression that there would be some fundamental difficulty.

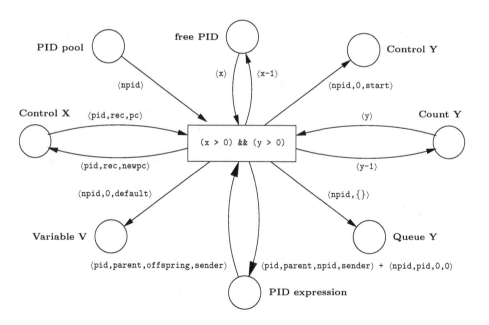

Fig. 3. A Create Net Transition

In Fig. 3 modeling the CREATE statement, a new instance of process Y is created by putting new tokens into places `Control Y`, `Queue Y`, `Variable V`, and `PID expression`. All these tokens are tagged with the identifier ⟨npid⟩ taken from the process identifier pool place `PID pool` (common for the whole system). The standard [11] in a sense assumes an unlimited supply of unique process identifiers, whereas in concrete reachability analysis, it is more or less necessary to have a sufficiently small upper bound on the number of available PIDs. The place `free PID` represents the number of currently available PIDs. On the other hand, SDL itself has an explicit mechanism for restricting the number of process instances associated with a process definition. The place `Count Y` represents the number of currently available PIDs within the restriction given in the SDL description.

A process may have *formal parameters*, which are replaced by actual parameters when the CREATE statement is interpreted. The process parameters are modeled as normal variables, and places are generated for each of them. The net transition corresponding to the statement is then responsible for updating the contents of those places.

A net transition for a STOP statement is essentially the opposite of the CREATE transition: all tokens with the given PID are removed.

4.5 Procedures

The SDL procedure body is translated in the same way as a process body, but a procedure call has a *unique wait number* which is used as a program counter value of the calling process. Thus the process cannot proceed until a RETURN net transition removes the wait number and replaces it with the number of the SDL statement following the procedure call.

Each procedure has a procedure place similar to the process place of a process, but the tokens in the procedure place also contain the wait number. This is necessary for distinguishing several calls to the same procedure. Each call to the same procedure in a process must have separate RETURN net transitions because they have different SDL statements as successors.

The procedure parameters are handled in the same way as process parameters. If a parameter should return a value, the RETURN net transition must move these values to the place of the actual parameters.

4.6 Timers

The modeling of timers in SDL can only be approximated using Petri nets because there is no concept of time in this formalism and the use of Timed Petri nets was not considered due to difficulties in analysis. It is, however, possible to have a useful approximation defined by *order* of execution. It is simple to define an *expiration window* using SDL statements and the corresponding net transitions. The basic idea of expiration windows is the same as in the Emma tool [4]. One net transition can "open" the window by putting a token into a special *timer lock place* and the timer is allowed to expire. Another net transition can "close" the window by removing the lock token from the timer lock place and the timer can no more expire. The reachability analysis will check all possible cases: it will let the timer expire in all possible states when the window is open.

5   Analysis of SDL Using Maria

Much effort in the design of SDL2PN has been put into ensuring that the tool can handle industrial-size systems. The *RLC* (*Radio Link Control*) protocol (a UMTS radio network layer protocol and an OSI data link layer protocol) has been and is being used as a test case. SDL2PN is expected to be able to handle an SDL/PR description that corresponds to the 56-page SDL/GR description [17] of the protocol. Since the end of the year 2001, SDL2PN has been able to handle most of the needed constructs.

In parallel with the development of SDL2PN, there was an explicit analysis project on RLC. In that project, several Maria models of the SDL specification of the protocol were manually constructed. Due to carefully selected abstractions, certain fundamental positive analysis results were eventually obtained [18, 19]. One of the lessons learnt in the project was that manual modeling and abstraction is is extremely error-prone, whereas even a single mistake can cause false positive or false negative analysis results. Proceeding towards more and more automatic analysis is reasonable in many respects. This does not mean that interactive analysis could or should be totally avoided.

6   Alleviating State Space Explosion

Here we consider basically two classes of methods that try to alleviate state space explosion: *partial order reduction methods* and *symmetry methods*. The primary motivation for this choice is that the HUT-TCS laboratory has long experience of these methods, including implementations. On the other hand, results reported by research groups in this field during the last two decades indicate that these two classes are "industrially relevant". Moreover, many contexts allow combining these two classes with other classes (including with each other) in such a way that the combination pays off in the form of a reduced verification cost.

6.1   Partial Order Reduction Methods

The semantics of SDL makes it possible to use a simple reduction method in the model. Because processes are completely independent of each other and in principle only communicate by sending messages, it is possible to remove unnecessary interleaving in the analysis by using a *resource place* containing a single token. One process only can take the resource token and proceed until it communicates with other processes. Then the resource token must be released and put back into the resource place where any other process can take it. The resource token implements a kind of static partial order reduction. Though the resource place technique is easy to implement and was implemented in Emma [5, 4], it tends to be blind to some typical forms of redundant interleavings: for example, reading from and writing to a queue when the queue is neither empty nor full. (Though full queues do not exist according to the standard [11], truly unbounded queues cannot be implemented. On the other hand, assuming some small capacity on a queue is a classical restriction technique in reachability analysis.) It is therefore motivation to provide some more powerful forms of partial order reduction implemented in the total tool formed by SDL2PN and Maria.

The term "partial order reduction method" can be understood in many ways, but here we assume that the method basically constructs a subgraph of the full reachability graph state by state in such a way that at each encountered state, the reduced set of immediate successor states is a subset of all immediate successor states, the subset being determined by an algorithm designed for the purpose. The requirements of such an algorithm depend on the verification task. For each infinite or terminal-state-ended path starting from the initial state in the full reachability graph, the constructed subgraph has a path that represents an equivalent observable behavior, the equivalence depending on the context. A characteristic feature in partial order reduction methods is that the action-based label of the "representative path" can be obtained from the action-based label of the "original path" simply by changing the order of some "important" actions and, optionally, by inserting some "unimportant" actions into arbitrary positions. The article [20] is a good state-of-the-art description, with emphasis on industrial applicability and on connections to other methods.

Much of the essence of partial order reduction methods is captured by the following naive characterization: "Some orders do not matter. Unfortunately, some orders do matter." Let us look at the message sequence charts in Fig. 4. The displayed charts illustrate the fact that as far as continuation of communication is concerned, the order of receptions of C and D is more important than the order of receptions of B and C. Note that there is no way to continue the behavior expressed by the rightmost chart.

Path compression means a sequence of graph transformation operations such that each single operation replaces some path by a single edge. Path compression can be used together with partial order reduction methods, whereas it is often the case that a path compression algorithm "induces" a partial order reduction algorithm (in the sense that a correctness proof for the former can be used as a correctness proof of the latter).

Let us consider the state-of-the-art of partial order reduction methods among SDL tools. SDLcheck [21, 22] uses COSPAN [23, 24] in such a way that all decisions concerning partial order reduction and path compression are made during the translation from SDL to the input language of COSPAN. IF [2, 26, 27] and PEP [13, 28] support partial order reduction in the sense that they produce input to SPIN [29, 30] that has various ways of partial order reduction and path compression. PEP itself has a partial order method based on net unfoldings, but certain combinatorial aspects complicate the practice of that method in the

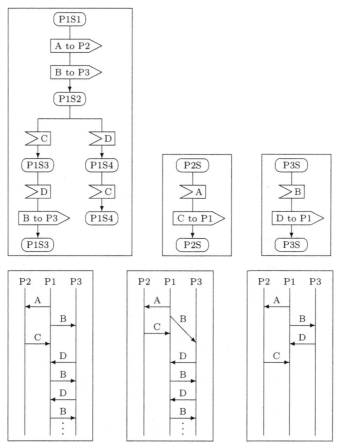

Fig. 4. Top: An SDL System Formed by Processes P1, P2 and P3. bottom: Three message Sequence Charts of the System

context of SDL. SPV [16] supports partial order reduction in the sense that it produces input to CPN/Tools [31] that has a partial order reduction method.

Considering the two latest high-level Petri net analysis tools developed at HUT-TCS (PROD [6, 7] and Maria [8, 9]) both tools have path compression, but only PROD has a "wide service" partial order reduction method. A explanation of this situation is that Maria is to have a partial order reduction method that is tailored for the case that the input comes from the SDL front-end. Due to fundamental similarity between SDL and the input language of SPIN, Maria is likely to have SPIN-style processes and SPIN-style algorithms. So far, the only considered true alternative to SPIN-style solutions is to split atomic actions and optimize the representation of data until there is a net that can be unfolded into a low-level net where PROD-style algorithms are both applicable and useful.

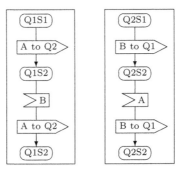

Fig. 5. An SDL system Formed by Processes Q1 and Q2 that are Symmetric via the Label Substring Mapping "Q1 $\mapsto$ Q2, Q2 $\mapsto$ Q1, A $\mapsto$ B, B $\mapsto$ A"

6.2   Symmetry Methods

Recognition of symmetries is a general mathematical way to reduce the amount of work needed for solving a problem. So, it is not surprising that they can be used for alleviating state space explosion as well. Several kinds of symmetries can be recognized and utilized, almost regardless of the modeling formalism. Figure 5 displays an SDL system where a symmetry is easy to recognize just by looking at the diagrams of the processes.

For convenience, let us skip the dynamics of symmetry methods and only consider the question of tool support. COSPAN has algorithms for symmetry reduction, and those algorithms apparently support SDLcheck via translation. CPN/Tools has a symmetry method, and the method apparently supports SPV via translation. Among tools that do not have any well known interface for SDL yet, Murϕ [32] and SMC [33] support reduction by symmetries. Maria is to have a symmetry method based on the work presented in [34].

7   Conclusions

The SDL2PN front-end for the Maria analyzer has been implemented to automatically transform standard SDL descriptions to high-level Petri nets which can be analyzed by Maria. Most of those features of SDL-96 that are not yet supported by SDL2PN were explicitly excluded in the supervising group meetings of the Maria and Anna-Maria projects where the overall design decisions on SDL2PN were made.

The front-end adds to the model net constructs which makes the analysis more efficient by reducing unnecessary interleavings. On the other hand, reduction methods are needed in the analyzer itself better in order to make the analysis useful also for real, industrial-size SDL descriptions.

Acknowledgments

In the versions up to the time of writing, the code in SDL2PN has been written by Annikka Aalto, Marko Mäkelä, André Schulz and Teemu Tynjälä (cf. [25]). Henna Ruusu and Teemu Tynjälä made an SDL/PR description of RLC on the basis of [17]. Ari Ahtiainen, Sari Leppänen, Matti Luukkainen and Vesa Luukkala represented Nokia Research Center in the supervising groups of the Maria and Anna-Maria projects and greatly affected the decisions concerning inclusion/exclusion of features of SDL-96 to be supported by SDL2PN.

References

[1] P. Leblanc. Simulation, verification and validation of models. VERILOG White Paper, Toulouse Cedex, France, March 1998. 285

[2] M. Bozga, S. Graf, L. Mounier. Automated validation of distributed software using the IF environment. Electronic Notes in Theoretical Computer Science, 55(3), 2001. 286, 294

[3] J. Fischer, E. Dimitrov, U. Taubert. Analysis and formal verification of SDL'92 specifications using extended Petri nets. Technical Report 43, Department of Computer Science, Humbolt University Berlin, Germany, 1995. 286

[4] M. Malmqvist. Methodology of dynamical analysis of SDL programs using predicate/transition nets. Technical Report B16, HUT-DS, Espoo, Finland, 1997. 286, 292, 294

[5] N. Husberg, T. Manner. Emma: developing an industrial reachability analyzer for SDL. Proc. FM'99, Vol. I, LNCS 1708, pp. 642–661. Springer, 1999. 286, 288, 294

[6] PROD 3.3.09—an advanced tool for efficient reachability analysis. Software, HUT-TCS, Espoo, Finland, http://www.tcs.hut.fi/Software/prod/. 286, 295

[7] K. Varpaaniemi, K. Heljanko, J. Lilius. prod 3.2—An advanced tool for efficient reachability analysis. Proc. CAV'97, LNCS 1254, pp. 472–475. Springer, 1997. 286, 295

[8] Maria—a modular reachability analyzer. Software, HUT-TCS, Espoo, Finland, http://www.tcs.hut.fi/Software/maria/. 286, 295

[9] M. Mäkelä. Maria: Modular reachability analyzer for algebraic system nets. Proc. ICATPN 2002, LNCS 2360, pp. 434–444. Springer, 2002. 286, 295

[10] T. Latvala. Model Checking Linear Temporal Logic Properties of Petri Nets with Fairness Constraints. Proc. ICATPN 2001, LNCS 2075, pp. 242–262. Springer, 2001. 287

[11] ITU-T. Z.100 (03/93) CCITT Specification and Description Language (SDL) *with* Z.100 Addendum 1 (10/96) Corrections to Recommendation Z.100 (10/96). International Telecommunication Union, Geneva. 287, 292, 294

[12] M. Mäkelä. Implementing the front-end of an SDL compiler. Master's thesis, HUT-TCS, Espoo, Finland, 1998. 287

[13] H. Fleischhack, B. Grahlmann. A compositional Petri net semantics for SDL. Proc. ICATPN'98, LNCS 1420, pp. 144–164. Springer, 1998. 288, 294

[14] N. Husberg, T. Tynjälä, K. Varpaaniemi. Modeling and analyzing the SDL description of the ISDN-DSS1 protocol. Proc. ICATPN 2000, LNCS 1825, pp. 244–260. Springer, 2000. 288

[15] A. Aalto. Automatic translation of SDL into high-level Petri nets. Master's thesis manuscript, HUT-TCS, Espoo, Finland, 2003. 289

[16] T. G. Churina, M. U. Mashukov, V. A. Nepomniaschy. Towards verification of SDL specified distributed systems: Coloured Petri nets approach. Proc. CS&P'2001, pp. 37–48. University of Warsaw, Poland, 2001. 291, 295

[17] 3rd Generation Partnership Project: Technical Specification Group Radio Access Network; RLC Protocol Specification, Version 3G TS 25.322 V3.5.0. 3GPP (3rd Generation Partnership Project), Sophia Antipolis, France, 2000. 293, 297

[18] T. Tynjälä. Combining abstractions and reachability analysis: A case study of the RLC protocol. Licentiate's thesis, HUT-TCS, Espoo, Finland, March 2003. 293

[19] T. Tynjälä, S. Leppänen, V. Luukkala. Verifying reliable data transmission over UMTS radio interface with high-level Petri nets. Proc. FORTE 2002, LNCS 2529, pp. 178–193. Springer, 2002. 293

[20] R. P. Kurshan, V. Levin, M. Minea, D. Peled, H. Yenigün. Combining software and hardware verification techniques. Formal Methods in System Design, 21(3):251–280, 2002. 294

[21] O. Başbuğoğlu, K. İnan. Compiling SDL into the finite state specification language COSPAN. Proc. ISCIS X (1995), Vol. II, pp. 643–650. Istanbul Technical University, Turkey, 1995. 294

[22] V. Levin, H. Yenigün. SDLcheck: A model checking tool. Proc. CAV 2001, LNCS 2102, pp. 378–381. Springer, 2001. 294

[23] R. H. Hardin, Z. Har'El, R. P. Kurshan. COSPAN. Proc. CAV'96, LNCS 1102, pp. 423–427. Springer, 1996. 294

[24] J. Katzenelson, R. P. Kurshan. S/R: A language for specifying protocols and other coordinating processes. Proc. 5th IEEE-PCCC (1986), pp. 282–292. IEEE, 1986. 294

[25] A. Schulz, T. Tynjälä. Translation rules from standard SDL to Maria input language. In Research Report A63, HUT-TCS, Espoo, Finland, 2000, pp. 105–114. 297

[26] D. Bošnački, D. Dams, L. Holenderski, N. Sidorova. Model checking SDL with SPIN. Proc. TACAS 2000, LNCS 1785, pp. 363–377. Springer, 2000. 294

[27] G. Jia, S. Graf. Verification experiments on the MASCARA protocol. Proc. SPIN 2001, LNCS 2057, pp. 123–142. Springer, 2001. 294

[28] C. Stehno. Real-time systems designs with PEP. Proc. TACAS 2002, LNCS 2280, pp. 476–480. Springer, 2002. 294

[29] G. J. Holzmann. The model checker SPIN. IEEE Transactions on Software Engineering, 23(5):279–295, 1997. 294

[30] G. J. Holzmann, J. Patti. Validating SDL specifications: an experiment. Proc. PSTV IX (1989), pp. 317–326. North-Holland, 1990. 294

[31] M. Beaudouin-Lafon et al. CPN/Tools: A tool for editing and simulating coloured Petri nets. Proc. TACAS 2001, LNCS 2031, pp. 574–577. Springer, 2001. 295

[32] C. N. Ip, D. L. Dill. Better verification through symmetry. Formal Methods in System Design, 9(1/2):41–75, 1996. 296

[33] A. P. Sistla, V. Gyuris, E. A. Emerson. SMC: A symmetry-based model checker for verification of safety and liveness properties. ACM Transactions on Software Engineering and Methodology, 9(2):133–166, 2000. 296

[34] T. Junttila. Symmetry reduction algorithms for data symmetries. Research Report A72, HUT-TCS, Espoo, Finland, 2002. 296

A   Using SDL2PN: A Simple Example

In the session below, the "###" lines are command lines. The output of the first command is an SDL/PR description of a system that is known to have exactly the same behavior as the system in Fig. 4. Therefore, the output of the last command corresponds to the rightmost message sequence chart in Fig. 4.

```
### cat p123.sdl
system M; signal A,B,C,D; block K referenced; endsystem;
block K;
  process P1(1,1) referenced;
  process P2(1,1) referenced;
  process P3(1,1) referenced;
  signalroute R12 from P1 to P2 with A;
  signalroute R13 from P1 to P3 with B;
  signalroute R21 from P2 to P1 with C;
  signalroute R31 from P3 to P1 with D;
endblock K;
process P1;
  start; output A; output B; nextstate P1S2;
  state P1S2; input C; nextstate P1S3;
             input D; nextstate P1S4;
  state P1S3; input D; output B; nextstate P1S3;
  state P1S4; input C; nextstate P1S4;
endprocess P1;
process P2;
  start; nextstate P2S;
  state P2S; input A; output C; nextstate P2S;
endprocess P2;
process P3;
  start; nextstate P3S;
  state P3S; input B; output D; nextstate P3S;
endprocess P3;
### sdl2pn -V
version 0.0.5
### sdl2pn -q1 -o p123.pn p123.sdl
0 infos, 0 warnings, 0 errors
Cleaning up: done
### echo 'deadlock fatal;' >>p123.pn
### maria -V
maria version 1.1
### maria -m p123.pn -e 'breadth; exit'
fatal deadlock state @19
"p123.pn": 21 states (12..12 bytes), 27 arcs
### maria -g p123 -e 'path @19; exit' 2>&1 | grep transition
transition "Output:M_K_P1:M_K_P2:M_A:0012"->@1
transition "Input:M_K_P2:M_A:0009:0020"->@3
transition "Output:M_K_P1:M_K_P3:M_B:0012"->@4
transition "Input:M_K_P3:M_B:0012:0024"->@8
transition "Output:M_K_P3:M_K_P1:M_D:0024"->@12
transition "Input:M_K_P1:M_D:0003:0014"->@15
transition "Output:M_K_P2:M_K_P1:M_C:0020"->@17
transition "Input:M_K_P1:M_C:0005:0016"->@19
```

Applying SDL
to Formal Analysis of Security Systems

Javier López, Juan J. Ortega, and José M. Troya

Computer Science Department, E.T.S. Ingeniería Informática
University of Malaga, 29071, Malaga, Spain
{jlm,juanjose,troya}@lcc.uma.es

Abstract. Nowadays, it is widely accepted that critical systems have to be formally analyzed to achieve well-known benefits of formal methods. To study the security of communication systems, we have developed a methodology for the application of the formal analysis techniques commonly used in communication protocols to the analysis of cryptographic ones. In particular, we have extended the design and analysis phases with security properties. Our proposal uses a specification notation based on MSC, which can be automatically translated into a generic SDL specification. This SDL system can then be used for the analysis of the desired security properties, by using an observer process schema. Apart from our main goal of providing a notation for describing the formal specification of security systems, our proposal also brings additional benefits, such as the study of the possible attacks to the system, and the possibility of reusing the specifications produced to describe and analyze more complex systems.

1 Introduction

Formal methods characterize the behavior of a system in a precise way and can verify its formal specification. In particular, the design and analysis of security systems can greatly benefit from the use of formal methods, due to the evident critical nature of such systems.

During recent years, the cryptographic protocol analysis research area [1] has experienced an explosive growth, with numerous formalisms being developed. We can divide this research into three main categories: logic-based [2], model checking [3, 4, 5], and theorem proving [6]. Although all three approaches have shown their applicability to simple problems, they are still difficult to apply in real, more complex environments such as distributed systems over the Internet.

Moreover, we believe that the results obtained in the analysis of cryptographic protocols do not have a direct application in the design of secure communication systems. Probably, one of the major reasons for that is the lack of a strong relationship between the analysis tools for security systems and the formal methods techniques commonly used in the specification and analysis of communication protocols. Trying to bridge this gap is one of the major contributions of our work.

R. Reed (Ed.): SDL 2003, LNCS 2708, pp. 300–316, 2003.

We have developed a methodology [7, 8] for the specification of secure systems, which also allows us to check that they are not vulnerable against both well-known and originals attacks. Our approach uses a requirement language (SRSL) to describe security protocols, which can then be automatically translated into SDL [9], a widely used formal notation specifically well suited for the analysis of protocols. In addition, we have developed some verification procedures and tools for checking a set of security properties, such as confidentiality, authentication, and non-repudiation of origin. In our approach we use a simple but powerful intruder process, which is explicitly added to the specification of the system, so that the verification of the security properties guarantees the robustness of the protocol against attacks of such an intruder. This is known as the Dolev-Yao's method [10].

Because SRSL is an extension of MSC [11], available editors for MSC and SDL can be used for writing SRSL specifications, as well as standard code-generators and SDL validation tools. In particular, we have built our translators and analyzing tools using Telelogic's Tau SDL Suite.

The structure of this document is as follows. After this introduction, Sect. 2 defines the security concepts and mechanisms used throughout the paper. Then, Sect. 3 provides an overview of our proposal. The SRSL language is presented in Sect. 4, while Sect. 5 discusses how the SRSL descriptions can be automatically translated into SDL, and how the SDL specifications produced can be analyzed for proving security properties. Finally, Sect. 6 draws some conclusions and outlines some future work.

2   Specification of Security Properties

A security protocol [12] is a general template describing a sequence of communications, which makes use of cryptographic techniques to meet one or more particular security-related goals. In our context we will not distinguish between cryptographic and security protocols, considering both to be equivalent. The international organization ITU-T has defined Recommendation Series X.800 [13, 14] to specify the basic security services. Among these, the ones provided by the basic security mechanisms (cryptographic algorithms and secure protocols) are authentication [15], access control [16], non-repudiation [17], data confidentiality [18], and data integrity [19].

The notion of *authentication* includes both authentication of origin and entity authentication. *Authentication of origin* can be defined as the certainty that a message that is claimed to proceed from a certain party was actually originated from it. As an illustration, if Bob receives a message during the execution of a protocol, which is supposed to come from Anne, then the protocol is said to guarantee authentication of origin for Bob if it is always the case that, if Bob's node accepts the message as being from Anne, then it must indeed be the case that Anne has sent exactly this message earlier. Authentication of origin must be established for the whole message. Additionally, it is often the case that certain time constraints concerning the freshness of the received message must also be met. *Entity authentication* guarantees that the claimed identity of an agent participating in a protocol is identical to the real one.

Access Control service. ensures that only authorized principals can gain access to protected resources. Usually, the identity of the principal must be established, hence entity authentication is also required here.

Non-repudiation. provides evidence to the parties involved in a communication that certain steps of the protocol have occurred. This property appears to be very similar to authentication, but in this case the participants are given capabilities to fake messages, up to the usual cryptographic constraints. Non-repudiation uses signature mechanisms and a trusted notary. We will distinguish two types of non-repudiation services: non-repudiation of origin (NRO) and non-repudiation of receipt (NRR). NRO is intended to prevent the originator's false denial of having originated the message. On the other hand, NRR is intended to prevent the recipient's false denial of having received the message.

Confidentiality. may be defined as the prevention of unauthorized disclosure of information. In communication protocols, this means that nobody who has access to the exchanged messages can deduce the secret information being transmitted.

Data Integrity. means that data cannot be corrupted, or at least that corruption will not remain undetected. Accepting a corrupted message is considered as a violation of integrity, and therefore the protocol must be regarded as flawed.

These services are commonly enforced using cryptographic protocols or similar mechanisms. It is worth noting that, To specify a security system, it is not necessary to know how the system is going to be analyzed, but it is essential to identify the security services required.

Now, considering the system from the attacker's perspective, additional security protocol vulnerabilities can be defined: (a) *man-in-the-middle*, where the intruder is able to masquerade a protocol participant; (b) *reflection*, where an agent emits messages and studies the system's answers; (c) *oracle*, where the intruder tricks an honest agent by inadvertently revealing some information (notice that such an attack may involve the intruder exploiting steps from different runs of the protocol, or even involve steps from an entirely different protocol); (d) *replay*, in which the intruder monitors a (possible partial) run of the protocol and, at some later time, replays one or more of the protocol's messages; (e) *interleave*, where the intruder contrives for two or more runs of the protocol to overlap; (f) *failures of forward secrecy*, in which the compromised information is allowed to propagate into the future; and (g) *algebraic attack*, where it is possible for intruders to exploit algebraic identities to undermine the security of the protocol. Please note that these kinds of attacks depend on the environment of the system (network, users, ...), and therefore not all of them are always achievable in a given context. However, we will study all potential situations, trying to cover them all in all cases.

To keep clear the focus of the paper, the following assumptions have been made. First, we suppose that cryptography is perfect, so no cryptanalysis techniques are used. Second, all agents may freely and perfectly generate random numbers. And finally, we do not consider interactions with any other protocols, because this is an open research topic.

3   Methodology Overview

Our approach (depicted in Fig. 1) performs the design and analysis of security protocols in the same way the design and analysis of a traditional communication protocols is accomplished, but including the security aspects.

In the first place, we need to gather the functional and security requirements of the system in any (usually informal) way. These informal specifications, together with the behavior about the kinds of possible attacks (if available), is the sort of information that can be described using our *Security Requirements Specification Language* (SRSL).

SRSL is an extension of MSC, augmented with textual tags. We make use of the MSC text area to include these tags, which are used to identify the security characteristics of the data being transmitted, the intruder's possible activities, and the security analysis goals. In case the attacker's behavior is not explicitly provided, we automatically generate a generic process that tries to examine all possible attacks.

For drawing the graphical SRSL specifications, any standard MSC and HMSC editor can be used. In our case, we have used Telelogic's TAU, which also allows the automatic translation of the graphical MSC diagrams into their corresponding textual form. A translator program is then used to obtain the SDL system

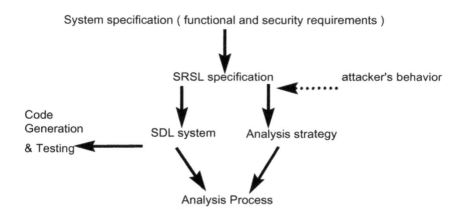

Fig. 1. Overview of Our Approach

from the SRSL descriptions. (This program has been written in C, using plain LEX and YACC tools.) The SDL system produced is composed of: (1) a package with the data types of the system for the analysis; (2) a package with one process type for each protocol agent; and (3) a collection of process types ("observer" and "medium") for the analysis strategy.

To analyze the security properties, we evaluate the behavior of the SDL system under different kinds of attacks (as specified by the medium processes defined in the analysis strategy). The observer process provided by the TAU Validator tool is used for these checks. Thus, we can check whether a specific state is reached, or whether a particular data is ever stored into the intruder's database knowledge.

We also make use of the TAU Validator *assert* mechanism, which enables observer processes to generate reports during the state space exploration. These reports are maintained by the Report Viewer, and can be examined to identify security flaws.

Currently, confidentiality and authentication [20] are the security properties usually analyzed. By analyzing confidentiality we prevent the intruder from being able to derive the plaintext of messages passing between honest nodes. Our analysis consists of checking if the secret item can be deduced from the protocol messages and the intruder's database knowledge.

```
Security_information ::= definition_section security_service_section

Defintion_section ::= Definition var_definition  knowledge_section

var_definition ::= <varlist> : Agent ;
        | <varlist> : Text ;
        | <varlist> : Random ;
        | <varlist> : Timestamp ;
        | <varlist> : Sequence ;
        | <varlist> : Public_key ;
        | <varlist> : Symmetric_key ;
        | <varlist> : Shared_key ;
        | <varlist> : Session_key ;

Knowledge_section ::= Knowledge <listagent_id> : <varlistasig> ;

Security_service_section ::= [intruder_strategy] security_property

intruder_strategy ::= Session instances [ <var>=<value> ] ;
        | intruder_knowledge [ <initial_knowledge> ];
        | intruder [ redirect | , impersonate | , eavesdrop ] ;

security_property ::= Security_service <security_service_list> ;

security_service_list ::= authenticated ( <agent> <agent> )
        | conf ( <data> )
        | NRO ( <agent> <data> )
```

Fig. 2. SRSL Security Section Syntax

An authentication protocol is considered to be correct if a user Bob does not finish the protocol believing that it has been running with a user Alice unless Alice also believes that she has been running the protocol with Bob. Our analysis consists of looking for a reachable state where Bob has finished correctly and Alice will never reach her final state.

We also analyze non-repudiation of origin. For that we define the evidence of origin and who produces it (the origin). Our analysis consists of checking that the evidence is digitally signed by the origin agent, and that it cannot be created by any other agent.

In addition, the SDL system generated from the SRSL specifications can be used to automatically generate C or C++ code, which can interact with exiting applications. In order to generate this code we need to replace the data types package with a corresponding package that defines the data types in ASN.1 or C. This prototype can also be used for testing, which is part of our future work.

4   The SRSL Language

The main aim of SRSL is to define a high-level language for the specification of cryptographic protocols and secure systems. As pre-requisites for this language we need to ask it to be modular to achieve reusability, to be easy to learn, and to incorporate security concepts.

As a natural base for SRSL we considered the requirements language most widely used in the telecommunications: the Message Sequence Chart (MSC) and its extension High-level MSC (HMSC). With MSC we can specify elementary scenarios, and compose them to define more complex protocols with HMSC. The version we have considered is previous to the MSC 2000 release [21], but we believe that some features of this release are very useful.

SRSL is divided into two main parts. The first one contains the definition of the protocol elements and the security analysis strategy. The second part describes the message exchange flow.

The first part is textual. The syntax of its main elements is shown in Fig. 2. These elements can be grouped into different categories, and are listed below (language keywords are written in *italics*):

- Main elements:
  - Entities: *Agent*, principal identification.
  - Message: *Text*, message text; *Random,* number created for freshness, also called nonce; *Timestamp*, actual time; *Sequence*, counter.
  - Keys:
    Public_key public-key cryptographic, formed by a pair of public and private keys;
    Symmetric_key used for symmetric encipher;
    Shared_key symmetric key shared by more than one entity;
    Session_key a fresh symmetric key used to encrypt transmission.
- The "knowledge" section contains the information needed to describe the initial knowledge of each party of the protocol.

- The "security service" section is split into the "intruder strategy" section and the "security property" section. The first one defines a possible attack scenario. The second one describes which security property we try to achieve with this protocol. We have used three different security statements: *Authenticated(A,B)*, stating that B is certain of the identity of A; *conf(X)*, stating that the data X cannot be deduced (also called confidentiality); and *NRO(A,X)*, or non-repudiation of origin, which states that the data X (the evidence) must have been originated in A. These statements have a formal description which is used to analyze them.

The message exchange flow is described using the standard MSC and HMSC facilities. MSC references are used to achieve reusability. We have specified a set of standard protocols in SRSL, that can be easily re-used in different contexts, and combined together to describe more complex protocols using their MSC references.

Messages consist of an identification name (either a text string describing the meaning of the message, or a simple counter sequence), and the message parameters (which define the message data type format).

Some cryptographic operations can be applied to messages: Concatenate (",") for data composition; Cipher ({<plaintext>} <key>) to cipher data; Decipher("*decrypt(<cipher_data>,<key>)*") to extract the plaintext; Hash("<hash-function> (<data>)"), result of a one way algorithm; and Sign([<plaintext>] <Public_Private_key>"), for getting a hash encrypted message with the signer's private key. Further cryptographic functions can be defined if required.

In addition, the MSC expressions constructed using the inline MSC operators *alt*, *par*, *loop*, *opt* and *exc* can also be used.

The keyword *alt* denotes alternative executions of several MSCs. Only one of the alternatives is applicable in an instantiation of the actual sequence.

The *par* operator denotes the parallel execution of several MSCs. All events within the MSCs involved are executed, with the sole restriction that the event order within each MSC must be preserved. An MSC reference with a *loop* construct is used for iterations and can have several forms. The most general construct, *loop<n,m>*, where n and m are natural numbers, denotes iteration at least n and at most m times. The *opt* construct denotes a unary operator. It is interpreted in the same way as an *alt* operation where the second operand is an empty MSC. An MSC reference where the text starts with *exc* followed by the name of an MSC indicates that the MSC can be aborted at the position of the MSC reference symbol, and instead continued with the referenced MSC.

To illustrate our approach we will specify here a typical secure web access to a data bank portal via the Internet. Figure 3 shows the SRSL specification of the system in SRSL, that uses two agents: "User_Browser" and "Bank_Portal". The "Bank_Portal" agent has a secure web service via the HTTPS protocol, which provides authentication of the server. This is represented by an MSC reference called "https_server_auth" that implements the server authentication and the key exchange protocol defined in HTTPS. This MSC reference is defined in a package of standard protocols. The results of this scenario is authentication

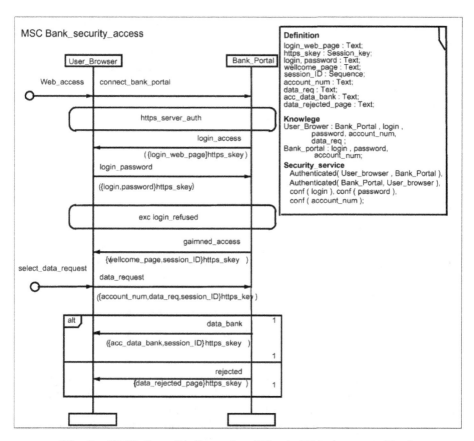

Fig. 3. SRSL Security Scenario of User's Web Access to Bank

of the server and a session key called "https_skey". The first security requirement *"Authenticated (User_Browser, Bank_Portal)"* is achieved with this protocol.

The second requirement means that the user must authenticate itself to the bank's portal. This is accomplished by a mechanism that asks for the user's identification (login) and password, and subsequently validates it. The exception MSC reference called "login_refused" is active if the login-password authentication process of the "Bank_Portal" fails. Notice that all messages are ciphered by the https protocol session key.

The last three requirements mean that the data transmitted is confidential. This goal is accomplished by making use of the session key established during the https connection.

Of course, other alternative security mechanisms could have been considered for specifying this system, which also met the five original requirements. The important point to note here is that we have chosen a form of specification that does not bind the developer to any particular security mechanisms, thus

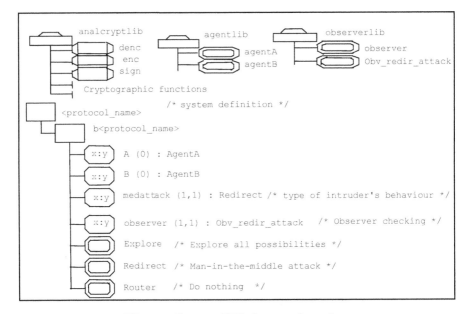

Fig. 4. Generic SDL System Overview

achieving separation of concerns and modularity. This is accomplished by allowing the security requirements to be defined at a higher level of abstraction, and independently from the system's functional requirements.

In the case of a system that is already implemented (a legacy system) that we want to analyze or document, we can describe instead the security mechanisms that have been implemented.

5   Security Analyses

We use SDL for the security analyses. In the first place, we need to build an SDL system from the SRSL specifications. We have developed a program that automates this process. The program is written in the C language, and uses LEX and YACC standard tools. The input file is a protocol specification written in SRSL, and the program produces a valid SDL system. The generated SDL system (depicted in Fig. 4) is composed of three packages, and contains several processes.

The SDL package that defines the system data types and their operators is called "analcryptlib". It also contains elementary security data types, and the message format definition used in the protocol. This information is used by the rest of the system.

Another SDL package defines a process type for each principal agent. They are implemented in a standalone fashion so they can be reused in different sit-

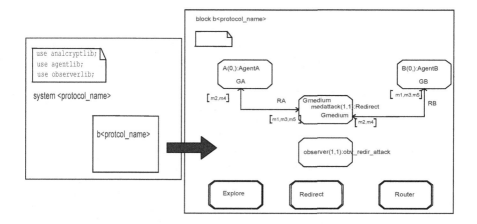

Fig. 5. SDL System Configuration

uations. Figure 4 shows two process types, which reference agents A and B respectively.

The last package is about the observer processes. They implement the assert mechanism used in the validation process, and depend on the medium process (called "medattack" in Fig. 4), and on the security services that will be evaluated.

The SDL system (shown in Fig. 5) is named after the protocol it defines, and consists of a single SDL block, which is composed of the process structure for analysis ("A", "B", "medattack"), an observer process ("observer") and several medium process types ("explore", "redirect", and "router"). The process structure for the analysis consists of a medium process that controls all transmissions among agent processes. This control implements the attacker's procedure.

Please note that medium process types have to be created inside this block because they implement the intruder's behavior, and therefore they may create process agent instances. The TAU tool we use requires all process instances to be defined within the same block. The following describes in detail all the system parts, and how the SRSL specifications are mapped onto the SDL description of the system.

5.1 Data Types Package

An SDL package contains the data types and the cryptographic functions used in the SRSL specification of the system. We may consider an SDL package for performing the analysis, and other package (written in ASN.1) for code generation. All cryptographic data and operators are standardized using ASN.1 notation, following PKCS standards [22].

Since the SDL data types do not support recursive definitions, we make use of enumerated and structured data types. The elemental data types defined in

Fig. 6. Example of translation of security data to SDL *struct*

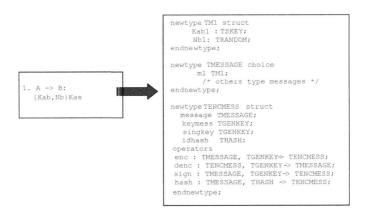

Fig. 7. Example of Translation Belonging to the First Message of a Security Protocol

Sect. 4 are then mapped to enumerated SDL *struct* sorts. An example is depicted in Fig. 6.

The messages, which are sent by protocol agents, are constructed by concatenation of elemental data types and cryptographic operations. We define a *struct* sort for each message, and set of elemental data types. The cryptographic functions are then applied to a set of elemental data types called "TENCMESS". This is shown in Fig. 7.

Freshness or temporary secrets are implemented by adding an item that references the process instance values. In particular, we use the SDL sort *PID* for this purpose.

Furthermore, we define a "set of knowledge" type for each data type. The analysis methods use these types to store message knowledge in order to prove the specified security properties.

5.2 Agents Package

The generic model identifies each protocol agent with an SDL process type. All process types are stored in a package called "agentlib" so they can be used in other specifications. An agent specification is totally independent from the rest of the system, so they are generated in separate modules. In addition, the specification allows concurrent instances, so we can evaluate this behavior in the analysis phase.

The generic state transition of an agent process is triggered when it receives a correct message (a message accepted by the agent). Then, either the next message is composed to be sent to the receiver agent, or the process stops if the protocol's final state is reached for this process. If the message is not correct, the process returns to the state where it is waiting for messages.

The MSC expressions used in SRSL are mapped into SDL as follows: an *alt* expression produces several signal trigger states; a *loop* expression makes all next transitions return to the initial section state; an *opt* expression is implemented by a *continue* signal; and finally, an *exec* expression is translated into an asterisk state.

An SDL process is a finite state machine, and therefore it finishes when it executes a stop statement, or provides a deadlock if no signal arrives. Our model has to explore all possibilities. Hence, we need to develop a mechanism to ensure that all signals sent must be processed. Consequently, we have added a state called "final" to indicate the end of the protocol execution, and a general transition composed of a common "save" statement and a continuous signal, with less priority than the input statement, that checks whether there are signals still waiting to be processed. By means of this structure we are transforming a finite state machine into an infinite one, just for analysis purposes.

At this point, if we instantiate the medium process with a "Router" process type, we can specify a security protocol in the same way as we might specify a traditional communication protocol, and therefore we can analyze some of the liveness properties of the system in a traditional way. In the next subsection, we are going to explain how the security properties can be checked.

5.3   Model Medium-Observer Processes

In our approach, the intruder's behavior is divided into two main aspects, the exploration algorithm and the check mechanism. The first one is provided by a medium process, while an observer performs the check mechanisms.

We can consider two kinds of medium processes. The first one is characterized by an exploration mechanism that tries to explore all possibilities. It starts by examining all combinations of the different initial knowledge of each agent. Afterwards, it checks the concurrent agents' execution, by first trying combinations of two concurrent sessions, and so on. Our algorithm finishes when an "out of memory" is detected, or when it detects that the significant intruder knowledge is not incremented. In general, the completeness problem [23, 24] is undecidable. Thus, the fact that the algorithm terminates without having found a flaw, is not a proof that there are no flaws.

The second kind of medium process uses an intruder process specialized in finding a specific flaw. If we are able to characterize a particular kind of attack, we can then evaluate the protocol trying to find such a specific flaw. Perhaps this is not the best solution in general (the only result we get is that a specific vulnerability does not occur in the cases we have examined), but it is very useful

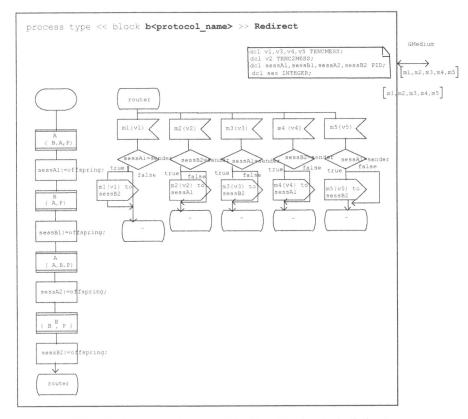

Fig. 8. Implementation of "redirect" Intruder's Behavior

for a protocol designer that wants to be sure that the protocol is not vulnerable with respect to that kind of attack.

The state transition of the medium process is triggered when it receives any message. After reception, the message is stored into the intruder's knowledge database. The intruder then decides which operation performs next, and proceeds to the next routing state. We have defined three different operations: *eavesdrop*, *redirect*, and *impersonate*. In an *eavesdrop* operation, the intruder intercepts the message but does not send it to any agent. A *redirect* operation means that the intruder intercepts the message but does not forward it to the original receiver. In an *impersonate* operation, the intruder sends a faked message to the original receiver.

Under the EU-funded project CASENET we are currently investigating the use of the protocol developer SAFIRE tool [25] to execute the medium processes. Even if we have to modify these processes to use the tool, we may easily obtain an environment for testing intruders' strategies. This is an open research item.

The security properties are proved using condition rules. These rules check different situations where protocol vulnerability is possible. The observer process

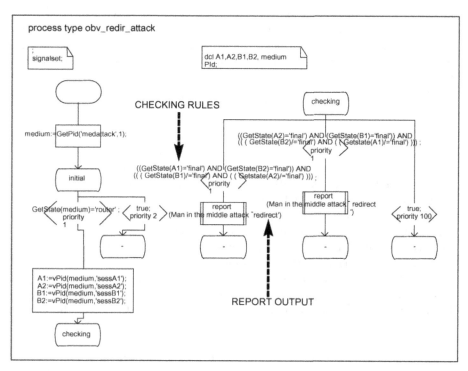

Fig. 9. Example of Observer Process Type that Checks Correspondence Flaw

carries out the checking mechanism. This is a special SDL process type that is evaluated in each transition of the protocol specification. It has access to all variables and states of all process instances, so we can test it automatically. To implement it we have to create an SDL *struct* sort with a "v" operator for each structured type that we want to evaluate. Figure 9 shows an example of an observer process. We can see the condition rules for checking the authentication property, and the report result. The report contains a security failure MSC scenario.

Currently, confidentiality, authentication, and non-repudiation of origin can be checked. For checking confidentiality, we examine whether a specific value (that we consider secret) can be deduced from the intruder's knowledge. Authentication is analyzed by checking that all the principal processes finish at the expected protocol step. Some authors [20] call this the correspondence (or precedence) property. Finally, non-repudiation of origin analysis consists of checking that, in the intruder's database knowledge, the evidence is signed digitally by the origin agent, and that it cannot be generated without this signature, and not even in another protocol run.

In order to validate our proposal we have carried out the analysis of some of the most classic cryptographic protocols, such as the Needham-Schroeder symmetric key, and the secure socket layer (SSL). Ref. [7] describes the results of the analysis for the authentication protocol Encrypted Key Exchange (EKE) [26]. This protocol was specified in SRSL, using a well-known "man in the middle" attack evaluating two executions running in parallel sessions. The attack followed the *redirect* intruder's behavior. The resulting scenario describes a situation where only one of the two agents in each session has finished (agent A of the first session, and agent of B of the second one), but not the other.

6   Conclusions

We have presented a new analysis method for analyzing and evaluating security protocols and their possible attacks. Security protocols are specified in SRSL, which can then be translated into a working SDL system. Attacks are implemented by SDL processes that specify the intruder's behavior and observer processes that check safety properties. One of the benefits of our approach is that protocol specifications are described independently from the analysis procedures, so they can be re-used in other environments as well.

Several kinds of security attacks can be analyzed using our approach. It is essential to study how they can be produced in a real environment. We examine the result scenario provided in an analysis procedure, and redesign the security protocol if necessary.

We have applied this method in complex systems, for instance in electronic contract signing. The SRSL specification helped to implement it and draw attention to security services and their related mechanisms. Furthermore, we have simulated several security critical scenarios in order to verify the security properties.

Currently we are extending SRSL so more complex protocols can be specified, and to analyze other properties. We are studying the use MSC-2000 features. Furthermore, we are developing a framework to implement for testing protocol attacks in the Internet environment.

Acknowledgments

The work described in this paper has been supported by the European Commission through the IST Programme under Contract IST-2001-32446 (CASENET).

References

[1] C. Meadows. Open issues in formal methods for cryptographic protocol analysis. Proceedings of DISCEX 2000,pages 237-250. IEEE Comp. Society Press, 2000. 300

[2] M. Burrows, M. Abadi, R. Needham. A logic of authentication. In Proceedings of the Royal Society, Series A, 426(1871):233-271, 1989. 300

[3] R. Alur, T. Henzinger, F. Mang, S. Qadeer, S. Rajamani, S. Tasiran. Mocha: modularity in model checking. CAV 98 Computer-aided Verification, Lecture Notes in Computer Science 1427, pages 521-525. Springer-Verlag, 1998. 300

[4] W. Marrero, E. Clarke, S. Jha. Model checking for security protocols. DIMACS Workshop on Design and Formal Verification of Security Protocols, 1997. 300

[5] J. C. Mitchell, M. Mitchell, U. Stern. Automated analysis of cryptographic protocols using Murphi. In Proceedings of IEEE Symposium on Security and Privacy, pages 141-151. IEEE Computer Society Press, 1997. 300

[6] L. Paulson. The inductive approach to verifying cryptographic protocols. Journal of Computer Security, 6, 1998. 300

[7] J. López, J. J. Ortega, J. M. Troya. Protocol Engineering Applied to Formal Analysis of Security Systems. Infrasec'02, LNCS 2437, Bristol, UK, October 2002. 301, 313

[8] J. López, J. J. Ortega, J. M. Troya. Verification of authentication protocols using SDL-Method. Workshop of Information Security, Ciudad-Real- SPAIN, April 2002. 301

[9] ITU-T Recommendation Z.100 (11/99). Specification and Description Language (SDL), Geneva, 1999. 301

[10] D. Dolev, A. Yao. On the security of public key protocols. IEEE Transactions on Information Theory, IT-29:198-208, 1983. 301

[11] ITU-T, Recommendation Z.120(10/96). Message Sequence Charts (MSC). Geneva, 1996. 301

[12] A. Menezes, P. C. Van Oorschot, S. Vanstone. Handbook of Applied Cryptography. CRC Press, 1996. 301

[13] CCITT Recommendation X.800. Security Architecture for Open Systems Interconnection for CCITT Applications. 1991. 301

[14] ITU-T Recommendation X.810 (ISO/IEC 10181-1). Information Technology – Open Systems Interconnection – Security Frameworks for Open Systems – Overview. 1995. 301

[15] ITU-T Recommendation X.811 (ISO/IEC 10181-2). Information Technology – Open Systems Interconnection – Security Frameworks for Open Systems – Authentication. 1995. 301

[16] ITU-T Recommendation X.812 (ISO/IEC 10181-3). Information Technology – Open Systems Interconnection – Security Frameworks for Open Systems – Access Control. 1995. 301

[17] ITU-T Recommendation X.813 (ISO/IEC 10181-4). Information Technology – Open Systems Interconnection – Security Frameworks for Open Systems – Non-Repudiation. 1995. 301

[18] ITU-T Recommendation X.814 (ISO/IEC 10181-5). Information Technology – Open Systems Interconnection – Security Frameworks for Open Systems – Confidentiality. 1995. 301

[19] ITU-T Recommendation X.815 (ISO/IEC 10181-6). Information Technology – Open Systems Interconnection – Security Frameworks for Open Systems – Integrity.1995. 301

[20] P. Ryan, S. Schneider. The Modelling and Analysis of Security Protocols: the CSP Approach. Addison-Wesley, 2001. 304, 313

[21] ITU-T, Recommendation Z.120 (11/99). Message Sequence Charts (MSC-2000). Geneva,1999. 305

[22] RSA Laboratory. Public-Key Cryptography Standards (PKCS), http://www.rsa.com/. 309

[23] G. Lowe. Towards a Completeness Result for Model Checking of Security Protocols. 11th IEEE Computer Security Foundations Workshop, pages 96-105. IEEE Computer Society, 1998. 311

[24] M. Rusinowich, M. Turuani. Protocol Insecurity with Finite Number of Sessions is NP-complete. 14th IEEE Computer Security Foundations Workshop June 11-13, 2001. 311

[25] Solinet GmbH. SAFIRE product, http://www.solinet.com/ 312

[26] S. M. Bellovin, M. Merrit. Encrypted key exchange: Password-based protocols secure against dictionary attacks. In Proceedings of IEEE Symposium on Research in Security and Privacy, pages 72-84, 1992. 314

Development of Distributed Systems
with SDL by Means of Formalized APIs[*]

Philipp Schaible and Reinhard Gotzhein

Computer Science Department, University of Kaiserslautern
Postfach 3049, D-67653 Kaiserslautern, Germany
{schaible,gotzhein}@informatik.uni-kl.de

Abstract. Due to their intrinsic complexity, the development of distributed systems is difficult in general and therefore relies on careful and systematic development steps. This paper addresses the design and implementation of distributed systems, using SDL as the design language. In particular, the refinements during implementation design are examined, and it is shown how SDL interfacing patterns can support these steps, even in a heterogeneous environment. Then, tool support to automatically implement the interfacing patterns by generating tailored APIs for the system environment is presented. Finally, these technologies are illustrated in the context of a comprehensive development of a distributed light control system in a heterogeneous environment, using various communication technologies.

1 Introduction

The development of distributed systems in heterogeneous environments is a difficult issue - despite the use of customized design languages, development methods, and tool support in this area. One reason certainly is the intrinsic complexity of these systems due to concurrency, synchronization, and cooperation of system agents. Especially in cases of large systems, this requires suitable structuring mechanisms as well as a careful and systematic system design.

For the *functional design* (the design covering the overall functionality of a distributed system) SDL [1] is a suitable specification language that is widely used in industry. SDL supports the hierarchical structuring of a complex distributed system into agent modules. Furthermore, the interaction behavior as well as the internal behavior of these modules can be specified. For closed SDL systems, implementation code can be generated automatically, which has positive effects on quality, development costs, and time-to-market.

When it comes to *implementation design*, where, for instance, direct interaction of agents is replaced by message exchange through an underlying communication service, an SDL system may have to be partitioned into several

---

[*] This work has been supported by the Deutsche Forschungsgemeinschaft (DFG) as part of Sonderforschungsbereich (SFB) 501, *Development of Large Systems with Generic Methods*.

R. Reed (Ed.): SDL 2003, LNCS 2708, pp. 317–334, 2003.

subsystems. Usually, such a communication service is provided by a local operating system, and thus is part of the environment from the view point of the SDL subsystems. This means that to interact, agents now send/receive messages to/from the environment.

To implement open SDL systems (systems interacting with their environment) only part of the code is generated automatically with the existing tools. In addition, an environment interface – also called *environment functions* – has to be supplied, requiring manual coding steps. On the one hand, this environment interface depends on the underlying communication service. On the other hand, it depends on the SDL subsystems using the interface. Thus, replacement of the underlying communication service or changes of the interaction behavior of SDL agents entail changes of the environment interface, which is a time consuming and error-prone task.

Our strategy to address this particular problem is twofold:

1. First, we define generic design solutions for the interaction of an open SDL system with different underlying communication services. This is done by defining, for each communication technology, an interfacing pattern, using the pattern description template and notation of the SDL pattern approach [2, 3, 4, 5, 6]. Interfacing patterns can then be applied during the implementation design, where the decision to use a particular technology is made. In this way, the interaction behavior of SDL agents can be controlled, reducing the need for modifications of the environment interface.
2. Second, we conceive and implement tool support for the automatic generation of the environment interface. This tool support is syntactically and semantically integrated with the interfacing patterns, and currently supports interfacing with TCP and UDP sockets, CAN, UART/TP, and QNX IPC.

In [7], two solutions for environment interfaces are described:

The first solution is based on so-called *light-weight APIs* and datagram sockets. The idea is to emulate the datagram sockets by representing them as SDL abstract data types with suitable SDL operators (Socket, SendTo, RecvFrom, Close). To send a signal, it is first encoded into a character string, and then sent by evaluating the expression "SendTo (<parameterList>)". This strategy is straightforward, as there is a one-to-one relationship between SDL actions and the service primitives of datagram sockets. However, it differs from the SDL communication paradigm that is based on explicit signal exchange.

The second solution is based on so-called *full-weight APIs* and again datagram sockets. The communication is based on specific SDL signals outPacket, bindPort, and inPacket. To send a signal, it has to be encoded into a character string, and is then sent by an explicit SDL output action, as one parameter of outPacket.

Both solutions have the disadvantage that the SDL designer has to specify the coding and decoding of SDL signals and signal parameters in the design. Another drawback is that there exists only one set of operations for different SDL signals, therefore, the receiver has to decode the packets first in order to distinguish between these signals. Finally, only datagram sockets are currently supported.

The paper is structured as follows. In Sect. 2, we elaborate on the systematic design of distributed systems, illustrated by a running example. In particular, we explain the refinements during implementation design, and show how these steps can be supported by SDL interfacing patterns. In Sect. 3, we introduce the tool APIgen for the automatic generation of environment interfaces. We show how the tool complements existing code generators, and explain the generated code. Section 4 presents a survey of the comprehensive development of a distributed light control system in a heterogeneous environment, where various interfacing patterns have been applied in the design phase, and APIgen has been used to generate the environment functions. Conclusions are drawn in Sect. 5.

2   Systematic Design of Distributed Systems with SDL

2.1   Stepwise Design

The design of distributed systems is often done in several steps, especially in cases of large systems. This requires that the system requirements be partitioned into subsets that can be dealt with one-by-one.

Horizontally The separation of system functionalities can lead to a proper partitioning, such that with each requirement subset, more functionality is added. For instance, phases of a communication service (connection setup, data transfer ...) or functionalities of a communication protocol (flow control, error control ...) can be identified.

Vertically The requirements can be partitioned into different levels of abstraction. For instance, on a high level of abstraction, direct reliable interaction between groups of system agents is assumed, while this assumption is later relaxed to unreliable, indirect interaction between pairs of system agents. This of course may influence the behavior of the system agents, which now may have to deal with loss or group management.

For the remainder of the paper, it is sufficient to consider *vertical partitioning*, by distinguishing two levels of abstraction:

- *Functional design* deals with the overall system functionality — a high level of abstraction.
- *Implementation design* addresses the mechanisms used to implement the system, in particular, the replacement of direct interaction between system agents by concrete communication services.

To illustrate these steps, we start with a simple example: the system pingPong. Figure 1 shows a *functional design*, where two agents called pingAgent and pongAgent interact via a common channel pingPongTable, directly exchanging signals ping and pong, each carrying a parameter of type Integer.

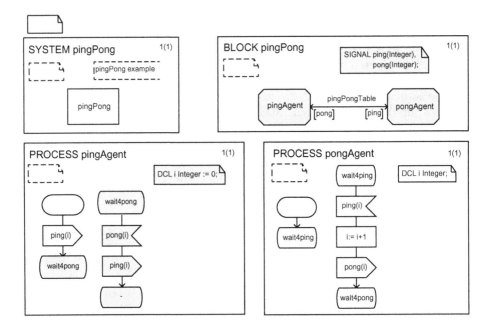

Fig. 1. Example "pingPong": Functional Design

In a distributed environment, it is intended that the agents of the system pingPong be placed on different hosts. Therefore, the direct interaction of the functional design has to be replaced by an underlying communication service. This leads to an *implementation design*, where this underlying service is made explicit, and the behavior of the interacting agents is modified such that the functional design is realized correctly.

Figure 2 shows an *implementation design* that is based on the decision to use the communication service provided by the transport protocol TCP. For this purpose, an SDL component called TCPserviceProvider is added, and interaction between pingAgent and pongAgent, now acting as service users, is redirected via this process. As TCP supplies specific service primitives, the behavior of the service users requires modification. For instance, to send a signal ping, a socket has to be created, and a connection must be established. Furthermore, the signal ping and its parameter have to be encoded before they can be sent, and to be decoded upon reception. Figure 2 shows the additional behavior of pingAgent resulting from these design decisions. The correspondence between Figs. 1 and 2 is highlighted by the shaded SDL symbols.

2.2 Pattern-Based Implementation Design

Analysis of several implementation designs has shown similarities in those parts where common channels have been replaced by an explicit service provider. To

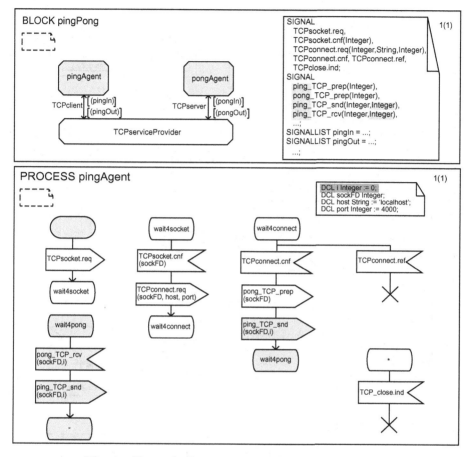

Fig. 2. Example "pingPong": implementation design

capture these similarities, we have defined *generic solutions* using the *SDL pattern approach* [2, 6, 8]. In particular, we have defined, for each type of communication service, an *SDL interfacing pattern*. Currently, interfacing patterns exist for the services provided by TCP, UDP, CAN, Bluetooth, UART/TP, AAL5, and QNX interprocess communication. Furthermore, SDL components representing these services have been defined in order to have complete implementation designs that can be simulated.

In Fig. 3, we show an excerpt of the generic solution defined by the SDL pattern TCPINTERFACING. The excerpt is taken from the *SDL Fragment*, the syntactical part of the design solution defined by the pattern, and shows the context, the adaptation, and the embedding for a TCP client (EFSM TCPclientAutomatonA) and the enclosing scope unit (SU TCP). To define the generic design solution, a language called PA-SDL (Pattern Annotated SDL, see [6] for details) is used. Solid symbols denote design elements that are added to the context specifica-

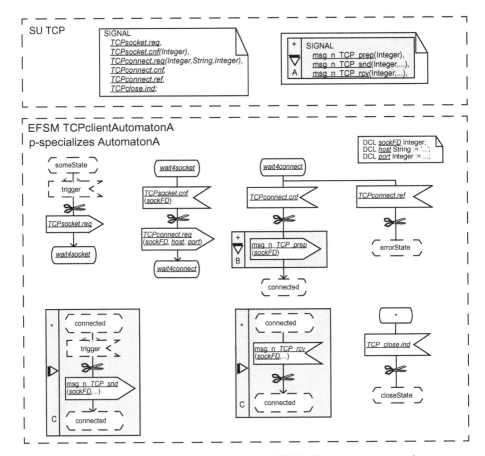

Fig. 3. TCPINTERFACING pattern (SDL Fragment, excerpt)

tion as a result of the pattern application. As a general rule, names may be changed. However, names in italics must be fresh, and if underlined, renamed in a unique way when adapting the pattern. SU refers to a structural SDL unit, for instance, a system, a block, a process, or a service. Scissor symbols indicate the possibility of refinements, for instance, by adding further actions to a transition, without disrupting the control flow. Finally, the shaded part called *border symbol* is an annotation denoting replications. The direction of replication (horizontal or vertical) is given by the arrow, the number of replications is specified by the multiplicity.

To apply a pattern, the context has to be identified first. In case of the TCPINTERFACING pattern a choice must be made of the enclosing structural unit, two active components (SDL processes), and matching transitions of these components. The SDL fragment then defines how to adapt the pattern, and how to embed it into the SDL context specification. Application of the TCPINTERFACING pattern to the functional design in Fig. 1 yields the implementation design in Fig. 2. In a similar way, interfacing with other types of communication services can be achieved.

3   Automatic Implementation of SDL Designs with APIgen

In this section, we introduce the tool *APIgen* (API generator), which supports the automatic code generation for distributed systems designed in SDL. API-gen is a supplement for *Cadvanced*, the SDL-to-C compiler that is part of the Telelogic TAU SDL suite [9]. In its present form, APIgen is syntactically and semantically integrated with the interfacing patterns of the SDL pattern pool (see Sect. 2.2). Starting point for the code generation is an implementation design, as shown in Sect. 2.1.

3.1   Architecture of APIgen

To run a system in a distributed environment, several implementation decisions have to be made. For instance, the target environment is determined, and the logical distribution given by the implementation design is mapped to physical components. In fact, this is also a decision between light and tight integration, in the sense that SDL processes are mapped to different OS processes or a single one. This may lead to a modification of the implementation design, such that components to be implemented on the same physical node are collected into one SDL system that is syntactically complete and therefore can be compiled.

Figure 4 shows the result of these implementation decisions for the pingPong system: pingAgent and pongAgent are assigned to separate nodes, therefore, separate SDL systems that interact with their local environment are introduced, each containing the corresponding declarations and process specifications. The resulting SDL systems are open in the sense that they interact with their environment. Here, interaction is by means of signals. Furthermore, it is decided to replace TCPserviceProvider by an OS TCP implementation.

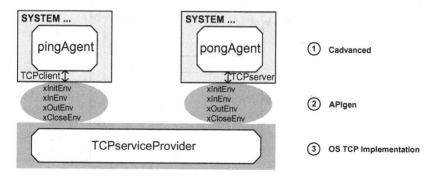

Fig. 4. Example "pingPong": light integration

From the implementation decisions, it follows that, from the view point of pingAgent and pongAgent, the communication service now belongs to the *environment*. This is important when it comes to automatic code generation: it is straightforward to generate C-code from SDL specifications, using *Cadvanced*, the SDL-to-C compiler [9]. However, interaction with the environment is not directly supported. For interaction between pingAgent and pongAgent with the OS TCP implementation, for instance, a set of tailored environment functions has to be provided: xInitEnv and xCloseEnv are called at system start and termination, respectively; xOutEnv is called when a signal is sent to the environment, and xInEnv is called periodically, polling for events in the environment leading to signals to be sent to the SDL system.

Conceptually, the environment functions can be understood as an API. They abstract from internal details, and serve as an interface to be used by SDL process implementations whenever interaction with the environment is necessary. Because the code of this API depends on both the environment (the type of communication service and its implementation) and the SDL system (the signal types to be exchanged with the environment, and, in particular, the signal parameters), it is commonly hand-coded. In our experience, this is a very time consuming and error prone task, due to several fundamental and conceptual differences between the physical environment representing a "real" world and abstract SDL specifications.

In the pingPong example, both SDL systems are compiled using Cadvanced, generating C-code that assumes the existence of this API. Furthermore, the TCP implementation is part of the operating system. To fully automate the code generation, we have conceived and implemented *APIgen*, a tool to create the environment functions (see Figure 5). APIgen takes the SDL specifications as input, and automatically generates C-code, supporting a variety of communication technologies (e.g., TCP sockets, UART/TP, CAN, QNX IPC). This fills the gap between code generation performed by Cadvanced and existing communication technologies, without requiring subsequent manual modifications or additions. Generated environment functions are stored in separate files named

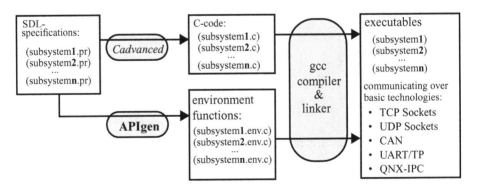

Fig. 5. Tool chain for automatic code generation

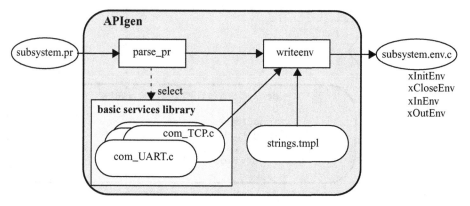

Fig. 6. Architecture of APIgen

subsystemn.env.c (see Fig. 5). They can be compiled separately and are linked with core modules subsystemn.c generated by Cadvanced.

When APIgen is started, there is no further interaction with the system developer. All communication specific information (such as selection of communication technology, host addresses, port numbers) is contained in the SDL implementation design specification, and is obtained from interfacing pattern applications (see Sect. 2.2). More specifically, APIgen takes SDL pr-files as input, and outputs env.c-files (see Fig. 6). Pr-files are processed in order to identify and collect signals sent to the environment. Furthermore, it is determined what basic technology is used to exchange these signals with other SDL systems (module *parse_pr* in Fig. 6). For this purpose, specific naming conventions have been defined. For instance, if an original signal sig is to be sent, then the corresponding signal to be sent via TCP sockets is to be named sig_TCP_snd (see Fig. 2). Please note that these naming conventions are enforced when applying the TCPINTER-FACING pattern (see Fig. 3).

The actual generation of environment functions is performed by the module *writeenv*, which uses general purpose strings from the library *strings.tmpl* and basic technology specific strings from the selected module of *basic services library* (see Fig. 6). Arranging technology specific strings into separate modules supports the extension of APIgen to incorporate further basic technologies, as well as its maintainability.

3.2 Auxiliary Signals

Before signals between processes of different open SDL systems can be exchanged, the underlying basic technology may have to be configured. For instance, a connection setup may be required, and messages to be exchanged may have to be registered. For these purposes, we introduce a specific set of SDL signals called *auxiliary signals*. These signals have predefined names and pa-

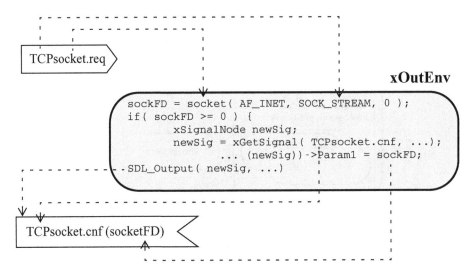

Fig. 7. API generation for auxiliary signals (example)

rameters, and must be sent to the environment prior to message exchange in accordance with the underlying service.

In Fig. 2, pingAgent first requests a socket, using SDL signals TCPsocket.req and TCPsocket.cnf, and then establishes a connection, using further signals TCPconnection.req, TCPconnection.cnf, and TCPconnection.ref. These are auxiliary signals following obvious naming conventions that are known to APIgen. Based on these naming conventions, APIgen will generate, for each signal, suitable environment functions xInEnv and xOutEnv. An example is shown in Fig. 7: an output of TCPsocket.req triggers the creation of a stream socket, where the file descriptor sockFD is returned as result.

The return of a result causes a problem in the context of SDL, because the output of a signal does not yield a return value. This is due to different interaction paradigms: in SDL, interactions are asynchronous notifications, while C-procedure calls are based on synchronous inquiry. To solve this problem, we model synchronous inquiry in SDL: after requesting a socket by output of a TCPsocket.req signal, the SDL process enters a waiting state until the result is returned. This result is received as a parameter of the predefined signal TCPsocket.cnf (see Fig. 2). To ensure that both naming and behavior conventions are followed in the SDL design, we have defined the TCPINTERFACING pattern (see Sect. 2). Please note that by using these conventions, it is straightforward to create multiple sockets, and to distinguish them by their file descriptors.

Figure 7 shows an excerpt of the API code that will be generated for the pingPong example. As the result will be returned upon completion of the socket request, the library function SDL_Output is called to return the TCPsocket.cnf signal to the SDL process. Usually, SDL_Output would be called in the environment function xInEnv, as this is an input to the SDL process. However, for efficiency reasons, it has been incorporated into xOutEnv.

3.3 Transfer Signals

Once the underlying basic technology has been configured, SDL signals can be exchanged between remote SDL processes. For this purpose, a specific set of SDL signals called *transfer signals* is derived from the original signals: that is, those signals that had been directly exchanged between SDL processes of the functional design (see Fig. 1). For instance, for an original signal ping, transfer signals ping_TCP_snd and ping_TCP_rcv are added to the signal definitions of the sending and the receiving process, respectively. The suffix distinguishes whether a signal is sent or received. The use of these signals in the SDL implementation design is shown in Fig. 2 and is in fact quite obvious.

To establish the interfacing between SDL processes and TCP sockets, several strategies are possible. For instance, a signal TCP_snd, parameterized with the file descriptor of the socket and a byte sequence containing the signal type and the signal parameter values, could be used for sending different SDL signals (see [7], full-weight API). This approach requires that coding and decoding of SDL signal type and parameter values is performed in the SDL implementation design. Without appropriate tool support, for instance, by Cadvanced, this strategy requires a very detailed design specification.

Alternatively, coding and decoding could be shifted into the application programming interface. We have adopted this strategy for two reasons. First, it relieves the SDL implementation designer of the tedious and error-prone details. Second, the routines for coding and decoding of signals can be and in fact is automatically generated by the tool APIgen. During the parsing phase, APIgen extracts all information necessary for this purpose from the input file subsystemn.pr. In particular, the naming conventions support the identification and collection of signals to the environment, and the assignment of the corresponding basic technology. We point out that different basic technologies may be used at the same time, therefore, this strategy also supports the development of large systems in heterogeneous environments. Furthermore, the naming conventions are again supported by interfacing patterns, e.g., TCPINTERFACING.

Figure 8 shows another excerpt[1] of the API code that will be generated for the pingPong example. In this example, an output of a signal ping_TCP_snd is mapped to the corresponding part of the environment function xOutEnv, and sent via an existing TCP connection. This TCP connection has already been established during the configuration of the underlying service, using auxiliary signals (see Section 3.2). The receiver prepares the reception of signals ping_TCP_rcv by first calling ping_TCP_prep, thus indicating where signals of this type should be

---

[1] For each SDL signal, approximately 1 page of C-code is generated and added to the environment functions. In addition, functions for encoding and decoding of signal parameters may be generated, depending on whether ASN.1 is used to define these parameters.

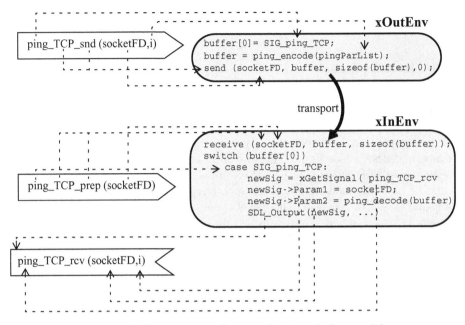

Fig. 8. API generation for transfer signals (example)

delivered. Afterwards, polling for actual receptions is done (environment function xInEnv). To support signal parameters, APIgen generated coding and decoding procedures, to be used by xOutEnv and xInEnv, respectively (ping_encode, ping_decode, see Fig. 8).

Please note that this is an excerpt of the code generated as part of xOutEnv. For each SDL signal sent via the environment interface, approximately 1 page of C-code is added to this function.

Some implementation details are worth mentioning:

– To generate environment functions (pingAgent.pr and pongAgent.pr), *APIgen* is started with a complete list of communicating SDL systems. This way, corresponding _snd and _rcv signals, (such as ping_TCP_snd and ping_TCP_rcv) can be associated and obtain a unique, system wide signal identification (such as SIG_ping_TCP, see Fig. 8) as well as matching coding and decoding procedures (ping_encode and ping_decode in Fig. 8) to be incorporated into xInEnv and xOutEnv as shown.
– Coding and decoding of signal parameter values is supported in different ways:
  • For certain basic SDL data types and some composite data types (including structures and arrays), APIgen automatically generates coding and decoding routines. The standard strategy is to encode all parameter values of a signal into a string.
  • For ASN.1 data types, coding and decoding routines are automatically generated with the ASN.1 utilities provided with the Telelogic TAU tool

suite. Both basic and packed encoding rules (BER and PER) are supported. These routines are then linked with the code generated by APIgen.

- When developing heterogeneous systems, it may be necessary to use specific routines for coding and decoding of signals. These routines can not be generated by APIgen. However, APIgen supports the system developer by creating template files (signaldefs.h and signaldefs.c) for coding and decoding routines, which are then completed by the system developer.

Development of *APIgen* started in 1998. After a first prototype with restricted functionality (few basic technologies, restricted use of signal parameters), it has been continuously improved and extended, and has been used in several case studies. The most comprehensive case study has been SILICON, where a distributed application in a heterogeneous environment has been developed from scratch. In the next section addresses this case study — especially the use of SDL interfacing patterns and APIgen.

4   The SILICON Case Study

In 1999, the problem description of a distributed light control system [10] was sent out with an international call for papers, soliciting the application of requirements engineering methods, techniques, and tools to this case study. The results have been published in [11]. We have taken a subset of this problem description as the starting point for another case study called SILICON (System development for an Interactive LIght CONtrol), covering not only the requirements phase, but all development activities. In particular, the objective of this case study has been to develop a complete, customized solution starting from an informal problem description, applying generic methods in all development phases.

The problem description of the SILICON case study consists of the building description and the informal needs from the view points of the user and the facility manager. Fig. 11 is an excerpt of the ground-plan, showing two offices and a hallway section as well as a number of installations. Each office is equipped with two light groups and switches to turn the lights on and off. The windows can be darkened by sun blinds that are controlled by further switches. Another light group is placed in the hallway section, it can be switched on and off. In addition, the light in the hallway is triggered by a motion detector.

In the following, we will focus on the design and implementation phases, and, in particular, on the interfacing with basic communication technologies at design and implementation level. According to the design steps explained in Sect. 2, we start with the functional design, which deals with the overall system functionality on a high level of abstraction. Nevertheless, we introduce a high-level system structure by identifying application components. For instance, we distinguish sensors, actuators, and control cells. Control cells are structured hierarchically, starting with the building level down to the room level, they receive sensor

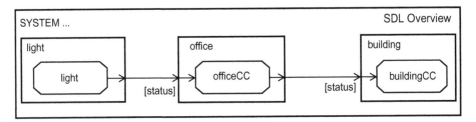

Fig. 9. SDL functional design (excerpt): system architecture (SDL overview diagram)

values and trigger actuators. This leads to a functional design with a logical system structure that follows the physical building structure.

In Fig. 9, an excerpt of the logical system structure as specified in SDL is shown. It contains three application components, namely a light sensor light, an office control cell officeCC, and a building control cell buildingCC. On the functional design level, these components interact directly through SDL channels. An interaction occurs, for instance, when the light sensor sends a signal status, which is received by officeCC and then forwarded to buildingCC. The status signal may then trigger further signals (not shown here), for instance, to display the light status on the facility manager control panel, or to trigger the light actuator.

In the implementation design, the channels between application components have been replaced by underlying communication services. In the SILICON case study, it was decided to group sensors, actuators, and control cells hierarchically, and, depending of the required throughput and real-time performance, to use different communication technologies on each level of the hierarchy. For instance, it was decided to use UART/TP and CAN to interconnect components of one room and one floor, respectively.

Figure 10 indicates how these design decisions have been incorporated into the SDL implementation design. While keeping the application components unchanged, further components representing the communication middleware (switchPE, UART_Codex_light ...) and the basic communication technologies (UARTservice Provider, CANserviceProvider) as well as the necessary channels are added, refining the functional design without modifying the behavior of the application components. In contrast to the example in Section 2, the communication middleware (switchMW, officeMW, buildingMW) is made explicit and not incorporated into the application components, in order to enclose all communication specific functionality. Otherwise, the approach is just the same: select an underlying service provider and apply interfacing patterns to replace direct communication. In the case study, we have applied several such patterns, including UARTINTERFACING, CANINTERFACING, TCPINTERFACING, and BLUETOOTH-INTERFACING.

Based on the implementation design, we have developed a complete, customized implementation, consisting of a physical building model, a new tailored communication technology, application hardware, communication middleware,

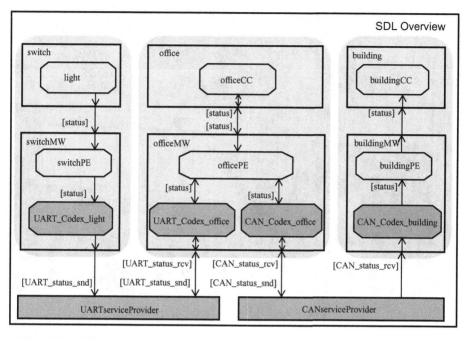

Fig. 10. SDL implementation design (excerpt): refined system architecture

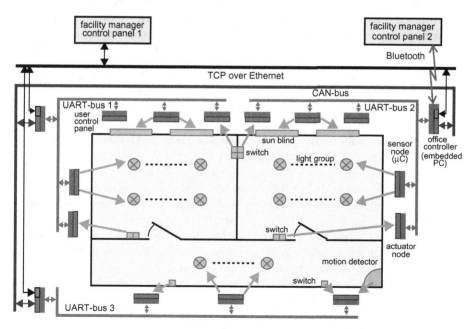

Fig. 11. Topology of the building model implementation

Fig. 12. SILICON building model

and application software. The implementation of the application components and
the communication middleware has been produced as described in Sect. 3, using
Cadvanced and APIgen. This provides evidence that the approach scales, and
that it works well also in the context of heterogeneous communication systems.
Figure 11 shows the building model topology laid out around the ground-plan:

- On the room level, the UART/TP-bus technology (Universal Asynchronous
  Receiver Transmitter/Token Passing) provides interconnection between micro controllers implementing switches, light groups, sun blinds, motion de-
  tectors, and user control panel, and embedded PCs implementing office and
  hallway controllers. We have installed 3 separate UART-buses, each associated with the devices of a single room.
- On the floor level, the CAN-bus technology (Controller Area Network) interconnects embedded PCs that act as office or hallway controllers.
- On the building level, Ethernet technology interconnects one or more embedded PCs of each floor. In this case study, this option is not fully exploited,
  however, we use this technology to download executables, and to visualize
  the communication system in operation. Furthermore, the facility manager
  control panel can be attached to this technology.
- In addition, Bluetooth technology provides wireless interconnection between
  the facility manager control panel and office controllers.

The hierarchical structure of the communication system in combination with
field bus technologies requires special purpose protocols with routing support,

as TCP/IP-solutions are not feasible here. Furthermore, these protocols have to support real-time communication.

The physical building model is shown in Fig. 12. It has been demonstrated at several industrial fairs including Embedded Systems 2001 in Nuremberg, and CeBIT 2001 in Hannover, in cooperation with Telelogic. In the front part of the building model, the windows equipped with sun blinds are visible. Below, micro controllers implementing the switches, sun blinds, and light groups are installed. User control panels are mounted in front of the building, and can be used to control each light group and sun blind separately. Furthermore, the panel can be used to set and recall one or more light scenarios. The embedded PCs are hidden under the building. To the left of the building model, two computer screens are placed. The front screen belongs to a laptop that acts as the facility manager control panel, and is used for control purposes as well as for visualization on the application level. The flat screen above provides the visualization on the communication level.

5   Conclusions

We have presented a methodology for the development of distributed systems through refinement of the functional design supported by SDL interfacing patterns. Interfacing patterns define generic solutions for recurring design problems, as do SDL patterns in general. In accordance with the underlying communication service, interface patterns are selected from the pattern pool, adapted, and embedded into the context specification. This is particularly valuable, as the quality of the design is improved, leading to a significant reduction of rework due to defects. Also, incorporating further basic technologies is straightforward.

In order to generate code from implementation designs, we have developed the tool APIgen, which complements existing SDL-to-C code generators. APIgen automatically generates environment interfaces for a variety of communication technologies, without the need of further user interaction, and is syntactically and semantically integrated with the corresponding SDL interfacing patterns. This way, several basic technologies can be used together, without the need for manual coding. This closes a gap in the development of distributed systems.

The methodology presented here is intended to support the communication system developer, who needs to preserve some control over the basic communication technology, even at the design level. For instance, the ability to make a proper selection between different technologies such as CAN, UART, or TCP, and to control their configuration (setting host addresses and port numbers) are crucial. Furthermore, when a particular selection, say TCP, has been made, the designer can control at which point in execution, connections are established and closed. This is different from other methodologies (such as the normal approach using Telelogic TAU) where interfacing with the environment is transparent on design level.

Currently, APIgen supports SDL-96, a pragmatic decision based on the available commercial tool support. It would be desirable to use the additional language features of SDL-2000, in particular, hierarchical states and exception handling. With these features, further abstractions can be introduced into design specifications, for example encapsulating generic design decisions captured by SDL patterns in general or SDL interfacing patterns in particular.

SDL interfacing patterns may be interpreted as design-level APIs, to be used during SDL implementation design. This way, the generic solutions captured by interfacing patterns may eventually lead to *standardized* design-level APIs, enabling interoperability. Furthermore, based on standardized APIs, tools for the automatic generation of program-level APIs (environment functions in the context of SDL implementations) can be developed. In fact, APIgen has been conceived and implemented for precisely this purpose.

References

[1] ITU-T. Recommendation Z.100 (08/02), Specification and Description Language (SDL). International Telecommunication Union, Geneva. 317

[2] B. Geppert, R. Gotzhein, F. Rößler. Configuring Communication Protocols Using SDL Patterns. SDL'97 - Time for Testing, Proceedings of the 8th SDL Forum, Elsevier, Amsterdam, 1997, pp. 523-538. 318, 321

[3] D. Cisowski, B. Geppert, F. Rößler, M. Schwaiger. Tool Support for SDL Patterns. Proceedings of the 1st Workshop on SDL and MSC (SAM'98), Berlin, 1998. 318

[4] F. Rößler, B. Geppert, P. Schaible. Re-Engineering of the Internet Stream Protocol ST2+ with Formalized Design Patterns. Proceedings of the 5th International Conference on Software Reuse (ICSR5), Victoria, Canada, 1998. 318

[5] B. Geppert, A. Kühlmeyer, F. Rößler, M. Schneider. SDL-Pattern based Development of a Communication Subsystem for CAN. Formal Description Techniques and Protocol Specification, Testing, and Verification, Proceedings of FORTE/PSTV'98, Kluwer Academic Publishers, Boston, 1998, pp. 197-212. 318

[6] B. Geppert. The SDL-Pattern Approach - A Reuse-Driven SDL Methodology for Designing Communication Software Systems. Ph.D. Thesis, University of Kaiserslautern, 2000. 318, 321

[7] T. Kim, R.L. Probert, I. Sales, A. Williams. Rapid Development of Network Software via SDL/Socket Interfaces, Proceedings of the $3^r d$ Workshop on SDL and MSC (SAM'2002), Aberystwyth, Wales, LNCS 2599, Springer, 2003. 318, 327

[8] R. Gotzhein. Consolidating and Applying the SDL-Pattern Approach: A Detailed Case Study. Journal of Information and Software Technology, Elsevier Sciences, 2003 (in print). 321

[9] Telelogic. Tau 4.4 SDL Suite, 2002. 323, 324

[10] S. Queins, G. Zimmermann, M. Becker, M. Kronenburg, C. Peper, R. Merz, J. Schäfer. The Light Control Case Study: Problem Description. Journal of Universal Computer Science (J.UCS), Special Issue on Requirements Engineering 6(7), pp. 586-596, Springer, 2000 . 329

[11] E. Börger, R. Gotzhein (Guest Eds.): Requirements Engineering: The Light Control Case Study. Special Issue of the Journal of Universal Computer Science (J.UCS), Numbers 6(7), Springer, 2000. 329

Validation of SIP/H.323 Interworking Using SDL/MSC

Ligang Wang, J. William Atwood, and Anjali Agarwal

Concordia University,
1455, de Maisonneuve Blvd. W., Montreal, Quebec, H3G 1M8, Canada
lgwang@cs.concordia.ca

Abstract. SIP and H.323 are complementary protocols used (by different communities) to provide signaling for Internet multimedia sessions. An Interworking Facility (IWF) between SIP and H.323 has been proposed within the Internet Engineering Task Force (IETF). The IWF, SIP User Agent, SIP Server, H.323 End Point, and H.323 Gatekeeper have been formally specified in SDL, and validated using a combination of MSC comparison and interactive simulation. SDL was found to be simple to use, and its object-orientation made model enhancement easy. Suggested improvements to SDL include more flexible ways to define data.

1 Introduction of SIP-H.323

In Internet telephony, call control and signaling are two main issues on which standards-setting efforts are focusing. Two standards for VoIP signaling protocols have already been defined, ITU-T Recommendation H.323 [1] and the IETF Session Initiation Protocol (SIP) [2]. H.323 and SIP both provide mechanisms for call establishment and teardown, call control and capability exchange. Currently H.323 is the most widely used protocol for PC-based conferences, while carrier networks using so-called soft switches and IP telephones seem to be built based on SIP. In order to achieve universal connectivity, interworking between the two protocols is desirable. Because of the inherent differences between H.323 and SIP, accommodation must be made to allow interworking between the two protocols. A proposed solution is specified by an Internet Draft of the IETF, SIP-H.323 Interworking [3, 4], which uses an Interworking Function (IWF) to provide protocol conversion between SIP and H.323. Based on H.323 version 2.0 and SIP version 2.0, the IWF provides transparent support of signaling and session descriptions between the SIP and H.323 entities.

Interworking between SIP and H.323 may involve the following entities: H.323 Endpoint (H323 EP), H.323 Gatekeeper (GK), Interworking Function (IWF), SIP User Agent (SIP EP) and SIP Server. The interworking function (IWF) that provides this translation between SIP and H.323 can be architected in a variety of ways: co-existence with H.323 gatekeeper (GK) and/or SIP server, or stand-alone. Figure 1 shows different types of configuration. Configuration 1 is

R. Reed (Ed.): SDL 2003, LNCS 2708, pp. 335–351, 2003.

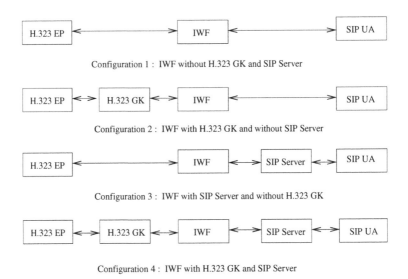

Configuration 1 : IWF without H.323 GK and SIP Server

Configuration 2 : IWF with H.323 GK and without SIP Server

Configuration 3 : IWF with SIP Server and without H.323 GK

Configuration 4 : IWF with H.323 GK and SIP Server

Fig. 1. Configurations of Interworking between SIP and H.323

a basic configuration, which has no H.323 gatekeeper or SIP server. The other three configurations contain one H.323 gatekeeper or one SIP server, or both. The way that the messages are generated during a call establishment between H.323 EP and a SIP UA is different depending on the configuration.

2   System Model of SIP-H.323 System

We formally specify the SIP-H.323 Interworking, as defined in the Internet Draft [3]. A new system model is established to verify the state machine and call flows proposed in the draft. We design and define the internal structure and behavior of five main components by SDL/MSC: H323 endpoint, H323 gatekeeper, Interworking Function (IWF), SIP server, and SIP user agent, which is called SIP endpoint or SIP EP in our model.

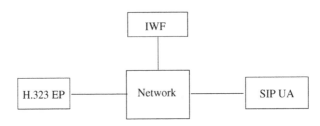

Fig. 2. Configuration 1: IWF without H.323 GK and SIP Server

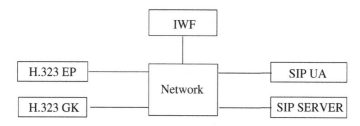

Fig. 3. Configuration 2: IWF with H.323 GK and SIP Server

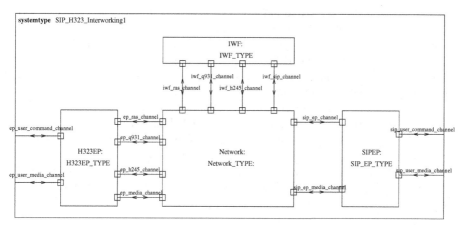

Fig. 4. SIP-H.323 Interworking Configuration 1 Interconnection Diagram

In our system modeling, we assume two configurations are used for the call scenarios. One is basic configuration, shown in Fig. 2, which includes an H.323 EP block, an IWF block, and a SIP EP block. The other configuration as shown in Fig. 3, contains, in addition, an H.323 GK block and a SIP server block, which reside respectively in an H.323 zone for address resolution and admission control, and in a SIP administrative domain for pre-call registration service and address resolution. Other configurations, such as the existence of only one H.323 GK or one SIP server with IWF, are to be considered as a combination of the above two configurations.

Figure 4 shows the SIP-H.323 system described by SDL without H.323 gate-keeper and SIP server. From the figure, H.323 EP block has four channels in connection with the network. The four channels are used for transmission of RAS messages, Q.931 [5] call signaling messages, H.245 messages, and media communication. RAS messages and media messages are transmitted by UDP. Q.931 messages and H.245 messages are sent using TCP. H.323 EP has two additional channels joined to the end user, which can instruct H.323 EP to start a call and exchange media messages with H.323 EP. SIP EP block has two channels in connection with the network. The two channels are for transmission of SIP session initiation messages and media messages. Both types of messages are

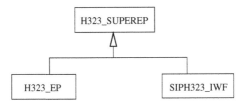

Fig. 5. Inheritance

sent by UDP. Two extra channels are used for SIP EP end user to instruct SIP EP to initiate a call and exchange media messages. As an interworking component between H.323 EP and SIP EP, IWF has four channels linked with the network. Three are for the H.323 side to exchange RAS messages, Q.931 call signaling messages, and H.245 messages with H.323 EP. One is for the SIP side as a session channel to communicate with SIP EP.

Another configuration of the SIP-H.323 system that includes an H.323 gatekeeper and a SIP server is similar to the SIP-H.323 system shown in Fig. 4 except that two extra components, H.323 GK block and SIP server block are introduced for registration service and address resolution service. Two channels from H.323 GK to the network are used to exchange RAS messages and Q.931 messages with H.323 EP while one channel from SIP server to the network is for session initiation messages exchange.

2.1   Inheritances and Reusability

We choose SDL [6] as an object-oriented and formal language to formally model our systems. SDL provides structuring concepts that facilitate the specification of large and/or complex systems. An SDL system comprises four main hierarchical levels: systems, blocks, processes, and procedures. The components are classified as system types, block types and process types.

Because both H.323 EP and IWF should support H.225 (RAS and Q.931) and H.245, we define H.323 EP super block type as an abstract super block type using SDL to depict the common features and internal interconnection structure of H.323 EP and IWF. H.323 EP block and IWF block can inherit from the H.323 EP super block type. Both can extend their own features and structures by adding new processes and new channels. Also, their internal behavior can be extended by redefining the behavior of each internal process in order to replace the behavior of their super block. Figure 5 shows the relationship of inheritance.

H.323 EP Super Block. Figure 6 depicts the internal structure of H.323 EP Super Block type in SDL. H323EP_SUPERTYPE includes common function modules for both H.323 EP and IWF. H323EP_SUPERTYPE has 12 processes.

RAS and RAS_Deliver processes are responsible for transmission of RAS messages. The RAS process mainly focuses on timer control because RAS messages,

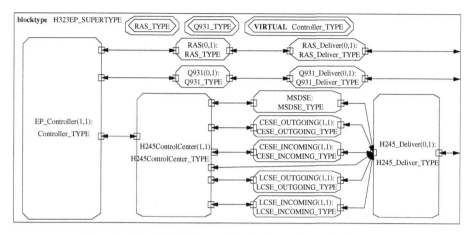

Fig. 6. H.323 EP Super Block Type described in SDL

being carried over UDP, may be subject to loss, while the RAS_Deliver process mainly focuses on forwarding RAS messages to the network.

The Q931 and Q931_deliver processes are responsible for collecting Q.931 commands. The Q931 process mainly focuses on Q.931 message flows, while the Q931_Deliver process focuses on forwarding.

The H245ControlCenter, MSDSE, CESE_OUTGOING, CESE_INCOMING, LCSE_OUTGOING, LCSE_INCOMING and H245_Deliver processes are involved in exchanging H.245 messages.

MSDSE is the main entity responsible for master and slave determination message flows, as well as returning back to H245ControlCenter the result of determination. It also keeps track of internal state when two H.323 Endpoints are negotiating their master/slave relationship.

CESE_OUTGOING, CESE_INCOMING are a pair of processes for capability exchange. CESE_OUTGOING negotiates outgoing capability, while incoming capability is negotiated by CESE_INCOMING.

LCSE_OUTGOING, LCSE_INCOMING are a pair of processes for opening logical channels bi-directionally. LCSE_OUTGOING opens outgoing logical channel, while LCSE_INCOMING opens incoming logical channel.

The H245_Deliver process collects H.245 messages from these processes and delivers them to the network, and vice visa.

The H245ControlCenter is responsible for coordinating these processes to accomplish the whole task of H.245. If one of these tasks cannot step further, H245ControlCenter will return H245fail to EP_Controller. By means of H245ControlCenter, each component under the control of H245ControlCenter can be modified, replaced, or extended without causing modification of other components [7].

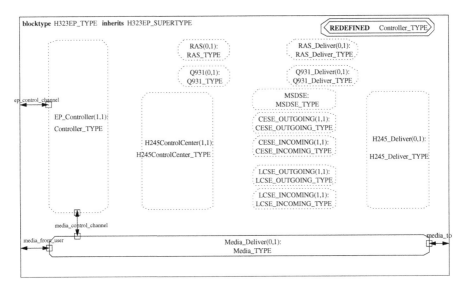

Fig. 7. H323 Endpoint Block described in SDL

H323 EP Block. H323 EP block inherits from H323EP_SUPERTYPE and extends its features by adding new channels and new processes. Figure 7 depicts the internal structure of the H323EP block in SDL. The ep_control_channel is added for communication with the user to start a call. A new Media_Deliver process is introduced to transfer media data between the user and the network. The media_control_channel is used by the EP_Controller to control media flows and media capability. The internal behavior of the EP_Controller process is redefined in the H323 EP block. The EP_Controller process in the H323 EP block is a core component that mainly maintains the state of the whole call procedure and coordinates RAS process, Q931 process, and H245ControllerCenter process.

IWF Block. IWF block also inherits from H323EP_SUPERTYPE, and extends its features by adding new channels and new processes. Figure 8 depicts the internal structure of the IWF block. The Transaction_Controller process is introduced for transaction management of SIP commands. The Timer_Controller process is to maintain the timer and inform the Transaction_Controller process of time-out or time-expiration messages. The to_transaction_route channel is added for exchange of SIP commands between the IWF_Controller process and the Transaction_Controller process. The timer_transaction_route channel is added to connect the Timer_Controller process and the Transaction_Controller process for exchanging timer control messages. The sip_to_network_channel channel is added for communication with the network.

The internal behavior of IWF_Controller process is redefined in the IWF block. The IWF_Controller process in IWF block is a core component that not only coordinates RAS process, Q931 process, and H245Controller Center process,

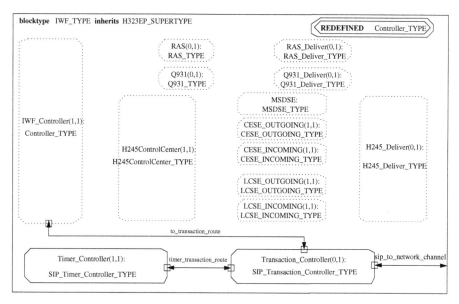

Fig. 8. SIP-H.323 IWF Block described by SDL

but also maintains the state of the whole call procedure and is responsible for message mapping between SIP and H.323.

Because SDL provides object-oriented features to design systems, we use inheritance to design the H323EP block and the IWF block. The common structure of both H323EP block and IWF block is described in the H323EP Super Block type. In this way, it improves our model without redundancy and reduces our work. However, because the inheritance is not compatible with parameterized block type in our SDL support tool, ObjectGeode 4.0 [8], we cannot pass a parameter into H323EP_Super block for EP_Controller process to perform different behaviors according to different modes: standalone and collaboration with H323 Gatekeeper. We will verify the advanced features and simplify our model as further study.

SIP EP Block. Figure 9 depicts SIP EP block, which represents a SIP Endpoint. SIP EP block has four processes. The Transaction_Controller process is used for transaction management by keeping in memory a list of SIP commands and SIP responses. It also starts a timer by sending a timer-start message to the Timer_Controller process when a SIP command is sent to the network. It will stop the timer by sending a timer-stop message when the final response of the SIP command is received from the network,. The Timer_Controller process is responsible for maintaining the timer. When a timer times out or expires, it sends timer-timeout and timer-expiration messages to the Transaction_Controller process. Command_Controller process in SIP EP Block is a core process that is responsible for keeping all state of the whole procedure of session initiation. The

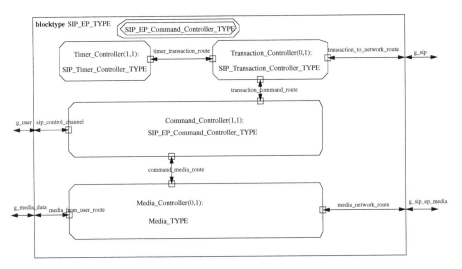

Fig. 9. SIP Endpoint Block

block type has four gates. The g_user and g_media_data are used for communication with the end user. The g_sip and g_sip_ep_media are for communication with the network.

The H.323 Gatekeeper Block. Figure 10 depicts H323_GK block. The H.323 Gatekeeper is not only responsible for assisting H.323 EP to register and resolve address, it also routes the call setup signaling (Q.931). Therefore, H.323 Gatekeeper also contains the module of Call Setup for H.323 EP to forward Q.931 messages. There are four processes in H323GK. GK_RAS process is used to maintain a registration table. GK_RAS_Deliver process is used to forward RAS messages and maintain a list of messages recently sent. The GK_Q931 process is used to query user information of H.323 EP or IWF from GK_RAS process, and sends Q.931 messages to the destination end user. GK_Q931_Deliver process is used to forward Q.931 messages.

The SIP Server Block. Figure 11 depicts SIP_SERVER block. SIP_SERVER block consists of three processes. Transaction_Controller is used for transaction management by keeping in memory a list of SIP commands and SIP responses. It also can enable or disable the timer in the Timer_Controller process by sending timer control messages. The Timer_Controller process is responsible for maintaining the timer. The Command_Controller process is used to maintain the user registration table and forward SIP messages from one SIP EP to the other one.

The Network1 Block. Two processes comprise the Network1 Block, which is used in the configuration where no H.323 gatekeeper and SIP server exist, The

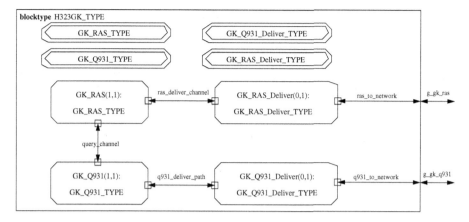

Fig. 10. H.323 Gatekeeper Block

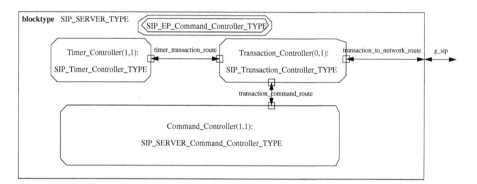

Fig. 11. SIP Server Block

TCP process is used to simulate the property of the TCP network, the UDP process is used to simulate the property of the UDP network that it will lose some UDP packets randomly.

The Network2 Block. Used in the configuration where the H.323 gatekeeper and the SIP server exist, the Network2 block inherits from Network1 block and extends Network1 block by adding channels in connection with H.323 Gatekeeper and SIP Server. Besides, the internal behavior of TCP process and UDP process are redefined in Network2 to adapt to the configuration with H.323 Gatekeeper and SIP Server.

2.2   Behavior Description

The dynamic behavior in an SDL system is described in the processes. Each process is described by an extended finite state machine (FSM). In our system

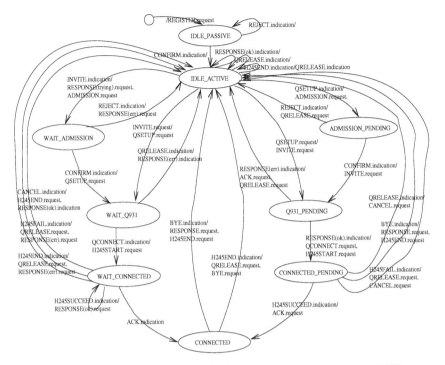

Fig. 12. The Finite State Machine of IWF_Controller in IWF

model, SDL can be used to realize the description of behavior of each process in terms of an FSM as follows.

Figure 12 shows the Finite State Machine of IWF_Controller in IWF. Figure 13 shows a part of Process Diagram of IWF_Controller in IWF. A call procedure is initiated when either QSETUP.indication is issued from the H.323 side or INVITE.indication is issued from the SIP side. When QSETUP.indication is received, if IWF is in registration mode (coexistence with H.323 GK and SIP Server), the admission procedure will begin by sending an ADMISSION.request message. If a REJECT.indication message is received, IWF_Controller will send QRELEASE.request to stop the call procedure. If a CONFIRM.indication message is received, it means the admission procedure succeeds. If IWF is not in registration mode, the above admission procedure is ignored. IWF_Controller will directly send INVITE.request to initiate session for the SIP side. If the final response is ok, it maps the SIP messages to H.323 messages by sending QCONNECT.request. By sending H245START.request it also begins the H.245 procedure. Once an H245SUCCEED.indication is received, it will then send ACK.request back to the SIP endpoint to inform that the H.323 endpoint is ready for media transmission. The media connection between the H.323 endpoint and the SIP endpoint is established at this time. Otherwise, if an H245FAIL.indication is received, it will send CANCEL.request to cancel the

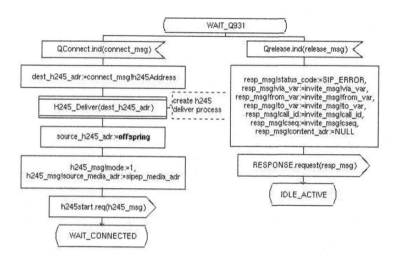

Fig. 13. A Part of Process Diagram of IWF_Controller in IWF

session and send QRELEASE.request to stop the call setup procedure. when INVITE.indication is received, the call procedure is similar to the above, but in reverse direction. Besides, IWF_Controller will map the H.323 messages to the SIP messages.

After both endpoints have established media connection and IWF_Controller is into connecting state, the connection can be terminated by either receiving BYE.indication from the SIP endpoint or H245END.indication from the H.323 endpoint. If BYE.indication is received, it sends a response with ok to the SIP endpoint, and sends an H245END.request to the H.323 endpoint to release the call. If H245END.indication is received, it sends a BYE.request to terminate the session, and sends QRELEASE.REQ to disconnect the connection at the H.323 side.

The "composite state" advanced feature of SDL 2000, can make our FSM simpler and more readable. However, due to the limitation of our tool, Object-Geode 4.0, which can only support up to SDL 96, we could not introduce such features to simplify our model.

2.3 Time Constraints

SDL has a timer that can easily add time constraint conditions. This feature is important for real-time systems.

In some processes of our model, we use timer as one constraint condition. For example, in the CESE_OUTGOING process of the H323EP block, if the timer expires then the user is informed with the REJECT primitive and the outgoing CESE_OUTGOING process sends a TerminalCapabilitySetRelease message. In the Timer_Controller process of the SIP_EP block, when the timer expires, it sends timer-timeout and timer-expiration messages to the Transaction_Controller process for instructing Timer_Controller process to resend the SIP commands since the SIP commands may be lost because it is carried over UDP. All in all, the timer feature of SDL is important and necessary for analyzing real-time systems.

2.4   Data

We use many new datatypes to define complex data, such as the list of transctions, defined by an array. During modeling, we find that we have difficulty in using those data types because SDL-92 only provides limited data types and limited operations for those data types such as the string operations. It could be better if SDL can be extended to use some data type similar to C/C++ or java although SDL and many tools provide operations or methods that can be programmed by C/C++. The diversity of data representation and operation also improve generating code and implementation.

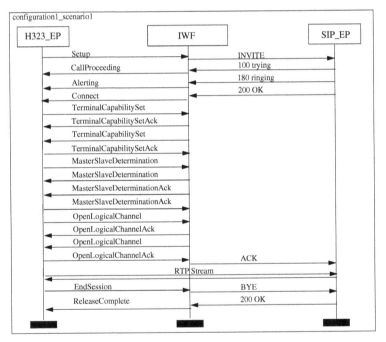

Fig. 14. Successful Scenario 1 Under Configuration 1 [3]

3   Simulation and Validation

3.1   Test Plan and Configuration

Once our system has been completely modeled by SDL, we can use Object-Geode [8] as a simulation and verification tool. ObjectGeode is a formal method toolset dedicated to analysis, design, verification and validation through simulation, code generation and testing of real-time and distributed applications. ObjectGeode can verify that the system works as expected with a limited number of nominal cases described by MSC. The aim of verification is to determine whether the SDL model will run reliably. In addition, model checking is achieved by ObjectGeode to run the model automatically to highlight errors such as deadlocks, livelocks or dead code.

ObjectGeode provides three techniques for simulation and verification: static checking, interactive simulation, and exhaustive simulation. Static checking is provided to check the SDL model against SDL static semantics: data type checking and connection checking. Static checking can also use MSC models to check against the SDL model from the point of view of static semantics. Interactive simulation can provide dynamic checking under the control of the user. The user plays the role of the environment to send external signals. Interactive simulation can provide a step-by-step way to simulate a model, and it can generate MSC. Exhaustive simulation provides automatic and random execution of state transitions and generates long simulation scenarios.

We use Message Sequence Chart (MSC) [9] to show interactions between system components. MSC diagrams provide a clear description of system communication in the form of message flows. A set of MSC diagrams cover partial system behavior. A collection of MSC diagrams may be used to give a more detailed specification of a system. These language constructs in MSC are instance, message, environment, action, timer set, timer reset, time-out, instance creation, instance stop, and condition. The standardized MSC language offers a powerful complement to SDL in describing the communication between different blocks and processes of an SDL-system.

Because one of our goals in this paper is to test the pre-determined scenarios specified in the draft of Interworking between SIP-H.323,we manually generated the following MSC scenarios based on the draft of interworking between H.323 and SIP for "simple call" to validate the model. Our MSC scenarios can also be used in simulation and validation with our SIP-H323 SDL model as the constraint conditions to verify against our model. More detailed MSC can be automatically generated by ObjectGeode during simulation and validation.

We use two configurations to simulate the system of interworking between H.323 and SIP. One configuration is without the assistance of H.323 gatekeeper and SIP server, i.e., no registration procedure is needed on either side. The other configuration includes H.323 gatekeeper and SIP server. Under this configuration, the H.323 endpoint and the SIP endpoint need to register in their administration domain area respectively before any call setup is attempted. The IWF should also register with both the H.323 gatekeeper and the SIP server

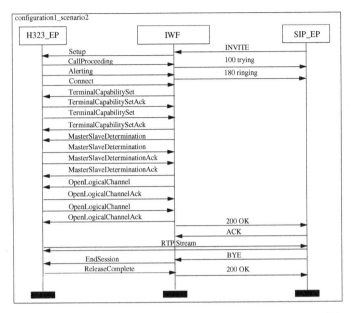

Fig. 15. Successful Scenario 2 Under Configuration 1 [3]

before it can be involved in any call setup or session initiation procedure. In this case, the IWF can be considered as an H.323 gateway in H.323 and a SIP endpoint in SIP.

Figure 14 shows a scenario case where a call is initiated from H.323 EP to the SIP EP under configuration 1 [3]. Figure 15 shows another scenario case where a call is initiated from SIP EP to H.323 EP under configuration 1 [3].

Figure 16 shows one successful scenario case of a call initiated from H.323 EP to the SIP EP under configuration 2. Figure 17 shows another scenario case of a call initiated from SIP EP to H323 EP under configuration 2.

3.2   Simulation

We use the system SIP_H323_Interwork1 to simulate our model. The system consists of one H.323 Endpoint block, one SIP Endpoint block, and one IWF block. We also include one network block as a modeling of the environment. Thus, the whole system is regarded as a closed system. The call establishment procedure can be initiated from both directions.

We use system SIP_H323_Interwork2, inherited from SIP_H323_Interwork1, to simulate our model. H323_EP and SIP_EP are configured as registration mode so that both can send registration messages to H323_GK and SIP_SERVER respectively. The system also adds an H323_GK block and a SIP_SERVER block. The Network block is extended to support H323_GK and SIP_SERVER. Likely, we chose the following two scenarios to validate the model.

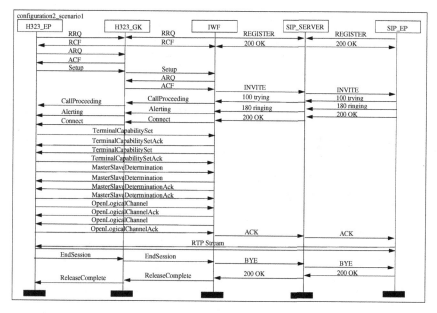

Fig. 16. Successful Scenario 1 Under Configuration 2 [3]

In our simulation, we use interactive simulation to simulate most of the successful scenarios as the above figures and unsuccessful scenarios specified in the draft of Interworking between H.323 and SIP under the different configurations. We use those scenarios as a case study to validate our design against some of the specific properties of our model.

3.3   Validation

We only did interactive simulation to verify if the pre-determined scenarios can be run by our model. It is not surprising no errors were found since we did not do exhaustive simulation and verification.

With the above scenarios, we have covered all the protocol primitives specified as well as all important scenarios. Furthermore, we have decided to send data along the media channel to verify that the call and media connections have been successfully established between the H.323 EP and the SIP EP, and that the session description has been successfully negotiated and exchanged between the H.323 EP and the SIP EP via the IWF. We generate a number of MSC for these scenario case studies to check the system protocol functionality at each stage. We also trace the exchange of signals between the processes. From the MSC, we are concerned with checking that the proper signal is being produced and transmitted from the module involved, e.g., IWF translates H.225 (Q.931) call signaling messages into session initiation messages. We verify the message mapping and state transitions mentioned in the draft of interworking between H.323 and SIP. We find that none was violated.

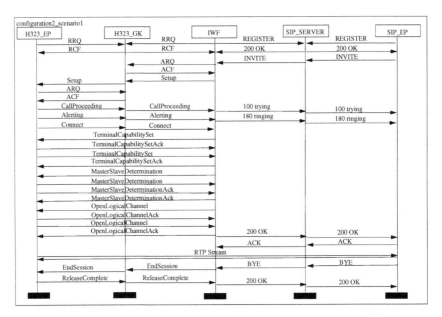

Fig. 17. Successful Scenario 2 Under Configuration 2 [3]

4   Conclusion and Future Work

As a case study of SDL, we have modeled and verified the proposed Interworking
Facility (IWF) between H.323 and SIP, for two different configurations, using
SDL and MSC. All critical components of the IWF, the H.323 endpoint, the
SIP endpoint, the H.323 gatekeeper, and the SIP server have been specified. We
have defined all the internal behavior of our processes by specifying the finite
state machine mentioned in the Internet Draft in SDL. Then, we use interactive
simulation to simulate and verify the properties of our model, by comparing
against the dynamic behavior specified in the MSCs. Moreover, the combination
of SDL and MSC provides a simple and very efficient method for validating the
design of the IWF. We have verified that the IWF, as specified in SDL, operates
in accordance with the various successful and unsuccessful scenarios given in the
Internet Draft, for two representative configurations. In addition to modeling the
call setup exchanges, we have modeled the media channels, to permit verifying
the entire operation.

The use of SDL has permitted us to describe H.323, SIP, and the IWF in a
precise, yet understandable way. We have found that the structure of SDL has
made model enhancement easy because SDL provides object-oriented features
to design systems. However, because the SDL tool ObjectGeode we used can not
support the inheritance with parameterized block type together, we could not
obtain more simplified model from ObjectGeode 4.0. We will simplify our model
as future work. Furthermore, due to the limitation of our SDL tool, which only
claims support up to SDL 96, we have no opportunity to use composite state and

other advanced features of SDL 2000 to simplify our model, but we do foresee its advantage and will study it further. As to data type, although SDL 2000 has introduced many new data type, we suggest that SDL can be improved more to manipulate a variety of data type similar to C/C++ or java by providing more default operation because the diversity of data representation and operation will improve generating code and implementation. Finally, we will also study our model further by using exhaustive simulation for validation.

Acknowledgments

J.W. Atwood and A. Agarwal acknowledge support provided by Concordia University, and by the Natural Sciences and Engineering Research Council of Canada through its Research Grants program.

References

[1] International Telecommunication Union, Packet based multimedia communication systems, Recommendation H.323, Telecommunication Standardization Sector of ITU, Geneva, Switzerland, Feb. 1998. 335

[2] M. Handley, H. Schulzrinne, E. Schooler, J. Rosenberg, SIP: session initiation protocol, Request for Comments (Proposed Standard) 2543, Internet Engineering Task Force, May 29, 2001. 335

[3] H. Agrawal, R.R. Roy, V. Palawat, A. Johnston, C. Agboh, D. Wang, H. Schulzrinne, K. Singh, J. Maeng, SIP-H.323 Interworking, draft-agrawal-sip-h323-interworking-01.txt, Internet Draft, Internet Engineering Task Force, July 13, 2001, work in progress. 335, 336, 346, 348, 349, 350

[4] H. Agrawal, R.R. Roy, V. Palawat, A. ohnston, C. Agboh, D. Wang, H. Schulzrinne, K. Singh SIP-H.323 Interworking Requirement, draft-agrawal-sip-h323-interworking-reqs-04.txt, Internet Draft, Internet Engineering Task Force, Feb, 2003, work in progress. 335

[5] International Telecommunication Union, Digital subscriber signalling system no. 1 (dss 1) - isdn user-network interface layer 3 specification for basic call control, Recommendation Q.931, Telecommunication Standardization Sector of ITU, Geneva, Switzerland, Mar. 1993. 337

[6] ITU-T, Recommendation Z.100(10/93) — Specification and Description Language (SDL). 338

[7] L. Wang, Modeling and Verification of Interworking between SIP and H.323, 2002. Master of computer science thesis, Department of Computer Science, Concordia University. 339

[8] Verilog, Toulouse, France, ObjectGeode, 1996. 341, 347

[9] ITU-T, Recommendation Z.120(10/96) — Message Sequence Charts (MSC). 347

Modeling IETF Session Initiation Protocol and Its Services in SDL

Ken Y. Chan and Gregor v. Bochmann

School of Information Technology and Engineering (SITE), University of Ottawa
P.O.Box 450, Stn. A, Ottawa, Ontario, Canada. K1N 6N5
{kchan,bochmann}@site.uottawa.ca

Abstract. This paper describes the formal approach to modeling IETF Session Initiation Protocol (SIP) and its services in SDL. The main objective is to discover the advantages and shortcomings of using a formal language such as SDL to model an IETF application signaling protocol: SIP. Evaluating the feasibility of using CASE tools such as Telelogic Tau in modeling a protocol as complex as SIP is also the interest of this study. By creating an "Abstract User" interface, we discover the importance of use case analysis in specifying SIP services more precisely. In addition, the object-oriented extension in SDL-96 has been applied to some extent in the modeling process; we create an SDL framework that allows us to reuse and to add SIP services to the core protocol more easily by applying SDL type inheritance in our model. Furthermore, we discuss enhancements that may be made to the SDL language and Tau tools to improve the modeling experience of IETF protocols.

Keywords: SIP, Internet Telephony, UML, Use Case, SDL, MSC, Telelogic, Software Specification, Design Methodology

1 Introduction

With the increasing popularity of voice chats and Internet long distance calls, many companies foresee Internet telephony and voice applications would be a high revenue growth segment of the telecommunication market in the next few years. In the Internet telephony world, many researchers believe the IETF Session Initiation Protocol (SIP) is the emerging Voice over IP (VoIP) signaling protocol that can compete against ITU H.323 protocol suites [1, 2]. SIP was originally designed as a simple call setup and handling protocol between user terminals. However, it has also been extended to address VoIP signaling at carrier-grade level and customer-premise telephony applications. Although researchers believe many new types of voice applications can be built with SIP, the flexibility of the SIP header and its unique user agent-proxy architecture would complicate the problem of feature interactions [4, 5, 6]. Thus, we have developed an SDL model of SIP and its sample services [1, 3] to investigate the feature interaction problem. However, the emphasis of this paper is to discuss our experience of modeling a semantic rich application protocol like SIP using

R. Reed (Ed.): SDL 2003, LNCS 2708, pp. 352–373, 2003.

the SDL language and the CASE tool called Telelogic Tau [7]. The feature interaction problem is beyond the scope of this paper. Furthermore, we have used version 4.3 and 4.4 of Telelogic Tau in our modeling exercise. The next generation version of Telelogic Tau called "Tau G2" was still under development by Telelogic Inc. and was unavailable to us.

This paper is organized as follows: Section 2 presents an overview of the SIP protocol. Section 3 gives an overview of our design methodology which is further detailed in the subsequent sections. Section 4 explains the steps of applying use case analysis and deriving our use case scenarios. Section 5 describes the process of converting sample service call flows into Message Sequence Charts (MSC) which represent important test case scenarios. Section 6 details the structural design of the model. Section 7 illustrates the behavior specification of the SIP model. Section 8 explains the steps of validating and verifying the SDL model using an SDL CASE tool called Telelogic Tau. Section 9 discusses potential enhancements to and our experience using SDL and Tau tools to model SIP. Finally, the paper ends with a conclusion and discussion of future work.

2   Overview of SIP

SIP (Session Initiation Protocol) is an application-layer multimedia control protocol standardized under IETF RFC 2543 [1]. Similar to most World Wide Web protocols, SIP has an ASCII-based syntax that closely resembles HTTP. This protocol can establish, modify and terminate multimedia sessions including multimedia conferences, Internet telephony calls, and similar applications. SIP can also initiate multi-party calls using a multipoint control unit (MCU) or fully meshed interconnections instead of multicast. SIP offers five facets of establishing and terminating multimedia communications [1] but we focus only on call setup and call handling in this research because they are the central functions of any telephony services and offer interesting behaviors for formal modeling. Call setup is defined as the establishment of call parameters at both called and calling party. Call handling is defined as the ability to manage mid-call and third-party call control such as call transfer and call waiting, after the initial call has been setup and to manage termination of these calls.

Under the SIP model, signaling parties communicate with each other through asynchronous messaging. Because SIP is a transport-independent signaling protocol, SIP messages can be transferred via UDP, TCP, or other transport protocols. There are three types of messages: request, response, and acknowledgment. In a basic two party call setup as illustrated in Fig. 1, the initiator 'A' sends an "INVITE" request to the called party 'B' to establish a unicast multimedia session (a conference call would require multicast sessions). The "METHOD" field in a SIP request message indicates the action to be performed, and in this case, "INVITE" is the typical call setup and handling SIP request action. Then, the called party would generally reply with one or more appropriate response messages, and the caller would finally acknowledge the final "OK" response by sending an "ACK" message (which is considered as a special request message) to

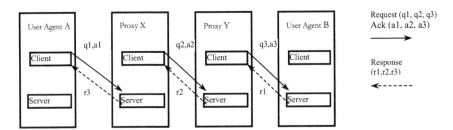

Fig. 1. User Agent A calls B via Proxies X and Y

the called party. Upon reception of the "ACK" message, the voice media would be established between the two parties [1].

To cancel a previous request, the request initiator may send a "CANCEL" request message to the called party. To terminate an existing session, the member of the session who desires to terminate the session can send a "BYE" request message to the other party. In an N-party call session, the initiator of a SIP request does not necessarily have to be a member of the session to which it is sending the invite. Media and participants can be added to or removed from an existing session by sending "INVITE" message(s) with new parameters in the SDP [8] after the initial call setup. To register the location of the session member, the member can send a "REGISTER" message to a SIP registrar that serves as a lookup directory. There are other SIP methods that have been defined, for example, "INFO". Additional SIP methods can also be added to the standard [1]; however, these are beyond the scope of this paper.

In SIP terminology, a call consists of all participants in a conference invited by a common source. A SIP call is identified by a globally unique call-id. Thus, if a user is, for example, invited to the same multicast session by several people, each of these invitations will be a unique call. However, after the multipoint call has been established, the logical connection between two participants is a call leg, which is identified by the combination of "Call-ID", "To", and "From" header fields. A point-to-point Internet telephony conversation maps into a single SIP call. In a call-in conference using an MCU, each participant uses a separate call to invite himself to the MCU. The sender of a request message or the receiver of a response message is known as the client, whereas the receiver of a request message or the sender of a response message is known as a server. A user agent (UA) is a logical entity, which contains both a user agent client and user agent server, and acts on behalf of an end-user for the duration of a call. A proxy is an intermediary program that acts as both a server and a client for the purpose of making requests on behalf of other clients. A proxy may process or interpret requests internally or by passing them on, possibly after translation, to other servers (Fig. 1). A reader should not confuse the SIP client and server with the initiator (caller or originator) and callee.

```
INVITE sip:ken@ee.uottawa.ca SIP/2.0
Via: SIP/2.0/UDP gtwy1.uottawa.ca;branch=8348
;maddr=137.128.16.254;ttl=16
Via: SIP/2.0/UDP gtwy.ee.uottawa.ca
Record-Route: gtwy.ee.uottawa.ca
From: Bill Gate <sip:bill@Microsoft.com>
To: Ken Chan <sip:ken@uottawa.ca>
Contact: Ken Chan <sip:ken@site.uottawa.ca>
Call-ID: 56258002189@site.uottawa.ca
CSeq: 1 INVITE
Subject: SIP will be discussed, too
Content-Type: application/sdp
Content-Length: 187


v=0
o=bill 53655765 2353687637 IN IP4 224.116.3.4
s=RTP Audio
i=Discussion of .Net
c=IN IP4 224.2.0.1/127
t=0 0
m=audio 3456 RTP/AVP 0
```

```
OK 200 SIP/2.0
Via:SIP/2.0/UDP gtwy1.uottawa.ca;branch=8348
;maddr=137.128.16.254;ttl=16
Record-Route: gtwy.ee.uottawa.ca
From:  Bill Gate <sip:bill@Microsoft.com>
To: Ken Chan <sip:ken@uottawa.ca>
Contact: Ken Chan <sip:ken@site.uottawa.ca>
Call-ID: 56258002189@site.uottawa.ca
CSeq: 1 INVITE
Content-Type: application/sdp
Content-Length: 187
```

Fig. 2. INVITE Request from Bill to Ken (left) and OK Response without SDP from Ken to Bill (right) Captured at gtwy.ee.uottawa.ca

A user agent or a proxy is said to contain both client and server and can act as either a client or a server, but not both simultaneously in the same transaction [1].

What makes SIP interesting and different from other VoIP protocols are the message header and body. Like HTTP, a SIP message, whether it is a request, response, or acknowledgment message, consists of a header and a body. A sample "INVITE" request message body is shown in Fig. 2:

The top portion of the message is the message header. The first line is the request line, which contains the Method name 'INVITE', the Request-URI (ken@site.uottawa.ca), and the SIP Version. The Request-URI names the current destination of the request. It generally has the same value as the "To" header field but may be different if the caller is given a cached address that offers a more direct path to the callee through the "Contact" field. The "From" and "To" header fields indicate the respective registration address of the caller and of the callee. They usually remain unchanged for the duration of the call. The "Via" header fields are optional and indicate the path that the request has traveled so far. This prevents request looping and ensures replies take the same path as the requests, which assists in firewall traversal and other unusual routing situations. Only a proxy may append its address as a "Via" header value to a request message. When the corresponding response message arrives at a proxy, the proxy would remove the associated "Via" header from the response message header. The "Record-Route" request and response header fields are optional fields and are added to a request by any proxy that insists on being in the path of subsequent requests for the same call leg. It contains a globally reachable

Request-URI that identifies the proxy server. "Call-Id" represents a globally unique identifier for the current call session. The Command Sequence ("CSeq") consists of a unique transaction-id and the associated request method. It allows user agents and proxies to trace the request and the corresponding response messages associated with the transaction. The "Content Type" and "Content-Length" header fields indicate the type of the message body's content and the length of the message body measured in bytes.

The sample response, excluding the associated SDP body in Fig. 2, indicates a success 2XX response (2XX is a success response code in the range of 200 and 299) returned by the callee. The first line of a response message is the status line that includes the response string, code, and the version number. It is important to note that "Via" header fields are removed from the response message by the corresponding proxies on the return path. When the calling user agent client receives this success response, it will send an "ACK" message that has a very similar format as the "INVITE" request message, except the Method name would be "ACK" instead of "INVITE" in the request line. Note that SDP is not required in the body of the "ACK" message.

We have discussed only some of the key header fields in SIP. There are many header fields available in SIP and the header can become very complex. The associated RFC [1] is recommended for further details on SIP. In addition, the SIP community has specified a variety of traditional telephony services for SIP in [3, 9, 10]: Call Forward Busy (CFB), Call Waiting (CW), Originator Call Screening (OCS), Terminating Call Screening (TCS), ... In the case of CFB, user 'A' calls user 'B' who is busy and replies with a busy response message. Then, the proxy will forward the call to user 'C'. Because we have implemented very few advanced Internet telephony services (such as Call Forking), we will use CFB as the sample SIP service to describe our modeling approach in the subsequent sections.

3   Design Approach

Though the end result of this formal modeling exercise is to produce an SDL [11] model that serves as a formal specification of SIP and some of the sample services, the modeling exercise fits into a bigger picture: the overall development process to develop reliable SIP implementation. Before we dive right into the details of the SDL model, we present the overall design approach that we use in this project. Not surprisingly, the process is highly iterative by nature because the specifications of SIP services are a collection of informal textual service descriptions and sample call flows that do not offer all the detailed requirements up front. The process is best described in Fig. 3, as a typical software development lifecycle, except it has incorporated formal modeling.

Tools that are based on formal methods can be used to ensure the final SDL model would meet these requirements. In a large project, we believe a system modeling team takes the responsibility of building system models and verifying that all requirements, particularly performance requirements, can be met. The

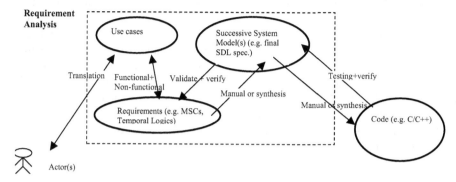

Fig. 3. Typical Software Development Lifecycle

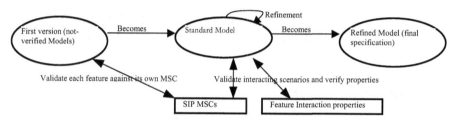

Fig. 4. Iterative Specification Process

system model serves as the final specification resulting from the requirement analysis. The design and implementation teams may use tools to synthesize the implementation or manually translate the specification to code. In this paper, the focus is on the generation of message sequence charts as both our use case scenarios and test cases, and the modeling of SIP and its services as a SDL system model. Synthesis is beyond the scope of this paper.

After the sample service scenarios are translated to message sequence charts, an SDL model of SIP and selected services is created. We found that it is useful to define three sets or versions of the SDL models:

1. the initial model;
2. the version that complies with the published specification (the standard model);
3. the refined (final) version that includes the preventive measures for feature interactions (the refined model).

In Fig. 4, we show that the initial models involve validation of each feature against MSC test cases. Then, the standard model is checked for feature interactions. Finally, the refined model is produced.

The approach to model SIP and its services begins with modeling the core signaling functionality of SIP; we call this the basic (telephony) service of SIP. The basic service includes establishing a two party call, terminating a two party call, suspending the call, presenting dial tone, busy signal, no answer signal, ringing, and alerting signal. The user agent and proxy are the only SIP entities that are modeled. After we complete the basic service, we add additional SIP services such as multi-party call signaling features (call redirection, forwarding, and holding (suspending)) to the model. These protocol features are essential to enabling the development of more complex telephony features such as CFB, CW, OCS, TCS, etc. Advanced Internet telephony features such as Call Forking (CF) and Auto-callback (ACB) will be added at the later stage. The complete SDL model consists of over 60 pages of diagrams, thus only selected diagrams will be presented in this paper.

4   From Use Case Diagrams to Use Case Scenarios as MSC

We begin our modeling exercise with use case analysis. The following subsections describe how use case diagrams and use case scenarios are derived from existing informal service specifications [3, 9, 10].

4.1   Defining Use Cases

Our use cases are defined in forms of use case diagrams [12]. They are based on the informal call flow diagrams and textual service specification described in various IETF documents [3, 9, 10]. Each actor in our use cases has a specific role in a service; Figure 5 shows the use case diagram of Call Forward Busy (CFB).

In this example, there are three distinct actors (originator, forwarder, and participant/forwardee). In Sect. 5, we show an originator corresponds to the user agent process SipUserAgent1_1. The forwarder corresponds to the user agent process SipUserAgent1_2. The forwardee corresponds to the user agent process SipUserAgent1_3. The "indicate busy" use case extends the "make a call" use case. The "extend" relationship is used to describe additional functionality that the extended use case has. We will show how use case scenarios can be derived from such user case diagram in the next section.

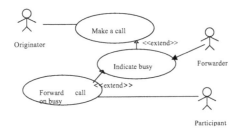

Fig. 5. Use Case Diagram of Call Forward Busy

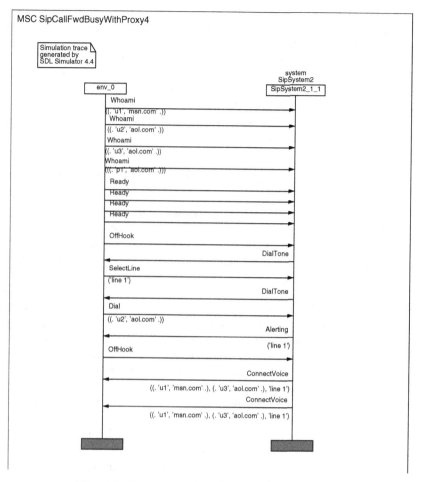

Fig. 6. Call Forward Busy Use Case Scenario

4.2 Defining Use Case Scenarios as MSC

Since the IETF drafts have provided a call flow diagram or success scenario for each sample service in graphical notation [9], we can translate these scenarios into message sequence charts. However, we note that these call flow diagrams only include the sequence of exchanged SIP messages at the protocol level. They do not represent service scenarios in the sense of use cases. In the previous section, we show how we apply use case analysis and come up with use case diagrams.

Following standard practice of software engineering, we think that it is important to define service usage scenarios at the interface between the user and the system providing the communication service. We have therefore associated each use case ("make a call", or "indicate busy", or "forward call on busy" ...) to a partial trace of a certain call flow scenario. Then, a use case diagram which contains the relationships between use cases and actors represents a full trace of a service. Thus, we can translate a use case diagram to at least one service usage scenario. As an example, Fig. 6 shows a use case scenario (service usage scenario) of CFB, which corresponds to the use case diagram in Fig. 5 and also to the call flow diagram of CFB found in [9]. We have also defined an abstract user interface (see Sect. 6.3) which represents the interactions at the service level. These interactions between the users and the SIP system describe use case scenarios of SIP services. The users are the actors of the use case scenarios and are represented by the environment env_0 in SDL.

5   Converting Call Flows to MSC as Test Case Scenarios

The combination of the use case scenario with the corresponding scenario of exchanged SIP messages from [9] is represented in Fig. 7. We may call such a combined scenario a service and protocol scenario. It can be used as a test case for validating the SDL specification of the SIP protocol, as explained in Sect. 8.

After having defined our use case scenarios, which correspond largely to the call flow diagrams that we found in [9], we can combine the use case scenario with the corresponding scenarios of exchanged SIP messages from [9]. Figure 7 shows such an MSC corresponding to the use case of Fig. 6. We may call such a sequence chart a "combined service and protocol scenario". Such a combined scenario may be used as a test case for validating the SDL specification of the SIP protocol, as explained in Sect. 8. The test cases are written as message sequence charts because we use the Telelogic Tau's Validator to verify our SDL model against the combined scenario.

The sample call forward busy described in the IETF SIP Service Example draft [3], which is shown in Fig. 7, is used to demonstrate our process of converting informal requirements to message sequence charts. In Fig. 7, user 'A' calls user 'B' who is busy and replies with a busy response message. Then, the proxy forwards the call to user 'C'. Because Fig. 7 can be used as a test scenario MSC against which the model is verified, such test scenario must be a complete trace which includes the initialization phase of the simulation. However, the initialization phase (sequence NewInstance, Whoami, Id, and Ready of operational management signals, see Sect. 6.1) is not part of the service specification; it is our invention to facilitate simulation and verification of the model.

The call flow diagram and the service requirements of call forwarding described in [10] can be used in conjunction for creating a formal call forward busy specification. Before we begin developing the SDL model, we need to articulate the requirements in formal notations. The first step is to convert the call flow diagram to a syntactically correct message sequence chart. In Fig. 7, the method name of the request message ('INVITE') is converted to an SDL signal (or MSC message). The SIP message parameters would become the signal parameters. Also, we can use co-regions to express the general ordering of messages because the SIP RFC indicates that the arrival of a call setup response message such

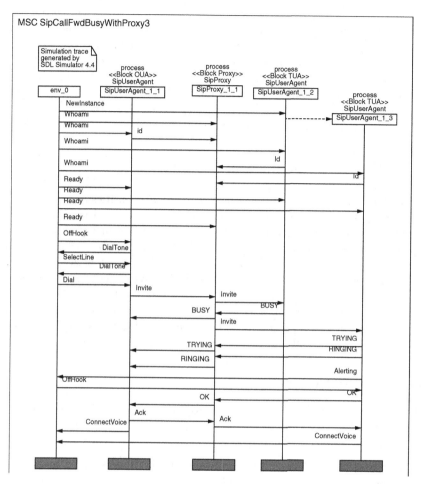

Fig. 7. Call Forward Busy Test Scenario in IETF SIP Service Examples Draft

as 'TRYING' or 'RINGING' can be out of order. However, we decided that we could not use co-regions in our message sequence charts because Tau does not support co-regions in the validation process. The symbol of instance end is used to end all instances in our message sequence charts because it defines the end of the description of an instance in MSC; it does not define the termination of the instance.

An action that describes the interaction between a SIP entity and a non-SIP entity is written as a signal/message from a SIP entity to the environment in our message sequence charts. For example, ConnectVoice is a signal that is sent from the user agent to the media controller to establish RTP voice streams. The SelectLine signal is used to select the line on the phone. Evidently, our use case scenarios written as message sequence charts together with the SDL model give a more precise formal service specification of SIP services than the IETF drafts.

After we have developed the SDL system model for SIP, we would verify the model against these message sequence charts which serve as the basic SIP compliant test cases for the system model. The final system model that includes all the preventive measures for feature interactions is the specification of the SIP protocol entities. The SDL model may also be used to synthesize the code base, but it is beyond the scope of this paper.

6   Defining the Structural Model

In this section, the structural definitions of the SIP entities are discussed. The relationship between modeled entities, their interfaces, and attributes are considered parts of the structural definition. A SDL system represents static interactions between SIP entities. The channels connected between various block instances specify the signals or SIP messages that are sent between user agents and/or proxies. Block and process types (SipUserAgentType, SipProxyType ...) are used to represent SIP entity types such as user agent and proxy. In addition, the Tau tool Organizer component [7] allows the service designer to partition the specification into a number of modules, called SDL Packages. SDL Packages are used to package SDL entities for reuse.

6.1   Core SIP Entities

The following subsections describe the two main SIP entity types in the model: User Agent and Proxy.

User Agent. A SIP User Agent contains both, what is called in SIP, a user agent client (UAC) and a user agent server (UAS). Since a user agent can only behave as either a UAC or UAS in a SIP transaction, the user agent is best represented by the inheritance of UAC and UAS interfaces. The inheritance relationship is modeled using separate gates (C2Sgate and S2Cgate) to partition the user agent process and block into two sections: client and server. The Envgate' gate manages the sending and receiving of "Abstract User" signals between the user agent and the environment (see Fig. 8). An instantiation of a block type represents an instance of a SIP entity such as user agent or proxy, and contains a process instance that describes the actual behavior of the entity. The process definition file contains the description of all the state transitions or behaviors of the features to which the SIP entity has subscribed. In addition, each SIP entity must have a set of permanent and temporary variables for its operations. In the case of a user agent, the permanent variables store the current call processing state values of the call session (To, From). The temporary variables store the values of the consumed messages for further processing.

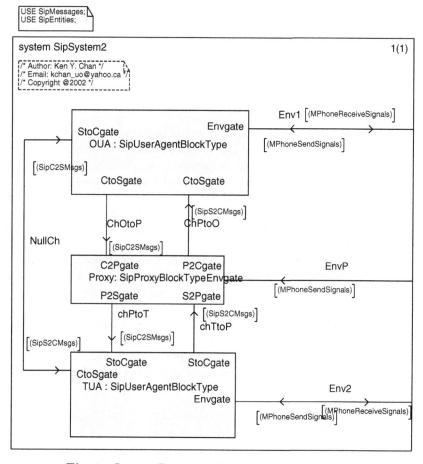

Fig. 8. System Diagram of Proxy and User Agents

Proxy. Similar to a user agent, a proxy consists of client and server portion. It tunnels messages between user agents but also intercepts incoming messages, injects new messages, or modifies forwarding messages on behalf of the user agent(s). A proxy is also a favorite entity to which features are deployed. If a proxy needs to keep track of the states of a session for a feature, it is considered a stateful proxy, and vice versa. A SIP Proxy has four gates that interact with user agents or proxies: client-to-proxy (C2Pgate), proxy-to-client (P2Cgate), server-to-proxy (S2Pgate), and proxy-to-server (P2Sgate). The Envgate gate manages the sending and receiving of "Abstract User" signals between the user agent and the environment (see Fig. 8).

In our SDL model, we use different SDL systems to represent different structural bindings between SIP entities and to simulate a particular set of call scenarios. The most complex system in our telephony model (see Fig. 8) realizes

the concept of originating and terminating user endpoints. It contains an originating user agent block, a proxy block, and a terminating user agent block. The
originating block contains all the user agent process instances that originate SIP
requests while the terminating block contains all the user agent process instances
that receive these requests. Upon receiving a request, a terminating user agent
would reply with the corresponding response messages. It is important to note
that only the originating user agent and proxy instances can send SIP requests
(including acknowledgments).

All blocks are initialized with one process instance. During the simulation,
a NewInstance "Misc User" signal can be sent to a process instance to create a
new process instance. Signals such as NewInstance, Whoami, Id, and Ready' are
not "Abstract User" signals. They are created for the purpose of operational
management, configuration and administration. We grouped all non-SIP signals
to the Envgate' gate. We believe it was an oversight. We should have created
different gates for different types of environmental signals. This would be a part
of our future work.

Before the first "INVITE" message is sent, the environment must initialize
each user agent and proxy instance with a unique Internet address by sending
them a message called Whoami. The user agent instances would in turn send an Id
message along with its Internet address and process id (Pid) to the proxy. Thus,
the proxy can establish a routing table for routing signals to the appropriate
destinations during simulation. Similar to the user agent, a proxy has a set of
permanent and temporary variables for its operations. In Fig. 9, we have a block
interaction diagram that describes the relationship between the process set and
its block.

6.2   SIP Messages

In this case, SIP messages are defined as SDL signals in the SIPMessage package. We have defined only the main header fields of the SIP header because we
are interested in only the operation (method) and the endpoints of the call session. These fields in a SIP message are represented by the corresponding signal
parameters. Since we could not find any SDL package that supports linked list
data structure in Tau, the number of variable fields such as 'Via' and 'Contact'
are fixed in our model. Complex data and array types of SDL have been tried
for this purpose, but were dropped from the model because they may cause the
Tau validation engine to crash. Instead, we used a fix number of parameters to
simulate these variable SIP header fields.

6.3   Abstract User Interface

As mentioned in Sect. 4, a set of user signals (see Fig. 10), that is not part of
the SIP specifications [1, 3, 9], has also been defined here to facilitate simulation
and verification. They represent the interface between the user and the local IP-
telephony equipment in an abstract manner; we call this interface the "Abstract
User interface". The modeling of these user-observable behaviors is essential to

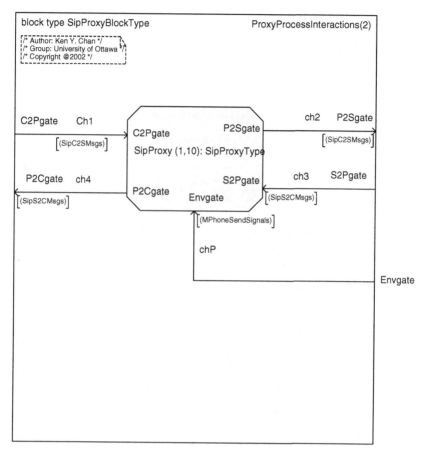

Fig. 9. Block-Interaction Diagram of Proxy Type

describe feature interactions; however, the SIP protocol messages described in the SIP standard do not describe these user interactions properly. For example, an INVITE message in SIP may play different roles. It is more than just a call setup message; for instance, it may be used for putting the call on hold in the middle of a call (mid-call features) [3]. To make the simulation as realistic to real phone calls as possible, the "Abstract User Interface" includes signals such as Offhook, Onhook, Dial, SelectLine, CancelKey, RingTone, AlertTone, TransferKey which relate to the actions that are available on most telephones units on the market (see Sect. 4 and Fig, 6).

The parameters of each "Abstract User" signal are designed to give an unambiguous semantics to a user action. For example, the ConnectVoice signal has five parameters: From's user and domain, To's user and domain, and call-id. These parameters mark the logical endpoints of a call segment, which is used by a media controller to establish a voice stream between the two hops. All the out-

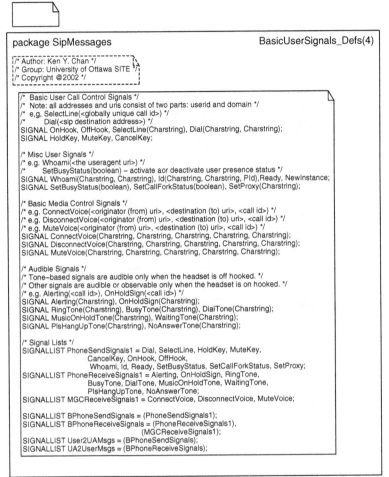

Fig. 10. "Abstract User" Interface (Signals)

put signals have the call-id as their parameter that represents the line number of the call.

Finally, one may ask how these high-level "Abstract User" signals are connected to the protocol's low-level primitives (SIP messages). We initially considered having a dedicated process in each SIP entity block (SipUserAgentBlockType and SipProxyBlockType) to map these user signals to SIP signals which are managed by another dedicated process (SipUserAgent and SipProxy). However, we found it would introduce unnecessary complexity to the design so we abandoned the approach. Instead, each block type has one process which contains all the behavior of the block type. The mapping between "Abstract User" signals and SIP signals is simple. In Sect. 7, Fig. 11 shows when the user agent receives a HoldKey "Abstract User" signal at the Connect_Completed state, it updates its state variables, sets the timer, and sends the corresponding Invite message to the destination. Then, the user agent would make a state transition from the Connect_Completed state to SentOnHold state.

Similarly, when the originating user agent receives a success response from the destination, the user agent would cancel the timer and send the corresponding OnHoldSignal signal to the environment (the caller phone alerts the user with an On-hold tone). Finally, the user agent would make a state transition from the SentOnHold state to the OnHold state. In general, the mapping between "Abstract User" signals and SIP signals is based on a relationship of trigger events and actions. For example, an "Abstract User" signal can trigger the sending of a SIP signal, and vice versa. We will explain this in more detail in Sect. 7.

7   Behavior Specification

7.1   User Agent Process Specifications

In general, a SIP feature or service is represented by a set of interactions between users and the user agent processes, and possibly the proxy processes. Each process instance plays a role in a feature instance. A process instance contains state transitions which represent the behaviors that the process instance plays in a feature instance. In our model, we capture the behavior of a SIP entity in an SDL process type (such as UserAgentType). The first feature we model is the basic SIP signaling functionality, also known as the basic service. Each process type has state transitions that describe the basic service. In the case of a user agent, the process includes the UAC and UAS behavior. We define a feature role as the behavior of a SIP entity that makes up a feature in a distributed system. A feature role is invoked or triggered by trigger events. The entry states of a feature role in a SIP entity are the states for which the trigger events are defined as inputs. For example, the on-hold feature can be triggered in the Connect_Completed (entry) state by an INVITE message with 'ONHOLD' as one of its parameters (Fig. 11). After the invite message is sent, a response timer is immediately set. Then, the user agent is waiting for the on-hold request to be accepted. When the other user agent responds with an OK message, the requesting agent would cancel or reset the response timer and inform the device to display the on-hold signal on the screen.

In general, trigger events are expressed as incoming signals; whereas precondition, post-conditions, and constraints are expressed as enabling conditions or decisions. Actions are tasks, procedure calls, or output signals. As a triggering event is consumed by the user agent process, the parameters of the event may be examined along with the pre-conditions of the feature. Then, actions such as sending out a message and modifying the internal variables may be executed. Post-conditions and constraints on the action may also be checked. Finally, the process progresses to the next state.

Although we have described the skeleton of the model (systems, blocks, data variables in processes), we have not defined the essential behavior of the model,

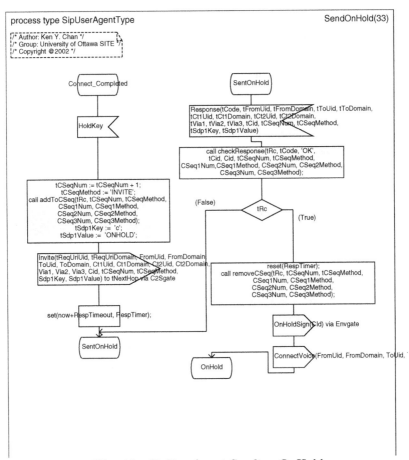

Fig. 11. SipUserAgent Sending OnHold

which is defined by the state transitions of the processes. The question is how to come up with the state transitions for the "initial" models. Since we have a message sequence chart describing the success scenario of a two party call, we assign a unique state to each input and output of the instance type (user agent or proxy type). For example, if Connect_Request state is the current state and we have received a HoldKey signal, we would send an Invite request to the other user agent. We do not put any timers in the *initial* model because we would like to produce a simple rapid prototype model that we can experiment with. However, we add timers (e.g. response timer) to the *standard* and *refined* models.

A state transition occurs when 1) an "Abstract User" signal is received from the environment, 2) a request or response message is received, or 3) a continuous signal is enabled. The so-called Continuous Signal in SDL is used to model the situation in which a transition is initiated when a certain condition is fulfilled. For example if the UAS is busy, the boolean isBusy would be true in the Server_Ring state. The UAS would immediately send the BUSY response to the caller. This way, we would not have to worry about the timer expiration because we do not need to send a busy toggling signal to simulate busy during a simulation. An asterisk '*' can be used in a state and signal symbol to denote any state or any signal; its semantics is equivalent to a wildcard. A state symbol with a dash '-' means the current state. Error handling, such as response timer expiration, can easily be modeled with SDL timers and a combination of '*' and '-' state symbols. For example, when the response timer expires, a timeout message would be automatically sent to the input queue of the user agent process. The expiration of the response message is generalized as the situation in which the receiving end does not answer the request in time. Thus, a NoAnswer signal is sent to the environment. Finally, the process can either return to the previous state or go directly to the idle state through the Jump_Idle connector in this case.

Moreover, we can add additional features or services such as CFB, OCS, and other services, to the system. To add behaviors of additional features to a process type, we can subtype a "basic" process type such as UserAgentType. The derived type has the same interfaces and also additional state transitions [13]. We do not want to add new interfaces (signal routes) to the process types because we do not want to change the interfaces of the block types. If a feature requires new SIP methods and response codes, we would not need to change the interfaces because method names and response codes are simply signal parameters in our model. Thus, we avoid the need to add new interfaces whenever a new feature is defined.

7.2   Proxy Process Specification

A proxy is different from a user agent because a proxy processes messages exchanged between user agents or proxies. We model the proxy also as an entity to which telephony features may be deployed. The proxy performs a predefined set of actions based on the header information (e.g. originator and destination addresses) of the incoming message(s). A proxy listens for response messages from the terminating user agent and forwards the response message to the originating agent based on the routing information that was set during the initiation phase of the simulation.

In summary, a state model of SIP and its sample services can be derived from message sequence charts. Many protocol features such as timer expiration, parameter checking, sending and receiving messages can be mapped to equivalent structures in SDL. The object-oriented extension to SDL allows specialization of telephony services. Thus, SDL is suitable in modeling telephony services. In the next section, we will examine the validation and verification process.

8   Verification and Validation

The SDL specification that has been discussed in the previous subsection was constructed using the Telelogic Tau tool version 4.3 and 4.4 [7]. Tau offers many verification or reachability analysis features: bit-state, exhaustive, random walk bit state exploration and verification against a given MSC. Bit-state exploration is particularly useful and efficient [14] in checking for deadlocking interactions because it checks for various reactive system properties without constructing the whole state space as the exhaustive approach does.

We verified our SDL model of SIP mainly by checking whether the model would be able to realize specific interaction scenarios which were described in the form of Message Sequence Charts (MSCs) [7, 15] (see Sect. 5). In fact, we used the scenarios described informally in [1, 3], and rewrote them in the form of MSCs. Then we used the Tau tool to check that our SDL model was able to generate the given MSC. An MSC is verified if there exists an execution path in the SDL model such that the scenario described by the MSC can be satisfied. Thus, an MSC in Tau is considered as an existential quantification of the scenario. When "Verify MSC" is selected, Tau may report three types of results: verification of MSC, violation of MSC, and deadlock. Unless Tau is set to perform 100% state space coverage, partial state space coverage is generally performed and reported in most cases. Verification of the model against an MSC in Tau is apparently achieved by using the MSC to guide the simulation of the SDL model. As a result, the state space of the verification has become manageable [16].

Although we could use MSCs as the test cases of our SDL model, MSCs have limitations in terms of expressing quantification of instances and their behaviors. For example, we could not find a way to write an MSC to verify this condition: For all user agents that receive an 'OK' response, they must reply to the sender of the response with an 'ACK' message. We note that such properties could also be checked during simulation using Observer Process Assertions [7], as discussed in Sect. 9. Also, Live Sequence Chart (LSC) [17], which has not been discussed much in this paper, appears to be a promising extension to MSCs in this context. However, Tau does not support LSC at the moment. Further research in the application of LSC would be a part of our future works.

9   Advantages of SDL & Tau and Possible Enhancements

In the course of modeling SIP services, we discovered not only the advantages but also some shortcomings of using SDL and CASE tools such as Telelogic Tau to model an IETF application protocol such as SIP. SDL is a good language to model SIP because SIP and its services can be easily expressed as interactions between extended communicating finite state machines. We can simulate a distributed SIP system a transition at a time using Tau. Other advantages of using Tau include 1) the ability to express test scenarios as MSCs and to verify these MSCs against the model, 2) the ability to verify the model does not violate system properties by writing these test properties (e.g. livelock) as Observer Process Assertions.

However, we find the lack of SDL packages that support a variety of abstract data types in Tau has been a problem in modeling SIP. Unlike bit-oriented protocols such as Ethernet and Token Ring, SIP is an ASCII-based, attribute-rich signaling protocol with mandatory, optional and variable size parameters. If we were to model SIP messages as SDL signals, we could not easily insert, remove, search, and modify values from the optional and/or variable size header fields. Although it is not impossible to model variable header fields with fixed size arrays in Tau, it is a very inconvenient task. Many programming languages offer the language feature of pointer (C++ [18]) and/or reference (Java [19], C++) so that a programmer could build his/her customized data structures. Pointer is a dangerous programming feature that is normally not included in formal languages. The SDL language could be extended with additional built-in ADTs[1]. We believe support for common abstract data types such as linked list and hash table should be made mandatory in SDL. This would be sufficient to enhance our modeling experience. A linked list can be used to describe a variable-length parameter list whereas a hash table can be used to store all the key-value pairs in an SDP body. These two abstract data types eliminate the need to re-index the content. Although SDL has the Vector type which is basically a subtype of Array, this Vector type does not have the properties of a Java Vector; it does not have insert, remove, and update operators.

Secondly, we believe the SDL language should be extended with string processing facilities. In programming languages such as Java and C++, the language definition comes with string processing libraries. For example, the int indexOf(String substring) operator of the String class in Java returns the index position of the first occurrence of the substring in that string object instance [19]. Similar operations can be added to the SDL language. Furthermore, regular expression operators may be added to the SDL language. These string processing operations would facilitate the checking and comparisons of SIP header values. Without these operations, it is difficult to develop a complete model of an IETF application protocol such as SIP.

Furthermore, we find that the Tau validation tool needs to offer more flexible verification features. For example, the ability to incorporate model checking of the SDL system using temporal logic formula would be a bonus. We may use temporal logic formula to verify more complex distributed system properties such as live-locks. In addition, we could not easily specify actors in our use case scenarios; we group all the actors together as the environment. We could create additional actor/user processes to simulate actors. However, if we were to show the interactions between actors in our use case scenarios, the message sequence charts would also display the exchange of internal SIP messages between user agent and proxy processes. We could probably develop an actor-layer to partition user signals from internal signals but it would not be a trivial task. Ideally, Tau could offer different environment instances for different channels to a system. This way, we would not need to develop our actor-layer in the model.

Last but not least, we find that the SDL editor lacks GUI context sensitive features, such as allowing a designer to select one of the existing state names

---

[1] Editorial note: implementation of the SDL-2000 data features added since SDL-92 such as **object** date types may meet some of these needs. Alternatively users could donate useful data type definitions to an open source library.

when he/she creates a new state label, that are normally found in other CASE tools such as Microsoft Visual Studio [20]. Cutting and pasting objects between pages is also not always allowed; these some the minor improvements that can be made to the tools.

10   Conclusion and Future Work

In this paper, we have described our approach to the formal modeling of the IETF Session Initiation Protocol (SIP) and its services in SDL. We have discussed the advantages and shortcomings of using a formal language such as SDL to model an IETF application signaling protocol: SIP. Moreover, we have shown that modeling a complex IETF protocol such as SIP using CASE tools such as Telelogic Tau is feasible. Also, we have explained that the "Abstract User" interface that we developed has allowed us to develop a more user-centric and precise formal service specification for SIP. We believe SIP or any IETF application protocols should be specified from a user-centric perspective. Currently, some of the IETF RFCs and drafts for the application protocols are not written with use case analysis in mind. Many researchers have found IETF documents difficult to read. In addition, we have shown that our SDL framework allows us to reuse and to add SIP services to the core protocol quite easily. Furthermore, we have discussed the enhancements that may be made to the SDL language and Tau tools to improve the modeling experience of IETF protocols.

As part of our future work, we would like to modify our model to support the new SIP standard which is specified under [21]. We intended to start the model with the latest standard but unfortunately the new RFC came to our attention only in the later stage of our project. We have some ideas on how to extend our model to support the new standard but it is beyond the scope of this paper. In addition, we would like to use the Target Expert tool included in Tau to generate target executables in the future.

Acknowledgments

This project would not be possible without the support of Communications and Information Technology Ontario (CITO) and Natural Science and Engineering Research Council (NSERC), Canada. The tools and the support we have received from Telelogic and Klocwork Inc. are appreciated. Furthermore, we would like to thank our colleagues at SITE, in particular Dr. Luigi Logrippo from Université du Québec en Outaouais and Dr. Daniel Amyot from University of Ottawa, for their insights in the domain of formal telephony specification and SDL.

References

[1] M. Handley, H. Shulzrinne, E. Schooler, J. Rosenberg, SIP: Session Initiation Protocol. Request For Comments (Proposed Standard) 2543, Internet Engineering Task Force, Mar. 1999. 352, 353, 354, 355, 356, 364, 370

[2] International Telecommunication Union. Packet based multimedia communication systems,Recommendation H.323. Telecommunication Standardization Sector of ITU, Geneva, Switzerland, Feb. 1998. 352

[3] A. Johnston, R. Sparks, C. Cunningham, S. Donovan, K. Summers. SIP Service Examples. Internet Draft, Internet Engineering Task Force, June 2001, Work in progress. 352, 356, 358, 360, 364, 365, 370

[4] K. Chan, G. v.Bochmann. Methods for Designing IP Telephony Services with Fewer Feature Interactions. Feature Interactions in Telecommunications and Software Systems VII, IOS Press, to be published, June 2003. 352

[5] J. Lennox, H. Schulzrinne. Feature Interaction in Internet Telephony. Sixth Feature Interaction Workshop, IOS Press, May 2000. 352

[6] E. J. Cameron, N. D. Griffeth, Y.-J. Lin, M. E. Nilson, W. K. Shure, H. Velthuijsen. A feature interaction benchmark for IN and beyond. Feature Interactions in Telecommunications Systems, IOS Press, pp. 1-23, 1994. 352

[7] Telelogic Inc.. Telelogic Tau SDL & TTCN Suite, version 4.3 and 4.4. http://www.telelogic.com, accessed on Dec 20, 2002. 353, 362, 369, 370

[8] M. Handley, V. Jacobson. SDP: Session Description Protocol. Request For Comments (Proposed Standard) 2327, Internet Engineering Task Force, April 1998. 354

[9] A. Johnston, S. Donovan, R. Sparks, C. Cunningham, D. Willis, J. Rosenberg, K. Summers, H. Schulzrinne. SIP Call Flow Examples. Internet Draft, Version 5, Internet Engineering Task Force, June 2001. Work in progress. 356, 358, 359, 360, 364

[10] J. Lennox, H. Schulzrinne, T. Porta. Implementing Intelligent Network Services with Session Initiation Services. http://www.cs.columbia.edu/ lennox/cucs-002-99.pdf, accessed on October 7, 2002. 356, 358, 360

[11] ITU-T. Recommendation Z.100 (08/02), Specification and Description Language (SDL). International Telecommunication Union, Geneva. 356

[12] Object Management Group Inc.. Unified Modeling Language. version 2.0. http://www.omg.org/uml/, accessed on Feb. 12, 2003. 358

[13] J. Ellsberger, D. Hogrefe, A. Sarma. SDL - Formal Object-oriented language for Communication Systems. Prentice Hall Europe, ISBN 0-13-621384-7, 1997. 369

[14] G. J. Holzmann. An improved protocol reachability analysis technique. Software Practice and Experience, Vol. 18, No. 2, pp. 137-161, 1988. 370

[15] ITU-T. Recommendation Z.120 (11/99), Message Sequence Chart (MSC). International Telecommunication Union, Geneva. 370

[16] Ø. Haugen, MSC Methodology. SISU, DES 94, Oslo, Norway, 1994. Access on 23Dec2002 http://www.informatics.sintef.no/projects/sisu/sluttrapp /publicen.htm. 370

[17] W. Damm, D. Harel. LSCs: Breathing Life into Message Sequence Charts*.Formal Methods in System Design, Kluwer Academic Publishers, pp. 19,45-80, 2001. 370

[18] B. Stroustrup. Stroustrup: C++. http://www.research.att.com/ bs/C++.html, accessed on Feb 10, 2003. 371

[19] Sun Microsystems Inc. The Source for JavaTM Technology. version 1.x. http://java.sun.com, accessed on Feb 10, 2003. 371

[20] Microsoft Inc.. Visual Studio Home Page. http://msdn.microsoft.com/vstudio, accessed on Feb 10, 2003. 372

[21] J. Rosenberg, H. Shulzrinne, G. Camarillo, A. Johnston, J. Peterson, R. Sparks, M. Handley, E. Schooler. SIP: Session Initiation Protocol. Request For Comments (Standards Track) 3261, Internet Engineering Task Force, June 2002. 372

Automated Generation of Marshaling Code from High-Level Specifications

Thomas Weigert and Paul Dietz

Global Software Group, Motorola Inc., Schaumburg, Illinois 60196
thomas.weigert@motorola.com

Abstract. This paper presents the application of program transformation to the development of marshaling code. Marshaling code amounts to about half of the signaling software in a subscriber radio, and as such constitutes about 20% of the total software in the radio. Development of marshaling code is considered to be a difficult, error prone, and laborious task. We have successfully developed significant portions of Motorola TETRA (Trans-European Trunked Radio) infrastructure and subscriber software through automated code generation techniques using the process outlined in this paper. This process, and the tools described in this paper, have subsequently been applied to the development of a number of communication applications and delivered tremendous cycle time and quality improvements.

1 Introduction

Any system in which components communicate over links is faced with the problem of bandwidth. There is a natural limit to how much data can be transmitted over various media. Much effort in developing communication systems is devoted to packing as much information as possible into the data passed over the communication links. The bandwidth limitations are particularly stringent for wireless communications.

The format of the data communicated between system components must be known so that both ends can correctly extract the communicated information. These formats used to be mostly proprietary, but are today largely governed by standards bodies. The communicated information is usually referred to as protocol data units (PDU). Standards and air interface definitions prescribe precisely how each bit in a PDU is to be interpreted by the sending and receiving components.

While the communicated information passes over the link in a tightly packed and publicly documented format, within the system components the information cannot be represented in that manner since:

- The byte order and alignment of the PDU may not agree with that of the computer equipment chosen to implement a component. For example, the TETRA standard assumes a "big endian" format and does not byte align the fields in a PDU.

R. Reed (Ed.): SDL 2003, LNCS 2708, pp. 374–386, 2003.

- The information contained in a PDU is hidden within several layers of the protocol stack and arranged to minimize space consumption. This is usually contrary to the needs of the applications utilizing that information, which have their own view of how that information should be represented.

Therefore, communication systems are riddled with code that converts data from the PDU format to an application-specific format. This process is commonly called "protocol header marshaling" or "PDU packing/unpacking." Marshaling code converts data encoded in the PDU format into some other format and vice versa. This may involve swapping bytes to change byte order, moving bytes to correct alignment, and changing representation from sequences of bits to more complex objects such as Integers, Booleans, enumerated values, or the like.

The correctness, performance, and portability of the marshaling code are critical. Marshaling has been characterized as the last remaining bottleneck for network software, with respect to both performance and development effort [1]. Marshaling code may constitute a significant amount of the total software in a component. For example, about half of the signaling related software (approximately 20% of the total software) in a Motorola TETRA subscriber radio is involved with header marshaling.

While stub compilers exist for some protocols to automatically generate header marshaling code (such as XDR [2] for Sun RPC), this code is typically written in large manual efforts. Unfortunately, due to the low-level nature of the task, marshaling code is very difficult to write and is highly error-prone. The goal of portability is also very difficult to achieve due to the radically different constraints that the communicating components are subject to. For example, a subscriber radio is severely limited in available memory but handles only one call at a time. A base station has ample memory available, but must handle many calls concurrently (up to 50 calls for a TETRA system, over 1000 calls for larger systems). Completely different code has to be written for both platforms, although the tasks of marshaling the protocol headers are identical.

Using the Mousetrap program transformation environment [3], we have developed domain-specific code generators to automatically generate marshaling code stubs directly from PDU definitions. The generated code is sensitive to the demands of the target platform and can therefore be used on both subscriber and infrastructure equipment. These code generators have successfully been utilized to develop marshaling code for the TETRA air interface. The developed code is shipping in a TETRA subscriber radio and a TETRA base station developed by Motorola.

2   Representing Protocol Data Units

The TETRA standard defines interoperability between components of advanced European trunked radio systems. [4] defines the format of the PDUs and the encoding and decoding rules that have to be obeyed to communicate with TETRA equipment.

Elements	Type	Length	Remark
PDU type	1	5	
Call ID	1	14	
TX grant	1	2	
TX req permission	1	1	
Encryption control	1	1	
Speech service	1	1	
Notification ind	2	6	
TX party type ID	2	2	
TX party address SSI	2	24	C[a]
TX party extension	2	24	C[b]
Proprietary	3		R

a. Present if TX party type ID is SSI or TSI
b. Present if TX party type ID is TSI

Note: information element names have been adjusted to match the subsequent figures.

Fig. 1. D-TX Granted PDU

As an example, Fig. 1 shows the definition of the *D-TX Granted* PDU from Table 74 of [4] which informs the mobile subscribers concerned with a call that permission to transmit has been granted to a particular subscriber. Each row in this table specifies an element in the PDU, the type of this element, and its length in bits. Any additional semantic information about this element is stated in the comment column. An element (or field) in a PDU is either a basic value (a sequence of bits that is given some meaning) or an embedded PDU. Three different types of fields may be contained in a TETRA PDU.

– Type 1 fields are mandatory and are thus always present. After all type 1 fields, a TETRA PDU will contain a bit, referred to as the O-bit, indicating whether any more bits will follow.
– Type 2 fields are optional. The presence of each such field is indicated by a flag bit, referred to as the P-bit. While the type 2 field itself may be missing, its correlated P-bit will always be present (provided that the O-bit indicates that there are any following bits). Type 2 fields may be omitted but their order cannot be changed. As a slight complication, the interpretation of PDU fields may also depend on the value of previous fields (see the *TX party address SSI* and *TX party extension* fields in the *D-TX Granted* PDU); such conditional fields are indicated by a "C" in the "Remark" column. The field on which conditional fields are dependent and the conditional fields themselves are treated as a unit. As a consequence, the dependent fields are not preceded by a P-bit. For both type 1 and type 2 fields, the length of the field is self-defined. That is, its length either is known statically, or can be deduced from its components.
– Type 3 fields may be of arbitrary length and must always be decoded dynamically. Another flag bit, referred to as the M-bit, indicates whether a type 3

Example 1: 59 0F C8 00
Example 2: 59 0F C8 C7 00

Fig. 2. Two Instances of a D-TX Granted PDU

```
d-tx-granted ::=
    SEQUENCE {
        pdu-type pdu-indicator ( SIZE(5) ),
        call-id INTEGER ( SIZE(14) ),
        tx-grant INTEGER ( SIZE(2) ),
        tx-req-permission INTEGER ( SIZE(1) ),
        encryption-control INTEGER ( SIZE(1) ),
        speech-service INTEGER ( SIZE(1) ),
        notification-ind INTEGER ( SIZE(6) ) TYPE2,
        tx-party-type-id INTEGER ( SIZE(2) ) TYPE2,
        CASE tx-party-type-id {
        [ssi] tx-party-address-ssi INTEGER ( SIZE(24) )
        [tsi] SEQUENCE {
                    tx-party-address-ssi INTEGER (
SIZE(24) ),
                    tx-party-extension   INTEGER (
SIZE(24) )
            }
        } TYPE2,
        prop Proprietary TYPE3
    }
```

Fig. 3. D-TX Granted PDU in the ASN.1-like Syntax

field will follow. Each type 3 field is encoded as a type/length/value tuple. The element stored in the type 3 field is identified by a four-bit element indicator and its length in bits is given in an eleven bit binary encoded integer. Moreover, type 3 fields may be repeated arbitrarily many times.

In Fig. 2 we show two examples of instances of a *D-TX Granted* PDU. The first sequence of bits (shown as hexadecimal numbers) represents a PDU with no type 2 or type 3 fields, the Call Id is "2174", and the *TX grant* information element is set to true. The second example adds an optional *Notification ind* information element with a value of "7" to this PDU.

We defined a domain-specific notation to express a TETRA PDU. We relied on a syntax close to ASN.1 [5], a notation familiar to protocol designers. As shown in Fig. 3, this notation allows a nearly literal transliteration of the definition as stated in the standards document. However, information that the standard kept in comments (such as the description of conditional fields) is made explicit.

We have further developed a domain-independent notation to express a PDU. While a PDU definition using the notation of Fig. 3 is specific to the TETRA standard and will not apply to other air interfaces, the domain-independent notation can express any PDU that conforms to very basic and fairly standard guidelines: Every field must have a unique name, the PDU is held in a contiguous

```
typedef D_TX_Granted
    varbits {
        Nat8 PDU_type :5;
        Nat16 Call_ID :14;
        Nat8 TX_grant :2;
        Nat8 TX_req_permission :1;
        Nat8 Encryption_control :1;
        Nat8 Speech_service :1;
        bool Obit;
        if (Obit) {
            bool Notification_ind_Pbit;
            if (Notification_ind_Pbit)
                Notification_ind Nat8 6;
            bool TX_party_type_ID_Pbit;
            if (TX_party_type_ID_Pbit) {
                Nat8 TX_party_type_ID :2;
                if (TX_party_type_ID == SSI)
                    Nat32 TX_party_address_SSI :24;
                if (TX_party_type_Id == TSI) {
                    Nat32 TX_party_address_SSI :24;
                    Nat32 TX_party_extension :24;
                }
            }
            bool type_3_Mbit;
            while (type_3_Mbit) {
                Proprietary_type_3 prop;
                bool type_3_Mbit = true;
            }
            bool type_3_Mbit = false;
        }
    }

typedef Proprietary_type_3
    varbits {
        Nat8 Element_indicator :4;
        Nat16 length :11;
        prop Proprietary : length;
    }
```

Fig. 4. D-TX Granted PDU in the Domain-independent Notation

area of memory, and dynamically encoded fields must be packed and unpacked in the order stated in the definition.

Figure 4 shows the same PDU in the domain-independent notation. We shall not discuss the details of this notation since it is beyond the scope of this paper. Note, however, how the peculiarities of the TETRA encoding rules have been made explicit in Fig. 4. There is explicit reference to P-bits and O-bits, and the fields following these flags are conditional upon their value. Values for the M-bit are stored with the type 3 field. The type/length/value encoding of the type 3 field is made explicit in the new type introduced to correspond to the type 3 field. Finally, Integer subrange or Boolean types have been assigned to the fields since the domain-independent notation correlates the sequences of bits in the PDU to types of the unpacked representation.

The domain-independent notation provides support for the techniques customary in protocol design:

- Constrain the length of data;
- Choose data fields depending on previously encountered data;
- Determine optional components;
- Add padding bits and control alignment of data components;
- Self-delimiting encoding.

3 Automated Generation of Marshaling Code

The development of TETRA marshaling code begins by expressing a PDU in the domain-specific notation. As specifications captured in this notation closely resemble the definition in the standards document, their verification is straightforward.

A TETRA-specific stub compiler that has been developed by us then translates these PDU specifications into the domain-independent notation as shown in Fig. 4. It also generates specifications for the routines that perform the packing and unpacking of a protocol data unit. This stub compiler embodies knowledge about the encoding rules of the TETRA protocol.

Finally, a second code generator compiles the packing and unpacking specifications into efficient C code optimized towards the constraints of the target platform. As an example, the automatically generated code stub that creates a *D-TX Granted* PDU is shown in Fig. 5. This stub is passed a pointer and an offset to a region of memory into which the PDU shall be packed. Macros allow access to the data that must be packed. This second code generator is completely independent of the details of TETRA and encapsulates knowledge about the translation of domain-independent specifications into highly efficient real-time code.

While a detailed discussion of the generated C code is beyond the scope of this paper, it can be seen that the resultant code is highly optimized and not a simple translation of the TETRA encoding rules. Where possible, several fields are written together into the memory representing the PDU. Much less shifting of bytes is thus required. The operations writing into the PDU are sensitive to the target machine word size (in this case the 16 bit words of the subscriber hardware). Because data may be corrupted, all writes into the PDU are protected by masking off unaffected bits.

Typically, SDL is used to define the call control applications on both subscriber radios and on the infrastructure. To support those situations, we generate a set of SDL type definitions corresponding to the PDU data structures. The generated SDL data types for the above example are shown in Fig. 6. These SDL data types are mapped onto the C types generated by the second code generator by the SDL code generator.

The development of marshaling code through program transformation described in this paper is applicable to any project in which system components

```
sint16 pack_D_TX_Granted (bsqrep_base_t * base216, bsqrep_offset_t offset217) {
    sint16 var168, var170; sint8 flag211, var196;
    __bitseq_addseq_int8 (base216, offset217, ACCESS_D_TX_Granted_Pdu_Type & 0x1f, 5);
    __bitseq_addseq_int16 (base216, offset217 + 5, ACCESS_D_TX_Granted_Call_ID & 0x3fff, 14);
    __bitseq_addseq_int8 (base216, offset217 + 19, (ACCESS_D_TX_Granted_TX_grant & 0x3) << 3

            (ACCESS_D_TX_Granted_TX_req_permission & 0x1) << 2 |
            (ACCESS_D_TX_Granted_Encryption_control & 0x1) << 1 |
            ACCESS_D_TX_Granted_Speech_service & 0x1, 5);
    if (ACCESS_D_TX_Granted_Notification_ind_Pbit) {
        __bitseq_addseq_int8 (base216, offset217 + 24,
                            (uint8) (ACCESS_D_TX_Granted_Notification_ind & 0x3f |
0xc0), 8);
        flag211 = 1; var170 = 32; }
    else { var170 = 24; flag211 = 0; }
    if (ACCESS_D_TX_Granted_TX_party_type_ID_Pbit) {
        var196 = ACCESS_D_TX_Granted_TX_party_type_ID & 0x3;
        if ((uint8) flag211 < 2) {
            static uint8 t125[2] = {5, 1}; static uint8 t126[2] = {3, 1};
            uint8 t127 = t126[flag211];
            __bitseq_addseq_int8 (base216, offset217 + var170, t125[flag211], t127);
            var170 += t127; }
        __bitseq_addseq_int8 (base216, offset217 + var170, var196, 2);
        flag211 = 2; var170 += 2;
        switch (var196) {
            case 1:
            {   union union32 val219;
                val219.rep3 = ACCESS_D_TX_Granted_TX_party_address_SSI & 0xffffff;
                __bitseq_addseq_int8 (base216, offset217 + var170, val219.rep1[1], 8);
                __bitseq_addseq_int16 (base216, offset217 + var170 + 24 - 16, val219.rep2[1], 16); }
                flag211 = 3; var170 += 24; break;
            case 2:
            {   union union32 val218;
                val218.rep3 = ACCESS_D_TX_Granted_TX_party_address_SSI & 0xffffff;
                __bitseq_addseq_int8 (base216, offset217 + var170, val218.rep1[1], 8);
                __bitseq_addseq_int16 (base216, offset217 + var170 + 24 - 16, val218.rep2[1], 16); }
                pack_TX_party_extension (base216, offset217 + (sint16) (24 + var170));
                flag211 = 4; var170 += 48; }
        }
    pack_INIT_D_TX_Granted_Proprietary_type_3();
    while (NEXT_D_TX_Granted_Proprietary_type_3 != 0) {
        if ((uint8) flag211 < 6) {
            static uint8 t125[6] = {9,1,1,1,1,1}; static uint8 t126[6] = {4,2,1,1,1,1};
            uint8 t127 = t126[flag211];
            __bitseq_addseq_int8 (base216, offset217 + var170, t125[flag211], t127);
            var170 += t127;   }
        var168 = pack_Proprietary_type_3(base216, offset217 + var170);
        var170 += var168; flag211 = 5;  }
    if ((uint8) flag211 < 6) {
        static uint8 t125[6] = {1,2,1,1,1,1};
        uint8 t127 = t125[flag211];
        __bitseq_addseq_int8 (base216, offset217 + var170, 0, t127);
        return t127 + var170;   }
}
```

Fig. 5. Pack Routine Generated for D-TX Granted PDU

communicate amongst each other via well-defined primitives. Significant cycle time, quality, and performance improvements can be expected when code is developed in this manner.

In detail, we suggest the following development process when producing marshaling code:

- Define a domain-specific notation to express protocol data units;
- Develop a translator from the domain-specific notation to the specification language for a code generator encapsulating the protocol encoding rules;
- Capture the protocol data units in the domain-specific notation;
- Using the translator and code generator, automatically produce marshaling stubs in the target language;
- Use the generated stubs when developing the application.

The final steps in this process are straightforward. However, the first two steps require significantly different skills than are usually available in a development organization. In this particular effort, the domain-specific notation and the stub compiler were produced by a team devoted to providing code generation support to our developers.

Fortunately, these two steps are required only once per major project. For example, once we captured the TETRA air interface in a specification language and a stub compiler, these tools could be used for any application that uses the TETRA protocol. The stub compilers can be used for any target platform, and it is not required that the rest of the development project relies on code generation or a particular methodology. For example, the TETRA subscriber teams develop their applications directly in C. The stub compiler produces C code that is integrated with the handwritten code. On the other hand, the base station team leveraged code generation from SDL design models to develop the application, and the stub compilers produced not only the C code for the marshaling routines but also the SDL data types corresponding to each PDU.

4   Practical Experience

We shall describe our experiences in applying the above process to the development of the marshaling code for the TETRA subscriber radio.

Once the TETRA air interface standard was thought to be understood, the domain-specific notation was defined. Studying the standards document and language definition required approximately one week.

We then produced the stub compiler, which translates PDU definitions into the domain-independent notation and generates packing and unpacking routine specifications. Although this effort was hampered by the fact that the involved teams were separated by an eight-hour time difference, the stub compiler was completed in less than a week.

The PDUs for TETRA Mobility Management (MM) and the Circuit Mode Control Entities (CMCE) were then specified. There were a total of 36 PDU objects in MM, and 43 PDU objects in CMCE. (Not all these data objects are

```
value type D_TX_Granted {
struct
    Pdu_type Natural ( 0..31 );
    Call_ID Natural ( 0..16383 );
    TX_grant Natural ( 0..3 );
    TX_req_permission Natural ( 0..1 );
    Encryption_control Natural ( 0..1 );
    Speech_service Natural ( 0..1 );
    type2group value {
        struct
            Notification_ind Natural ( 0..63 ) OPTIONAL;
            TX_party_type_ID_choice value {
                struct
                    TX_party_type_ID Natural ( 0..3 );
                    TX_party_type_ID_choicebody value {
                        choice
                            fld0 value { };
                            fld1 value {
                                struct
                                    TX_party_address_SSI Natural ( 0..16777215 ); };
                            fld2 value {
                                struct
                                    TX_party_address_SSI Natural ( 0..16777215 );
                                    TX_party_extension Natural ( 0..16777215 ); };
                    };
            } OPTIONAL;
            type3group value
                Array <Natural, value {
                    struct type3field value { prop Proprietary_type_3; }
OPTIONAL;
                    }>;
    } OPTIONAL;
}
value type Proprietary_type_3 {
struct
    Element_indicator Natural ( 0..15 );
    length Natural ( 0..2047 );
    prop Propietary;
}
```

Fig. 6. SDL data type generated for the D-TX Granted PDU

referred to as PDU by the standard. However, the same notation and marshaling considerations apply to all of them, and we shall not make a finer distinction.) Translation of the standards document into the domain-specific PDU notation and reviewing the resultant specifications required approximately three days.

Finally, it took one day to generate target code for the pack and unpack routines from the PDU definitions.

In our initial attempt, we did not arrive at the understanding of the TETRA protocol as described above. In particular, due to vagueness in the standards document [4] our initial software interpreted the encoding rules differently:

– Dependent type 2 fields were coded with a preceding P-bit;
– Embedded PDU structures which did only contain type 1 fields were coded without a final O-bit.

When the ETSI conformance tests were disclosed for public inquiry it became clear that the understanding of the standards body was different from our interpretations. While these changes affected many of the generated marshaling routines, the corrections nevertheless were accomplished in less than a day (from the time the change was initiated to the delivery of corrected software). Both changes could be handled by a simple change in the manner the encoding rules were represented in the translator and regenerating the target code. No change to the PDU specifications was required. Had we written the packing and unpacking software manually, we would have to find the places were these bits were written or read from the PDU data structures and change the rather intricate code. (To judge the difficulty of this undertaking, the reader may want to examine the pack routine in Fig. 6 and attempt to find the locations in the code which had to be changed.)

It was then discovered that the lower protocol layers on the subscriber hardware were not able to transfer "long" PDUs, because the fragmentation operation would not be supported for this release. There were four uplink PDUs which would be longer than the limit of 56 bits even without type 3 fields. To deal with this problem, the affected PDUs were slightly changed to allow all necessary information to be transmitted while staying within the restrictions imposed by the lower protocol layer.

These changes were minor modifications of the specifications of each affected PDU. No other modifications were required, and the corrected software could be delivered by simply regenerating the marshaling code for the affected functions.

A total of 153 packing and unpacking routines for MM and CMCE were developed. These routines have a total complexity of 878 using McCabe's cyclomatic complexity metric [6]. Using published estimation techniques, we expect that around 85 staff weeks would be necessary to develop the marshaling routines by hand. It took us a total of 11 staff weeks to develop the marshaling routines following the process outlined in this paper. This time includes developing the translators, interfacing the resultant packing and unpacking routines to the rest of the MM and CMCE software, modifying the specifications and the translators in response to the requirement changes, preparing test suites, and executing the test suites. Therefore, we estimate that this process resulted in an 8X cycle time reduction.

The approach to the development of marshaling code advocated in this paper is similar to the "little languages" discussed in [7]. A small language expressive over the distinguishing characteristics of a particular problem domain is used to capture the specifications. A translator (or a set of translators) transforms the domain-specific notation into product code. [7] lists the following advantages of domain-specific languages:

- Domain experts themselves can understand, validate, and modify the software;
- Modifications are easier to make and their impact is easier understood;
- Domain-specific knowledge is not hidden in code written in a conventional programming language;

– The explicitly available knowledge can be re-used across different applications and is independent of the implementation platform.

In this project, we have experienced all these benefits. The protocol experts have developed the PDU specifications quickly and validated them directly against the standards document. When a new interpretation of the standard surfaced, these changes were easily integrated into the existing specification. The encoding rules of the TETRA protocol are not hidden in a C program, and the specifications of the TETRA PDUs are not hidden in C type declarations. The PDU specifications have been reused to generate code for both the subscriber and infrastructure platforms. Similar empirical evidence suggesting that the use of domain-specific languages increases flexibility, productivity, reliability, and usability is presented in [8].

We expect to gain further benefit from this approach when new releases of TETRA products and changes in the standard require modifications of the marshaling routines. Significantly impacted by this approach are the source maintainability attributes (understandability, modularity, encapsulation, cohesion, portability, etc.) which are considered as the predominant maintenance factors [9]. In addition, our specifications are much smaller than their C counterpart would be, and their descriptive nature and closeness to the standards document reduces the need for extensive commenting.

Since the release of the TETRA product described in this paper, many projects have adopted the process outlined above. We have developed notations and translators customized towards the key protocols supported by Motorola products, such as GSM, CDMA, UMTS, or iDEN, as well as for a number of protocols internal to the network. Marshaling routines for these protocols are now customarily developed using the development process outlined in this paper.

5   Other Approaches

The prevalent approach to developing protocol header marshaling code in the industry is manual coding.

USC [10] is a flexible stub compiler that can generate stubs to marshal headers, devices, and IPC arguments. USC generates C stubs. It requires that users annotate the C types used in their application with the precise layout within the USC type system. Impressive performance results for stubs generated by USC for standard networking protocols have been reported [10]. Unfortunately, USC does not provide support for dynamic encodings. In a dynamic encoding the value of a field can affect subsequent data layout. The TETRA protocol relies extensively on dynamic encoding for type 2, type 3, and conditional fields. Therefore, USC cannot be used to generate stubs for the TETRA protocol. Many of the air interfaces in telecommunication products rely on dynamic encodings.

The only data representation format we are aware of that supports dynamic encodings is ASN.1. Public domain [11, 12] and commercially supported compilers exist for ANS.1 into C or C++, as well as other languages. Unfortunately, the standard encoding of ASN.1 representations (BER or PER encodings) is completely different from the encoding rules prescribed by the TETRA standard. None of the air interfaces examined by us utilize BER encoding and only UMTS relies on PER encoding for most, but not all, its PDUs. Often, the standard encoding rules are perceived to not be efficient or flexible enough to support the high-performance needs of modern communication protocols. In addition, the conditional fields possible in a TETRA PDU cannot be expressed in ASN.1 and thus could not be handled conveniently in an ASN.1 compiler.

The ASN.1 community has since recognized the need for supporting encoding rules other than the standard BER and PER encodings. Recently the ASN.1 Encoding Control Notation (ECN) has been standardized [13]. ECN allows users to define their own encoding rules or modify existing encoding rules. ECN allows the specifier to separate the "pure" data definitions of ASN.1 from an "encoding object" which defines the encoding of a corresponding ASN.1 type. When an encoding object is applied to an ASN.1 type, it inserts the auxiliary fields that are specific to the defined encoding. At least one commercial implementation of the ECN is already available. However, ECN is quite complex and requires intricate understanding of minute details of the ASN.1 standard.

6   Conclusion

We have described a process and supporting tools that allowed us to produce complex software of high quality in a rapid fashion. Software developed by automated generation from high-level specifications as described in this paper has been shipping in Motorola products for a number of years.

References

[1] D. D. Clark and D. L. Tennenhouse. Architectural Considerations for a new Generation of Protocols. Proceedings of the SIGCOMM '90 Symposium (1990). 375
[2] Sun Microsystems, Inc. XDR: External Data Representation (1987) 375
[3] T. Weigert, J. Boyle, T. Harmer, F. Weil. The Derivation of Efficient Programs from High-Level Specifications. Artificial Intelligence in Automation. World Scientific Publishers (1996). 375
[4] European Telecommunications Standards Institute. Radio Equipment and Systems: Trans-European Trunked Radio, Voice Plus Data Part 2: Air Interface. ETS 300 392-2 (1995). 375, 376, 382
[5] International Telecommunication Union. Abstract Syntax Notation One (ASN.1): Specification of Basic Notation. Recommendation X.680 (2002). 377
[6] T. J. McCabe. A Complexity Measure. IEEE Transactions Software Engineering, 2 (1976). 383
[7] A. v.Deursen, P. Klint. Little Languages: Little Maintenance? Proceedings of the First ACM SIGPLAN Workshop on Domain-Specific Languages. Paris (1997). 383
[8] R. B. Kieburtz et. al. A Software Engineering Experiment in Software Component Generation. Proceedings of the 18th International Conference on Software Engineering (1996). 384

[9] T. M. Pigoski. Practical Software Maintenance–Best Practices for Managing Your Software Investment. John Wiley (1997). 384

[10] S. O'Melley, T. Proebsting, and A. B. Montz. USC: A Universal Stub Compiler. Proceedings of SIG-COMM '94 Symposium (1994). 384

[11] C. Huitema. MAVROS: Highlights on an ASN.1 Compiler. Project RODEO Tech. Rep., INRIA (1991). 384

[12] M. Sample, G. Neufeld. Snacc 1.0: A High Performance ASN.1 to C/C++ Compiler. Tech. Rep., Univ. of British Columbia (1993). 384

[13] International Telecommunication Union. Abstract Syntax Notation One (ASN.1): Encoding Control Notation. X.692 (2002). 385

The Winning Entry of the SAM 2002 Design Contest:
A Case Study of the Effectiveness of SDL and MSC

Alan W. Williams[1], Robert L. Probert[1], Qing Li[1], and Tae-Hyong Kim[2]

[1] School of Information Technology and Engineering, University of Ottawa, Ottawa
{qli,awilliam,bob}@site.uottawa.ca
[2] School of Computer & Software Engineering, Kumoh National Institute of
Technology, Gyeongbuk 730-701, Rep. of Korea

Abstract. The SDL Forum Society holds workshops on the languages SDL (Specification and Description Language) and MSC (Message Sequence Charts). At the 2002 workshop (SAM2002), held at Aberystwyth, Wales, an SDL design contest was held to promote discussion about the use of SDL. The contest challenge was to use SDL and MSC to specify a railway crossing system. Our team from the University of Ottawa, consisting of Qing Li, Alan Williams, Robert Probert and Tae-Hyong Kim won the contest. In this paper, we outline our design approach including requirements analysis, high-level design, iterative design construction, design verification, design validation against high-yield scenarios, and design maintenance based on new and changed requirements which arrived close to the end of the design cycle. We also describe the rationale for some of the decisions we had to make during the process. Based on our experience, we provide some comments on the strengths and weaknesses of the methods and tools that we used.

1 Introduction

A workshop on the languages SDL (Specification and Description Language) and MSC (Message Sequence Charts) – called the SAM (SDL And MSC) workshop – is held by the SDL Forum Society once every two years. The Society organized an SDL design contest to promote discussion about the use of SDL at the 2002 workshop (SAM2002) held at Aberystwyth, Wales. The contestants were asked to produce an executable specification for an informal description of a railway crossing system. This paper is based on the work done producing the winning entry.

1.1 Background

Traditionally, specifications are written in natural language, which normally contains ambiguities. This causes confusion for end users and customers, and can result in inappropriate design decisions. These specifications themselves may

R. Reed (Ed.): SDL 2003, LNCS 2708, pp. 387–403, 2003.

also contain errors or defects, but no direct, automatic verification or validation can be made at this early stage of gathering Functional Requirements. The Specification and Description Language (SDL) [1] and Message Sequence Charts (MSC) [2], as formal specification languages, provide precise mechanisms to write unambiguous specifications. This makes it possible to verify and validate specifications automatically. Minimizing errors and ambiguities at this early stage can save considerable unnecessary rework at later stages.

1.2   The Languages and the Supporting Tools

The first version of the SDL standard was published in 1976, followed by improved versions in 1980, 1984, 1988, 1992, and 1996. SDL-2000 is the newest version, which introduces some major revision of previous versions to apply object-oriented concepts.

Following the releases of each SDL version, supporting tools were developed and distributed by tool vendors. At the time this contest was undertaken, the tool we used, Telelogic Tau 4.3, only supported most of the features of SDL-96. Due to tool limitation, we cannot exercise the new features in SDL-2000. When we discuss SDL features through out this paper, mostly we mean the features supported by Tau 4.3.

1.3   Contest Description

The contest specified the use of SDL-2000 and MSC-2000[1] to design a railway crossing system, based on ten requirements expressed in natural language [3]. This section provides a summary of the contest procedure, example items in the initial list of requirements, plus some changes and additions that were added by the contest organizer and distributed approximately one month before the contest deadline.

1.4   Contest Organization and Objectives

The contest was designed by a subgroup of the Program Committee in consultation with experts. To simulate a realistic experience, initial, purposely incomplete, and informal natural language requirements were posted as a request for proposals in February. Competitors had about 6 weeks to develop an initial design and documentation. Then, additional requirements were posted. Finally, a set of compulsory test scenarios were posted. The time pressure was significant, which is an important factor of verifying how a SDL system that can be evolved is designed.

---

[1] Editorial note:At the time the contest rules were set (October 2001) it was expected SDL-2000 would be substantially supported by at least one tool by SAM-2002.

The objectives of the contest were:

– To submit an SDL/MSC specification for a Railway Crossing System;
– To use the key features of the latest version of the languages, SDL-2000 and MSC-2000;
– To validate the design using available tools;
– To document the design using graphical notation;
– To present the design to the SDL forum committee for assessment.

2   The Requirements

The task is to specify a railway crossing controller with the following characteristics (see [3] for more details):

1. There are a number of tracks for the trains. The specification should be generic in the number of tracks.
2. There is a controller, taking into account the number of cars waiting and the trains approaching.
3. There is a gate for cars, which must be controlled. The pattern of cars approaching is simply given by a constant delay between the cars.
4. Each track has two sensors: one sensor when a train is approaching and one sensor when the train is leaving the gate. Another sensor indicates when there is more than one car waiting.
5. There is a signal on each track informing the trains if they are allowed to pass or if they have to stop.
6. The controller can act either by closing the gate or by stopping a train (setting a closing signal). Each of these actions has to be finished before the train reaches the gate.
7. Trains: the solution should be generic in the number of trains. A train will start the braking phase as soon it sees a stopping signal and restart when the stopping signal goes off. All trains on the same track are supposed to run in the same direction and with a minimal delay between them depending on their speed. (A train must be able to stop even if the preceding one stops immediately). There are regular trains, which have a small (maximal) speed and fast trains, which can run faster. Regular and fast trains never run on the same track.
8. The active elements of the system are the trains, the sensors, the controller and the gate. The cars are not considered to be in the system.
9. The solution should allow several strategies of the gate controller to be checked.
10. At least the following strategies should be possible: trains take precedence – at least those with high speed; cars take precedence if there are too many waiting cars. Furthermore, each specification should provide a strategy.

Later on, the following additions were specified, and part of the contest was to explain what modifications were needed to incorporate the changes:

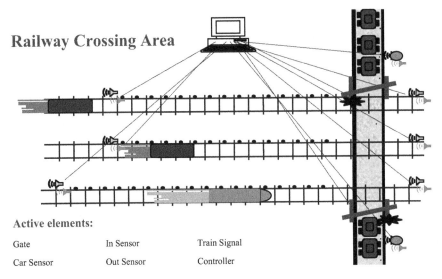

Fig. 1. Railway Crossing Area

1. It is not allowed to set the stopping signal for a track when a train is between the two sensors.
2. It should be possible to manually control the crossing. In this case, unsafe actions should be rejected.
3. A sensor does not produce one signal, but a sequence of signals (one for each of the wheels). The end of the sequence is given by a delay of a certain size after the last signal.

Figure 1 is a simplified illustration of the railway crossing area described in the requirements:

3   Requirements Analysis and Design Decisions

3.1   Guiding Principles

A railway crossing is a safety-critical real-time system. First, we decided upon guiding design principles, namely: safety, simplicity, and flexibility/extensibility.

- **Safety** – Because this is a safety-critical real-time system, safety is the basic and most important aspect in the design.
- **Simplicity** – Simplify the design by bringing it to a certain abstract level and save details for later design stages. This way we can specify the requirements more clearly and increase testability.
- **Flexibility/Extensibility** – To be cost effective, the system should allow for different numbers of tracks and traffic situations, such as big city, small town and countryside.

3.2   Multiple Strategies

As specified in requirements 9 and 10, several strategies are needed. To make the system flexible and safe, we provide four strategies to handle a variety of situations. The users should be able to switch among the strategies dynamically when the system is running. The four strategies are:

- Strategy 1: Manual override;
- Strategy 2: Trains take precedence;
- Strategy 3: Normal – Priority order: fast trains – many cars – slow trains;
- Strategy 4: Many cars take precedence.

Strategy 1: Manual Override.

Here, the system is controlled manually. This provides a means of guaranteeing the system continues to run, even if a part of the system does not function properly. For example, suppose the gate is closed, but it cannot send a "Closed" signal properly. In this case, the "Green" track signal will not be sent automatically by the controller. Therefore, it should be able to be sent manually, to allow the trains to proceed.

To assure safety, any unsafe manual actions should be rejected. As an example, when an "Open" signal is sent to open the gate, the system should first check if there are any trains still in the crossing area. If there are none, it should first set track signal to "Red" on all tracks, and then send an "Open" signal to open the gate. If there are one or more trains, it will wait until all the trains have passed the crossing area or have stopped, and then open the gate.

Strategy 1 provides complete flexibility to handle any traffic situations. It allows the system not to be constrained by pre-set control options.

Strategy 2: Trains Take Precedence.

Here, trains take precedence, including fast trains and slow trains. The gate is normally closed. It only opens when more than one car is waiting and no train is in the crossing area. It closes again after all cars have passed, or when a train is approaching, even if there are still many cars waiting.

This strategy is useful in areas far from cities, where there are normally not many cars at the crossing (long delay between cars). It allows trains to pass faster, and the gate does not need to open and close very often.

Strategy 3: Normal Strategy. — Order of Priority: Fast train – many cars – slow train.

Here, fast trains take precedence, then many cars, and then slow trains. The gate is normally open for cars. When a fast train approaches, close the gate, no matter how many cars are waiting. When a slow train approaches, and there are more than one car waiting, stop the train. Close the gate after all cars have passed. After all trains have passed the crossing area, even if no cars are waiting, open the gate.

This strategy is the major portion of the RCS system. It is used in most real railway crossing systems, and is applicable to a variety of locations and traffic densities.

Strategy 4: Many Cars Take Precedence.
In this strategy, "many cars" take precedence. The gate is normally opened for cars. When a train approaches, the system first checks if there are cars waiting. If so, stop the train until all cars pass the crossing area, then close the gate. As soon as all moving trains pass the crossing area, the system will check whether there are cars waiting. If so, it sets the track signal to "Red" on all tracks, and then opens the gate, even if many trains stopped and are waiting or a train is approaching.
This strategy is useful in big cities or during rush hour in areas where there is heavy car traffic.

4   System Architecture

By nature, SDL and MSC require a global, early view of the system architecture. In particular, for SDL, major signals need to be defined globally. For MSCs, processes and signal names must be identified at the beginning of design.

4.1   General Structure

The elements of the crossing area are: cars, car sensors, the gate, trains, train approaching sensors, train departing sensors, train signal lights, and the central controller.

A car sensor is used to detect if more than one car is waiting. The gates are used to control car traffic by opening or closing the gate arms.

On each track, a sensor is used to detect if there is a train approaching the crossing area, and a second sensor detects when the train has left the crossing area. A train signal is used to control train traffic with signals to stop (red) or proceed (green).

There are multiple tracks. The central controller is the central component of the system. It controls traffic of the crossing area by communicating to the other components.

As specified in requirement point 8, the cars are not considered to be in the system.

All communications between components are through exchanging of signals. As a result, the system structure is modeled in SDL as shown in Fig. 2.

4.2   How to Make the Number of Tracks Generic?

As specified in requirement point 1, the number of tracks should be generic.

Unless the crossing is re-constructed, the number of tracks in a specific railway crossing does not change, therefore, we can define a block type Tracks. Each

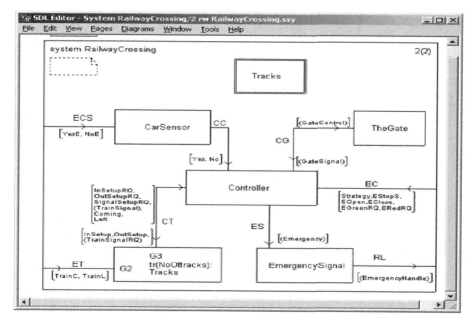

Fig. 2. System Diagram

track is an instance of the block type. The number of instances can be given at system initiation, which allows a different number of tracks at different crossing.

On each track, there is a train approaching sensor, a train departing sensor, and a train signal (lights). To associate these three independent devices, we added a multiplexor process TrackControl, which acts as an intermediary between the central controller and the three process. The Block type *Tracks* diagram is shown in Fig. 3.

4.3 How to Model the Trains?

Some of the requirements implied that we would need to model the mechanics of the system. Two aspects of this are the length of the train, and what distance the train would need to brake to a halt. It seemed the only way to achieve this is to model the physical properties of the train: current position, speed, and acceleration. We would also need to model the distances of the sensors from the crossing, as well as the position of the train signal light. To meet the modified additional requirements, we also need to track the number of axles on a train to indicate how many times the train sensor is activated.

Taking this approach would result in a rather complex physical model of the entire system. Furthermore, with only two sensors per track, the system would not have enough information to do this reliably unless the trains were continuously reporting changes in acceleration to the system.

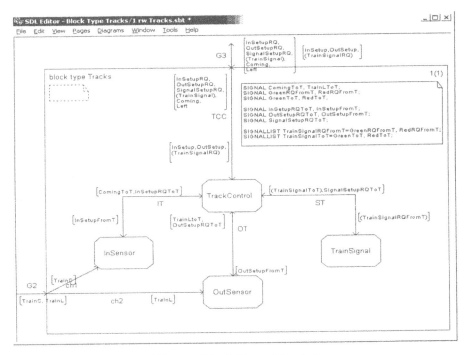

Fig. 3. Block Type "Tracks"

Therefore, we decided not to model the trains as a process, but signals from the environment. The system would communicate with the trains through the available sensors and train signal lights.

4.4   Behavioral Design Aspects

- All system behaviors are categorized as normal behavior and exception handling behavior (abnormal). They are handled differently.
- The system is controlled either automatically or manually, but not both simultaneously.

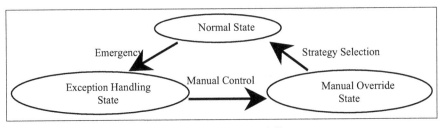

Fig. 4. System Functional Diagram

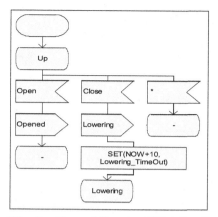

Fig. 5. Part of Process "TheGate"

- The System Functional Diagram is shown in Fig. 4.
- All system behaviors are specified as finite state machines. In SDL, they are process diagrams. See Fig. 5 as an example.
- A State Diagram is used to give a big picture of complicated processes. Figure 6 is an example of the state diagram of the Controller process.

4.5 Implementing Strategies – A Problem in SDL

To implement multiple strategies, we encountered difficulties with a limitation of SDL.

It seemed to be a good idea to use the object-oriented features of SDL where we could have a superclass with the common behavior of various strategies, and different subclasses that implement the specifics of each strategy. However, we also wanted to be able to change strategies while the system was running, so that a strategy change would not require re-initializing (or worse, re-compiling) the system. This is where dynamic binding would be useful: the controller process could switch from being of one type to another, as long as each instance was a subclass of the generic controller. What this requires is that the controller process be declared to be of the type of the superclass, but instantiated as one of the subclasses. Unfortunately, SDL has only static binding, and one has to know the exact type of the process at compile time.

As a result, changes in strategy were implemented in the "traditional" way: using a 'flag' variable to indicate which strategy is currently in effect. On transitions where the choice of strategy results in differing behavior, an SDL decision construct was used to choose alternate control flow paths on a transition. With this model, strategies can be changed dynamically while the system is running, although it also results in more complex state diagrams.

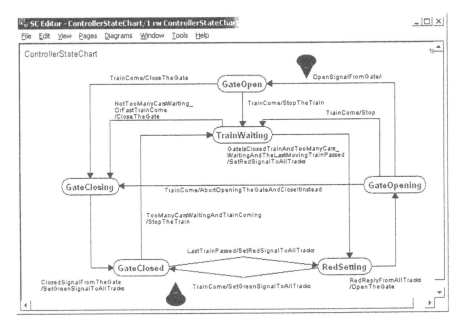

Fig. 6. State Diagram of process "Controller"

5   Validation

As a safety critical system, a railway crossing needs to be thoroughly tested.

5.1   Test Scenario Design

To cover as many paths as possible, we designed over 100 test cases, but path coverage is still not 100 percent. We will discuss this in more detail in later sections.

Test cases are designed using State Transition Charts. As an example, Fig. 7 is a high-level system behavior inspired by HMSC [2], which shows how physical components react with each other by exchanging signals.

Figure 8 illustrates a detailed test case design of the same test case using a State Transition Chart. Only the states in the box are specific to this test case. The other states are a preamble to make this test case feasible. While the MSC in Fig. 7 shows high-level system behavior, the state chart in Fig. 8 can be executed using the Simulator.

5.2   Test Execution

We used a simulator tool, called "Simulator" [4].

By manual input of signals using Simulator, we generated a set of MSCs. If the generated MSC matches designed test case result, this test case passes;

Test case A

Situation:

There are no trains between the sensors, and the controller triggers the opening of the gate. Then, a train passes the first controller.

Expected behaviour:
The opening of the gate is aborted, and the controller triggers its closing.

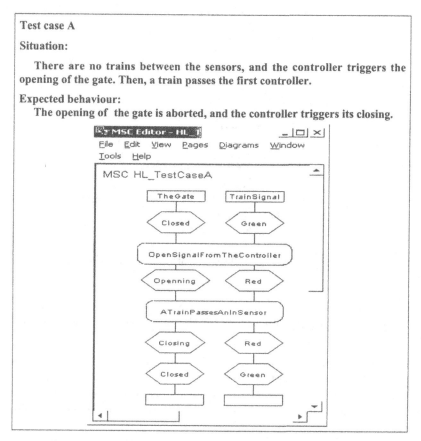

Fig. 7. Test Case Design – High Level System Behavior

otherwise, it fails. By 'matches designed test case result', we mean the end state of each entity in generated MSC is the same as in designed state transition chart.

Figure 9 is an example of a simulation trace MSC. The end state of Controller is "GateClosing", which matches the result shown in Fig. 8.

We used a verification tool, called "Validator" [4].

Validator was used to debug the specification. Its error and warning reports help to locate dead lock, queue overflow and implicit symbol consuming. Its "Coverage Viewer" indicates uncovered symbols, which helps in test case design. It also helps to locate unreachable branches. This makes optimizing the design easier.

5.3   Test Results

Using Simulator: Because test cases are difficult to implement automatically in Simulator in Tau, to manually test every test case is very time consuming.

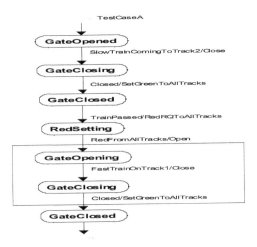

Fig. 8. Test Case Design – State Transition Chart

We only implemented approximately 60 test cases for high-risk scenarios. After iteratively modifying the design and simulation, all the test cases passed.

Using Validator: In the Validator, exception-handling actions cannot be triggered, therefore they cannot be validated. This means all the exception-handling paths, such as timeout, become unreachable and cannot be tested. As a result, symbol coverage is 60 percent. We will discuss this in more detail in later sections.

For non-exception handling scenarios, symbol coverage is 100 percent.

5.4   Validation Decisions and Their Rationale

As mentioned earlier, we designed over 100 test cases based on State Transition Charts such as the one shown in Fig. 8. The target was to cover as many paths as possible. Since 100 percent path coverage is almost impossible (discussed in more detail in a later section), we chose high risk critical race scenarios first. With the help of Validator's "Coverage Viewer", we created more test cases base on uncovered paths.

6   Adapting to Changes

Because one of the intentions of our design is its evolvability, all the modifications were handled very easily.

– Modification 11: It is not allowed to set the stopping signal for a track when a train is between the two sensors

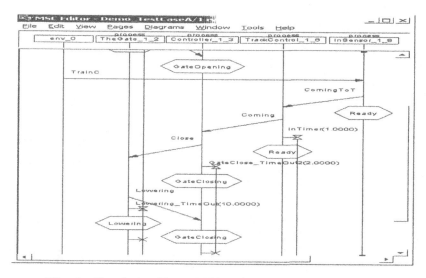

Fig. 9. Simulation Trace MSC – Actual System Behavior

This is a basic requirement for a safety critical system. It was specified explicitly to make sure all entries meet the basic safety requirements, in our understanding, because we already met this requirement without any modification.

– Modification 12: It should be possible to manually control the crossing. In this case, unsafe actions should be rejected.

Intuitively, to make this modification in the simplest way, the strategies should be modeled as a class. This way, a manual control strategy can be created by simply instantiating another object from the class. However, the operation with Manual control has nothing similar to the other strategies. So we need to model a whole set of new scenarios. These are normally used for exception handling.

Because exception scenarios cannot be triggered with the tool, we cannot simulate any exception scenarios and cannot verify the design. Therefore, we did not give a detailed design for exception handling. For the new Manual control, we added a new path parallel with all paths with strategies involved. See Fig. 10 as an example.

– Modification 13 : A sensor does not produce one signal, but a sequence of signals (one for each of the wheels). The end of the sequence is given by a delay of a certain size after the last signal.

This modification is handled easily. In the old requirements, a sensor produces one signal for the whole train, so when the InSensor detects a train, it sends a "Coming" signal to the TrackControl. To make the modification, we added a timer. Before time out, if the sensor receives a "Coming" signal (another wheel), it will reset the timer. After time out, which means the whole train has passed the sensor completely, if the sensor receives another

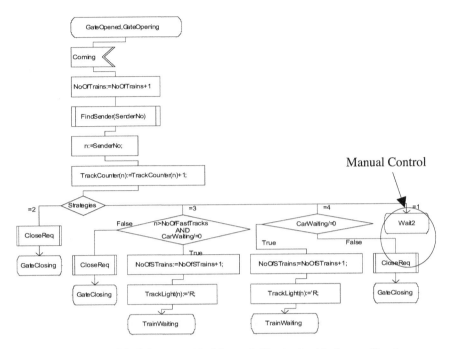

Fig. 10. Modification 12: Manual Control added as a Strategy

"Coming" signal, it means this is a new train, and it will send a "Coming" signal to the TrackControl. The modifications are shown in Fig. 11. The only added symbols are enclosed within circles.

7   Observations

SDL and MSCs were appropriate for representing real-time reactive systems, and integrated well with the test scenarios for validation purposes. However, MSCs generated from simulation are very complex and difficult to read.

With respect to the use of the TAU toolset, simulation and validation were of enormous benefit to us. However, we encountered some challenges.

For example, we had inadequate tool support for SDL/MSC-2000. Other concerns follow.

7.1   Exhaustive Validation Impossible

When the number of states increases, the number of paths increases exponentially. When it reaches a certain level, exhaustive validation becomes impossible.

However, for some safety critical systems, exhaustive validation is necessary. One solution is to simplify the design. At specification stage, it is possible to

Process TrackControl

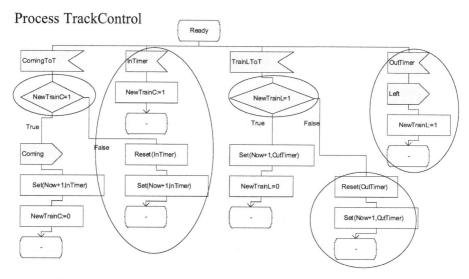

Fig. 11. Modification 13: Manual Control added as a Strategy

simplify the design and bring it to a certain abstract level. This can largely eliminate the number of states needed, and also specify the requirements clearly. All unnecessary details can be saved for later design stages.

7.2   Lack of Exception-Handling

Exception-handling actions cannot be triggered in the tools, so they cannot be validated. As a result, all the exception-handling paths, such as timeout, become unreachable and cannot be tested. This can be a high risk in real safety critical applications.

7.3   Conclusions and Recommendations

In this paper, we have summarized how we utilized the best features of SDL and MSC in the context of a toolset Tau 4.3 from Telelogic to design a safety-first railway crossing controller as part of the SAM International Design Contest for 2002. Our entry was judged to be the best of several excellent submissions by experts in these two languages. Accordingly, we have tried here to explain the design decisions we made, and the benefits and disadvantages of these decisions, but more importantly, the support we received from SDL, MSC, and the toolset in the validation and analysis of these decisions.

7.4   Experience

We hope that our experience will assist others in their evaluation of the suitability of these languages and toolset for their design and development environment. Briefly, it was our experience that:

- The time we spent on analysis of the initial requirements was invaluable. During this time, we recognized which actors were essential and which were secondary. Also, our initial diagram of the crossing, which was relatively primitive, was central to coming up with our initial versions of states and signals. For example, we "discovered" that traffic crossed the tracks in one direction only. This also helped us in deciding how not to model cars specifically (as in requirement 8) and yet capture the case of many cars waiting.
- A good specification can be written easily by using just simple SDL features. We also found it useful to iterate between the simple SDL and a multi-state transition chart similar to those used by Bræk and Haugen. This approach was found to be more efficient than the use of MSCs.
- As a graphical design language, simple SDL is easy to learn, especially with a good support toolset. Formal design tools do not need to be harder to understand than other languages. However, some of the features of SDL-2000 were not supported in our version of the toolset.
- SDL-2000 has become a very powerful language. It can do almost everything that other design languages can do. However, using the advanced features required a significant amount of learning.
- In practical applications, it is critical to find an appropriate mapping from requirements to design. We selected our mapping based on the simplicity, extensibility, and safety of the design. In the case of deciding not to model specific attributes of trains, for example, number of cars, we were able to simplify the requirements, resulting in a simpler, more robust design.

This design may be a good tutorial example for the implementation and validation of real life applications in SDL. To that end, the editors of SAM 2002 have put the requirements, our design, and critical validation scenarios (referred to as test cases by the organizers) on the SDL forum website at

  http://www.sdl-forum.org/SAM_contest/Li_Probert_Williams/.

We welcome comments and questions sent to any of the first three authors.

7.5   Recommendations

The following are some recommendations based on our experiences:

- Spend a significant amount of project time on the analysis and verification of requirements, especially in conjunction with the use of graphical methods and tools, preferably at a simple level. Get the basic requirements right first, then consider necessary complexities and refinements.
- Use tools and languages that fit the design team. We found for example that MSCs were too bulky to utilize for making design decisions, or even for analysis of requirements. However, the MSCs used by the contest organizers were necessary to allow objective comparisons between design solutions. Perhaps some MSC simplification tool is required.
- Try to encourage the timely availability and distribution of tools for the requirements and design languages of choice, in our case, SDL-2000.

- Encourage an egoless design environment. We listened and respected all suggestions, and selected the best on the basis of extensive analysis.
- Set design priorities early. In our case, safety was paramount. This helped us to design the Manual Strategy with safeguards against human error or sabotage, for example.
- Implement traceability from the start. Check and maintain coverage of requirements by design decisions. Relate scenarios to requirements and review the affected scenarios with respect to every new design decision in order to limit the "ripple effect" of any design omissions or errors.

We hope these recommendations will assist others in developing effective real-time designs, and we welcome comments and suggestions, especially those based on the use of the languages SDL and MSC, and supporting toolsets for real-time design.

Acknowledgments

The authors wish to acknowledge the support of Nortel Networks, Telelogic, CITO (Communications and Information Technology Ontario), and NSERC (the Natural Sciences and Engineering Research Council of Canada). We are grateful for comments and encouragement from Hasan Ural and several graduate students of the ASERT Laboratory. As well, we appreciate the comments of the referees which have improved the presentation in this paper.

References

[1] ITU-T. Recommendation Z.100 (08/02), Specification and Description Language (SDL). International Telecommunication Union, Geneva. 388
[2] ITU-T. Recommendation Z.120 (11/99), Message Sequence Chart (MSC). International Telecommunication Union, Geneva. 388, 396
[3] http://www.sdl-forum.org/SAM_contest/Li_Probert_Williams/ 388, 389
[4] http://www.telelogic.com 396, 397

Author Index

Lecture Notes in Computer Science

For information about Vols. 1–2649
please contact your bookseller or Springer-Verlag